The Last and Greatest Battle

The Last and Greatest Battle

Finding the Will, Commitment, and Strategy to End Military Suicides

JOHN BATESON

OXFORD
UNIVERSITY PRESS

OXFORD
UNIVERSITY PRESS

Oxford University Press is a department of the University of
Oxford. It furthers the University's objective of excellence in research,
scholarship, and education by publishing worldwide.

Oxford   New York
Auckland   Cape Town   Dar es Salaam   Hong Kong   Karachi
Kuala Lumpur   Madrid   Melbourne   Mexico City   Nairobi
New Delhi   Shanghai   Taipei   Toronto

With offices in
Argentina   Austria   Brazil   Chile   Czech Republic   France   Greece
Guatemala   Hungary   Italy   Japan   Poland   Portugal   Singapore
South Korea   Switzerland   Thailand   Turkey   Ukraine   Vietnam

Oxford is a registered trademark of Oxford University Press
in the UK and certain other countries.

Published in the United States of America by
Oxford University Press
198 Madison Avenue, New York, NY 10016

Library of Congress Cataloging-in-Publication Data
Bateson, John, 1951–
The last and greatest battle : finding the will, commitment, and strategy to end military
suicides / John Bateson.
     pages cm
Includes bibliographical references and index.
ISBN 978–0–19–939232–2 (hardback)
1. Soldiers—Suicidal behavior—United States—History.   2. Veterans—Suicidal
behavior—United States—History.   3. Soldiers—Mental health—United States.
4. Veterans—Mental health—United States.   5. Combat—Psychological aspects.
6. Suicide—United States—Prevention.   7. Military psychology.   I. Title.
HV6545.7.B37 2015
362.28088'35500973—dc23
2014017942

9 8 7 6 5 4 3 2 1
Printed in the United States of America
on acid-free paper

To Suzan

Our greatest foes, and whom we must chiefly combat, are within.

—Miguel de Cervantes

Contents

About the Author

John Bateson was executive director of a twenty-four-hour crisis intervention and suicide prevention center in the San Francisco Bay Area for sixteen years. He served on the steering committee of the National Suicide Prevention Lifeline and was appointed to a blue-ribbon committee that created the California Strategic Plan on Suicide Prevention. His previous books—*The Final Leap* and *Building Hope*—focus all or in part on suicide.

Preface

If someone had told me when I was younger that one day I would write a book sympathetic to members of the U.S. Armed Forces, I would have been skeptical. I attended college in Berkeley at a time when protests against the Vietnam War were at their peak and the military was castigated. Every person of any prominence who opposed the war spoke at local rallies, from Beatnik poets to Jane Fonda. There were large marches in the streets, mass demonstrations on campus, riots in People's Park, car burnings, tear gas sprayings, clashes with the National Guard, and more. I didn't participate in all or even most of the demonstrations, but I supported them. Like many of my peers, I didn't see any purpose to the war, only senseless carnage.

In 1970, when I was a freshman, the lottery was held to draft young men to fight in the war. Those who got a low number, based on their birthday, were the first ones drafted, while those who got a high number—all the way up to 366 (leap-year births included)—were spared, at least for the time being. I remember watching the news on television in a dormitory lounge when the results of the lottery were reported (few students had televisions in their own rooms those days). I wasn't all that worried even if my number turned out to be low because I had a student deferment. Still, it was a jolt when my birthday was announced as number forty-five. All men my age with numbers under fifty who didn't have a medical or student deferment were certain to be drafted.

Four years later, when I graduated from college, the war had ended. With the fall of Saigon, the fighting was over and everything in this country returned to normal—or so I believed. No one in my family had served. Only one of my close friends served (as a helicopter pilot, a high-risk assignment, but he survived). No one from my high school was killed in action or, as far as I knew, had been physically wounded. True, many veterans came home with serious, visible scars—missing limbs that put them on long waiting lists for prosthetics, spinal cord injuries that necessitated permanent confinement to a wheelchair, eye patches that covered the hole left after shrapnel exploded in their face. I averted my gaze when I saw them, thankful in my selfish and uncaring way that they weren't me. I never shouted invectives or otherwise disrespected these troops, but neither did I hold them in high regard. If anything, I pitied them for being pawns in a deadly game that had no redeeming value.

Beyond reading periodic news stories about the dangers of Agent Orange, I was oblivious to the war's impact on people who served, and totally ignorant to the impact on families. I was unaware of the psychological damage, knowing nothing about the trauma and horror that these veterans were exposed to. My friend and I lost touch after he enlisted, and even though we renewed our friendship years later, I didn't ask. I was more aware of the social impact—high postwar incidences of alcoholism, unemployment, and homelessness—but only because I saw tangible evidence of it, mainly crippled vets on street corners begging passersby for money. I made sure to put a few coins or a folded-up bill into their collection tins, but that was the extent of my compassion. Lacking any window into their world, and seeking none, I didn't have the slightest idea about what their lives were like. Even though the majority of service members who returned from Vietnam were my age, their existence was as alien to me as if they were from another country or another time period. Post-college, I was more focused on finding a job and launching a career than on the hardships of people with whom I perceived I had little or nothing in common.

For many years, my thinking didn't change. In 1983, when President Ronald Reagan sent 8,000 troops to the small Caribbean island of Grenada to liberate a handful of American medical students who were thought to be at risk when a new government took power there, I was incensed. Nineteen U.S. soldiers were killed, one hundred sixteen were wounded, four hundred Grenadians died or were wounded (including eighteen mental patients who were killed in their hospital beds), and $135 million was spent on Operation Urgent Fury,[1] for what? The students were never in any real danger. In 1991, when President George H. W. Bush committed more troops to roust Saddam Hussein's army from Kuwait than the United States deployed at the height of the Vietnam War, with the stated purpose of protecting U.S. oil interests in the area, I was livid. Nearly 300 American service members were killed (including 15 women), more than 450 were wounded, more than 100,000 Iraqi soldiers were dead and another 300,000 wounded, while $60 billion was spent on Operation Desert Storm.[2] Yet gas prices continued to rise and Hussein remained in power. In 2003, when President George W. Bush declared war on Iraq[*] for reasons that subsequently proved to be manipulated, I was outraged. Don't our leaders ever learn? Every conflict seemed so senseless to me that I not only blamed our presidents for getting the country into these wars, but I also blamed those who participated in the fighting. From the luxury of distance and ignorance, I felt that they were equally at fault. After all, you can't wage a war without soldiers. Someone has to drop the bombs, launch the grenades, fire the missiles, and shoot the bullets that result in war's casualties. Politicians may issue declarations of war, but it's people in the military who carry them out. The fact that since Vietnam every U.S. soldier who has been killed or injured in battle has volunteered for service—he or she wasn't drafted—was proof in my mind that they bore much of the responsibility for what happened to them and to others. If they hadn't enlisted, they wouldn't have suffered.

Then I was hired as executive director of a twenty-four-hour crisis intervention and suicide prevention center in the San Francisco Bay Area. During my sixteen years there, and especially since 2010, the agency's client load included an increasing number of people who

---

* Technically, we're not in a war because Congress has the sole authority to declare war. Congress approved the use of military force in Iraq, though—a type of war declaration—and after 9/11 gave the president general authority for the War on Terror. I don't think most members of the general public, the media, or deployed troops believe that what's going on in the Middle East is anything other than a war.

served in the military, as well as their families. My eyes were opened in a way they hadn't been before to the anguish, depression, guilt, and grief that these individuals experienced. In addition, I learned about PTSD (posttraumatic stress disorder), TBI (traumatic brain injury), and other aftereffects of war.

One thing that is substantially different about the fighting in Iraq and Afghanistan today as compared with either of the world wars or Vietnam is that it's possible to forget today we are even in a war. Fewer than 1 percent of people in the United States—about 2.7 million out of 314 million—has served in a current war zone. Another 1 percent represents these troops' immediate families. For 98 percent of the population, neither the reality of the war nor the possibility of deployment is a personal concern. According to a 2011 study by the Pew Research Center, "A smaller share of Americans currently serve in the U.S. Armed Forces than at any time since the peace-time era between World Wars I and II."[3]

For most of us, our daily lives continue as always, and what happens abroad is something we read or hear about, but that is all. Moreover, whether the fighting goes on for another three years, five years, ten years, or longer really doesn't matter. The vast majority of us will remain unaffected.

It wasn't always so. The Civil War consumed the lives of everyone in this country. Every member of society had a stake in it, from those who fought to those who worried about the safety of their loved ones, from those who saw their property destroyed and their businesses bankrupted to those who cheered or feared the end of slavery. No one was immune to the impact.

Similarly, nearly every community was affected by World War I, and nearly every household was affected by World War II. Able-bodied males from all walks of life were drafted into service and sent overseas to fight. Women worked in factories and helped produce supplies and arms for the war. Families posted maps of Europe and the Pacific on their walls, noting the locations of loved ones with pushpins in order to track their movements and know which news stories to pay the most attention to.

During Vietnam, thanks in large part to CBS anchor Walter Cronkite, there was war coverage almost every night, not just for days or weeks but for months and years. Media attention didn't come and go depending on whether there were any new developments—it was constant, every day, for the duration of the fighting. Even if one didn't serve, it was impossible to forget that the United States was at war and the consequences of that. A primary reason for this was because the majority of troops who fought in the war didn't volunteer; they were drafted. As a result, nearly every community, rich and poor, had a vested interest because its children were the ones whose lives were on the line.

Today, what's going on in various war zones around the world only concerns the people who enlisted and their immediate families. The rest of us have the luxury of not thinking about it if we choose.

Laurie B. Slone and Matthew J. Friedman head the National Center for PTSD. They also are professors at Dartmouth Medical School and authors of *After the War Zone: A Practical Guide for Returning Troops and Their Families*. They offer this advice to the American public:

> Take a moment in your busy schedule to think about the fact that there is a war going on and how it has affected individuals, families, and communities. Think about what troops and their families are going through. Think about all of the children who are separated from their parents and about all of the partners who must now take full responsibility for their households while also worrying endlessly about whether their loved ones will return safely home. Consider how reunited couples must get reacquainted or learn to deal with the returned partner's agitation, silent withdrawal, or continual nightmares.[4]

To those of us on the outside, we see or read in the news about happy homecomings during which veterans are reunited with loved ones, and we think that their lives will return to normal after that. We fail to think, even for a minute, about what really awaits them. The training that these warriors completed to become killing machines of the U.S. government, the experiences that they have endured putting this training into practice, the atrocities that they have witnessed and, in many instances, participated in because that is where their training has led, and the consequences of it all can't be simply cast aside or compartmentalized when they return. As individuals they are changed, and so are their families.

This change means that they need a lot more than medals, monuments, accolades, and parades. Many need help, real help, the kind that soldiers in combat have always needed and, to this point, rarely received—behavioral health care counseling for themselves, re-adjustment support for their families, employment opportunities, housing, and more. This help isn't short term, and it isn't cheap. The consequence of not providing it, though, is the continuing destruction of our veterans by alcohol, drugs, and suicide.

It is rare today for a week to pass without at least one news story related to PTSD, depression, and suicide in the military. At the same time, it's all too easy for most of us to gloss over the headlines or tune out the details because civilian life continues uninterrupted. American soldiers are dying every day in a war that has cost our country more than $1.4 trillion to date[5] and may well end up costing several times that amount, according to Linda Bilmes. She is a professor at Harvard's Kennedy School of Government and coauthor of the book *The Three Trillion Dollar War: The True Cost of the Iraq Conflict.* An investment of that magnitude could revitalize our economy and help us get out of debt, provide health care and a college education to everyone who wants it, or put every able-bodied citizen to work at a meaningful wage. Yet the fact that it's being diverted barely crosses our minds.

As a society, it behooves us to be aware of the devastation we are causing, not only in our economy and in the countries where we choose to wage war, but in the homes and lives of those who do our fighting. The psychological toll exacted by combat is real, serious, and often unrelenting. Like war itself, it must not be taken lightly.

Acknowledgments

I am deeply indebted to the families of active-duty troops and veterans whose loved ones died by suicide and who have talked publicly about it. This has taken enormous courage, given the stigma that suicide carries in our society, and it has made a difference. The stories they tell shed more light on the problem than any report can and speak powerfully of the need to acknowledge, understand, and commit to preventing these tragedies.

I also am indebted to the many people whose encouragement, support, and expertise made this book possible. This includes suicide researchers, military officials, individuals who counsel active-duty service members and veterans, and numerous others.

Early reviewers of the manuscript added a much-needed critical eye, as well as much-appreciated validation. If any errors remain, they are mine alone.

I want to thank the staff at Oxford University Press for the enthusiasm with which they embraced this book and express gratitude to my agent for placing it there. I am honored to be among the writers whose work OUP is publishing.

Lastly, and most important, I want to thank my wife and children. The richness and meaning they add to my life is greater than words can describe.

The Last and Greatest Battle

The Problem Defined

"Even grasshoppers hate me."

I N *PATHWAY TO HELL*, BY DENNIS W. BRANDT, AS WELL AS IN THE HBO
documentary *Wartorn: 1865–2010*, the horror, stress, and consequences of the Civil War are related through the experiences of
one soldier, Corporal Angelo Crapsey of Roulette, Pennsylvania.
Considered "lively and cheerful" by friends, and popular with young
women because of his handsome looks, Crapsey believed wholeheart-
edly in the Union and vowed to "fight for its protection as long as
I can breathe."[1] In April 1861, within days after Confederate forces
fired on Union troops at Fort Sumter and ignited the war, Crapsey
enlisted. He was eighteen years old and filled with romantic notions
of "fighting for the Stars and Stripes."[2] He wrote to a family friend,
"You may think it seems strange for me to leave my work when I was
getting such wages [he was working oil fields, boring wells]. Strange
it was, but I love the old flag dearly."[3]

As reality set in, however, dreams of glory vanished. Subsisting
on poor food and dirty water, sleeping on wet ground, and marching
long distances over rugged terrain, Crapsey soon realized what he
had committed to. Still, he remained confident.

"Camp life is not home," he told his family. "I knew that before I started. A soldier's life is hard, but I should be able to take care of myself."[4] (Crapsey's letters constitute some of the most vivid and articulate accounts of the Civil War; however, he was a poor speller. I have corrected his spelling for the sake of readability.)

Then his unit began to suffer casualties, and the flag he loved so much turned "red with the blood" of all the soldiers "who have died fighting to protect it."[5] One casualty was a soldier who killed himself.

"He had been unwell for a few days and seemed to be a little shattered," Crapsey wrote. "He took a rifle and loaded it when there was no one about, and put the muzzle into his mouth and tucked the gun off with his shoes. I heard the gun when he shot himself."[6]

In the following weeks the fighting grew even more intense. Bullets flew in every direction, and "cannon balls came whirring through the air and smashing down everything that was in range."[7] Crapsey's thoughts became more troubled, and his mood darkened. "I don't know as my courage is so very good," he wrote. "Many was the time I saw things that will be remembered until death."[8]

By August 1862, any hope he had for a quick resolution had disappeared, and he couldn't stop thinking about what he had seen. At the Battle of Cedar Mountain in Virginia, his unit arrived too late to fight. Crapsey joined a burial party, dumping the bodies of Union soldiers into shallow graves. "It was a terrible sight," he said. "I saw hundreds of dead men."[9]

A month later he was at Antietam for the bloodiest day in U.S. history. "Shot and shell and grape and canister were flying like hail. Men fell like weeds. The battle raged all day with a deafening roar."[10]

He worked burial detail again and contemplated his own mortality. "I don't know how I have escaped death or a wound. I thank my Heavenly Father for my life being spared this far. I know not how soon I will follow my comrades who now lie slumbering in an unknown grave."[11]

The bravado he exuded early on was gone. He lamented, "So many of our noble men have been laid cold in death and so many thousands are crippled for life."[12] He added, "No one except he [who] has been a soldier can imagine what one has to endure."[13]

Crapsey's experiences intensified after the Battle of Fredericksburg on December 13, 1862. There, his company succumbed to Confederate forces, and he was taken prisoner. The next few weeks were a nightmare. Libby Prison in Richmond, Virginia, had been a ware-house at one time, and the odor of as many as 1,000 men, unwashed and diarrheic, crammed into two large rooms that still smelled of fish was overwhelming. In addition, food was almost nonexistent—men were fed a six-ounce ration of bread twice a day. Worst of all, lice were everywhere. Crapsey exchanged his boots for food to try and appease his hunger, but there was no relief from the parasites.[14]

After three weeks, Crapsey was moved to Camp Parole, a hold-ing area in Annapolis, Maryland, for Union prisoners of war. Five months later, he was among those exchanged for Confederate POWs. When he returned to his unit, Crapsey was welcomed back by old comrades, but they noticed immediately that he had changed. His gregariousness had disappeared, he didn't say much, and when he did it was to comment on the suffering of prisoners. He also had devel-oped a disturbing habit—scraping at phantom lice.[15]

Angelo Crapsey participated in six battles. The last was on the biggest stage of all—Gettysburg. Once again he emerged unscathed, but within days he developed a high fever and dysentery. (Dysentery and diarrhea were common because soldiers lacked access to toilet facilities. Union doctors attributed 57,000 deaths to dysentery and diarrhea, and it's likely that thousands of Confederate soldiers died from it as well. By 1865, according to historian Drew Gilpin Faust, the sick rate for diarrhea and dysentery was 995 per 1,000.)[16] Doctors thought Crapsey would die and summoned his father for last rites. Crapsey survived, though, and came home in October 1863.

Family members knew at once that he was different, however. "His mind was weak," his stepmother said. "He hadn't been home five minutes before I noticed that."[17] Friends remarked that he was a "perfect wreck in mind and body" and was "wild and wandering in his memories all the time."[18] More than once he jumped to his feet, threw up his hands, and shouted, "I surrender!"[19] He said that he had killed so many men, "Even the grasshoppers hate me."[20]

In an effort to rid himself of imaginary lice, Crapsey hacked his arms with the blade of a broken scythe. He also dove through the front window of a friend's home, drank poison, and tried to drown himself, only to be saved each time. Doctors suggested that he be placed in a mental institution, but his father wouldn't hear of it. On August 4, 1864, longtime friends didn't let him hunt with them, so Crapsey went off on his own. He sat under a tree, put the barrel of his rifle in his mouth, and used a branch to pull the trigger, imitating almost exactly the suicide he had witnessed three years earlier in his unit. He was twenty-one.

There are casualties in every war. Some are obvious, such as soldiers* who are killed in battle or related action. Their bodies, if identified and recovered, are sent home, oftentimes from distant lands and in flag-draped coffins, to be honored in solemn military ceremonies and buried in vast military cemeteries like Arlington and Calverton. Depending on the war and where the deceased are from, they also may have their names etched on national monuments and small-town plaques. Their service to our country is forever recognized, as is the fact that they made the ultimate sacrifice.

Other casualties, such as civilians who are caught in the crossfire, are less obvious. Typically referred to as *collateral damage*, they are nameless, faceless people—at least by U.S. military and media standards—characterized as being in the wrong place at the wrong time. Their deaths are considered unfortunate but also unavoidable. No doubt our attitude toward them would be different if they were American citizens. Then we would be moved by the tragedies of our fellow countrymen. As it is, when we send solders off to fight, they engage the enemy on foreign ground. It's one of the luxuries that we have enjoyed and also taken for granted. Roadside bombs, grenades, and sniper fire don't strike loved ones who are stateside. The children who are rendered orphans and the families who are suddenly homeless are casualties of another nation.

There is a third group of war casualties, though, whose numbers are growing and in recent years have exceeded the number of U.S. troops killed in battle. This group consists of American service members who die by their own hand. Oftentimes these deaths happen far away from any war zone and long after the person's last military tour of duty has ended. Many of these victims suffer, in one form or another, from posttraumatic stress disorder (PTSD) that is treated inadequately or not at all. Exposed to horrors that the average

---

* I use the words *soldiers* and *troops* interchangeably, as most members of the general public do. Among military personnel, however, there is a clear distinction. Soldiers are in the Army, while sailors are in the Navy, airmen are in the Air Force, and Marines are in the Marine Corps.

American who lacks wartime experience can't possibly comprehend, perhaps missing limbs or bearing other physical and psychological scars, these individuals are expected to return home and, within a short period of time, adjust naturally to everyday civilian life, almost as if the war never happened.

It's an impossible task for many. The intensity of their experiences, the development of their senses to imminent danger, and the focus they must have on the here and now—daydream for a second in a war zone and you may die—can't be easily dismissed.

Imagine, if you can, what it's like to experience the constant threat of death or serious injury, to witness killings and maimings on a regular basis, to believe that no place is safe, no duty is without risk, no stranger or situation is to be trusted. Out of necessity, soldiers develop a heightened sense of vigilance. Every setting presents risks. For present-day service members in Iraq and Afghanistan, crowds and open-air markets aren't safe because they are targets for suicide bombings. Trash on the side of the road isn't safe because it may hide an improvised explosive device (IED). Cars and nonmilitary trucks aren't safe because they could be carrying a vehicle-born improvised explosive device (VBIED).

When soldiers in Iraq see someone on a cell phone, they don't know whether the person is having an innocent conversation or is coding a bomb to kill them. Since roadside bombs made from hand grenades, mortar rounds, TNT, or other explosive elements can be detonated from a cell phone as easily as from a pressure switch or charge wire, the latter is always a possibility. (At the height of the war in Iraq, more than 60 percent of all U.S. military deaths were from IEDs.)[21] When a child approaches a soldier, is it because he or she wants to play or is it because the child has been strapped with explosives that will be triggered when the soldier is close enough to kill?

There is no letup, no chance to relax. Soldiers today live on high alert the whole time they are in a war zone, referring to it as 360/365—that is, it's all around them every day.[22] They sleep little because they have to be on guard against the possibility of incoming mortar fire, an ambush, an IED, or a suicide bomber. Violent deaths are common, especially "in theater"—an odd way to refer to the geographic area where war takes place, but that's the military term for it—and surviving the ever-present threats of danger becomes a 24-7 job. Even when they are behind walls in a forward operating base

(FOB), presumably safe, soldiers carry their weapons at all times, including when they go to the bathroom.

Soldiers learn to sit with their backs to a wall so that any attack comes from in front of them. They learn to drive fast and employ evasive maneuvers to reduce the likelihood of being struck by a rocket-propelled grenade (RPG). They learn that women and children may be armed, so never let down your guard or assume that anyone is innocent.

They also learn to avoid lighted areas at night because their bodies are more exposed. They avoid dark areas as well because the enemy is more hidden. They avoid confined spaces, too, such as stairwells, because it's possible to be trapped without an exit.

In addition, soldiers endure harsh climatic conditions, from extreme heat to bitter cold. In the desert, wearing full body armor, they operate in 130-degree weather. Even the water they drink can be 90 degrees or more. They are weighted down by firearms and ammunition and ride in airless Humvees with bulletproof windows that are closed tight.

They also deal with harsh elements, from giant insects to raw sewage. Moreover, they accept, because they have no choice, poor sleep accommodations (sometimes hard ground or a ditch), poor food (oftentimes packaged and bland MREs [Meals Ready to Eat], which soldiers jokingly refer to as Meals Rejected by Ethiopia), and the constant discomfort of dirt and sand in their clothes (Iraq is called "the sandbox"). The only social support they have is other soldiers in their unit. These comrades are the only people they can trust, the only ones they can count on to protect them. If a buddy is killed or seriously injured, there is the grief of losing a friend and also the guilt that they didn't adequately protect the person, that they were responsible in some way for what happened.

On top of all this, there is the stress of being separated for long periods of time from loved ones, separations that test marriages and families. Until recently, soldiers had only limited communication with family members. Today, they can communicate readily via cell phones, Skype, blogs, e-mail, and other electronic means; however, this is both a blessing and a curse. Easy communication provides a source of comfort, reassuring soldiers that their families are all right while letting families know that their loved one is alive and—at least for the moment—safe. At the same time, it has drawbacks. For one thing, bad news travels faster than ever—everything from minor problems, such as a broken washing machine that needs to be fixed but the deployed person isn't there to help, to a spouse's infidelity. With access to frequent communication, it's tempting for loved ones to talk about challenges on the home front, which has the adverse consequence of distracting soldiers from their military duties. At the same time, family members may be exposed to the harsh realities of war that time and distance, historically, have hidden. To hear gunfire or explosions in the background tends to trump whatever a soldier might be telling you about the relative security of his or her environment.

"It's Like a Diesel Smell"

Returning home presents challenges for soldiers and their families that are beyond the grasp of ordinary citizens. While they are in country (that is, serving in foreign lands), soldiers live on the edge. There is constant excitement and danger. They feel that what they are doing is important, they have each other's back, and they are in control, especially emotionally. They know what to do, where to go, and who to listen to. Their lives are organized and structured, nearly every minute planned. Tasks are clear, and responsibilities—to themselves, to their unit, to the service, and to their country—have been drilled into them ad nauseam to avoid any hesitation or confusion. When something happens, they react immediately, without thought, because that is how they have been trained. Then they come home, and none of that exists. There is no commander giving orders, no uniform to wear, no group of buddies to protect. There is no stated mission— whether it makes sense or not—of a hill to climb, river to cross, jungle to hack through, or town to liberate. There is also nowhere near the same level of accountability, with every job performed to the highest standards because that is how the military operates. "Good enough" isn't good enough when you are a soldier. Whether it's something as mundane as making a bed or shining shoes, or more complex such as patrolling a neighborhood or establishing a base of operations, it has to be done exactly right. There is no excuse for an incomplete report, sloppy dress (outside a combat zone), or a poorly executed salute. Yet in civilian life—particularly in a household—such precision is neither sought nor welcomed by others.

Troops go from driving Humvees down the middle of the road in order to avoid IEDs to steering shopping carts down supermarket aisles in order to buy groceries. Instead of selecting weapons, they are selecting cereals. Instead of deciding survival strategies, they are expected to make small talk with people at a party. Instead of suppressing feelings, being suspicious of others, and dealing with conflict through violence—as they have been trained—they are supposed to express emotions, trust others, and defuse conflict with tact.

Is it any wonder when soldiers come back from war today that they don't want to go anyplace where there are lots of people, such as a shopping mall, discount department store, movie theater, or farmers' market? That they tend to drive fast and aggressively, tailgating and not waiting for other cars that have the right of way because that is how one avoids being killed in Iraq? That they can't enjoy a vacation or even a picnic in a mountainous area because the terrain reminds them too much of Afghanistan? That they feel a strong need to have weapons nearby for protection, to make multiple perimeter checks around the house to ensure their family's safety, and to constantly search rooftops for snipers, even in sleepy residential neighborhoods? This is what they have been trained to do. It has been ingrained in them because their survival and the survival of others depends on it. Yet to find oneself not fitting in at home as a result of these ingrained responses can be a source of anger, frustration, and despair for everyone, soldier and family members alike. To flinch when someone approaches you from behind, or to drop to the floor whenever there is a loud noise—a door being slammed, heavy object falling, or car backfiring—sends a strong signal to others that you aren't like them. Nor can you be.

"There's a certain kind of smell, it's like a diesel smell," says Iraq veteran Kevin Powers, author of the novel *The Yellow Birds*, which focuses on the experiences of two U.S. soldiers in Iraq. "If I'm walking down the street and a city bus goes by, I'll catch a whiff and [it will] immediately put me back there."[23]

The highs of being home and reunited with loved ones wear off quickly and aren't nearly as high as the adrenaline-charged moments of combat. The experience of being fired at and discharging your own weapon in return while there is chaos all around you—shells exploding, people yelling, trees being uprooted, smoke billowing, shadows moving, the earth buckling—can't be reproduced, although some soldiers try by engaging in risk-taking behaviors such as motorcycle racing, rock climbing, and skydiving. Ironically, the lows back home are infinitely worse. In the midst of war, there is little opportunity to think about a friend hunched over next to you one minute, eyes peering through the darkness at an unknown enemy, then lying dead the next minute, the victim of a random bullet or roadside bomb. This is because your survival instincts kick in, and you are scampering for safety, dragging your buddy's body with you. There is little opportunity, too, to think about enemy combatants you have killed or, worse, innocent civilians who died because, in the moment, they didn't seem innocent at all. There is too much else to focus on. Months later, though, when you are back home and all you seem to have is time on your hands, the images won't go away. The scenes of shock, grief, and guilt form a continual loop in one's mind, winding and rewinding no matter how hard a person tries to stop them from playing. At some point it can become too much. Untreated, it can lead to suicide.

Thanksgiving Day, eight months after returning home from Baghdad where he patrolled Airport Road, one of the most dangerous assignments, Army reservist Tom Bowman shot himself. He was twenty-three. According to his mother, he came back a different person. "His eyes," she said, "were just dead. The light wasn't there anymore."[24]

Charles Edward Dane ("Eddie" to family and friends) served six combat tours—three in Iraq, two in Kosovo, and one in both Bosnia and Afghanistan. A staff sergeant in the Marines, he received medals and ribbons for achievement, good conduct, and combat action. He also battled depression and PTSD. After a second arrest for drunk driving, his fifteen-year military career ended with a dishonorable discharge. Subsequently, he killed himself.

Linda Michel was a Navy medic at Camp Bucca, the largest U.S. military prison in Iraq until it was dismantled in 2011. Named after a New York City fire marshal and former soldier who died in the September 11, 2001 terrorist attacks, Camp Bucca housed more than 6,000 people, nearly all of them Iraqi civilians. Following the prisoner abuse scandal at Abu Ghraib, many Abu Ghraib detainees were transferred to Camp Bucca. Today, it's a hotel, turned over by the Pentagon to the Iraqi government as part of the withdrawal of U.S. troops from the country. When Michel was there, however, it was still a prison. (In its first year as a hotel, the renamed Basra Gateway hadn't changed much. Guard towers remained, there was "still a jumble of concrete blocks, sandbags, and barbed wire" at the front gate, and trailers that once housed U.S. military personnel now accommodated oil company executives who were on business trips.)[25]

In 2006, two weeks after she returned home to Clifton, New York, and only a few weeks before she was scheduled to be discharged after five years of duty, Michel shot herself. She had been treated for depression and prescribed Paxil, but was not evacuated.

"If somebody needs Paxil in a combat zone," her husband, an Iraq War veteran, told a reporter afterward, "you either send them to a hospital or you send them home."[26]

Neither happened. Her death at age thirty-three left her husband widowed and her three young children motherless.

"Suicide Mania"

It isn't just the current war, though. If one goes back through history, there has always been a strong correlation between war and suicide.

In the Civil War, many people resorted to suicide before, during, and after the fighting. According to historian Diane Miller Sommerville, young men who didn't want to acknowledge their fears because they would be labeled cowards for the rest of their lives chose to kill themselves instead, sometimes en route to the front. Married women who suddenly found themselves alone, no longer protected by their husbands, who were off fighting somewhere or already dead, killed themselves rather than flee or try to safeguard their homes and children from marauders. Southern men who returned from battle to find their homes destroyed and their slaves emancipated, facing enormous debt and being unable to provide for their families, killed themselves.[27] The phenomenon was so frequent that news stories of "suicide mania" were common in the South.[28] "Not a day passes without from five to ten cases," one North Carolina newspaper reported in 1882.

Sommerville is a history professor at Binghamton University in New York. In 2011 she received a fellowship award from the National Endowment for the Humanities to examine how two current problems—suicide and mental illness—were handled in the past. Since the Civil War is the defining moment historically and psychologically in the South, it was natural for this event to become the focus of her research.

In an article titled "A Burden Too Heavy to Bear," a portion of which she was kind enough to share with me prior to publication, Sommerville talks about the "community of suffering" that existed in the South during and after the Civil War. This suffering included soldiers who died by suicide and those who ended up in insane asylums due to the psychological trauma they experienced.[29]

Unfortunately, no comprehensive data exist on suicides in the United States during the nineteenth century, much less data on suicides by soldiers and veterans. Uniform death certificates weren't introduced until the 1880s, and even after states starting using them, they didn't always reflect accurately whether the cause of death was suicide. In some states, legal consequences for killing oneself were never enacted so coroners weren't required to investigate suicides. In many counties, inquest records weren't retained or they disappeared from archives long ago. In the South, as the war went on and the Confederacy weakened, records stopped being maintained. Then, at the end of the war, any data that might have been helpful disappeared because no one took responsibility for collecting it. Added to this is the fact that suicides tend to be underreported due to stigma. As a result, no one knows how many people died by suicide during and immediately after the Civil War.

Then again, no one knows how many American soldiers killed themselves during and after World War I, World War II, the Korean War, Vietnam, or the first Persian Gulf War. It was only with the advent of the second Gulf War in 2003 and the fighting in Iraq and Afghanistan that the military began to monitor the suicide rate of troops. This is why it is virtually impossible to compare the number or percentage of military suicides currently with those in other eras—no data for previous wars exist. There is piecemeal information, considerable anecdotal evidence, and knowledge of psychiatric casualties in wars past, but no concrete data on suicides specifically. All one can say with certainty, as Richard A. Gabriel does in his book *No More Heroes: Madness and Psychiatry at War*, is that "in a modern war, the chances of becoming a psychiatric casualty are more than twice as great as being killed by enemy fire."[30]

Still, historians like Sommerville, David Silkenat (author of *Moments of Despair*, which focuses in part on Civil War suicides in

North Carolina), and Eric T. Dean, Jr. (author of *Shook Over Hell*, an examination of posttraumatic stress during and after the Civil War), have been able to piece together information based on asylum records, newspaper accounts, letters, and diaries. In Sommerville's words, their work and the work of others demonstrate "a near epidemic of emotional and psychological suffering" experienced by Civil War soldiers and veterans.[31]

In recent years, two University of Hawaii professors, B. Christopher Frueh and Jeffrey A. Smith, have added some details. After examining thousands of Union records, they believe that they have determined the number of suicides by Union soldiers during the war. This was possible because in 1862 the U.S. War Department Surgeon General's Office began compiling what came to be called the *Medical and Surgical History of the War of Rebellion*, subsequently referred to as the *MSHWR*. All Union army medical directors were ordered to provide data on the "morale and sanitary conditions of the troops," past and present. Later the scope was broadened to include general hospitals that treated military personnel. By early 1864, the Surgeon General's Office had a comprehensive system in place for tracking the medical condition of all Union soldiers. Three years after the war ended, Congress commissioned the publication of the first part of the *MSHWR*—a massive tome of 6 volumes, 3,000 pages, and more than 700 tables that took nearly 20 years to produce in full.

To understand the work of Frueh and Smith, as well as other suicide researchers, it's important to know the meaning of suicide rates. These rates are based on the number of deaths per 100,000 people. In the past 30 years, the suicide rate in the United States has averaged 11.8 (that is, 11.8 people out of every 100,000 kill themselves). It was 12.0 in 1981, rose to a high of 12.9 in 1986, and ended the decade at 12.2. In 1990 it was 12.4, then dropped gradually to a low of 10.5 in 1999. Starting in 2000, the rate began increasing, ending at 11.9 in 2008, 12.0 in 2009, and 12.4 in 2010, the last year for which data are available. No one has been able to explain satisfactorily yearly variations in the country's suicide rate. There is a relationship between unemployment and suicide that accounts for some of the fluctuation, but not all. What is known is that men have a suicide rate three times higher than women, whites have a higher suicide rate than other ethnicities, and the elderly have the highest rates of any age group. Also, the three states with the highest suicide rates are Alaska, Montana, and Wyoming. Not coincidentally, these states have the largest percentage of gun owners, according to the Harvard Injury Control Research Center, and also of white men. In addition, these states have a scarcity of mental health services because much of the population lives in rural areas.

In assessing Civil War suicides, Frueh and Smith determined that the suicide rate for white men in the Union army was 14.5 in the first 12 months of fighting (July 1, 1861–June 30, 1862), 13.9 the second year, dropped to 8.7 the third year, and rose to 11.8 the fourth year (ending June 30, 1865). These rates are based on a total of 270 suicides by white soldiers. Frueh and Smith also noted thirty-two suicides by Union soldiers in the first year after the war—thirty-one by whites—although they couldn't ascertain a rate because it was unclear how many troops remained on active duty once the war ended. Blacks didn't participate in battle on the Union side the first two years. In the third year, 1863–1864, eight black Union soldiers killed themselves, according to Frueh and Smith, a suicide rate of 17.7. There were no reported black suicides in the fourth year (1864–1865).

Frueh and Smith decided that their yearly calculations were somewhat inflated, however, because the "mean unit strength," a figure they used to determine the number of combatants, didn't include casualties, deserters, and replacement soldiers who fought for a portion of the year but weren't present the whole year. Also, many soldiers served more than one year. Taking these into account, Frueh and Smith came up with an overall rate of 6.6 per year during the war for Union soldiers.

This is a better estimate than anyone else has been able to produce. Even if it's accurate, though, it's difficult to draw a comparison between this number and the suicide rate of civilians at the time because no national data existed. Psychiatrist R. Gregory Lande cites census information that indicates the suicide rate of male civilians in 1870 was 10.0;[32] however, there are no other data sources, and census information at that time in regard to suicide is unreliable. At best there are only aggregated data for specific regions of the country. Massachusetts, for instance, was one of the first states to record suicides, starting in 1843. At the beginning of the Civil War, the state averaged 95 suicides per year. The number dropped to an average of 79 suicides per year from 1861 to 1865. By 1870 there were fewer suicides than a decade earlier—84. Ten years after the war ended, however, the number had increased to 126 per year, and in 1880 it was 140. Looking at the number of suicides alone, it's easy to argue that they were increasing. This is why suicide rates are important. Because they account for population growth, they provide a truer picture. In Massachusetts, for instance, the suicide rate in 1860 was 7.7 based on a population of 1,231,066. In 1870 it was 5.8 based on a population of 1,457,351. In 1880 it was 7.9 based on a population of 1,783,085. In other words, while the number of suicides increased, the number of people increased, too, so that the suicide rate vacillated over forty years, ending near where it had started.

Similarly, in New York City the number of suicides nearly doubled from an average of 64 per year in the first three years following the Civil War to 120 per year three years later.[33] Here, though, the increase reflects an increased rate as well, from 7.9 in 1860 based on a population of 805,658 to 12.7 in 1870 based on a population of 942,292.

"Don't Worry If Your Man Screams at Night"

In many respects, Angelo Crapsey's suicide was typical of those during the Civil War. He was young and enlisted out of a sense of patriotic fervor—the same fervor that has compelled young people to enlist in recent years, following 9/11. While he knew that he would be putting his life at risk, he also exuded an air of invincibility that is common among youth. When he began to witness first-hand the brutality of war, however, and see soldiers killed and wounded in battle, his own mortality became evident. In addition, he contributed to the slaughter, firing his weapon and shooting others. Coming home, he couldn't forget what he had seen and done, and no help was offered that enabled him to deal with the psychological trauma he endured.

Based on the American Psychiatric Association's *Diagnostic and Statistical Manual of Mental Disorders*, Angelo Crapsey's behavior met all of the present-day criteria for PTSD. He was exposed to a horrific event, relived the event, was estranged from others, was unable to sleep or concentrate afterward, experienced impaired social functioning, and had these symptoms for a month or more.[34] If Crapsey were alive today, there is no doubt that a diagnosis of PTSD would be confirmed.

"Angelo Crapsey never spilled a drop of blood defending his ideals," says author Dennis W. Brandt, "but he did expend his mind."[35]

So have soldiers in other wars. In World War I and World War II, the country was united rather than divided, and all fighting took place overseas, so U.S. factories, homes, and civilians were spared. In addition, returning soldiers were treated as heroes and conquerors, and their military service was celebrated in newsreels, parades, and movies. Yet while family members and friends who didn't fight embraced the peace that followed, the minds of many returning World War I and World War II soldiers weren't at peace. They had to live with the fact that they had committed and witnessed atrocities. They had killed others and watched good friends get killed.

No one wanted to talk about the changes—least of all with loved ones who wouldn't understand the situation but might judge a soldier's actions harshly regardless. Instead, it was common for veterans of these wars, behind closed doors, to become aggressive with spouses and children, to be quick to argue, intolerant of any pushback, and insensitive to others' feelings. The war had changed them. Subject to flashbacks (unwanted memories that seem real) and nightmares, vets no longer were the innocent boys and men who had picked up arms to protect their country. Now they carried deep, hidden wounds.

Writer Doris Lessing's father was a young bank clerk in England when World War I broke out. After he came home, others talked about his kindness and compassion, but they didn't see him the way she did. "I do not think these people would have easily recognized the ill, irritable, abstracted, hypochondriac man I knew," she wrote in *A Small Personal Voice*.[36]

Following the Battle of Dunkirk in 1940, in which 11,000 Allied soldiers were killed and 40,000 were captured, the British Army offered terse advice to soldiers' wives when their husbands came home. "Don't worry if your man screams at night or throws himself down when a plane flies over the back garden,"[37] the Army said, implying that this behavior was normal and nothing to fret over.

The problem was that while this behavior might have been considered normal, it was hardly inconsequential. In California alone, according to one analysis, 532 veterans over age 80 (placing them in their prime in World War II) killed themselves between 2005 and 2008.[38] That's nearly four times as many World War II–era veterans dying by suicide as people the same age who never served in the military. Coming home, their mental condition wasn't recognized, much less treated. No one knew then that there was such a thing as posttraumatic stress, or that it could have a devastating impact. Certainly it wasn't something that vets could seek care for from hospitals or clinics of the Veterans Administration (in 1989, the Veterans Administration was renamed the Department of Veterans Affairs). The only recourse was the one that most veterans took—to self-medicate with alcohol.

For Vietnam veterans, it was worse. Fighting in a war that didn't have a concrete purpose, that the American public didn't support and—in fact—grew to oppose, they returned home to a lukewarm reception. In most instances it wasn't a hostile reception, according to Jerry Lembcke in his book, *The Spitting Image*. Despite the myth that Americans spit at returning Vietnam veterans, it rarely happened, says Lembcke. In *Homecoming*, however, syndicated newspaper columnist Bob Greene tells of a request he made to Vietnam vets to share their stories of being spat upon, and receiving more than 1,000 letters in response. In any event, the new veterans—many of whom went to war unwillingly—weren't treated as heroes the way that U.S. service members in World War I and World War II were treated, or with anywhere near the same level of respect as is shown to troops today. The prevailing opinion was that Vietnam represented the first U.S. military defeat, which made the war something that people wanted to forget as quickly as possible. In fact, if one lived in the South, Vietnam wasn't the first war lost—the Civil War was. Nevertheless, Vietnam was a crushing defeat in many ways, and few people who weren't involved had any interest in hearing stories of the war or exhibited much sympathy for the battle scars (internal and external) that soldiers brought home with them. At best, the message Vietnam vets heard was, "Forget the war. Move on. Deal with life now." At worst, they were regarded as drug addicts, whiners, and—because of atrocities like My Lai—baby killers. (My Lai was a small Vietnamese village where Army soldiers, in 1968, ordered inhabitants to a village square, then mowed them down with automatic weapons. Afterward, huts in the village—some with people still in them—were blown up with grenades, and the few survivors were herded into a ditch where they, too, were gunned down. In all, more than 560 unarmed and defenseless villagers—children, women, and old men—were murdered. The story came to light only because a

U.S. helicopter pilot tried to intervene, and another witness, an Army photographer, recorded the slaughter on a secret camera, after being ordered to turn in his official camera. Subsequently, thirteen soldiers were accused of war crimes, but only the commander, Lieutenant William L. Calley, was found guilty. His prison sentence was reduced to house arrest by President Richard Nixon, and later Calley was paroled, expressing remorse but also justifying his actions by saying that he was just following orders.)

Many Americans know that more than 58,000 U.S. troops died in the Vietnam War. Their names are engraved on the Vietnam Memorial, one of the most popular and poignant tourist destinations in our country. People run their fingers reverently over the names, silently acknowledging their connection to a loved one, friend, or stranger. No one knows, though, the number of Vietnam veterans who have since died by suicide. This is because the best source for this information, the U.S. government, whiffed when presented with the opportunity to make it known.

The *National Vietnam Veterans Readjustment Study* (NVVRS), published in 1990, is considered to be the premier epidemiological study of the impact of psychological problems on American veterans who served in Vietnam. Funded by Congress, and conducted primarily by government agencies, the study is massive. The executive summary alone is more than 300 pages. Then there is a large companion volume of tables and appendices. Despite its heft, however, there is a serious omission. As Penny Coleman first noted in her book *Flashback*, nowhere in the NVVRS, as it is known, is there any reference to suicide. In fact, the word *suicide* doesn't appear in any context, and the fact that thousands of Vietnam vets had killed themselves fifteen years after the war ended, when the NVVRS came out, is never mentioned.[39]

How did the hundreds of so-called experts who contributed to the NVVRS miss this? Why did none of them note a link between the psychological traumas experienced by soldiers in Vietnam and incidences of suicide by these same soldiers after the war? At best, Coleman says, the omission was irresponsible. "At worst, it was a cynical strategy to avoid taking responsibility for a population that was emotionally incapable of protecting itself."[40]

Two factors support the latter view. First, for years government officials refused to admit any connection between the effects of

Agent Orange—dropped in massive quantities by U.S. helicopters to defoliate jungles in Vietnam and flush out the enemy—and subsequent health problems experienced by soldiers who were exposed to the deadly chemical. Veterans' claims related to Agent Orange were denied routinely. More than 100,000 soldiers—at their request— were examined in VA hospitals and clinics for Agent Orange exposure by 1983,[41] yet fewer than 1,500 were awarded compensation. Moreover, those who were compensated received nominal amounts, and only for skin rashes that they were able to prove had been caused by the dioxin.

The second factor is that the Australian government commissioned a similar study of its Vietnam War veterans, but conducted it much differently. In the *Retrospective Cohort Study*, each of the 60,000 Australian veterans who had served in the war was contacted and a master roll was created. It was a significant investment of time and resources, although as one of the authors of the study noted, "Once you have built it, you have it forever."[42] The result was more information and a greater level of detail than in the American study, despite the latter's voluminous final product. Among other findings, the Australian study reported a 21 percent increase in suicides by Vietnam veterans between 1982 and 1994.[43] In addition, the death rate of children of Vietnam vets from accidents and suicide was 250 percent higher than for other Australians in the same age group.[44]

In defense of the U.S. military, the argument can be made that tracking 3 million American veterans would have required a much greater commitment of time and resources than the *Retrospective Cohort Study* in Australia. Yet it would have indicated a genuine willingness to try and understand the war's short-term and long-range impact on troops. The irony is that the U.S. government, by virtue of commissioning the *Medical and Surgical History of the War of Rebellion*, willingly made a substantial investment during and immediately after the Civil War to track 2.1 million Union soldiers (the absence of records made it impossible to track the 900,000 Confederate troops), but not the 3 million U.S. soldiers who fought in Vietnam.

The lack of any reference to suicide, suicide deaths, suicide attempts, or suicide ideation in the *National Vietnam Veterans Readjustment Study* is all the more baffling because of research reported elsewhere. In 1986, an article in the *New England Journal of Medicine* noted that veterans were 65 percent more likely than nonveterans to die by suicide.[45] In 1988, psychiatrist Jacob Lindy's book, *Vietnam: A Casebook*, made a direct connection between war and suicide. Specifically, Lindy noted that every person in a treatment sample of Vietnam veterans reported having suicidal thoughts in the previous seven days, as did 72 percent of Vietnam veterans in a clinical sample conducted by the National Institute of Mental Health. Moreover, 37 percent of vets in the clinical sample had attempted suicide, as had 8 percent in the treatment sample.[46] Lindy's work was well known in the field, yet its results never made it into the *NVVRS*, issued two years later. Consequently, none of the suicides by Vietnam veterans were acknowledged, much less examined.

Because neither the Department of Veterans Affairs nor the Department of Defense (DoD) has maintained information on Vietnam vets who have died by suicide, the number is unknown. A front-page story in the *Seattle Times* in 1981 said that there had been 50,000 suicides of Vietnam veterans up to that time.[47] Four years later, *Discover* magazine put the number at 58,000—equivalent to the number of battlefield casualties.[48] In 1987, it was 100,000, according to a *60 Minutes* report.[49] In 1988, it was between 26,000 and 100,000 according to *CBS News*.[50] The same year, psychiatrist Lindy claimed that there had been "tens of thousands more" suicides after the war than combat deaths.[51] In *Nam Vet: Making Peace with Your Past*, former Vietnam paratrooper, one-time drill sergeant, and Army chaplain Chuck Dean says that it's 150,000 suicides.[52] Other sources think it's even higher.

All are just guesses, though, and sometimes biased. From the government's point of view, undercounting the number serves to lessen the problem and reduce the liability of military payouts. If the impact is minimized, so is the responsibility. From the viewpoint of veterans groups, it's the opposite. The greater the number of veteran suicides, and the more that they can be connected with trauma from the war, the more it strengthens their case for increased compensation.

Whatever the number is, in each instance no crisply folded American flag was presented to a grieving spouse. No monetary payout (however modest) was made to a dead soldier's family. No condolence letter was sent by the president. Every casualty was the result of invisible wounds, wounds that may have been sensed but were never fully known. It's not surprising that more than half of all

Vietnam vets abuse alcohol at some point in their lives.[53] The bottle offers a way to escape the mental ravages of war that no other avenue except street drugs and prescription medication provides.

Eighteen to Twenty-Two

Worldwide, about one million people are murdered and killed in wars—big and small—every year. The same number of people die by suicide annually.[54] For veterans, the killing continues long after the last battle shot is fired. In locked hotel rooms, garages, and closets, in parks, secluded woods, and other outdoor spaces, the casualties mount, a hidden cost of war. As hard as it is to survive the harrowing experiences of battle, it's even harder sometimes to find enjoyment and meaning in life when the shooting stops and depression, despair, and hopelessness set in. Even if you are surrounded by family, you are alone in your mind.

For a long time, officials with the Department of Veterans Affairs said that the agency didn't track suicides by veterans. It was only in 2008, as the result of a lawsuit, that the VA disclosed a startling truth: An average of eighteen veterans per day killed themselves. That equaled 1 suicide every 80 minutes, 126 suicides every week, more than 6,500 suicides every year. It meant that nearly 20 percent of all people in the United States who killed themselves were veterans—yet vets comprise only 7 percent of our population.

Subsequently, a federal appeals court noted that eighteen suicides per day was evidence of the VA's "unchecked incompetence."[55] The VA, in response, said that the number wasn't reliable because it was based on old and incomplete data. In particular, the VA could only collect information on veterans who were enrolled in the Veterans Health Administration (VHA). Since two-thirds of vets aren't enrolled, no one was tracking what happened to them. (Many vets don't enroll in the VHA because they have jobs that provide private health care or because they are frustrated with the VA's services and pay for other care or go without.)

In 2010, at the behest of Eric Shinseki, secretary of the VA, who requested support from the governors of all fifty states, the department entered into a data-sharing agreement with each state and began compiling more complete and accurate information on suicides by veterans. Robert Bossarte, an epidemiologist at the VA's

Canandaigua Medical Center in Rochester, New York, led the effort. For two years, starting in October 2010, he and his team accessed death records for more than 400,000 Americans who had died by suicide since 1999. In February 2013, the initial VA Suicide Data Report was issued, based on information that had been tabulated from twenty-one states. According to the report, twenty-two vets die by suicide every day—20 percent more than was thought previously. About 8,000 veterans kill themselves annually. Two-thirds of the victims are age fifty or older, a fact that suggests the number isn't related solely or even primarily to suicides by active-duty troops.[56]

In reporting his initial findings, Bossarte downplayed the notion that the number of military suicides was reaching epidemic proportions. He noted that overall suicide rates in the United States rose nearly 11 percent between 2007 and 2010. Thus veterans weren't the only people who were killing themselves with greater frequency. While this was true, it didn't account for the fact that the increase among veterans was twice that of the civilian population.

In January 2014, the VA issued an update to the previous Suicide Data Report. The first report was based on data through 2009, while the second report included 2010 and 2011. The latter indicated an increase in the suicide rate of all male veterans who were enrolled in the Veterans Health Administration from 37.4 in 2010 to 40.0 in 2011. More than that, though, the rate for male VHA users ages 25 to 29 rose from 37.0 to 48.3, and for male veterans ages 18 to 24 it rose from 46.1 in 2009 to 79.1 in 2011. Those are large increases, and well above civilian rates. As for female veterans in the VHA, the rate increased from 12.9 in 2009 to 14.4 in 2011—again, above the civilian rate. The report also noted that veterans comprise 22 percent of all suicides in the United States now, as well as supported the earlier estimate of twenty-two veterans dying by suicide each day.

In an effort to find a silver lining, the 2014 report noted that between 1999 and 2010 the suicide rate for male VHA users age 35 to 64 decreased 16 percent, while it increased in the general male population by 27 percent. That would be meaningful if this was the primary age group in the military, but it's not. VA officials also took a measure of solace in the fact that veterans who aren't enrolled in the department's health care system are at even greater risk of suicide. According to the report, the suicide rate among non-VHA veterans increased 61 percent between 1999 and 2010.[57]

As hard as it is to collect data on suicide deaths among veterans, it's nearly impossible to compile information on suicide attempts, at least attempts by those outside the system. Within the system, data are available—and alarming. Based on the latest information, a veteran in the VHA attempts suicide every half-hour now.[58] The number of suicide attempts increased 63 percent in recent years, from 10,888 in 2009 to 17,754 in 2011.[59]

The goal of Bossarte and others is to complete the analysis of suicide data from all fifty states, as well as from Pentagon service records, VA hospital and clinic files, and information from the VA Crisis Line (a joint project of the National Suicide Prevention Lifeline, the federal Substance Abuse and Mental Health Services Administration, and the VA). Once this is done, the VA will be able to report the number of veterans who served in combat before they killed themselves, the military positions they held, the amount of time that elapsed between the end of their military service and their deaths, whether they contacted the VA Crisis Line for help, and the kinds of treatment that they received—if any—from VA physicians, psychologists, and counselors. This information, which hasn't been available to this point, will be integrated with information from other sources, including the VA's universal electronic medical records system, to identify gaps in existing knowledge, opportunities for intervention, and ways to more accurately measure the effectiveness of VA-sponsored suicide prevention programs. In addition, the VA is collaborating with the Department of Defense in developing a Joint Suicide Data Repository to further understand the problem.

All of it undoubtedly will be useful in determining causes and developing strategies for reducing and preventing military suicides. The question one has to ask, though, is why it has taken the government so long to begin collecting this data. In the VA's case, why was a lawsuit required to jump-start the process, and why was it necessary for an appeals court to issue a harsh finding before the VA decided to act? Was it because political leaders, Pentagon brass, and VA officials were worried that what they discovered would prove untenable to the public? No one I've talked to has even hinted at this. They have only said that going forward the information is being gathered and studied.

For active-duty troops, the Department of Defense didn't begin to systematically track suicides until 2001. In 2003, the first year of today's Gulf War, DoD reported 79 suicides by current service members. In 2004, the number dropped to 67, leading military leaders to congratulate themselves on implementing effective prevention strategies. Then the number began to climb, to 87 in 2005, 102 in 2006, 121 in 2007, 140 in 2008, and 162 in 2009. In recent years it has skyrocketed, nearly doubling to 310 in 2010 and hitting a new record of 349 in 2012. These increases have come despite the fact that the military's official involvement in Iraq has ended and troops are being withdrawn from Afghanistan in efforts to wind down the war there.

The Army has had both the highest number of suicides and the highest suicide rate. Of the 343 suicides in 2012, more than half—182—were in the Army. This isn't all that surprising because the majority of ground forces in Iraq and Afghanistan are in the Army. The second highest number of suicides and second-highest suicide rate are in the Marines, whose members comprise the second-highest number of ground forces. There were forty-eight Marine suicides in 2012, up 50 percent over 2011. (In 2012 the Marine Corps commissioned a study by the American Association of Suicidology to collect more information on Marine suicides using psychological autopsy techniques.) Third is the Navy (sixty suicides in 2012, up 15 percent), and fourth is the Air Force (fifty-nine suicides, up 16 percent). Each branch of our armed forces has suicide rates that are above the national rate, even when demographic factors such as age, gender, and ethnicity are considered. Of greater concern is that the military rates have been climbing in all branches, and in the Army it has doubled in recent years.

Since 2003, the number of deaths by suicide among enlisted men and women has been greater than the number of battlefield deaths, sometimes substantially.[60] In 2012 in Afghanistan, there were 18 percent more deaths by suicide (349) than battlefield deaths (295). As a point of reference, the situation has been much the same in England. In 2003, the British Ministry of Defense released figures showing that four times more veterans of the first Gulf War killed themselves (107) than died in combat (24). A year earlier, in 2002, *BBC News* reported that "more veterans of the Falklands War have killed themselves in the years since the 1982 conflict ended than died during hostilities."[61]

Based on a 12-year study of more than 320,000 men, a third of whom served in the U.S. military between 1917 and 1994, the suicide rate of veterans is 2.1 times higher than those who never served. Veterans are also twice as likely to use a firearm to kill themselves. Veterans age twenty to twenty-four are at greatest risk, with a rate three to four times higher than civilians of the same age.[62] (The study, which was published in 2007 in the *Journal of Epidemiology and Community Health*, found that veterans who are white, older, and better educated are at greatest risk, along with men who are physically or emotionally disabled. Curiously, vets who are overweight are less likely to die by suicide than those whose weight is normal, researchers found.)

Among active-duty troops, the risk appears to be highest for those who see heavy combat. According to new research, the more exposure a soldier has to severe combat, the more likely he or she is to attempt suicide later. This might seem obvious, but it hadn't been validated before. In one study, 93 percent of veterans who saw heavy combat had symptoms of posttraumatic stress, and nearly 70 percent had attempted suicide.[63]

At the same time, combat exposure and the number of deployments aren't the sole causes of military suicides. More than one-third of active-duty troops who have killed themselves in recent years never deployed, and for members of the National Guard and military reserves—who comprise a majority of America's fighting force today—it's more than half. Because a smaller percentage of U.S. troops have engaged in actual combat today than in the past, one might reasonably conclude that the incidence of suicides should decline. In fact, though, it has increased. Whereas 90 percent of troops in the Civil War fought in battles, only 30 percent of American soldiers in World War II experienced combat, and the ratio dropped to 15 percent in Vietnam.[64] Today it's about 20 percent.[65] According to the Armed Forces Health Surveillance Center, 84 percent of service members who died by suicide between 2008 and 2010 had no documented combat experiences.[66]

Extra Burdens for Women

For women, who comprise more than 17 percent of our current armed forces,[67] exposure to combat hasn't been as strong a link to psychiatric stress and suicide as another element—sexual assaults. Incidences of rape in the military occur almost twice as often as in the civilian population, with 90 percent of the victims being junior-ranking women whose average age is twenty-one, while their assailants tend to be non-commissioned officers whose average age is twenty-eight.[68] In a 2010 study by the VA, 90 percent of female respondents reported that they had been sexually harassed while in the military.[69] A subsequent Pentagon report indicated that an estimated 26,000 people—mostly women—were sexually assaulted (raped or victims of attempted rape) in fiscal year 2012. This represented nearly a 37 percent increase over the 19,000 service members who were sexually assaulted in fiscal year 2011. Overall, fewer than 17 percent of sexual assaults in the military are reported, according to the Department of Defense—3,374 in fiscal year 2012 and 3,192 in fiscal year 2011. The larger number of estimated assaults is based on anonymous surveys conducted by the Department of Defense of active-duty military personnel. In the military, one in three female service members is sexually assaulted, compared with one in six in the civilian population.[70] Of those who are raped, it has happened more than once for 20 percent, and for 14 percent they are gang raped.[71] Oftentimes, male perpetrators in the military go unpunished, which adds to a woman's trauma. Of the total number of reported assaults, only 6 percent of perpetrators spend any time in jail.[72]

A 2010 study published in the journal *Psychiatric Services* provided the first large-scale review of suicide among female veterans.[73] Researchers collected data from sixteen states and concluded that women in the military were three times more likely to die by suicide than female civilians the same age.[74] Reasons included sexual harassment and rapes, the fact that women in general tend to develop PTSD at a rate two times greater than men, and the increased exposure of women to combat.

As of 2012, more than 130 women had been killed in combat in the two Gulf wars, with 800 others wounded.[75] The numbers are likely to go up as a result of the Department of Defense's decision in January 2013 to permit women to serve in combat positions. Historically, war has been considered a man's business. No women fought in the Civil War or in World War I, no women saw combat in World War II or in the Korean War, and only a small number of women served in Vietnam. Today, though, the sight of female soldiers in the U.S. military is common. Although they have been assigned duties that usually don't require them to fire a weapon, jobs like convoy drivers, medics, photographers, and translators, their lives have been just as much at risk as the lives of men who serve alongside them. In fact, driving a convoy is considered one of the most dangerous assignments. The threat of an improvised explosive device planted along the roadside is ever-present, as is the possibility of a vehicle-born IED or crossfire coming from any direction. In addition, not only is a medic exposed to enemy fire when treating injured soldiers on the battlefield, but he or she also is exposed to gruesome sights.

Private Galina Klippel, age twenty-four, shot herself in the head in 2010 at a military base in Hawaii. She had returned to the states recently, after serving thirteen months in Afghanistan, where she accompanied a chaplain on rounds at a local hospital. The hospital was filled with wounded soldiers and Afghan civilians, including children. Some were missing arms, legs, or both. It was hardly the adventure that Klippel envisioned when she joined the Army. The morning that she killed herself, Klippel called her staff sergeant, also a woman, to ask how she was doing. Little did the staff sergeant know that Klippel really was calling to say good-bye.[76]

On the plus side, the Pentagon's decision means that women qualify now for promotions and pay increases that weren't available to them previously because they didn't officially serve in combat. On the negative side, it means that their risk of suicide most likely will increase, in large part because war zones continue to be male-dominated worlds, and women in them are expected to exhibit the same tough, aggressive warrior mentality as their male counterparts, even though they tend to be more anxious than male soldiers about leaving children and spouses behind. As Daryl S. Paulson and Stanley Krippner note in *Haunted by Combat*, "Women have the extra burden of having to defy stereotypes, especially those marking them as too fragile for military duty."[77]

Women also are at a disadvantage when they come home from war because our country historically has defined "veteran" as male. The 2010 study noted previously was a start, but as the Institute of Medicine reported in 2013, "Research on the health of veterans has focused on the health consequences of combat service in men, and there has been little scientific research…of the health consequences of military service in women who served."[78]

A further challenge is that many of the 280,000 women who returned from post-9/11 deployments as of 2013 have had even more trouble than their male counterparts accessing services and care, as well as finding jobs.[79] In addition, they are much more likely to be single parents with children to support. At least 40 percent of women on active duty have children, and 30,000 single mothers have deployed to Iraq and Afghanistan since 2009.[80]

A Life of "Brutal Compression"

The increasing number of women now serving in combat zones is only one of many differences between the current war in the Middle East and previous wars that the United States has fought. Another difference is that the enemy today isn't clearly defined. Labels are used—jihadists, Al Queda, the Taliban, terrorists—but who they apply to isn't always obvious. Without a central command, enemy attacks occur spontaneously and anonymously by small groups of people whose actions lack sophisticated planning and high-level oversight. In addition, uniforms aren't worn by insurgents, and lines become blurred when farmers are fighters, women are suicide bombers, and teenagers are snipers. Who is innocent, who should be feared, and how can one tell the difference instantly, without making a mistake that could prove to be fatal? This was the situation to some extent in Vietnam as well, except that in the Middle East today most of the fighting is taking place in urban environments where the chances of injuring civilians are much greater. (It's worth noting that some experts believe the term *suicide bomber* is misleading. The fact that these individuals—like Japanese kamikaze pilots in World War II—are willing to die in order to kill others makes them homicidal rather than suicidal, motivated by a sense of nationalism and potential rewards in an afterlife rather than by depression and feelings of hopelessness or despair.)

Related is the fact that there no longer is a clear battlefield. In military parlance, it's asymmetrical, meaning that there isn't a defined beginning, middle, or end. Whereas in previous wars there was an established front line, today that isn't the case. Today, everyone in a war zone is vulnerable, everyone is at risk. It doesn't matter what the person's role is or what he or she is doing—using a latrine, eating in a mess hall, or trying to sleep. The risk never goes away.

Moreover, enemy forces have moved away from engagements by small units to hit-and-run attacks in which the primary weapons are improvised bombs, mortars, and rocket-propelled grenades, which kill without discriminating among the victims. Public places that draw a crowd, particularly outdoor markets and churches, are prime targets. Institutions of authority, such as police stations, also are subject to attacks. No street is secure due to the possibility of snipers, and even military bases, protected by concrete barriers, are susceptible to incoming fire. As a result, in Iraq and Afghanistan there is no safe place for soldiers to be and no safe role for them to perform. With night vision equipment and attacks coming from anywhere, troops must maintain constant vigilance; they always have to be on guard. Fatigue and sleep deprivation are so common that they are taken for granted.

The conditions of combat have changed, too. Up to and including World War I, troops generally fought when the sun was up. In addition, they maintained fixed positions of battle. With World War II, much of the fighting moved to nighttime with the hope that the enemy would be caught by surprise. Twenty-four-hour watches were implemented with soldiers sleeping in shifts. Vietnam introduced the concept of guerrilla warfare, where the enemy was constantly on the move, making quick hits and then disappearing into the jungle before a counterattack could be mounted. Today, conventional rules of warfare are ignored—at least by the other side. Enemy soldiers dress like civilians, use civilians as shields, and are just as likely to target noncombatants—medics, journalists, and relief workers—as they are those who are holding weapons.

Another difference is that today's conflicts in Afghanistan (referred to by the military as Operation Enduring Freedom or OEF) and in Iraq (now called Operation New Dawn or OND in recognition of the military's reduced role in the country) have been going on for more than ten years. This is longer than any war that the United States has engaged in, including the Civil War, both world wars, and Vietnam. Despite all of the lives that have been lost and altered, buildings turned to rubble, weaponry fired, and money spent, no end is in sight, even though George W. Bush declared six weeks after he launched the war that it was over already, and even though his successor, Barack Obama, continues to promise that the country won't continue a state of "perpetual war," yet during his watch the war in Afghanistan escalated, the number of drone strikes in Pakistan, Yemen, and Somalia increased dramatically, and U.S. intervention in Syria has—more than once—appeared imminent. In addition, the stability that our government has long sought for the region seems no closer today than it was before we launched combat operations there.

In the Civil War, it was clear who the enemy was and why the Union and Confederate armies were fighting. When General Robert E. Lee surrendered to General Ulysses S. Grant at Appomattox Court House in April 1865, the shooting ended. In World War I, the combatants and reasons for fighting were equally clear. So was the end, signified by the Treaty of Versailles. In World War II, the enemy was obvious—Hitler's Nazis, Mussolini's Italian Fascists, Hirohito's Red Army—as was the threat that they posed. The agreements reached at the Potsdam Conference ended the war.

In contrast, there is no agreed upon definition today of what a U.S. victory in Iraq or Afghanistan will look like or how we will know it. As a result, it's difficult for soldiers and their families, as well as the public, to determine whether we are winning the war or losing it, how close or far away the end is, and what will happen after that. Soldiers in their second or third or fourth tours of duty are no more hopeful that it will be their last deployment than they were when they first enlisted. This adds to their stress, as well as to the stress of their loved ones.

A further difference is that there are fewer battlefield deaths today, mainly because body armor is improved and medical care is better. In Vietnam, three U.S. soldiers were wounded for every one who was killed. In Iraq and Afghanistan, fifteen U.S. soldiers have been wounded for each one killed.[81] The survival rate for troops who are wounded has increased from 75 percent in previous wars to 90 percent today. A consequence, though, is that many more soldiers are coming home with mental health problems. In past wars they might have died; now they survive but suffer serious psychological injuries. When a soldier's body armor or Kevlar helmet deflects a bullet or shrapnel, protecting vital organs, it doesn't deflect the psychological trauma of being so close to death.

A final difference is the way that deployments are handled today. The typical tour of duty is twelve months. When it ends, troops are flown home and reunited almost immediately with their families. Then they go through a period of reintegration (the Army calls it "dwell time"[82]), usually lasting a year, during which it's presumed that they adjust from the front line to the home front. Just as they are reintegrated, however, they may be deployed again and need to adopt a battle mindset once more. A soldier who has multiple deployments must make multiple transitions. Each transition is quick, marked by a plane flight to or from a war zone that offers little time to prepare for what follows.

In contrast, soldiers in Vietnam served one twelve-month tour of duty, then came home. They didn't go back and forth. While any transition from home to war is difficult, every deployment is different and the transitions don't get any easier. In fact, they often get harder. Service members may join new units in new locales, and thus have to adjust to new peers, new leaders, new duties, new languages, and new local customs.

In World War I and World War II, soldiers served one tour of duty that lasted the duration of the war. While they didn't benefit from periodic trips home or have access to today's systems of near-instant communication to stay in touch with loved ones, they had only two transitions to deal with—going abroad and coming back—as in Vietnam. Additionally, when the war ended, they couldn't come home right away. Instead, they boarded large troop ships that took several weeks to cross an ocean. The trip provided opportunities for soldiers to process their experiences with fellow soldiers—the only people who knew what combat was like—as well as time to acclimate themselves mentally and emotionally to a new, changed life.

This isn't something that today's soldiers get in the age of aviation. Today, troops leave the battlefield (referred to as "taking the pack off") and within twenty-four hours are stateside. They have a few days to debrief, fill out paperwork, and complete a written psychological assessment, but that is all. They are home within the week. Most soldiers are unwilling to admit any problems in the assessment for fear that it will delay their reunion with families. Also, when you have been taught to be tough and take care of yourself, it can be seen as a sign of weakness to ask for help. Moreover, it could cause others to lose confidence in you, and potentially jeopardize career opportunities.

On page one of a 2010 Army report on suicide, there is a stunning summation of what it's like to be a soldier today. "At twenty-four years of age," according to the report, "a soldier, on average, has moved from home, family, and friends and has resided in two other states; has traveled the world (deployed), been promoted four times, bought a car and wrecked it, married and had children, has had relationship and financial problems, seen death, is responsible for dozens of soldiers, maintains millions of dollars worth of equipment, and gets paid less than $40,000 a year."[83]

As Jennifer Senior noted in *New York Magazine*, "even without deployments, the life of a soldier is a model of brutal compression and, therefore, almost certain to cause distress."[84]

Taking it one step further, at thirty-four years of age the same soldier, if he or she is still in the military, will have accumulated another ten years of crammed experiences. He or she will have lived in additional states and spent more time in distant countries, witnessed new deaths and gruesome injuries, been prescribed medication for depression and posttraumatic stress while being denied other benefits, been divorced, had one or more drunk driving arrests, received multiple speeding tickets, contemplated and possibly attempted suicide, and known more than one soldier or veteran who has died by suicide.

In their book *Haunted by Combat*, Vietnam veteran Daryl S. Paulson and psychologist Stanley Krippner describe the same disparity between soldiers and civilians, but in a different way. A civilian goes through life, they say, in a manner that is more or less predictable. He or she graduates from high school, goes to college, gets married, has children, works, buys a house, and in the end retires to a life of leisure. In contrast, a soldier's life is subject to constant threats and continual change. He or she "has seen so much death, so much suffering, and has been forced to live so closely with insecurity that he can no longer feel secure," write Paulson and Krippner. "Often, the veteran feels his life has no positive meaning, no purpose, and no direction, once he has experienced war."[85]

The difference is borne out by the experiences of U.S. soldiers in Iraq. In Operation Iraqi Freedom (OIF), the U.S. military's name for the fighting in Iraq up to September 2010, 95 percent of Army soldiers and Marines were shot at, 85 percent knew someone who had been seriously injured or killed, 75 percent saw ill or injured women or children whom they were unable to help, 56 percent killed an enemy soldier, 53 percent handled human remains, and 20 percent killed a noncombatant.[86] How could they not be affected by these experiences? Nowhere else but in combat does someone go through a range of emotions so quickly, deeply, or frequently, alternately feeling mad, glad, sad, scared, relieved, powerful, and guilty.

Time Is Running Out

One of the dangers of engaging in war is to initiate combat without first understanding the cultures and traditions of the enemy. This is especially true when all of the fighting takes place in foreign lands and the enemy isn't one that you have fought before. Military leaders focus on an adversary's technology and weaponry while paying little or no attention to the values and norms behind them.

As Dexter Filkins noted in the *New Yorker*, Iraq is a tribal society, and the payment of blood money—called *fasil*—is the way that deaths are expunged. "A man is killed, the tribes meet, a price is agreed on, and the act is, if not forgotten, then at least set aside," Filkins wrote. "Life goes on."[87]

Not understanding this, or at least failing to acknowledge it, the United States offered no remuneration in the beginning to the families of Iraqi civilians who were mistakenly killed by U.S. troops. As a result, says Filkins, a small insurgency became large by virtue of families and tribes vowing revenge. Ultimately, this oversight was corrected, and requests could be made to the office of the Judge Advocate General (JAG) for reparation, the going rate being $25,000 for a wrongful death.[88] The ill will that was created before then, however, couldn't be undone, and it continues to contribute to feelings of animosity toward the United States, despite humanitarian efforts by soldiers to overcome them.

The other, even larger danger of engaging in war is to underestimate the enemy by believing that the fighting will be quick and decisive and produce few casualties on our side. The way wars are conducted today, a small number of poorly trained and ill equipped yet fanatic militants can stymie even the most powerful of armies, engaging in random attacks that result in numerous deaths of U.S. troops. The willingness of insurgents to sacrifice their own lives in the process, as well as their cunningness in using our own cultural values against us, such as forcing U.S. soldiers to kill grenade-wielding children, make for far different combat situations than in the past, with far different repercussions.

It probably will be many years before the effects of the current conflicts in Iraq and Afghanistan are fully known. Unlike other wars, however, we are receiving strong hints already of the human toll. Nearly every day now there is a new report of one or more soldiers who have been killed because an IED exploded, a mortar landed, a rocket-propelled grenade was launched, a suicide bomber struck, or an enemy sniper fired. Nearly every day, too, there are stories of veterans who are killing themselves, many suffering from PTSD.

These stories aren't good for recruitment efforts, which is why it's in the military's best interests that they aren't widely told. The fact that they are appearing anyway, and that the military is forced to do something about them by implementing additional training programs, developing new assessment tools and protocols, hiring more psychologists, counselors, and social workers (1,900 in 2012 alone, bringing the total number of mental health workers in the VA to nearly 23,000), and collecting more empirical evidence is an indication of just how serious the problem has become. Not only is it not going away, but it's growing worse.

At the same time, suicide is preventable. In fact, it's the most preventable form of death. Recognizing warning signs, knowing about resources, being unafraid to ask someone if he or she is feeling suicidal, probing to assess intent—the level of hopelessness that a person is feeling and whether he or she has a plan and access to means—then doing safety planning is required. That and a commitment to saving every individual who is at risk, not just the few who reach out for help.

Preventing suicides among active-duty troops and veterans is more difficult than in the general population for a variety of reasons, all having to do with the nature of war. The first time someone pulls the trigger, sees a friend killed, or kills someone himself, everything changes. The person isn't the same after that. Whether it's learning to fire a weapon in order to inflict bodily harm on someone else, grieving the death of a buddy who you not only cared about but felt responsible for safeguarding, or living with the psychological burden of killing—in recent years referred to as suffering a "moral injury"—the consequences are irreversible.

Then there is the fact that soldiers develop a fearlessness of death because it's so common in their world. The average citizen rarely witnesses death, and when we do it's usually in a hospital where the situation is controlled, the outcome is inevitable, the dying person is elderly, the cause of death is sickness, loved ones are gathered around, and doctors and nurses are present to inform and comfort us. For soldiers, it's the opposite. Death is sudden, unpredictable, and uncontrollable. The person who dies is young and in good health up to the moment when he or she is struck, the cause of death is violent and human-induced, the location is a battlefield that is thousands of miles from family and home, and the only sources of support are overworked military chaplains (there is one for every thousand troops in the field)[89] and fellow soldiers who, in all likelihood, are trying themselves to cope with similar feelings of loss.

Added to this, soldiers have easy access to lethal means. Each one is issued at least one firearm and taught, through endless hours of training, how to clean it, load it, aim it, and shoot it. Most soldiers learn to handle multiple kinds of weapons, from handguns and carbines to submachine guns and rocket launchers. Even after they leave the service, many veterans continue to keep weapons around them for comfort and security (so do police officers, who also have high suicide rates). According to *JAMA*, the American Medical Association's primary publication, reducing access to lethal means is one of the two most effective ways to prevent suicides (the other is to require physicians and mental health professionals to be trained in suicide prevention).[90]

It's no coincidence that the qualities troops learn to use in combat—controlled aggression, suppressed emotions, tolerance to pain, and fearlessness in the face of death—are the same qualities that make an individual more at risk for suicide.[91] When a person has a strong desire to die, combined with the capacity to kill himself or herself, some kind of intervention becomes paramount. To date, the military hasn't implemented proven ways to gauge a person's suicidal intentions, much less ways to intervene effectively. Each branch of our armed forces has gone about it separately, producing mixed results at best. Even the Air Force, which has been the most aggressive and had the most success, has suicide rates higher than the general population.

Time is running out, at least for some service members. Nearly every day now an active-duty soldier resorts to suicide, and nearly every hour a veteran does the same. This can't continue. Our troops deserve better, and their families deserve better. The question is whether they will get it and, if so, when?

The casualties don't end when the fighting stops. Indeed, in many instances they are just beginning.

The Effects of PTSD

"It's 1999, and my husband just died from the Vietnam War."

WHEN DENNIS FISHER CAME HOME FROM VIETNAM IN 1974, FEW people had any understanding of PTSD. It wasn't something that families talked about—certainly not with others whose loved ones hadn't served in the war. Most spouses didn't know that there was even a name for the behavior exhibited by their husbands, the restlessness, sleeplessness, hyperalertness, nightmares, shutting off of emotions, lack of concentration, irritability, and increased use of alcohol that had become the new norm. For Fisher and many others like him, the only treatment he received was delivered—padded envelopes filled with Paxil, Vicodin, and other medications.

In Penny Coleman's book *Flashback*, Fisher's wife Maryallyn and daughter Jean-Marie describe what it was like to live with a Vietnam veteran who had PTSD. Although Dennis Fisher rarely talked about his wartime experiences, even when prodded, they pieced together some of it. In doing so they learned that he had been exposed to more trauma than many veterans. A grenade was thrown into his military vehicle, and everyone but him was killed. He befriended a young girl after an American officer raped her. He took control of a machine gun in a helicopter after the gunner was shot to death, and in turn was hit in the shoulder and neck with shrapnel.

After the war, Fisher's anxiety level was high. According to his wife, "He would go into rages over nothing" and wouldn't sleep for several days. The holidays were especially difficult because of the celebrations. Anytime planes or helicopters flew overhead, they added to his nightmare as he thought he was back in Nam.[1] Jean-Marie remembers her father sitting in their garage with a BB gun "shooting at mice that weren't there. I was scared out of my mind."[2]

Dennis Fisher drank heavily, at home and in bars. He abused the medications he received and smoked marijuana much of the time. For his physical injuries, the shrapnel in his shoulder and neck, he was awarded 100 percent disability. For his PTSD, he was awarded 10 percent.

In 1997, feeling exhausted, drained, and unable to take it anymore, Maryallyn Fisher packed up Jean-Marie and left Dennis. She still loved him, but she couldn't live with him. It was too much.

Two years later, on Father's Day 1999, Fisher shot himself. At first, his wife didn't want anyone to know. "It was the shame—on top of everything else, it was the shame," she told Coleman. "When something like this happens, you are so wide open and vulnerable, you have absolutely no defenses. I didn't want my husband's suicide being discussed over coffee at the diner. I didn't want a lot of people knowing, because I couldn't stand to have his death treated casually. And I couldn't defend him because I had nothing. I was just totally, completely an open wound."[3]

For months afterward, Jean-Marie was a mess, too. A classmate filled her water bottle with vodka, and the two of them would get drunk at school. She went to classes stoned. She cut herself. She smoked.

Later, she began reading war books and watching movies like *Platoon* and *Full Metal Jacket*. They gave her new insight into her father.

"No wonder he was weird," she said. "And no wonder he was an atheist because a lot of people gave up on God with what they saw. My dad actually killed people. He was trained to kill people. You're trained to kill people, you get shot a lot, and then you come home to a regular family. How weird is that?"[4]

Eventually, the mother and daughter found support through a grief group for families of veterans. They became able to say publicly that Dennis had killed himself. They came to understand that as much as they had tried, they couldn't help him. His pain was too deep.

Maryallyn Fisher had no doubt about the cause of her husband's death. When he took his life she said, "It's 1999, and my husband just died from the Vietnam War."[5]

Today, most people know what PTSD is and what the initials stand for—posttraumatic stress disorder. We read or hear about it almost every day, usually in conjunction with a news story about American soldiers who have PTSD and haven't been diagnosed for it, or have been diagnosed but haven't been treated, or have suffered so severely that they killed themselves, usually after they returned home, and in a few instances after they killed others. In recent years PTSD has been expanded beyond the battlefield to include exposure to other horrific events such as natural disasters, sexual assaults, violent crimes, kidnappings, and torture in which the affect of this exposure has been life-altering and the symptoms—recurrent, uncontrollable, and unwanted memories; social withdrawal; emotional numbness; hyperarousal; inability to sleep; and frequent displays of irritability—have lasted at least one month and interfered significantly with a person's daily functioning. At the same time, PTSD continues to be associated most often with active-duty service members and veterans, particularly those who have seen combat.

Our ability to recognize, understand, and treat PTSD has increased dramatically since the Vietnam War. While some things about it remain unknown—most notably why PTSD afflicts certain people who are exposed to trauma and not others who have experienced the same catastrophic event—training programs now exist in all branches of the military to improve soldiers' resiliency and ability to cope with stress. In addition, there are assessment tools to test for PTSD, plus multiple treatment options.

It wasn't always so. Prior to Vietnam, PTSD had other names, names that weren't clinical, sometimes weren't even psychologically based, and in almost every instance carried considerable stigma. Then again, there has been a growing movement in recent years to eliminate the "D" from PTSD because of stigma, because calling something a "disorder" gives it a negative label and discourages those who are afflicted from seeking help. Thus, PTSD as an acronym may not remain in use forever.

During the Civil War, what we now know as PTSD was referred to as *nostalgia* and *melancholia*—terms that, on the face of it, sound so benign it was as if the person were merely homesick. The condition also was called—less commonly—*hysteria, neuralgia, soldier's heart, irritable heart syndrome,* and *DaCosta syndrome,* the latter after a cardiologist and medical researcher named Jacob Mendes DaCosta, who first observed it in Civil War soldiers.

DaCosta's research sample was small—only 200 cases—with each man complaining of physical symptoms such as shortness of breath, heart palpitations, abnormal sweating, and chest pains. Treatment was simple, consisting of rest, an assortment of drugs (including tonics whose high alcohol content reduced anxiety), and the expectation that the soldier would return soon to military duty. If a soldier thought that his medical condition justified a discharge, DaCosta told him that he would recover fully and could continue serving. In this way malingering was discouraged.

It's worth noting that while DaCosta acknowledged the motivation of soldiers to avoid battle by feigning illnesses, he believed that "irritable heart" couldn't be faked. Even if a man wound a bandage tightly around his abdomen to simulate shortness of breath, DaCosta said, once he undressed and lay down, his heartbeat returned to normal. After that, the man could stand or walk around, and his breathing remained the same, unlike someone with "irritable heart" whose irregular rhythm continued.[6] It's also worth noting that while seventy-six of the men who DaCosta treated ended up returning to service,[7] the majority did not, indicating that their condition probably was genuine.

As for a cause, DaCosta considered a number of factors, including tobacco use, fevers, diarrhea, and masturbation, all of which drained a body's defenses, he believed. In general, physical injuries weren't the source, he maintained, unless they occurred near the heart. He also found no connection between "irritable heart" and a soldier's occupation prior to the war. "Painter, butcher, blacksmith, carpenter, the city-bred man who had left his desk in the counting house, the farmer fresh from tilling the fields, were all fully represented in the long list of sufferers," he said.[8] Ultimately DaCosta concluded that hard field service was to blame. Long marches and extended fighting weakened the hearts of some soldiers.

According to B. Christopher Frueh and Jeffrey A. Smith, who examined Union records in detail and published their findings in a 2012 article in the *Journal of Anxiety Disorders*, during the four years of the Civil War there were 5,129 cases of nostalgia. In the peak year, July 1, 1862–June 30, 1863, there were 2,057 cases. While that might seem like a lot, it actually means that fewer than 0.3 percent of Union troops were affected by what might be considered PTSD—an unusually low number given that 30 percent or more of active-duty troops today are diagnosed with PTSD. Moreover, while the majority of current troops don't experience combat, 90 percent of soldiers during the Civil War engaged in the deadliest fighting in U.S. history. One would expect them to have higher incidences of posttraumatic stress than today's troops, not lower. It's also telling that Frueh and Smith found no mention of classic PTSD symptoms like nightmares and flashbacks in any of the records that they reviewed, although there are possible reasons for this.

Richard J. McNally, a psychology professor at Harvard University, says that mental disorders were underestimated and oftentimes undiagnosed during the Civil War. This isn't surprising since PTSD was unknown at the time so doctors didn't ask about related symptoms. In addition, individuals with psychiatric problems may have had other injuries or diseases that were considered more serious and preempted the notation of a mental disorder. McNally notes, too, in a 2012 article in the *Journal of Anxiety Disorders*, that despite the absence of PTSD-type symptoms in records that Frueh and Smith reviewed, evidence of hypervigilance, nightmares, concentration problems, and apathy is found in letters, memoirs, and other documents of Civil War veterans and their families.[9]

These documents contradict the widely held belief that psychological problems manifest themselves merely by suggestion and can spread out of control like a wildfire if they aren't extinguished immediately. In their writings, afflicted soldiers, their spouses, and parents rarely referenced other soldiers who were traumatized. Instead, they lamented the veteran's newly acquired abnormalities, abnormalities that were shocking to behold, mystifying to treat, and—to most minds—largely unexplainable. Family members weren't looking at the big picture; they were only concerned at the individual level, about the erratic behavior of a veteran after he came home from the war.

It was the military that looked at the big picture. Military leaders worried that they would find virtually all of their soldiers in hospitals rather than on battlefields if they didn't take prompt action. The action they took was based on the assumption that soldiers who presented psychiatric illnesses were scheming to be discharged. To discourage this practice, the punishment for being officially labeled a malingerer or a coward was the same as for desertion—execution. Not only that, but the offender was shot in front of his comrades and buried where he fell with no grave marking, as if he had never existed. Such severe measures were intended to discourage other soldiers from engaging in imitative behavior. In all likelihood, what they really did was prevent soldiers from disclosing any kind of psychological condition unless they intuited that their commanding officer would be sympathetic and assign them lighter duty.[10] Since the penalty for malingering was the same as for desertion, it meant that if a soldier ran away, he at least had the chance of not being caught. During the Civil War, 10 percent of both the Union and Confederate armies deserted, about 300,000 men altogether.[11] Other soldiers, knowing the hardships, often sympathized with them.

"Several of the boys in our Regiment said 'no use going any further,' and they started East," one soldier wrote. "I saw them leave, and never thought hard of them for leaving. Oh war, war!"[12]

The punishment for desertion and malingering was harsh, but it was a different time. Sigmund Freud was five years old when the Civil War started, and the study of psychiatry was in its infancy. Recruitment standards were written by bureaucrats rather than physicians, and medical exemptions—before and during the war—were frowned upon because they limited the number of soldiers who qualified to fight. Even men with myopia, for instance, weren't exempted from service. (Oddly enough, healthy young men who presented themselves to enrollment boards were turned away if they were toothless—a common occurrence in those days since dental care was poor. A possible rationale, according to R. Gregory Lande, was that eating hardtack required strong teeth.[13])

It's not surprising that although the number of deserters was high, the number of soldiers who received the "Surgeon General's Certificate of Disability" was extremely low. During the whole course of the war, only 1,300 Union soldiers were formally discharged,

853 of them for insanity, 266 for neuralgia, 150 for alcoholism and delirium tremens (alcohol poisoning), and 31 for nostalgia.[14]

A study published in 2006 and sponsored by the National Institutes of Health and the National Science Foundation reached a different conclusion than Frueh and Smith. Researchers determined that 44 percent of Union soldiers who survived the war suffered from some form of mental illness that today would be considered PTSD.[15] The study was based on an analysis of health and pension records of 15,000 Union soldiers. The lack of comparable war records for Confederate soldiers limited the study, although it's reasonable to conclude that the frequency of psychiatric disorders among Confederate troops was at least as high as for Union soldiers, if not higher.

Eric T. Dean, Jr. analyzed case histories of 291 Civil War veterans who were committed to the Indiana Hospital for the Insane between 1861 and 1920. In terms of occupation, religious affiliation, and marital status, they were representative of the overall adult male population at the time, he says. In at least one respect, however, they were different. All had symptoms, according to Dean, that today would be diagnosed as posttraumatic stress disorder. At least 10 men in the sample went on to kill themselves,[16] a suicide rate of 3,436—astronomically high.

"Many of these men," Dean says in his book *Shook Over Hell*, "continued to suffer from the aftereffects of the war and, along with their families, often lived in a kind of private hell involving physical pain, the torment of fear, and memories of killing and death." He notes that "exposure in the army" was listed as the most common cause of insanity in soldiers. Other causes also were related to combat, including "shock of battle," "shell explosions," and, simply, "The War."[17] (The title of Dean's book refers to a Union soldier named Jason Roberts who was a prisoner of war in several southern prisons. By the end of the war Roberts was so weakened that he had to be carried home on a stretcher. Subsequently, he lost all of his teeth due to scurvy and suffered the rest of his life from diarrhea and rheumatism. In time he was committed to the Indiana Hospital for the Insane because, in his words, he had been "shook over hell.")

About 8,500 people were housed in mental asylums at the beginning of the Civil War. By the end of the war, that number had doubled, even though the country's population increased only 2 percent.

Moreover, the number of mental patients continued to swell for the next fifty years, doubling every ten years. Says Lande, "Johnny was coming home, disabled and distraught."[18]

The surge in mental patients resulted in an expanded system of institutional treatment. Large hospitals that functioned as both clinical laboratories and asylums were set up to house the afflicted. They served an even more important social role, though, by removing insane people from public view, thus hiding an unseemly problem. Eventually, however, when their hallways overflowed with patients and public funding declined, they merely warehoused individuals who had nowhere else to go.[19] At that point the hospitals were dismantled, and mentally ill patients were left to roam the streets, uncared for and on their own.

In *Flashback*, Penny Coleman notes that many Civil War soldiers complained of and were treated for physical ailments that seem rather minor. For instance, 145,000 soldiers were hospitalized for "constipation," and 66,000 were hospitalized for "headaches."[20] Politically and socially, it was more acceptable for both armies to admit that soldiers were suffering from minor physical problems rather than devastating psychiatric ills. Minimizing the impact of battlefield exposure kept up morale and aided recruitment efforts. Physical problems also were difficult to refute, while psychiatric problems are invisible. In addition, few army doctors at the time had any clinical training or experience in mental health, so there was little chance that they would attribute a soldier's condition to mental trauma.

Historian Joseph T. Glatthaar determined that after the war many white Union soldiers exhibited symptoms of PTSD, while black soldiers in the Union army did not, even though the latter were exposed to the same horrifying combat experiences. Glatthaar concluded that black soldiers had developed greater resiliency to war-induced trauma, most likely as a result of "the excitement of freedom, the vision of genuine equality, and the enthusiastic response of the black population for their work."[21]

Proximity, Immediacy, Expectancy, Simplicity

From the outset of World War I, England suffered heavy casualties. Battles at Aisne, Antwerp, Gallipoli, Marne, Ypres, and elsewhere resulted in many deaths, but it was in 1916 in the Somme Valley of France where the toll was greatest. On the first day of fighting 60,000 British soldiers out of 110,000 were killed. Over the next four months, another 500,000 died.[22]

British soldiers marched in rows and attacked in daylight. This made them easy targets for slaughter. Those who were lucky enough to survive physically weren't so lucky mentally. "Exposed to such a horrific environment," writes Dean, "ruled by the machine gun, poison gas, the artillery barrage, and the smell of rotting human flesh, a world in which one's comrades were routinely cut down, decapitated, or blown to bits before one's eyes, many World War I soldiers seemed to go mad."[23]

When British soldiers weren't marching, they engaged in trench warfare, which, in many respects, was even worse. Trapped below ground level for weeks at a time, they were subjected to the constant explosions of incoming artillery and the helpless screams of comrades who were struck. They had to deal with mud and cold, rats and lice, meager rations of food, widespread dysentery, and the fear that the next enemy howitzer to hit had their name on it.

Given these conditions, the number of psychiatric casualties isn't surprising. According to Denis Winter in *Death's Men: Soldiers of the Great War*, in 1914 there were 1,906 hospital cases in England of "behavior disorder without physical cause." In 1915 this number had grown to 20,237, or 9 percent of all battle casualties.[24]

That same year, 1915, a forty-two-year-old psychiatrist named Charles Myers became chief "Specialist in Nervous Shock" to the British Army in France. On the face of it, he was an odd choice, since he had never practiced medicine and had no experience with asylum psychiatry. Indeed, his background consisted almost exclusively of assisting colleagues in the small psychology department at Cambridge. Yet he was eager to support the war effort, and readily offered his services.

In Boulogne, on his first day on the job, Myers observed a dozen cases that he considered "most interesting, including one of incessant terror bordering on acute mania." The soldier, Myers noted in his diary, was "absolutely impervious to his surroundings, dodging shells from under the bed clothes."[25]

Soon Myers was handling hundreds cases of soldiers who, he said, were suffering from "shell shock." The cause, he believed, was primarily physical, the result of brain vibrations and nerve disruptions due to exploding artillery shells. Later the condition was ascribed to both brain concussions (now known as traumatic brain injury or TBI, in which high-pressure blast waves caused by an explosion rattle a person's brain regardless of whether he is wearing a helmet) and psychological stress. Soldiers who had "shell shock" were thought to lack the mental ability to deal with the horrors they had witnessed and participated in, either because their minds were physically damaged or because they were emotionally traumatized. Symptoms included anxiety, depression, insomnia, nightmares, intense fear, inability to concentrate, and panic attacks.

The problem with "shell shock," from the Army's point of view, was that it didn't fit neatly into the clear-cut labels in use at the time. Officially, men were either well, sick, physically wounded, or mad. Anyone who didn't fit into these categories, but was unwilling or incapable of fighting, was considered a coward, subject to being shot. Myers argued that shell shock was a new category, and soldiers with it needed to be treated in facilities that were separate from those that were for soldiers with other injuries. Reluctantly, higher-ups approved Myers's request for a separate facility and amended the way that injured soldiers were labeled. If a soldier incurred shell shock or a shell concussion due to enemy fire, his record read "Shell-shock W" for "wounded." He received a "wound stripe" and, if he couldn't fight anymore, was eligible for a pension. If his breakdown didn't follow a shell explosion that was caused by the enemy, however, the soldier's record read "Shell-shock S" for "sickness." In this instance there was no wound stripe or pension.

Autopsies subsequently discredited the theory of brain lesions as the cause of "shell shock," and Myers himself discouraged use of the phrase when he no longer believed that it had a physical explanation. Instead, his staff were instructed to use the acronym NYDN—Not Yet Diagnosed (Nervous).[26] Too many others already were referring to the condition as "shell shock," however, so the name stuck anyway. The only change was that by September 1918 "Shell-shock W" was abolished, and soldiers either suffered from shell shock or they didn't. Well before that, though, incidences of psychiatric trauma were common. By 1916, shell-shocked men constituted 40 percent of the casualties. In England, 80,000 cases of shell shock were treated by the British Army Medical Service.[27]

In 1916, Myers was named consulting psychologist to the Army. In a long memo to superiors he articulated a strategy for dealing with "shell shock" that today is known as forward treatment. Instead of being evacuated, Myers said, traumatized soldiers should remain near the front, in special hospitals where they would be served hot meals and receive a good night's rest. The restorative power of this approach, Myers believed, in combination with positive encouragement from a psychiatrist, were sufficient to boost a soldier's morale and hasten his return to the front. The French employed a similar strategy, he noted, and it seemed to be effective.

Today, Myers's principle of "proximity" is the basis of military psychiatry, but at the time it met considerable resistance. The traditional view of generals was simple. "We can't be lumbered with lunatics in Army areas," one said.[28] Despite their opposition, Myers's plan was approved, although shortly thereafter Myers was demoted for reasons he never understood and that, today, can only be surmised. Probably they had to do with the fact that he focused on underlying psychological issues when the prevailing opinion was that military doctors needed to deal with physical symptoms. The way Myers operated, every soldier could end up in a hospital, and there would be no one left to fight—an untenable situation if one is waging war.

In 1917, when the United States entered World War I on the side of the British, French, Russians, and Belgians, psychiatric training for U.S. Army medical officers consisted of a mere twenty-four hours. Included in this total was time spent attending lectures on military law and malingering.[29] A member of the U.S. Surgeon General's office, Major Thomas Salmon, developed a program for treating "war neurosis," which was the new name for shell shock. Based on Myers's model, Salmon's program was known as PIE, which stood for proximity, immediacy, and expectancy (later an *S* was added for "simplicity," and the acronym became PIES). It placed psychiatrists near the front lines, backed by forward hospitals. This way, affected soldiers could be treated at the scene and as quickly as possible. Treatment was simple and followed the British model of warm food and rest. The expectation was that troops would return to their units sooner if they received prompt attention instead of being evacuated. Prompt attention was seen as being in the best interests of both the soldier and the war effort. Removing a soldier from his unit delayed treatment, isolated him, and made it less likely that he would recover. It also hindered the country's fighting interests by reducing its available manpower.

On the face of it, PIE seemed effective. Of the soldiers who were treated, 70 percent ended up returning to their units within five days, and half the remainder returned within two weeks.[30] The number of soldiers who needed to be evacuated for psychiatric stress was reduced dramatically, thereby enabling the United States to maintain an adequate fighting force.

The assumption that wartime neuroses would end when the war ended proved to be false, however. While the civilian population rejoiced that the Great War was over, that Germany and Austria-Hungary had been defeated, and that America could return to the safe shell of isolationism that it had enjoyed prior to the start of the war, thousands of troops who survived the fighting were reeling from the nightmare of battle.

As Philip Gibbs, a British war reporter, wrote in his World War I memoir, *Now It Can Be Told*, "All was not right with the spirit of the men who came back. They put on civilian clothes again and looked to their mothers and wives very much like the young men who had gone…but they had not come back the same men. Something had altered them. They were subject to queer moods, queer tempers, fits of profound depression….Many were bitter in speech, violent in opinion, frightening."[31]

No programs or services existed to treat them; instead, they and their families were left to fend for themselves. At the time, the United States didn't have a health care system dedicated to veterans. In theory, the U.S. Public Health Service was supposed to provide care, but by 1921 the number of people seeking help was eight times greater than it had been before the war.[32] No new facilities had been built to accommodate this unanticipated surge in patients, and existing facilities were inadequate to meet the demand. Many disabled veterans ended up sleeping on cots or on the floors in the halls of overcrowded hospitals.[33]

Over the next two decades, the problem would only grow worse. By 1944, World War I veterans occupied nearly 50 percent of the VA's 67,000 hospital beds.[34] Meanwhile, in England, which entered the war earlier than the United States and suffered heavier casualties, 120,000 veterans of World War I had received awards or pensions for psychiatric disabilities.[35]

The Infamous Slaps

The heavy losses of World War I led the Allies to seek major reparations from the vanquished in the form of financial reimbursements and forfeiture of land, even though both sides helped start the war, and the economic terms imposed on Germany, Austria, and Hungary through the Treaty of Versailles were impossible for those countries to meet. The Allies never collected financially, but they did divide the spoils—land in Europe, the Middle East, and Africa. France took Alsace-Lorraine back from Germany and claimed Lebanon and Syria, Great Britain took Palestine, Jordan, and what is today Iran and Iraq, and new independent states—Yugoslavia, Czechoslovakia, and Poland—were carved out. Hungary lost two-thirds of its land, Austria was reduced to a small country, and the Ottoman Empire (now Turkey) was similarly shrunk and left impoverished.[36]

The realignment was seen as just compensation for the victors, but it also would prove to be short-sighted and costly. A reshaped world map caused another global war barely twenty years later when two dictators—Adolf Hitler in Germany and Benito Mussolini in Italy—rose to power by blaming their countries' smoldering ruins and economic woes on foreign influences. In addition, a third despot—General Hideki Tojo, who had gained power in Japan—had ambitions to expand his country's resources, which were limited by virtue of being a small island nation. Moreover, the Allies' postwar presence in the Pacific and Asia was getting in his way. The stage was set.

Between the two world wars, the belief arose in this country that screening troops before they went off to fight would eliminate most cases of combat stress. The screening, it was believed, would single out those soldiers who lacked the mental toughness to withstand the strain of battle, thereby reducing or eliminating altogether future cases of psychological trauma related to the war. The result was that when the United States entered World War II, the lessons learned twenty years earlier in World War I were ignored. Salmon's PIE model was abandoned, and psychiatrists no longer were assigned to forward units.[37]

The results of pre-enlistment screening proved to be a failure in two ways. First, incidences of war-related trauma increased as the fighting wore on. Over the course of World War II, there were 2.4 times more psychological casualties than in World War I.[38] With no place to go for help, some troops gradually lost their minds. Second, so many potential soldiers were deemed unfit for military service due to psychiatric reasons that they negated recruitment efforts. In

September 1943 alone, the U.S. Army inducted 118,600 men and discharged 112,500 others for psychiatric reasons. Ben Shephard notes in *A War of Nerves* that at this rate the Army would have had to induct one hundred in order to secure a net increase of five enlisted men.[39] Altogether, 800,000 men were rejected for service, and more than 500,000 others who were admitted initially ended up being discharged because of subsequent psychiatric and emotional problems. It was no way to win a war.

The United States entered World War II reluctantly, just as it had World War I. Germany's invasion of Austria, Czechoslovakia, Poland, Norway, Denmark, Luxembourg, Belgium, the Netherlands, Greece, Yugoslavia, and Russia, combined with Italy's invasion of Albania and Japan's invasion of French Indochina, had propelled Britain and France to declare war on the Axis Powers. Even so, the United States tried to stay out of it. Embargoes were imposed, German, Italian, and Japanese assets in the Unites States were frozen, and embassies were closed. These actions did nothing to stop Hitler's march across the Continent, however. Moreover, it wasn't long before the resources of England and France were depleted. At that point President Franklin D. Roosevelt announced a shift in U.S. policy from neutrality to "non-belligerency." The country didn't join the fight, but it began supplying weapons to the British and the French. In addition, all men ages twenty-one to thirty-five in the United States were mandated to begin military training, because it appeared to be just a matter of time before the country would have to commit combat troops as well.

In May 1941, a German U-boat sunk an American merchant ship. In October, two U.S. destroyers were torpedoed by the Germans. In December, the Japanese attacked Pearl Harbor. With that bombing, it no longer was possible for the United States to remain isolationist.

World War II is referred to in this country as "the good war," producing in its aftermath "the greatest generation." Americans were united behind the war even more than in World War I, and most people committed with relatively little complaint to do their part. Men went off to fight, women worked in factories that produced equipment, munitions, and supplies, and everyone at home endured the sacrifices that were necessary to support the war effort (rationing, blackouts, and so on). Great pride was taken in each new Allied victory, and everyone believed that Hitler would be turned back and democracy would prevail.

Behind the stories and reports of U.S. soldiers valiantly conquering their enemies, however, there was a dark side. It was more than battlefield deaths and physical injuries, as tragic as those were. The darkness was hidden, invisible, but no less real. Whereas in World War I it was given a graphic name—"shell shock"—in World War II it was called "combat fatigue" or "battle fatigue," implying that some troops were physically and emotionally exhausted. They weren't sick or broken, just tired. The assumption was they would rebound quickly, without treatment, once they were home—safe, sound, and rested. Unfortunately, this wasn't to be the case.

In 1942, not even a year into the war for the United States, the number of American troops who suffered from war-related psychiatric causalities already exceeded the number in World War I.[40] The reason was due, at least in part, to the fact that in planning for war, the military hadn't considered having treatment centers near the front. As a result, when soldiers suffered war-zone trauma, the only options were to evacuate them or force them to continue fighting. Neither option was desirable. The military couldn't afford to remove men from their posts when the fighting was at its peak, nor were soldiers of much use when they were psychologically damaged. An effort was made to rush recruits with psychiatric training to the front, not to provide therapy but to emphasize to soldiers how important it was that they return to their units as quickly as possible. To this end, soldiers were told that rest would cure them, that no sort of neurosis was involved. In 1943, the Army went further, officially instructing mental health workers that all psychiatric cases were to be diagnosed as "exhaustion" from that time forward, and treated accordingly.[41]

The highlight—or rather low point—of this unenlightened approach came in August 1943. General George S. Patton, visiting wounded American soldiers in a Sicilian hospital, struck two of them who were being treated for psychiatric injuries. According to Patton, the commanding officer of all U.S. Army forces, such injuries didn't exist. He called the first soldier a "goddamned coward" and slapped him across the face with his gloves. The second soldier he not only slapped but also threatened with a gun.

"Your nerves, hell," Patton said. "You are just a goddamned coward, you yellow son of a bitch. . . . You're going back to the front lines and you may get shot and killed, but you're going to fight. If you don't, I'll stand you up against a wall and have a firing squad kill you on purpose. In fact, I ought to shoot you myself, you goddamned whimpering coward."[42]

That same month, Patton sent a memo to soldiers under his command. "It has come to my attention," the memo said, "that a very small number of soldiers are going to the hospital on the pretext that they are nervously incapable of combat. Such men are cowards and bring discredit on the army and disgrace to their comrades, whom they heartlessly leave to endure the dangers of battle while they, themselves, use the hospital as a means of escape. You will take measures to see that such cases are not sent to the hospital but are dealt with in their units. Those who are not willing to fight will be tried by Court-Martial for cowardice in the face of the enemy."[43]

The incidents led General Dwight D. Eisenhower to relieve Patton of his command, partly out of compassion for what Eisenhower called Patton's "abuse of the 'sick,' "[44] and partly out of concern that Patton's actions would fuel German propaganda.[45] Regardless, Patton's well-publicized attitude played to the troops' fears of disclosing mental breakdowns. It also perpetuated the belief that war-related trauma would end when the war ended. Just as in World War I, though, it was the opposite. In the immediate aftermath of World War II, the number of soldiers with psychiatric problems overwhelmed U.S. hospitals. By the late 1940s, the Veterans Administration had 102,000 hospital beds, and not only was every one filled but nearly 21,000 veterans were waiting to be admitted.[46] The majority of patients—60 percent—sought treatment for psychiatric problems.[47] How the country dealt with the problem is one of the most shocking stories to come out of the war.

"It's Like the Devil Presides in You"

Walter Freeman was a neurology professor at George Washington University. He took the psychosurgical practice of lobotomies, which had been invented prior to World War II, and applied it to cases of psychosis. He believed that not only could he identify the nerve connections responsible for a patient's problem, but that severing these connections would solve it. His proposed surgery, performed under local anesthesia, involved driving an ice pick with a hammer through the corner of a person's eye socket and into the prefrontal cortex of the brain. The prefrontal cortex controls a person's thoughts and actions. Although there was no compelling evidence to support the effectiveness of such a drastic procedure, it did have economic benefits. Freeman's ice-pick lobotomy could be done for $250, while a year's stay in a hospital would cost $35,000.[48] And the results, while not curative, did rid problem patients of their aggressive tendencies. Unfortunately, and not surprisingly in light of what is known today, most ended up worse off than before, lacking emotions, social skills, and the ability to make decisions.[49] (Egaz Moniz, a Portuguese neurologist, is credited with inventing the practice of lobotomies. In 1949, he was awarded the Nobel Prize for Medicine, an award he accepted in a wheelchair because he had been shot in the spine and paralyzed years earlier by a patient he had lobotomized.)

The number of lobotomies surged from 150 in 1945 to more than 5,000 in 1949. By 1948, nearly fifty operations per month were being performed in VA hospitals. Overall, between 1936 and 1951 about 18,000 lobotomies were performed in the United States, with 12 percent being done by the VA.[50] (The majority of those not done on veterans were done on women, including John F. Kennedy's sister, Rosemary Kennedy.) Lobotomies ended in 1954 when the drug Thorazine was discovered and was subsequently used to treat schizophrenia, bipolar disorder, and other psychoses, but the impact would be felt for years.

During World War II, about 800,000 infantry soldiers saw direct combat. Of these, 300,000, or 37.5 percent, experienced psychiatric problems that were serious enough for them to be discharged. In addition, there were 596,000 instances where a soldier was hospitalized for days or weeks for psychiatric reasons and wasn't discharged.[51] (Some soldiers were hospitalized more than once.) On top of this, 464,000 soldiers reported psychiatric problems but weren't hospitalized; instead, they were told to return to action immediately, and complied.[52]

Famed writer J. D. Salinger was among those who experienced a nervous breakdown in the aftermath of the war. His battlefield service began on D-Day, June 6, 1944, with the Allied invasion of Normandy and ended nine months later, in April 1945, with the liberation of the Kaufering IV concentration camp in Germany (a subcamp of Dachau). Two months later, when he was home, he exhibited symptoms of PTSD, although no one knew it as such. He told his daughter, "You can never really get the smell of burning flesh out of your nose entirely, no matter how long you live."[53]

Counting all branches of the military, nearly 1.4 million of 8 million (17.5 percent) U.S. World War II service members suffered PTSD-like symptoms and were removed from duty, at least temporarily.[54] By comparison, in World War I about 106,000 service members out of 2 million (5.3 percent) were hospitalized for psychiatric reasons, with 69,000 permanently evacuated.[55]

In 1946, legendary filmmaker John Huston produced a documentary movie, paid for by the U.S. War Department, that focused on seventy-five psychiatric patients at Mason General Army hospital in Long Island, New York. All of the patients experienced combat in World War II and suffered debilitating emotional trauma and depression. That wasn't what viewers were supposed to think, however. Huston was hired to make a movie that would assure the public that American soldiers were all right, even those who suffered temporarily from war-induced trauma. The Army's chief psychiatric adviser, General William Menninger, pressed for the movie after he received numerous letters from the parents of discharged soldiers who complained about their sons' psychiatric condition. Menninger wanted the letters to stop, and he figured that the movie would produce that result.

The War Department hired the wrong filmmaker, though. While *Let There Be Light* excluded any footage of the closed wards at Mason General where schizophrenic and psychotic patients received shock therapy, it was hardly the positive public relations tool that the military thought it was getting. The images that viewers were treated to weren't rosy, despite attempts by the military to orchestrate individual stories in such a way as to imply that amazing recoveries were taking place. Instead, the men filmed by Huston were incoherent, wide-eyed, and confused, while the psychiatrists who treated them appeared brusque and uncaring. Meanwhile, the film's narrator offered a stark fact for an uninformed public. "Twenty percent of our army casualties," said the narrator, "suffered psychoneurotic symptoms—a sense of impending disaster, hopelessness, fear, and isolation."[56]

According to film critic Kenneth Turan, Huston's movie was "one of the first to document the terrible things combat did to the minds of soldiers."[57] Once it was finished, however, the military suppressed it, ostensibly because it violated patient confidentiality.[58] For thirty-five years it was locked up just like the patients it featured. It finally was released to the public in 1981—five years after the Vietnam War ended.

At the same time that *Let There Be Light* was being filmed, *JAMA* reported that "each moment of combat imposes a strain so great that men will break down in direct relation to the intensity and duration of their exposure." *JAMA* concluded that "psychiatric casualties are as inevitable as gunshot and shrapnel wounds in warfare."[59]

According to later research, published in the 1950s and 1960s in the *Journal of the American Psychiatric Association*, persistent symptoms related to posttraumatic stress—depression, insomnia, nightmares, headaches, irritability, and anxiety disorders—were present in veterans twenty years later, which led to the label "veteran's chronic stress syndrome," the precursor to today's PTSD.[60]

During this time, more than 475,000 World War II veterans with psychiatric disabilities were receiving pensions from the VA, and an additional 50,000 were in VA hospitals. Two and a half decades later, in 1972, 44,000 veterans were still in VA hospitals.[61]

In a 1989 study, 54 percent of World War II combat veterans who had psychiatric problems met the clinical definition of PTSD, and 27 percent were still suffering more than forty-five years later.[62] In 1993, 22,273 veterans ages sixty-five to seventy-nine (squarely in the middle of the World War II era) collectively spent more than 2 million days in VA hospitals for psychiatric illnesses, with an average length of stay of ninety days.[63]

"What you don't know going in," wrote Edward "Babe" Heffron in *Brothers in Battle, Best of Friends*, a memoir of World War II, "is that when you come out, you will be scarred for life. Whether you were in for a week, a month, or a year—even if you come home without a scratch—you are never, ever going to be the same. ... Living with it can be hell. It's like the devil presides in you."[64]

Heffron was an Army private. He said, "Any soldier who lived through combat, whether it was in 1776, 1861, 1918, 1944, any war, will never be entirely free of the war he fought. Some are just able to brush it off better than others."[65]

The Forgotten War

The lessons learned in World War I and World War II regarding the psychological impact of combat, the importance of unit cohesion, and the value of forward treatment weren't retained when it came to Korea a mere five years later. United States military leaders decided at the outset of the Korean War in 1950 that psychiatrists weren't needed. The fact that troops would be exposed to the same horrors as soldiers in previous wars, and might suffer the same fate—to be killed, physically injured, or mentally scarred by what they witnessed and experienced—was ignored, at least in the early stages of the war. The consequences were predictable.

About 1.7 million U.S. service members fought in Korea, and more than 36,000 were killed there. Another 8,000 are still missing. In addition, nearly 1 million Korean and Chinese soldiers were killed, plus 2 million Korean civilians.[66] Were it not for the TV series *M*A*S*H*, however, and the movie on which it was based, most Americans would know little or nothing about what is often referred to now as "the forgotten war." They wouldn't know that the war started when North Korean troops, who were trained and equipped by the Soviet Union, invaded the Republic of Korea in a civil conflict aimed at the country's reunification. They wouldn't know that it was, in many respects, a proxy war, with the United States supplying the majority of troops on the South Korean side and the North Korean military being boosted substantially by Chinese forces. They wouldn't know that when the war ended three and a half years later, virtually nothing had changed in Korea—the same division existed between North and South, and peace would be fleeting. (In 2013, on the sixtieth anniversary of the armistice agreement that stopped the fighting, President Obama urged Americans to stop referring to it as "the forgotten war" and consider it "the forgotten victory."[67] It's hard to consider any war a victory, however, when we feel a need to have 30,000 troops in the area 60 years later to keep the peace.[68])

Although not much was different in Korea after the war, a lot changed in the United States. Specifically, the Korean War led to a massive buildup of U.S. conventional and nuclear forces, which prompted Dwight D. Eisenhower, who was elected president in 1952 on the strength of his military service in World War II and Korea, to issue his famous warning against "the military-industrial complex."[69] In his last public speech as president, Eisenhower noted that 3.5 million men and women were "directly engaged in the defense establishment" and that the country spent more on military security "than the net income of all United States corporations." While acknowledging "the imperative need for this development," he said, "we must not fail to comprehend its grave implications" and "the potential for the disastrous rise of misplaced power."[70] (In *Unwarranted Influence: Dwight D. Eisenhower and the Military-Industrial Complex,* James Ledbetter notes that Eisenhower was born to Mennonite parents who were pacifists and considered war a sin. When the future five-star general and U.S. president was young and showed undue fascination with military history, his mother tried to hide the family's history books in order to quell his interest.)

In the first year of the Korean War, the rate of U.S. psychiatric casualties—250 per 1,000 men—was 7 times greater than in the first year of World War II.[71] One-fourth of all combat zone evacuations were for psychological reasons.[72] Realizing that it had to do something—and do it fast, before the problem grew worse—the Department of Defense turned to Albert Glass for help. Glass had been a psychiatrist in the Army Medical Corps during World War II. He knew firsthand what combat was like, the psychological toll it took on troops, and the success that had been achieved by having mental health professionals stationed near the front. His approach relied on resurrecting the notion of prompt forward treatment, albeit with two significant changes. First, psychiatrists didn't just visit soldiers at the front; they stayed there, living among them, socializing with them, and being part of their unit. Glass believed that evacuating a psychically wounded warrior was detrimental to the individual as well as damaging to the war effort and should be avoided at all costs. It caused soldiers to feel guilty about abandoning their comrades. Glass reasoned that treating a soldier immediately so that he could return to his unit had the benefit of restoring his self-respect. Treatment mainly involved rest and relaxation (R&R)—brief time away from the fighting so that troops could become reenergized again.

Glass's approach was embraced by the military for an obvious reason—it kept soldiers on the front lines. It also resolved a long-standing dilemma for military psychiatrists. While professional ethics dictated that they provide treatment that was in the best interests of a patient, it was unclear whether returning a soldier to battle as quickly as possible was consistent with this. A strong argument could be made that it wasn't. Now, according to Glass, the best interests of patients also happened to be the best interests of the military, thus there no longer was a conflict.

The second change Glass made was to implement a point system that attempted to quantify both the degree of trauma a soldier had been exposed to and the intensity of that exposure. An infantry soldier, for instance, accumulated four points per month, an artilleryman three points, and a soldier closer to the rear two points. After thirty-six points, the soldier was sent home. It didn't matter where he was at that time or the status of the war. What mattered was minimizing the possibility of a mental breakdown by putting a cap on a soldier's wartime experiences.[73]

On the face of it, the combination of quick, in-the-field treatment and the new point system worked. Whereas 23 percent of World War II troops had psychiatric problems, the number dropped to 6 percent at the end of the Korean War.[74] Moreover, 90 percent of troops treated for psychiatric problems during the war returned to battle.[75]

One problem that wasn't anticipated, though, was that as the Korean War went on, troops in the rear, who previously had been protected from the worst fighting by virtue of their distance from the front, ended up in situations that were equally dangerous. The combat zone had been expanded, yet the focus of mental health treatment was on forward troops. Soldiers in the rear were ignored, and they would become psychiatric casualties of the next major war, in Vietnam.

Operation Rolling Thunder

Hundreds of books have been written about the Vietnam War. Much of the focus has been on why we lost the war—the first military defeat in U.S. history if one doesn't count the Civil War for the South. How Vietnam could have been won is a popular topic of debate, as is the morality of the war—whether the United States should have been involved at all. Less attention has been cast on the physical and psychological injuries of soldiers who survived the fighting, and virtually no attention has been focused on the havoc the war created for people in Vietnam, where four million civilians were killed. (People in Vietnam don't refer to it as the Vietnam War. They call it the American War.)

Vietnam was different from every war preceding it, at least for the United States. Roger Spiller, a military historian, says that the United States has fought many kinds of wars: "revolutionary wars, guerilla wars, punitive wars, imperial wars, limited wars for the finer points of policy, wars marked by low and grudging social support, wars that consumed disproportionately younger men, wars whose supposed nobility was spoiled by atrocity, wars in which the rhythms of life at home were hardly interrupted, and wars in which the soldiers had only the most meager idea of why they were fighting." The Vietnam War is unusual, he says, because it "has been described in all these ways."[76]

Vietnam was the last war for which this country had a draft. Many men of eligible age (myself included) avoided it because of student deferments. Others failed medical screenings—to their relief. Still others fled to Canada. Those who didn't have the same options, or who chose not to exercise them, either voluntarily enlisted or waited to receive their induction notice. Among them was a disproportionate number of men who were unusually young, undereducated, largely poor, and predominantly from ethnic minorities.

In 1967, two years after the United States began Operation Rolling Thunder, the name for President Lyndon B. Johnson's sustained bombing of North Vietnam, fewer than half of the enlisted men in the U.S. Armed Forces had been drafted. The majority entered the military voluntarily, although not necessarily willingly. If conscription was inevitable, there were benefits to volunteering because a person had some say regarding his branch of service and field of interest. By 1969, however, the war had escalated to the point where the country needed more manpower to sustain the fighting, which took place in hot, humid jungles with dense vegetation that offered cover and escape routes to the enemy. At that time, the proportion of conscripted troops increased to 88 percent.[77] (Overall, 2.2 million of the 3.1 million American troops who served in Vietnam—71 percent—were drafted.[78]) This increase was due in large part to reduced standards, so that individuals who previously were ineligible because of their lack of education now qualified for military duty. Through Project 100,000, the recruitment plan implemented by Johnson's defense secretary, Robert McNamara, 350,000 new recruits were added. Most of them—80 percent—were high-school dropouts, and 40 percent read below a sixth-grade level.[79] Promised a job, housing, the chance to learn important skills, travel, and educational opportunities, they signed up and were assigned to infantry units, which had the highest casualty rates. Whereas the average age of U.S. combat soldiers in

World War II was twenty-six, in Vietnam it was nineteen. (Today, the average age of active-duty troops is twenty-seven, with officers averaging thirty-five. Among reservists, the average age is thirty-one for enlisted members and forty-one for officers. Roughly half of all service personnel are married, and 43 percent have children.[80])

The youthfulness of American troops is why Vietnam is referred to as America's first teenage war, although that isn't entirely accurate. As historian Gerald Linderman notes in *Embattled Courage*, eighteen-year-olds constituted the single largest age group for both armies in the first year of the Civil War.[81] Among Confederate soldiers, one-fourth were teenagers.[82] Nevertheless, more than 60 percent of U.S. troops who died in the Vietnam War and have since been memorialized on the Vietnam Wall were ages seventeen to twenty-one.[83] Among those who survived, youth and lack of other experiences made them less able to deal with the psychic wounds of war than previous generations of American soldiers. Most people barely out of their teens have minimal exposure to death and dying—certainly not on the scale of the carnage seen in Vietnam.

According to the Department of Veterans Affairs, 31 percent of Vietnam veterans suffer from posttraumatic stress.[84] Other studies peg the number at 70 percent—equal to two million service members—based on longitudinal data rather than a snapshot in time.[85] Symptoms of PTSD, such as the re-experiencing of traumatic events through nightmares, unwanted memories, and flashbacks; avoiding situations or people that trigger thoughts of a traumatic event; being numb to all emotions (even positive feelings toward others); being uninterested in activities one used to enjoy; and being hypervigilant, on high alert at all times, constantly on the lookout for danger and consumed by thoughts of one's safety and the safety of others, aren't always evident right away. They can take weeks, months, or even years to develop. Two decades after the war in Vietnam ended, fewer than 40 percent of troops who had been diagnosed with PTSD had sought help.[86] Either they thought real help didn't exist, they didn't trust the military to provide it, or they didn't want to admit that they needed help.

"Still in Saigon in My Mind"

In *Flashback*, several women who, like author Penny Coleman, were married to Vietnam veterans and subsequently became widowed because their husbands killed themselves tell their stories. In each instance, the festering malignancy of depression and despair related to a soldier's combat experiences created a ticking time bomb that, without intervention or adequate treatment, ultimately exploded. In its aftermath, the hopes and dreams of loved ones were reduced to rubble.

Ben James was one of only 18 men in his unit of 350 to survive the Vietnam War. He had received the Air Medal and Purple Heart—both of which he threw away. Haunted by nightmares, he stockpiled food and guns, avoided public places, and exploded in anger periodically at his wife and daughter. Despite having a good job, supportive family, and being treated for PTSD, he remained depressed. Before he died, he sorted through financial files and left everything in order on his desk, apologizing in a suicide note to his wife that he didn't have more money to leave her. When he killed himself, it was twenty-six years after he had come home from Vietnam.[87]

Bobby Garcia was twenty-five when he died. A former paratrooper, he "saw a lot of the war from the air," according to his wife. Once he was home, however, he realized "that the Vietnam War was not going to leave him just because he left it." He drank heavily, couldn't sleep, was irritable much of the time, and went through manic periods. Like Ben James, he left everything in order before he killed himself, making the bed and doing all of his laundry. Unlike James, he didn't leave a note. "He did not say goodbye," his wife said. "He just went quietly away."[88]

Emilia Perrish's husband, Noel, served in a tank battalion in Vietnam. When he came home, the only thing that provided any relief from the horrors he had witnessed was alcohol. Then that wasn't enough. Three months before his son was born, he shot himself. "Vietnam ripped his heart apart," his wife said. "The bullet just finished what the war had started."[89]

Any one of these widows, or Linda Robideau, could have offered testimony about the lingering effects of the war, if anyone in the military had been interested. In Robideau's case, her husband's suicide occurred on Father's Day 1996. Father's Day is a popular day for veterans with children to kill themselves. It serves as a painful reminder of their perceived inadequacies as parents and the burden they consider themselves to be for loved ones.

When Donald Robideau met Linda in 1982, she was a single mother with two young sons, one of whom had special needs. "If men were interested in me," she said, "after seeing the kids they weren't."[90]

Except Donald. He loved her children, and he and Linda married. It wasn't long after that, though, that she started witnessing his nightmares and saw him wake up covered in sweat. He talked about suicide and was prescribed antidepressants. They helped him cope but also frustrated him because they seemed like a crutch.

On June 16, 1996, in Royalston, Massachusetts, where they lived, Robideau put shutters over the windows in their bedroom and locked the door. Then he donned his camouflage shirt with his war medals, applied camouflage paint to his face, and told Linda that he was going to kill himself. She begged him not to, telling him of the pain it would cause her and her sons. He wouldn't listen, instead barricading himself in the house with six semiautomatic rifles and a homemade bomb that he fashioned from a propane tank rigged with gunpowder. Shortly after 1 p.m., following a two-hour standoff with police, Robideau emerged from the house, seemingly ready to give up. Then, on their front lawn, as the police chief—a man he reportedly liked—approached him, Robideau said, "Sorry," and shot himself.[91] He had been a teenager in Vietnam and was forty when he died.

In 1990, the same year that the massive *National Vietnam Veterans Readjustment Study* was published, which provided an in-depth examination of the psychological impact of the war on those who fought in it without ever referring, even in passing, to suicide, the *American Journal of Psychiatry* reported that about 9,000 Vietnam vets had died by suicide as of the early 1980s. The information came from the federal Centers for Disease Control, which some critics claimed was hardly impartial since it was another branch of government.

Even so, the absence of any mention of suicide in the *NVVRS* is inexcusable. What did make it into the report was the projection that 31 percent of the three million men who served in Vietnam had or would develop PTSD as defined by the new standards set forth in the American Psychiatric Association's *Diagnostic and Statistical Manual of Mental Disorders* (DSM).[92] The primary way to help them, it was decided, was to establish storefront vet centers. These centers were designed to assist psychologically damaged veterans who distrusted the VA and wouldn't seek help from VA facilities. At the centers, soldiers received emotional support and referrals. Equally important, they learned that it was common for veterans to develop PTSD and that it could be treated successfully. It might not go away entirely, but it could be managed.

In 1980 there were ninety vet centers in the United States. When Ronald Reagan became president in 1981, he tried to close the centers—which had expanded in number to 200—and channel patients to VA hospitals. Veterans complained loudly and effectively, calling it another betrayal of vets by the government.[93] Reagan relented, and by the middle of his first term the centers were treating about 150,000 veterans per year. Another 28,000 vets were being treated for PTSD in 172 VA hospitals and clinics across the country, 13 of which had special PTSD units.[94] (Today, there are more than 300 vet centers in the United States. In addition to dealing with combat stress, staff and volunteers there provide counseling to veterans who are sexually assaulted or harassed while on active duty, as well as grief counseling to the families of service members who are killed.)

Fifteen years after the last American combatant left Vietnam, 479,000 of the 3.1 million men who served there still had PTSD, and almost a million veterans in all had "full-blown" PTSD. Only 15 percent, or about 300,000, actually had been in combat,[95] but that didn't matter. As the lyrics of the song "Still in Saigon," by the Charlie Daniels Band, proclaimed, the war was inescapable anyway.

> Every summer when it rains
> I smell the jungle, I hear the planes.
> Can't tell no one, I feel ashamed,
> Afraid someday I'll go insane...
> Cause I'm still in Saigon...in my mind.[96]

Post-Vietnam, there would be differences the next time American troops were deployed. For one thing, the military would implement better screening practices to identify prospective soldiers who had or were likely to develop psychological problems. Screening would be far from perfect, but it would be an improvement over what had been done previously. In addition, the country would go back to having an all-volunteer force, which would result in older, better educated, and generally more mature enlisted personnel. Also, more resources would be made available by the Department of Defense and the VA to help soldiers cope with the trauma of combat, including drug screening and treatment programs, and benefits would be increased for all veterans.

What wouldn't be different was even more important, however. The battlefield would continue to be asymmetrical with no beginning and no end. Whereas in World War I and World War II soldiers rotated to the rear lines periodically for relief, that wasn't possible in Vietnam and it's not possible today. There are no rear lines to move to, no way to escape the constant stress of combat. In World War II, the average infantryman experienced forty days of battle in four years of service.[97] Today, the average soldier who deploys to Iraq or Afghanistan experiences battle every day that he or she is there, with few opportunities to rest, mentally or physically.

What also wouldn't be different after Vietnam was that enemy combatants and civilians would remain virtually indistinguishable from each other. Both would be comprised of women and children as well as adult men, and they would dress not in uniforms of war but in the clothing of peasants and farmers. It's much more difficult for today's soldiers to know at a glance who is innocent and who presents a threat. In addition, training would prepare troops to fight, but not to return to a normal life afterward. Token efforts would be made to provide support to soldiers and their families, but military culture wouldn't change. The stigma associated with mental health problems would continue to make troops resistant to seeking help.

The result would be even greater incidences of posttraumatic stress and an alarming increase in the number of suicides by active-duty service members. The former would overwhelm military hospitals and clinics that weren't prepared to deal with them. Only the development of new drugs such as chlorpromazine (used on schizophrenics) and lithium (used on manic patients) would stem the tide. They wouldn't solve the psychological problems induced by the war, but they would make it possible to clear U.S. mental wards of many psychotic patients. In 1955 there were 560,000 patients in state and county mental hospitals in the United States. By 1970, the number was down to 338,000, and by 1988 it was 107,000.[98] As for the growing number of suicides by America's veterans, they would leave military leaders and family members searching for answers that neither would find.

Surviving Combat, but Not Combat Demons

A number of influential people, most notably psychiatrist and author Robert Jay Lifton, argued in the aftermath of Vietnam that PTSD should be included in the DSM. This massive tome is the bible of modern-day psychiatry, and PTSD's inclusion in it would legitimize the condition, Lifton and others believed. It also would facilitate diagnoses and help guide treatment. No longer would psychological trauma be considered inconsequential or something that time alone would heal. It would stand on its own as a clinical condition with bona fide symptoms and prescribed cures.

The first edition of the *Diagnostic and Statistical Manual*, subsequently referred to as DSM-I, was issued in 1952 and included a condition called "gross stress reaction." It was commonly found in soldiers, according to the manual, and was short term. By the time that DSM-II came out, in 1968, the condition had been dropped and there no longer was any reference to the effects of psychiatric disorders produced by battle. In the third edition, referred to as DSM-III, published in 1980, PTSD was added. Since then, information about posttraumatic stress has been expanded, starting with DSM-IV, published in 1994, and most recently in the fifth edition, published in May 2013. Even so, there is disagreement among mental health professionals today about whether PTSD stands alone as a psychiatric disorder or whether it coexists with anxiety disorders, personality disorders, and depression. In *Shook Over Hell*, Eric T. Dean, Jr., says, "It would appear that all soldiers subjected to combat suffer some incidence of psychiatric breakdown (categorized as PTSD, shell shock, psychoneurosis, or outright insanity), both of an acute variety on the battlefield and in delayed form after the end of hostilities; although a lack of the use of consistent diagnostic categories over time makes direct comparisons impossible." Dean also notes that while the DSM refers to posttraumatic stress as "extraordinary" stress "outside the range of usual human experience," it's not clear what this means. How can it be measured and differentiated from "ordinary" stress that often cripples someone emotionally, such as a divorce, job loss, or a loved one's death? Without a strong definition, it's difficult to say how many people have PTSD, much less the best ways to treat it, especially when there may be as many as 175 variations, according to Herb Kutchins and Stuart A. Kirk in *Making Us Crazy: DSM*.[99]

Questions abound, too, regarding the exact process by which impressions of danger and death end up becoming traumatic memories, the role of genetics, and whether some troops have predisposed immunity to the effects. Mental health professionals can't determine in advance and with anywhere near 100 percent accuracy which individuals will be able to cope with the stress of combat and which will break down psychologically. They also can't say with certainty whether the impact of PTSD dissipates over time, even without treatment, or whether it's permanent, even with treatment. As Barry R. Schaller, author of *Veterans on Trial: The Coming Court Battles over PTSD*, points out, the study of PTSD has been rife with fallacies, misunderstandings, and paradoxes.[100] For example, it's unclear whether PTSD is a normal reaction to abnormal circumstances or whether it represents abnormal behavior in normal times. Good arguments can be made that it's both. Many people, if thrust into a war zone, would be psychologically traumatized, and if they spent any amount of time there they would have trouble adjusting to their former way of life when they returned home.

Virtually every soldier—even the toughest one—has a breaking point. In recent years, mental health professionals have begun to realize that most people aren't predisposed to psychiatric meltdowns; instead, such meltdowns are the normal reaction of normal people to the extraordinary stresses of war. Indeed, instead of asking why some soldiers break down, a more logical question to ask is why some soldiers don't break down. Why aren't they as affected by the psychological stresses of combat as everyone around them?[101]

While almost anyone who is exposed to a traumatic event can develop PTSD, there is a significant difference between civilians and soldiers. As Schaller notes, civilians who are victims of an accident, assault, or natural disaster may not feel confident or safe anymore, but their identity isn't threatened. They remain the same people they were before the event, less complacent and secure perhaps, but otherwise unchanged. Individuals who experience combat, however, who are trained to kill and see others killed, oftentimes aren't the same people afterward. Their experiences change them in fundamental ways. The things they have learned and had to do in order to survive are contrary to the ethical and moral standards by which civilians operate. Moreover, they don't stay distant the way that other memories do.

Once troops are away from the war, they can have a hard time living with themselves. According to Laurie B. Slone and Matthew J. Friedman of the National Center for PTSD, "Service members with PTSD often state that they have lost the person they used to be. They feel that they have become unrecognizable to themselves and to others. What is worse, they don't like the person they have become. People with PTSD often feel that they are unlovable or don't deserve the love of partners and family. Because of this, they often experience depression as well. When considering the losses that may lead to depression, the PTSD-related loss of self may be the most unbearable loss of all."[102]

It's this fact that makes veterans as well as active-duty troops more susceptible to suicide. Even if they suppress painful memories in the moment, they usually can't suppress them forever.

"Today a soldier can go out on patrol, kill someone or have one of his friends killed, and call his girlfriend that night and talk about anything except what just happened," says Karl Marlantes in his book *What It Is Like to Go to War*. A soldier may continue to be inured to his combat experiences when he returns home as well, but that doesn't mean it will last.

"Ask the twenty-year-old combat veteran at the gas station how he felt about killing someone," says Marlantes, an Army officer in Vietnam. "His probable angry answer, if he's honest: 'Not a fucking thing.' Ask him when he's sixty, and if he's not too drunk to answer, it might come out differently."[103]

One development that occurred between Vietnam and the Persian Gulf war today is that soldiers now know about PTSD. It's not unfamiliar to them, as it was for Vietnam veterans, nor is it questioned as a genuine psychiatric condition. Whether someone actually has PTSD may be subject to debate, but the fact that it exists and that it's disabling is beyond doubt.

In a 2008 report by the RAND Center for Military Health Policy Research, 14 percent of veterans returning from Iraq and Afghanistan—about 300,000 troops—were estimated to have PTSD.[104] RAND, like the VA, didn't take into account the fact that PTSD sometimes develops over years, however. If it had, the estimate, according to other sources, would be at least 35 percent, or 700,000 troops.[105] In addition, with continual deployments, the number keeps increasing.

In a September 2012 report by the VA that wasn't issued to the public but instead was posted without fanfare on the VA website and found accidentally by veterans who were searching for other information, new numbers were provided. Of the more than 1.6 million Iraq and Afghanistan veterans to that point (not counting current, active-duty troops), 834,000 had sought medical services from the VA and 247,000 were diagnosed with PTSD.[106] Among those with PTSD diagnoses, 109,000 weren't receiving any help, despite efforts by the VA to boost clinical staff. The VA added 1,600 mental health professionals in April 2012, and 300 others during the year, making a total of almost 22,000 VA clinicians. Even so, the department hasn't been able to keep up with demand. Moreover, 10,000 new Gulf War vets are pouring into VA medical facilities every month now.[107]

Recent research by the University of Utah's National Center for Veterans Studies indicates that the more exposure a soldier has to combat, the more likely he or she is to attempt suicide later. The research was led by David Rudd, an Army psychologist who served in the first Gulf War. Through Student Veterans of America, Rudd surveyed 244 veterans. Of those who had seen heavy combat, 93 percent had PTSD symptoms. Nearly 70 percent had attempted suicide.[108]

In releasing the results, Rudd said, "One of the primary shifts from World War II to Vietnam to the current wars is that psychological injury is undeniably the most significant consequence of war. It impacts far more veterans than any other kind of injury today....I don't think there's anything more tragic than to have someone serve multiple tours in combat and survive and then kill themselves."[109]

"I Deserve Hell"

As telling as they are, combat exposure and the number of deployments aren't the sole causes of military suicides. According to former Defense secretary Leon Panetta and others, more than half the active–duty soldiers who have died by suicide have no history of deployment.[110]

This is especially true for National Guard members and military reservists. They account for over half the suicides of Iraq war veterans, even though for much of the war they comprised only one-quarter of U.S. troops there.[111] Many didn't expect to be deployed when they enlisted, and they haven't received anywhere near the same level of combat training as active-duty troops. Moreover, they don't live on military bases, so they and their families aren't surrounded by others who share their plight. In addition, unlike active-duty units, their commanders see them only during drills, which can be sixty days apart. Finally, they may be assigned to units where they know no one, and their civilian job may be threatened by their absence.

The correlation between posttraumatic stress and suicides in the military is well established now. The incidences of both have risen dramatically in recent years, seemingly in lockstep with each other. According to the *Journal of Traumatic Stress*, most authorities view the escalating rate of military suicides as an indication that the departments of Defense and Veterans Affairs are dealing with both problems poorly.[112] Granted, sincere concern is expressed from the top down. Also, more study and media attention are being devoted to PTSD and military suicides today than ever before. In addition, new resources continue to be directed to treatment and prevention; for example, the VA spent $5 billion on mental health services in 2011 alone.[113] Nevertheless, it hasn't been enough. Combat changes people, and processes need to be in place that make it possible for them to lead relatively normal lives again.

It doesn't help that Pentagon and VA officials have discouraged military physicians from making new diagnoses of PTSD, or that they are challenging existing diagnoses. Each diagnosis costs the military money.

Perhaps the single most egregious act occurred in August 2005. That month the VA announced that 72,000 veterans who were receiving full disability benefits for PTSD would have their claims reviewed and possibly revoked. Meanwhile, until this review process was completed, more than 580,000 previously approved cases would be tabled. A public backlash forced the VA to retreat from its position; however, the reversal happened too late for at least one veteran. Greg Morris, age fifty-seven, was found dead in the New Mexico home he shared with his wife. The gun he used lay next to him, along with the Purple Heart that he had received. Also near his body was a folder of articles that described the VA's plan to review the claims of veterans like Morris to make sure that they deserved continuing compensation.

Before his suicide, Morris wrote letters to his local congressman, Representative Tom Udall, asking whether he would lose the VA's financial support for his disability, on which he had long depended. According to Udall, Morris believed, "As so many veterans do, that he was being forced to prove himself yet again. It is that belief that makes veterans so angry and so frustrated with this process."[114]

It's not enough that veterans sacrifice so much by fighting for their country. They also have to fight for their right to essential services such as health care for military-related conditions, even though these services are supposed to be guaranteed to them.

Michael Ecker was an Army veteran who served in Iraq. He suffered from PTSD and a traumatic brain injury that left him unable to hold a steady job after he was discharged. The $974 per month that he received in partial disability benefits wasn't enough to live on, so he moved in with his parents, who lived in Champion, Ohio. Ecker's application for an increase in benefits was denied due to a VA doctor's assessment that Ecker was "over-reporting both mood disturbance and impaired memory difficulty."[115]

Shortly after he received the VA's determination letter, Ecker stood in the woods behind his parents' home, holding a loaded gun. He called out to his father, who saw him salute and then shoot himself in the head before his father could stop him. Ecker was twenty-five. Since then, his father has been tempted to find the doctor who ruled on his son's case, give him Ecker's death certificate, and say, "Over-reporting?" Meanwhile, his mother continues to wonder if better treatment or a job suited to his condition would have prevented her son's death.[116]

The wife of Major Jeffrey Hackett has similar thoughts. After serving twenty-six years in the Marine Corps, Hackett came home in 2007 following his second deployment to Iraq. In his first deployment, in 2005, he led a team of Marines whose job it was to search for roadside bombs and destroy them. Eight men under his command were killed doing this highly dangerous work, and Hackett saw each body seconds after it had been blown apart. He also spoke at each victim's memorial service. Afterward, he had anxiety attacks, heart problems, and high blood pressure, and he couldn't sleep. He requested early retirement but instead deployed again. This time five more of his men were killed by IEDs, and Hackett incurred a damaged eardrum and severe migraines as a result of a concussion from one of the bombs. In an e-mail to his wife, Hackett said, "Don't know what to do. Feel responsible, feel angry, and I feel numb." He noted that the wife of one man who was killed "just had a baby three weeks ago," adding, "Every day I have in the Corps now is miserable and painful." In another e-mail Hackett said, "I failed! I failed everyone! My men in the Corps died unnecessarily."[117]

When he retired from the Marines in 2008, Hackett was given a 40 percent disability rating based on "ankle, shoulder, and knee strains," hearing loss, and a hiatal hernia (in a hiatal hernia, part of the stomach sticks through the diaphragm into the chest and affects a person's breathing). No mental health problems were noted, in large part because Hackett received no mental health treatment from the Marines despite his increasingly erratic and abnormal behavior.[118] Following retirement, he was unable to find work and ended up accepting a job as an unskilled laborer at an oil refinery near Cheyenne, Wyoming. The only requirements were that he have a high school diploma and be able to lift fifty pounds. It was quite a comedown for a man who once commanded highly-trained Marines in volatile and dangerous combat situations.

With a wife and four children to support, Hackett was barely able to get by on his pension of $1,755 per month and hourly salary of $16. Worse, after fifteen months he and other refinery workers were laid off. Hackett was forced to cash in a $150,000 civilian life insurance policy in order to make overdue mortgage payments, after he had already let a $400,000 military life insurance policy lapse. Without a salary, however, he fell deeper into debt. When he shot himself, in an American Legion Hall in Cheyenne after calling his wife and telling her that he loved her, he owed $460,000. On the front seat of his truck, Hackett left a terse note: "I deserve Hell."[119]

Following Hackett's death, his wife lost their home, and both of their cars were repossessed. A generous and anonymous former Marine bought her a house, and the VA—at a private attorney's urging—ruled that Hackett died as a result of "chronic and severe" PTSD caused by his service in Iraq. The latter meant that Danelle Hackett didn't have to pay taxes on his pension, saving her $100 per month. That was all that the VA would do, however. His 40 percent disability wasn't increased, nor was the lapsed $400,000 life insurance policy restored, even though he paid premiums on it for twenty-six years. If the VA had ruled retroactively that Hackett was "totally disabled," his wife would have received the $400,000. Because he had a job for fifteen months, however, her claim was rejected. Similarly, if Hackett had been killed in battle or died by suicide prior to his retirement, the policy would have been honored. Neither was the case, although Danelle Hackett believes otherwise. She believes that her husband was, in fact, killed in battle. "It just took him two years to die," she says.[120]

The Morality of Killing

"I'm a murderer."

D ERRICK KIRKLAND WAS TWENTY WHEN HE ENLISTED IN THE ARMY in January 2007. He had a wife and young child to support, and he couldn't do it by continuing to work minimum-wage jobs as a line cook at Steak and Shake and the International House of Pancakes. When a recruiter promised him an array of benefits—special training, health care, educational opportunities, travel, and a meaningful career—Kirkland signed up. His father had been in the Army, and his two grandfathers had been in the Army and the Navy. He grew up with the notion that serving in the military was honorable. So did his younger brother, who subsequently enlisted.

When Kirkland returned home to Indiana after his first fifteen-month tour of duty in Iraq, it was clear to members of his family that he wasn't the same person. No longer joking and happy-go-lucky, he was sullen and withdrawn and had trouble sleeping. The sparkle in his eyes had disappeared and his interest in skateboarding and playing the guitar was gone. More than once he told his mother, "I'm a murderer."

"No, Derrick, you're in a war," Mary Kirkland said. "There's a difference between being in a war and killing somebody, and just going up on the street and killing somebody."[1]

Derrick wasn't convinced. He had seen and done terrible things, things he didn't want to talk about, things he didn't want family and friends to know. It was true that he had changed. It also was true that he didn't like the person he had become.

In Iraq, Kirkland had been part of a search and destroy unit that was charged with rooting out insurgents. At one house, soldiers burst through the front door and shot an Iraqi man. The wounds were fatal, but the man wasn't dead yet. Kirkland's sergeant told him to stand on the man's chest. "We've got to move, and he's got to die before we move," the sergeant said.[2] Standing on the man's chest would cause him to bleed to death faster. Kirkland looked at his sergeant helplessly. It was clear he had no choice but to obey.

A short time later, Kirkland fell asleep while on guard duty. It happens to soldiers who are sleep deprived. He woke up when he heard a car driving through his checkpoint. He shouted for it to stop, but the family inside didn't speak English. Kirkland's orders were to open fire on any vehicle that failed to stop, so he did. In the military, orders must be followed; it doesn't matter if innocent people die as a result. (In his book *The Things They Cannot Say*, Kevin Sites recounts a similar story of an Iraqi father who was killed after he failed to stop at a checkpoint. It was learned later that the father had poor eyesight and the brakes on his truck were bad.)

After coming home, Kirkland started drinking heavily. In addition, his marriage unraveled, and his wife filed for divorce. When he was sent to Iraq a second time, he had reached the breaking point.

In Iraq, early in his second deployment, he stuck a gun in his mouth only to have a fellow soldier intervene before he could pull the trigger. Afterward, Kirkland was sent to a psychiatric unit in Germany where he attempted suicide again, this time by overdosing on medication. That resulted in him being flown back to his home base, Fort Lewis (now Lewis-McChord), in Washington State, where he was seen at Madigan Army Medical Center. There, soldiers in Kirkland's unit observed their sergeant calling him a "coward" and a "pussy" for seeking mental health services.[3]

Despite having attempted suicide twice, being diagnosed with posttraumatic stress disorder, and losing so much weight that he was down to 110 pounds, Kirkland was deemed "a low-moderate risk" for suicide, according to reports, and "did not require any further supervision."[4] He was released after just two days and one night in the psychiatric unit, with the only restriction being that he wasn't supposed to be around any weapons. He also was moved, to his own barracks room.

Three days later, Kirkland made another attempt. In the privacy of his room, he sliced his arms and ingested antidepressants and sleep medicine while drinking rum. This attempt wasn't fatal, either, and he bandaged himself sufficiently so that the next day, at morning formation, no one noticed anything wrong. No one checked his room, so the bloodstains that were everywhere went unnoticed, too.

That night, Kirkland made a fourth and final attempt. He hung himself in his closet with white nylon rope. Previously he had written, "I feel invisible. I feel like I'm transparent." In case anyone should fail to find his body, he left a note on his locker: "In the closet, dead."[5]

On March 20, 2010, the day that Kirkland was buried at Marion National Cemetery in Indiana, his mother stopped at a gas station and bought a newspaper to see if anything had been written about her son. To her surprise—and anger—the article on his death said that according to the Department of Defense, Kirkland had been killed in action and his family declined to comment.

"That started two lies off right there," Mary Kirkland told a reporter. "No, Derrick was not killed in action. He was killed because of failed mental health care at an Army base at Fort Lewis. And I would have commented. From day one, I would have commented."[6]

When she sought clarification, Mary Kirkland was told that the newspaper probably made a mistake, or the military "didn't want to embarrass the family."[7] That made her even madder, as did the fact that the Army wouldn't give her letters that Derrick had left. She was told that the letters couldn't be released because the military hadn't verified Derrick's handwriting.

In May 2012, Mary Kirkland participated in an antiwar protest in Chicago. She said she wasn't ashamed to tell people that her son had killed himself. It was a fact. What made her ashamed was that the military failed him. More should be done, she said, much more, to honor the dead, heal the wounded, and stop the fighting taking place. Too many lives were being lost. Too many bodies and minds were being damaged, sometimes beyond repair. Too many families were being torn apart by the effects of combat.

It was a demand, an appeal, a plea that countless others had made, both in recent years and in the past. For the most part, it continues to be ignored.

When the Civil War began, it wasn't expected to last long. In the first sixty days, fewer than fifty men died altogether, a third of the casualties occurring in the attack on Fort Sumter.[8] Then the fighting intensified, and soon the number of deaths on both sides became staggering, unimaginable.

Civil war is in some respects a misnomer. To the extent that the fighting took place between citizens of the same country, it was, of course, a civil war. Yet the fighting was hardly civil. When you are trying to kill or maim people before they kill or maim you, there is nothing well-mannered about it. It isn't a duel; it's butchery.

A Union soldier, recalling his first taste of heated combat, realized that it was much more gruesome than he ever imagined. "The men, infuriated and wild with excitement, went to work with bayonets and clubbed muskets, and a scene of horror ensued for a few moments. It was the first time I had been in the midst of a hand to hand fight, and seen men bayoneted, or their brains dashed out with the butt of a musket, and I never wish to see another scene."[9]

The Civil War is portrayed as the first modern war because locomotives and warships had a role. Even so, rifled muskets were the primary weapons. Because the guns had a short range, the enemy was no more than one hundred yards away, and oftentimes much closer. Soldiers confronted each other in the most personal and direct way possible. One saw the other's face, registered the look in his eyes, smelled his odor, perhaps felt his grip, heard his scream, which made the grisly aspects even more pronounced. Added to this was the fact that soldiers didn't wear any kind of protective armor. There weren't any medics to help either, to treat wounds or provide solace until the battle ended. Soldiers who were too injured to move lay where they fell, gasping for air, grimacing in pain, while the fighting continued around them.

Early on, there was a rush by eager men on both sides to join the fighting. It was fueled, on one hand, by economic and social interests, and on the other hand by romantic notions that the war offered opportunities for glory, honor, and heroic deeds—a chance to prove one's mettle. As if that wasn't enough, many women encouraged their husbands and sons to enlist, despite being fearful for their safety. The cause that they were fighting for—to maintain the Union or preserve Confederate values—was considered even greater than the threat of personal harm. According to one soldier, "I would be disgraced if I staid at home."[10] Another man who was hesitant to enlist received a special package from his fiancée containing a skirt and pantaloons along with a note telling him to "Wear these or volunteer."[11]

The reality of war changed things, however. It didn't take long before stories began to emerge about the massive number of casualties, the likes of which the country had never witnessed. Whereas fewer than 2,000 U.S. soldiers died in battle in the Mexican War of 1846–1848,[12] that many were killed in mere hours on battlefields in the Civil War.

On September 17, 1862, at the Battle of Antietam in Maryland, 23,000 men and countless horses and mules were killed or wounded. It was the single bloodiest day of war in U.S. history.

On July 4, 1863, at the conclusion of the three-day Battle of Gettysburg in Pennsylvania, there were 7,000 dead soldiers and 3,000 dead horses. As Drew Gilpin Faust describes it in *This Republic of Suffering*, "Six million pounds of human and animal carcasses lay strewn across the field in the summer heat, and a town of 2,400 grappled with 22,000 wounded who remained alive but in desperate condition."[13] The corpses created a powerful stench that lasted for days and left survivors reeling.

On September 20, 1863, after two days of intense fighting at the Battle of Chickamauga in southern Tennessee and northwestern Georgia, 4,000 men lay dead and 24,000 others were wounded. It was the highest number of casualties after Gettysburg, and the scene of the Union army's biggest defeat of the war.

Soldiers tried to explain the horrors that they witnessed, but many were at a loss for words. After the Battle of Fredericksburg, a Union chaplain said, "A battle is indescribable, but once seen it haunts a man till the day of his death."[14]

Following two days of fighting at the Battle of Shiloh, there were 1,700 dead on each side and more than 20,000 others who were severely wounded. Observing the scene, Ulysses S. Grant said, "I saw an open field...so covered with dead that it would have been possible to walk across the clearing, in any direction, stepping only on dead bodies without a foot touching the ground."[15]

It wasn't unusual for men to break down and weep uncontrollably at the carnage. Others repressed the horror, presenting a hardened face and calloused attitude to all of the suffering.

Faust notes the consequences, both immediate and long term, of the war. "Killing produced transformations that were not readily reversible," she writes, "the living into the dead, most obviously, but the survivors into different men as well, men required to deny, to numb basic human feeling at costs they may have paid for decades after the war ended."[16]

Ambrose Bierce was the most significant writer to participate in the Civil War. Enlisting in the Union army at age eighteen, he fought for four years and received multiple commendations for bravery. His combat service ended in 1864 when he suffered a serious head wound at the Battle of Kennesaw Mountain, near Atlanta. From that point on he focused on journalism, gaining fame and a broad audience with his barbed wit. In writing about the war, though, he didn't attempt to be clever, nor did he try to romanticize it. Instead, his central theme was death—"A thing to be hated" he said, "hideous in all its manifestations and suggestions."[17] As for surviving, he felt "sentenced to life,"[18] haunted "by visions of the dead and dying."[19] He also said, "When I ask myself what has happened to Ambrose Bierce the youth, who fought at Chickamauga, I am bound to answer that he is dead."[20]

Future Supreme Court Justice Oliver Wendell Holmes, Jr. also fought in the Civil War, as a Union captain. He concluded that "many a man has gone crazy since this campaign begun from the terrible pressure on the mind and body."[21] At Antietam, Holmes was shot and taken to a field hospital. Fearful of dying in anonymity, he wrote his name on a piece of paper so that he could be identified. When he recovered, he kept the paper for the rest of his life.[22]

Reports by people like Holmes, Bierce, and other soldiers opened people's eyes to what was going on. The reality was brought home even more, though, by a new, powerful technology—photography. The images of soldiers lying dead on battlefields were rendered with startling and disturbing clarity. Mathew Brady's studio on Broadway featured photos of Antietam, prompting the *New York Times* to comment that if Brady "has not brought bodies and laid them in our dooryards and along the streets, he has done something very like it."[23]

Although many Americans didn't view actual war photographs because newspapers and magazines of the day lacked the technology to reproduce them, they did see engravings based on the photos, which were powerful enough. Once the notion of glory and valor was dispelled, the number of men who volunteered for duty dropped significantly, to the point where in 1862 the Confederate army was forced to pass a draft law, and in 1863 the Union army did the same. The laws proved controversial in that there were numerous loopholes. Most professionals were exempted, and able-bodied men who could afford it had the option of paying someone else to take their place. As a result, some observers referred to it as "a rich man's war and a poor man's fight,"[24] and there were riots in many cities. With so many casualties, however, the two sides could sustain forces only through mandated military service. Thus, men who wanted no part in the fighting were conscripted anyway, including those whose mental stability might have been questionable to begin with. If they could point and shoot a gun, that was sufficient. The state of a person's mind was of lesser concern.

"It's Our Duty to Get It Right"

Just like in subsequent wars, the suicides of Civil War soldiers aren't included in the final tally of the dead. Then again, the number of men who were killed fighting for the North and South isn't known either, because prior to the Civil War, the United States didn't have any kind of bureaucracy regarding deaths. National cemeteries didn't exist, and no system was in place to identify men who died in battle, much less procedures for burying them. Unless they arranged in advance for a fellow soldier to notify family members if they were killed, and the fellow soldier survived to do so, men died anonymously on distant battlefields. This meant that all of the factors that people at the time—as well as today—considered essential to having a "good death" were absent. Not only was there no corpse, but in many instances there wasn't even a reliable report of a soldier's death. As a result, people didn't know what happened to their loved ones; they simply disappeared. Family members and friends couldn't mourn because they still hoped that their husband, son, or father would show up safe one day. Then, after months passed and the likelihood of their return seemed more and more remote, they were left without closure. Sacred texts that typically provide a small measure of comfort as a person's body is being lowered into the ground for eternal rest couldn't be read with the same effect. Most Civil War soldiers were buried in mass graves or in various cemeteries with tombstones listing their identity as "Unknown."

After the war ended, a massive reinterment program was launched to excavate the bodies of Union soldiers, identify them, and rebury them in seventy-four newly established national cemeteries. When the project was completed in 1871—at a cost of $4 million—about 300,000 soldiers had been reinterred, of which 54 percent were identified. This included 30,000 black soldiers, a third of whom were identified. They were buried in designated areas, thus continuing the segregation that they experienced during the war when they served in "Colored Troops."

Only Union soldiers were reinterred. The thinking was that they had served on the winning side, the side to preserve the Union, and thus merited this honor. Because Confederate soldiers had fought to destroy the Union, it was left to private citizens to reinter and acknowledge them. (The work of naming casualties continues to this day. According to Drew Gilpin Faust, the United States spends $100 million or more each year searching for and identifying 88,000 people who are considered missing in action from World War II, the Korean War, and Vietnam.[25])

In 1889, William F. Fox, an amateur historian, pegged the number of Civil War casualties at 620,000 after an exhaustive review of muster lists, battlefield reports, and pension records. Fox fought on the Union side at Antietam, Chancellorsville, and Gettysburg and knew the horrors of war firsthand. His estimate was substantiated by another Union veteran and amateur historian, Thomas L. Livermore, and has been accepted by historians for more than 100 years. It's nearly equal to all deaths suffered by American troops in the Revolutionary War, War of 1812, Mexican War, Spanish-American War, World War I, World War II, and the Korean War combined. In the largest battles—at Antietam, Gettysburg, Petersburg, Richmond, Chickamauga, Chancellorsville, Chantilly, Shiloh, Stones River, and Fredericksburg—the losses were especially staggering. Overall, 2 percent of the U.S. population was killed in the war, equivalent to six million today. The toll was especially high in the South, where 18 percent of men of military age died.[26]

In 2012, J. David Hacker, a history professor at Binghamton University, put forth a new estimate of the dead based on a sophisticated recalculation of census data that Fox didn't have access to. Hacker's estimate—750,000—is 20 percent higher that Fox's and is gaining widespread acceptance. Eric Foner, a noted Civil War historian, told the *New York Times*, "It [Hacker's estimate] even further elevates the significance of the Civil War and makes a dramatic statement about how the war is a central moment in American history. It helps you understand, particularly in the South with a much smaller population, what a devastating experience this was."[27]

In explaining why he attempted a new methodology, Hacker said, "Wars have profound economic, demographic, and social costs." He noted that the new estimate means there were 37,000 more widows and 90,000 more orphans than originally thought, making the losses even more profound. One hundred and fifty years later, the correction might not mean much. Then again, says Hacker, "It's our duty to get it right."[28]

In addition to all of the deceased, more than 450,000 soldiers were wounded in the war. Their bodies weren't torn apart by roadside bombs the way they are in the fighting today, but the extent of their injuries and gruesomeness of their wounds were similar given the lack of body armor and medical practices that bordered on medieval. In *Moments of Despair*, David Silkenat reports that over a two-month period Confederate doctors in Virginia performed more than 500 amputations. Few if any were done with anesthetics, and nearly half of those operated on didn't survive.[29]

Drew Gilpin Faust writes, "Witnesses at field hospitals almost invariably commented with horror on the piles of limbs lying near the surgeon's table, dissociated from the bodies to which they had belonged, transformed into objects of revulsion instead of essential parts of people."[30]

Minor injuries became serious when wounds became infected, a common occurrence since sanitation was poor and it sometimes took weeks for injured soldiers to be delivered in mule-drawn carts to overwhelmed hospitals. After the Battle of Perryville in 1862, Union surgeons didn't wash their hands for two days because water was scarce, yet they continued to perform amputations.[31] (Today, few wounds are closed on a battlefield because of the risk of contamination. Instead, they are left open until the wounded soldier can be treated in a sterile setting.)

Twice as many Civil War soldiers died from disease as from wounds suffered in battle.[32] In many respects it was worse to be injured than killed outright. Death was likely to come anyway, especially for victims with head and abdominal injuries, and the time that elapsed between receiving a wound and succumbing to it tended to be filled with excruciating pain.

Responders to traumatic events also can suffer from PTSD the same as participants in those events. According to a September 2007 study in the *American Journal of Psychiatry*, 14.4 percent of rescue and recovery workers who aided victims of the 9/11 World Trade Center attacks developed PTSD, as did 6.3 percent of police officers and 21.1 percent of unaffiliated volunteers.[33] During the Civil War, doctors and nurses developed symptoms that are consistent with the present-day definition of PTSD, based on a detailed review of their letters and memoirs.[34] One Confederate nurse, Kate Cumming, noted in a diary that as much as a colleague tried to prepare her for what she would see, the experience was still a shock. "Nothing that I had ever heard or read had given me the faintest idea of the horrors witnessed here," she wrote. "I do not think that words are in our vocabulary expressive enough to present to the mind the realities of that sad scene."[35]

Still, Cumming persisted, despite being plagued by nightmares for years afterward. "Visions of the terrible past would rise in review before me—the days, weeks, and months of suffering I had witnessed—and all for naught. Many a boyish and manly face, in the full hey-day of life and hope, now lay dying in the silent tomb."[36]

John G. Perry, a Union surgeon, wrote about operating virtually nonstop for four successive days. "I am heartsick over it all," he said, describing war as a "perfect maelstrom of horror" characterized by one thing—"slaughter."[37]

A Confederate doctor, Charles T. Quintard, described working nearly fifteen hours without food or a break until he practically collapsed. "I could do no more," he said. "I went out by myself and leaning against a fence, I wept like a child.... All that day I was so unnerved that if any one asked me about the regiment, I could make no reply without tears."[38]

Despite the enormous bloodshed, one of the challenges for Civil War officers was getting troops to fire their weapons. The combatants were untrained in matters of war and hadn't developed the ability to distance themselves emotionally from the act of killing. In addition, they were fighting people who, for the most part, were just like them, who looked the same, came from similar walks of life, and who—other than having a different opinion about slavery—shared many of the same values. If they weren't brothers literally, they were close to it metaphorically.[39] In the *Civil War Collector's Encyclopedia*, F. A. Lord noted that 27,574 muskets were recovered from the Battle of Gettysburg, and nearly 90 percent, or 24,000, were loaded.[40] They represented "soldiers who had been unable or unwilling to fire their weapons in the midst of combat and then had been killed, wounded, or routed."[41]

Civil War casualties were so great not because the firing was so deadly but because it lasted so long. Five hundred soldiers shooting at each other with muskets from thirty yards away resulted in a mere handful of men actually being hit every minute. Spread out over hours, however, "dragged on until exhaustion set in or nightfall put an end to hostilities," says Dave Grossman in his book, *On Killing*, the casualties added up.[42]

As for accounts of soldiers rushing each other with bayonets, this in fact was rare. Faust says that 94 percent of Union injuries resulted from bullets, 5.5 percent from artillery, and fewer than 0.5 percent were caused by saber or bayonet.[43] Not only is it much harder to kill someone at close proximity to you, Grossman says, but the average human resists the idea of piercing someone's body with a knife, preferring instead to club or slash at the enemy.[44]

"I Sleep Clearly Every Night"

Charles Whittlesey was voted one of the brightest men in his 1905 class at Williams College in Massachusetts. He went on to graduate from Harvard Law School and begin a law practice in New York City. With the outbreak of World War I, he took charge of a battalion that saw heavy fighting. At one point, in the Argonne Forest of northeastern France, companies in the battalion were cut off from support. For five days, without food or ammunition, the men in Whittlesey's battalion were vulnerable to German attacks and suffered heavy casualties. Whittlesey refused to surrender, and even refrained from using white panels to signal Allied planes for help because they might be misconstrued as surrender flags. Eventually, Allied troops broke through, and the men who were alive and able to function—194 out of the original 554 who had been trapped—were rescued.[45]

Shortly thereafter, Whittlesey was promoted from major to lieutenant colonel and then full colonel. He also was awarded the Medal of Honor—the Army's highest award—and honorably discharged. Back in the United States, he resumed his law practice, but with many interruptions. As a war hero he was in demand to make frequent public speeches. It wasn't something he felt comfortable doing, since he was, by nature, modest. He felt he couldn't refuse, however, just like he couldn't refuse when asked to be one of the pallbearers in ceremonies to honor the Unknown Soldier at Arlington National Cemetery.[46]

Whittlesey's wartime experiences, especially the losses suffered in Argonne, continued to haunt him, however. Some people blamed what came to be called the Lost Battalion on Whittlesey's inexperience and overzealousness. He wrote to a friend, "Not a day goes by but I hear from some of my old outfit, usually about some sorrow or misfortune. I cannot bear it much more."[47]

In 1921, Whittlesey booked passage on a steamship to Havana. None of his friends knew about it, nor did they know that prior to traveling he put all of his affairs in order, including prepaying the next month's rent. Late one night, after drinking with other passengers, he walked to the ship's railing and jumped. The letters that he left to be delivered to relatives didn't explain his suicide, and theories ranged from guilt over leading more than 250 men to their deaths to depression over the exalted position he had been forced into upon returning home.[48] One thing that was clear was that his wartime experiences contributed to his demise.

Many American schoolchildren learn that the first World War, referred to as the Great War until, twenty years later, World War II began and the two global conflicts took on numbers, started with the assassination of Francis Ferdinand, an Austrian archduke, in 1914. Although this is a simplistic explanation—Ferdinand's murder just set in motion events that had been brewing for some time—there is no denying that his death ignited a war that touched every corner of the planet. A small group of Serbian students plotted the murder when Ferdinand was visiting Sarajevo, and one of them, Gavrilo Princip, fired the fatal shot as the archduke rode in his car. Using the assassination as a pretext, the Austro-Hungarian government immediately declared war on tiny Serbia, whereupon Russia rushed to Serbia's defense. After that, other international powers—Germany, France, and Great Britain—bound by mutual defense treaties, mobilized troops and joined the fighting, Germany on the side of Austria-Hungary and France and Great Britain on the side of Russia. (In addition to having a mutual defense treaty, Great Britain and Russia were joined by bloodlines in that King George V of England and Tsar Nicholas II of Russia were related.)

The United States declared neutrality, and for the first couple of years of the war Americans watched from the sidelines as the European powers engaged in massive bloodshed. At the Battle of the Marne, each side lost more than 500,000 men. At the first two battles of Ypres, 350,000 soldiers were killed, wounded, or missing. At the Battle of Gallipoli, the combined casualty count was nearly 500,000. At the Battle of Verdun, French and German troops sustained losses of 700,000.

By the end of the war, the physical casualties were staggering. Germany lost 1.8 million men. Russia 1.7 million, France nearly 1.4 million, and Austria 1.2 million. Great Britain lost 900,000, and the Ottoman Empire 300,000. In Germany, France, Russia, and Austria, nearly a whole generation of young men was wiped out. Another 20 million people died of war-related causes, such as disease and hunger.[49]

American losses were smaller—130,000 killed or missing—mainly because U.S. involvement was shorter, given the country's later entry into the war. Nonetheless, the casualties were significant, representing about 7.5 percent of our fighting force. In addition, the war cost America $32 billion[50]—equivalent to $400 billion in today's currency.

Despite all of the deaths and injuries, the same phenomenon that existed in the Civil War regarding soldiers' reluctance to point their weapons at the enemy and fire occurred in World War I. One Allied lieutenant said that the only way he was able to stop his men from shooting high was to threaten them with his sword. He walked down the trenches and beat them on their backside until they fired low.[51]

Up to and through World War II, U.S. troops were less likely to fire at enemy soldiers, vessels, and aircraft that they could see with the naked eye than on ones that appeared on long-range scopes and radar screens. When the enemy was in sight, combatants were less

aggressive. "Intellectually," Dave Grossman says, "warriors understood that they were killing humans just like themselves and that
someone wanted to kill them, but emotionally they could deny it."[52]

More than any other factor, physical distance is tied to a soldier's
willingness to fight and his or her subsequent psychological state.
Grossman, a former Army Ranger, paratrooper, and psychology
professor at West Point, asserts that in his extensive experience and
wide-scale research, he has never encountered a soldier who refused
to fire at the enemy when a great distance separated them, nor did
any soldier suffer psychological trauma as a result. Whether it's
artillery crews or missile men, naval gunners or Air Force bombers,
soldiers show little hesitation in pulling the trigger—or any compunction later—if the enemy isn't visible. Part of their conditioning
is to focus on objectives rather than kills. For gunners, this means
firing at grid references. For airplane pilots, it means launching missiles at targets that may appear no bigger than a pin print on a screen.
For submarine crews, it means firing torpedoes at ships that are only
visible in periscopes. Of course, a ship that is sunk has people on it,
just as a building that is blown up likely has human occupants, but
a psychological distance is created when ships, planes, and buildings
are thought of as targets rather than people.

Even the individuals who were responsible for dropping atomic
bombs on the Japanese cities of Hiroshima and Nagasaki in 1945,
instantly incinerating tens of thousands of men, women, and children and leading thousands of others to die excruciating deaths in
the days that followed, didn't suffer psychologically afterward. In
a 1975 interview, General Paul Warfield Tibbets, Jr., who piloted
the *Enola Gay* (the plane was named after his mother, Enola Gay
Tibbets), which dropped the bomb on Hiroshima and flew weather
reconnaissance for Nagasaki, said, "I'm proud that I was able to start
with nothing, plan it, and have it work as perfectly as it did." He
added, "I sleep clearly every night."[53]

In 2005, on the sixtieth anniversary of Hiroshima, Tibbets and
the two other surviving crew members issued a joint statement: "The
use of the atomic weapon was a necessary moment in history. We
have no regrets."[54]

The only thing that bothered Tibbets was when the Smithsonian
Institution planned an exhibit that put the bombing of Hiroshima
in context with the suffering it caused. He considered it an insult

and said that too much attention was being placed on Japan's suffering when the real focus should be on atrocities committed by its military.

"Kill, Kill, Kill, Kill"

At the conclusion of World War II, U.S. Army Brigadier General S. L. A. Marshall interviewed thousands of soldiers and learned a surprising fact: Only 15 to 20 percent fired their weapons in combat. Even when they had the chance, most soldiers didn't fire, or if they did fire they deliberately aimed high or to the side.

"The average and normal healthy individual," Marshall determined, "has such an inner and usually unrealized resistance toward killing a fellow man that he will not of his own volition take life if it is possible to turn away from that responsibility.... At the vital point, he becomes a conscientious objector."[55]

This reluctance to shoot a fellow human being was even more surprising since the Japanese, in particular, were demonized by military brass and U.S. propaganda as being a lower form of life, on the order of animals rather than people (this thinking, in part, contributed to the mass interment of Japanese American civilians during the war). Even though soldiers knew that enemy bullets were responsible for the deaths of their comrades, 80 to 85 percent of U.S. troops resisted pulling the trigger.

To U.S. military leaders, this meant one thing: Training needed to be improved so that service members became habituated to shooting others without questioning the morality of it. They needed to overcome their fear of killing, which, in some respects, was even stronger than their fear of being killed. It wouldn't do if soldiers just showed up for battle when called; they had to show up with guns blazing.

And they did. In the Korean War, 55 percent of soldiers fired their weapons at the enemy. By Vietnam, the number was up to 95 percent.[56] Today it's close to 100 percent.

This doesn't that mean all weapons were aimed at the enemy, however. In Vietnam firefights, more than 50,000 bullets were fired for every enemy soldier killed.[57] One Vietnam medic who crawled out under the hail of enemy and friendly fire to aid wounded soldiers marveled at how many bullets could be fired during a firefight without anyone getting hurt.[58]

In World War II, fewer than 1 percent of fighter pilots accounted for 30 to 40 percent of all enemy aircraft that were shot down. Most fighter pilots never shot down anyone or even tried to.[59]

From the Pentagon's point of view, that had to change. It didn't further America's war effort if its soldiers weren't firing their weapons at the enemy. Starting with Vietnam, soldiers weren't just trained to kill, they were conditioned to do it.

Individuals who have never experienced combat assume that being fired at is the motivating factor causing soldiers to fire their weapons in return. In fact, it's not. Being told to fire is the key. Soldiers are trained to follow orders, and they are much more likely to shoot another human being when someone in charge tells them to.

It starts in basic training. The drill inspector's job is to train former civilians to abandon the beliefs and values they have developed to that point and adopt a military mindset. This means, among other things, that "physical aggression is the essence of manhood," Dave Grossman says, and "violence is an effective and desirable solution for the problems that the soldier will face on the battlefield."[60]

It's analogous, one might say, to a religious conversion, a repudiation of one's old way of thinking in favor of a new mentality. It's why soldiers no longer shoot at bulls-eye targets on firing ranges. Instead, they aim at man-shaped silhouettes that pop up briefly, then disappear. (Soldiers who knock down enough targets are awarded marksmanship badges and, in some instances, receive a three-day pass.)

"Kill, kill, kill, kill," a U.S. soldier in Iraq told a *Los Angeles Times* reporter. "It's like it pounds at my brain." "We talk about killing all the time," another soldier told the reporter. "I never used to be this way...but it's like I can't stop." He added, "I'm worried what I'll be like when I get home."[61]

In some respects, the military functions like a cult. Individuals are trained to respond to a leader's commands without questioning them. They also stop being individuals and instead become part of a group, physically indistinguishable from other group members by virtue of their newly shorn hair and military-issued uniforms.

When cult members are young and impressionable, it's easiest to shape them into followers—a process that Marines call "forming." As they mature, people learn to analyze, question, and make decisions based on personal experiences and information they have gleaned from a variety of sources. The younger people are, and the less educated, the more malleable they are. Getting to recruits early on means having a cleaner slate to work with.

There are other advantages to recruiting people eighteen and nineteen years old. For one thing, they tend to be in better physical shape than older soldiers. For another, they are less likely to have dependents. In addition, young people from poor neighborhoods don't have outside income sources, so the lure of government salaries and benefits is stronger. The biggest advantage, though, is that they are less inclined to think for themselves.

To kill a stranger—especially if that person is an unarmed civilian—means overcoming everything that one has learned about what it means to be human. It means setting aside all personal and social morals and following orders without hesitation or thought. It means not thinking of the act as murder but as simply doing your job, a job on which your own survival and the survival of others in your unit depends.

The moment he enlisted, a Vietnam veteran told Penny Coleman that he learned things about himself he never wanted to know. "When I stepped forward all I thought was, 'Can I do this? I will do it! I'll kill somebody if I have to. I'll kill somebody I don't even know. I'm going over and I'm coming home.' If you swear the oath, what you are saying to yourself is, 'I'll go and do whatever I have to do to survive. I'll be the worst person in the world, because if I'm the second worst, I will die. So I gotta be the worst person there is.' "[62]

Kevin Sites recounts the story of Army Staff Sergeant Mikeal Auton, who was twenty-one when he deployed to Iraq in 2004. "When I got here," Auton said, "I found out that pulling the trigger wasn't as hard as I thought it would be. All except for the first one."

The first one was on the streets of Baghdad. In the middle of a firefight, Auton saw through the optical scope of his M4 rifle a man heading in his direction. The man had his hands in his pockets, and it wasn't clear whether he had a weapon. His squad leader told Auton to shoot him, and Auton did. The man didn't die, though, and when they stood over him the squad leader told Auton to finish him off. Auton fired two rounds into the man's ear from two feet away, splattering his brains across the street. After that, subsequent kills weren't a problem. "You just get over it. Move on," he told Sites.

"Life Is Cheap in the Orient"

One way to deal with killing an enemy soldier is to think of it as stopping a threat and saving others in your unit. Instead of taking a life, you are preventing the deaths of comrades. Another way is to think of the enemy not as a person but as a lower form of being, lacking the same depth of feelings as the person who is holding a loaded firearm and has the license to pull the trigger. In Vietnam, U.S. soldiers were encouraged to dehumanize the enemy, to think of North Korean and Chinese soldiers as "gooks" and "dinks." This way, killing them was no different than killing a wild animal that is dangerous or an insect that is annoying. Just point, shoot, make sure your adversary is dead, then move on.

This attitude started at the top. In the Academy Award–winning documentary film *Hearts and Minds*, General William Westmoreland, who commanded all U.S. military operations in Vietnam, tells his staff, "Orientals don't place the same value on human life as does a Westerner. Life is plentiful. Life is cheap in the Orient."[63] Westmoreland insisted that separate toilet facilities be built at his headquarters for Americans and Vietnamese.[64]

It was no different in England. In 1942, Britain established a special battle school to prepare new soldiers for war. The school's course began with a lecture on hate. As Ben Shephard notes in *A War of Nerves*, "The commandant explained that you kill your enemy more quickly and efficiently if you hate him, and it saves time if the men go on the battlefield already hating, if they have pictures in their minds of the things he's done, ready to be remembered."[65]

General Marshall's report on the firing rates of U.S. soldiers in World War II indicated that the main reason that troops didn't discharge their weapons even when faced with an immediate threat was because they continued to think of the enemy as human. From the military's point of view, that had to change. Lost amid the hurrahs over the increase in firing rates in Vietnam, however, was the fact that more firing meant more instances of killing, more witnesses to these deaths, more gruesome physical injuries, and more psychiatric problems.

"Soldiers who kill reflexively in combat will likely one day reconsider their actions reflectively," says former major and West Point philosophy instructor Peter Kilner. "If they are unable to justify to themselves that they killed another human being, they will likely, and understandably, suffer enormous guilt. This guilt manifests itself as posttraumatic stress disorder."[66]

Added to this was the way that military and political leaders measured success in Vietnam. It wasn't based on territory conquered and occupied, as it had been in previous wars. Instead, it was based on a single statistic: body count. The number of dead enemy soldiers became the yardstick by which military leaders justified their commands and political leaders informed the public of the effectiveness of American war efforts.

Measuring success by body count resulted in three big problems. First, it was difficult to authenticate. The enemy didn't wear uniforms or engage in conventional tactics, and civilians not only looked the same as soldiers but also sometimes had weapons and engaged in the fighting. Even when civilians were innocent and unarmed, they were used as shields by insurgents and oftentimes ended up as casualties. In short order, all dead Vietnamese, including women and children, came to be considered "Viet Cong" whether they were soldiers or not. According to military historian E. B. Riker-Coleman, "The focus on enemy casualties created a casual attitude towards Vietnamese lives that contributed to the My Lai slaughter and countless other less dramatic incidents of civilian casualties."[67] When enemy combatants aren't separated from civilians, and everyone on the other side is considered a subhuman form to begin with, war takes on a different meaning.

According to Nick Turse in his book *Kill Anything That Moves: The Real American War in Vietnam*, "The whole Pentagon strategy centered on portraying My Lai as a one-off aberration, rather than part of a consistent pattern of criminality resulting from policies at the top." Thus, when other, similar atrocities came to light, they had to be suppressed.

In 1971, Major Carl Hensley of the Army's Criminal Investigation Division was assigned to lead the examination into charges by Lieutenant Colonel Anthony B. Herbert that two of Herbert's superior officers in Vietnam engaged in war crimes not unlike those at My Lai. Hensley found that Herbert's allegations were true; however, he was pressured not to divulge them. Hensley told his wife that he "could get four to ten years for what he knew," and that the cover-up went "all the way up to the highest."[68]

Depressed, sleepless, and unable to live with himself, Hensley took his life with a shotgun in April 1971. He was thirty-six. Afterward, the commander of the Criminal Investigation Division, Colonel Henry Tufts, said that there was no connection between Hensley's death and the Herbert investigation.

The second problem with body counts was that they were easy to manipulate. The media and the public had to rely on military leaders for their information, and the latter had a vested interest in inflating the numbers. In the military, the rewards for reporting high kill counts were commendations and promotions, while the consequences for less impressive results were stalled careers and assignments with less responsibility. Tangible benefits could be gained from submitting optimistic counts, counts that one's superiors could forward up the chain of command and keep the funding for military operations flowing. For President Johnson and members of his administration, it didn't look good to be losing a war in "some fourth-rate, ragged-ass little country," as Johnson called Vietnam.[69] The more enemy deaths that he and other members of his administration reported, the more they were able to convince the public that the United States was winning the war. People didn't need to know that American troops were dying, too, or that they had no training in guerrilla warfare, wore uniforms that weren't suited to a humid, jungle climate, or depended on a weapon, the M16 rifle, whose plastic grip was so cheap that soldiers joked it was made by the Mattel toy company (in the 1960s Mattel sold a reproduction of the actual weapon, called the M-16 Marauder, that not only looked real but had realistic sound effects).[70] All they needed to know was that enemy soldiers were being killed, which implied that U.S. troops were prevailing. The real truth could be hidden. (As a psychological weapon, or simply as a show of force, some U.S. troops left the ace of spades playing card on the bodies of dead Vietnamese soldiers and littered the jungles with it, believing that it symbolized death and misfortune in local lore. A U.S. card company supplied crates of the ace of spades in bulk.)

The third problem with body counts was that everyone's attention focused on the number of dead Vietnamese, not on U.S. casualties. Search and destroy units, which comprised 95 percent of combat troops in Vietnam,[71] flushed out enemy soldiers so that helicopter gunships could mow them down. Inviting enemy ambushes was highly dangerous work for the men on the ground, but that was of lesser concern. What mattered was that it created more opportunities for enemy killings.

Becoming "Progressively Numb" to One's Humanness

Reverend Rita Nakashima Brock is co-director of the Soul Repair Center at the Texas Christian University divinity school. The center helps veterans recover from what have come to be called "moral injuries," as well as teaches congregational leaders to address moral injuries.

The concept of moral injury is based on the guilt that soldiers feel when they perpetuate, fail to prevent, or witness acts that are contrary to socially held beliefs. It is not PTSD. In fact, one of the reasons that moral injury is controversial is because it shifts the focus from what gets done to members of our armed forces to what they do to others. The things they do or didn't do haunt their consciences. As *Newsweek* reporter Tony Dokoupil wrote in a December 2012 article, no matter how just a war seems to be, "It will leave many of the men who fight it feeling like they've dirtied their souls."[72]

Reverend Brock coauthored *Soul Repair: Recovering from Moral Injury after War*, in which she tells, in part, the story of her father, who was a POW in World War II. He received electroshock treatments for psychological distress after he was freed and subsequently served as a medic in Vietnam, where numerous comrades, including his translator, were killed. She notes that the kind of counterinsurgency war that the United States is fighting today in the Persian Gulf leaves soldiers struggling with the effects of split-second decisions that have no good options. For instance, if a soldier sees a child on the side of the road holding something, it might be a grenade that, if thrown, kills someone in the soldier's unit, in which case the soldier has failed his or her buddies. If, however, it's a rock, then the soldier has just shot a kid with a rock. Either way, there are lasting and immutable consequences.[73]

"Killing is always traumatic," Dave Grossman says. "But when you have to kill women and children, or when you have to kill men in their homes, in front of their wives and children, and when you have to do it not from twenty thousand feet but up close where you can watch them die, the horror appears to transcend description or understanding. . . . The standard methods of on-the-scene rationalization fail when the enemy's child comes out to mourn over her father's body or when the enemy is a child throwing a hand grenade."[74]

Daryl S. Paulson is a Vietnam veteran and a psychologist who has consulted for the Department of Defense on homeland security. He writes in *Haunted by Combat* about his first two weeks of combat. The unit's radio man was shot in the head just in front of Paulson while they were on patrol. "He was gone," Paulson says. "Just like that. He was simply 'tagged' and 'bagged,' "—that is, identified and then sent home in a body bag. Also during those first two weeks, Paulson saw six seasoned veterans killed by an incoming mortar round as they ate their C rations and a U.S. helicopter blown up by a direct hit of a 121-millimeter rocket, obliterating seventeen fellow soldiers in an instant.[75]

Afterward, Paulson says, he became "progressively numb to my humanness" and turned into "a true killing machine."[76] He marvels at how quickly the transformation happened for him and other members of his unit. "It is incredible that we could have regressed to such a primitive way of functioning in such a short time. Life had no value except the saving of our own."[77]

Following the war, Paulson had trouble socializing with anyone other than his Marine buddies. How could he tell a woman, he says, how vulnerable and afraid he had felt, not knowing whether he would still be alive from one day to the next? How could he tell her how angry he had been after his comrades had been killed and how much he wanted to kick dead "gooks" because they were the ones who were responsible for it? How could he relax at picnics—even taking tranquilizers beforehand—when he thought the enemy was all around, hiding in trees and stalking him?

One night Paulson held his loaded .38-caliber revolver and thought "with perverse pleasure" that putting a bullet in his brain would "end it all." The only reason he didn't, he says, is because killing himself would leave no one to tell the story of his lost comrades.[78]

In his best-selling memoir, *American Sniper: The Autobiography of the Most Lethal Sniper in U.S. Military History*, published in 2012, Navy SEAL Chris Kyle writes that he was only two weeks into his first of four tours of duty in Iraq when he was confronted with a difficult choice. Through the scope of his .300 Winchester Magnum rifle, he saw a woman with a child pull a grenade from under her clothes as several Marines approached. Kyle's job was to provide "overwatch," meaning that he was perched in or on top of bombed-out apartment buildings and was responsible for preventing enemy fighters from ambushing U.S. troops. He hesitated only briefly before pulling the trigger. "It was my duty to shoot, and I don't regret it," he wrote. "My shots saved several Americans, whose lives were clearly worth more than that woman's twisted soul."[79]

Kyle was credited with 160 confirmed kills—not only an astounding number but an indication that the U.S. military today still considers counting dead enemy something worth doing. Kyle was so good at his job that Iraqi insurgents nicknamed him the "Devil of Ramadi" and put a bounty on his head. They never collected, but the war took its toll anyway. Kyle, who learned to shoot a gun before he learned to ride a bike, saw the face of his machine gun partner torn apart by shrapnel, witnessed another comrade die when an enemy bullet entered his open mouth and exited the back of his head, and lost a third friend when an enemy grenade bounced off his chest and he jumped on it before it exploded in order to save everyone around him. Kyle also was among the many Marines who were sent to Haiti in 2010 to provide humanitarian relief following the devastating earthquake there. According to Nicholas Schmidle, whose lengthy profile of Kyle appeared in the *New Yorker* in June 2013, Kyle was overwhelmed by all the corpses in Haiti that were piled up on roadsides. He told his mother afterward, "They didn't train me to go and pick up baby bodies off the beach."[80]

These and other experiences led to many sleepless nights when Kyle returned home, as well as days in which he lived in an alcoholic stupor. It didn't help that in each of his sniper kills, Kyle could see through the lens on his rifle, "with tremendous magnification and clarity," wrote Schmidle, his bullet piercing the skull of his target.

According to his medical records, Kyle sought counseling for "combat stress" after his third deployment. Like most soldiers, however, in his exit physical he said he had "no unresolved issues."[81]

Kyle longed to return to the war, to the world he knew the best, where everything made sense and he was in the company of others who understood him and appreciated his talents. His wife, however, said that if he reenlisted she would take their two young children and leave him. Trying to find a sense of purpose outside of combat, Kyle participated in various activities for veterans, primarily hunting trips. In addition, he started a company that provided security at the 2012 London Olympics, helped guard ships near Somalia from pirates, and served briefly as a bodyguard for Sarah Palin.

When Kyle was approached by the mother of a distressed twenty-five-year-old Iraq War veteran named Eddie Ray Routh, who was suffering from PTSD and taking eight different medications, Kyle agreed to help. He told Routh that he, too, had had PTSD. In February 2013, Kyle and a friend drove Routh to a gun range near Kyle's home in Texas. Kyle thought that shooting a firearm might offer some kind of therapy for Routh. Instead, Routh shot and killed both Kyle and his friend with a semiautomatic handgun before fleeing in Kyle's pickup truck. Afterward, Routh told his sister that he killed the two men before they could kill him and that he didn't trust anyone now.

From an outside perspective, it's difficult to believe that a combat veteran like Routh would think he couldn't trust one of the most revered soldiers in recent years, a man who gave his time freely to assist other veterans. Yet Routh learned from his training as well as from his own experiences in war that many people who seemed friendly or innocent really weren't. While it's rare for this distrust to include a soldier's comrades, when one's mind is warped by a combination of trauma and a cocktail of pharmaceuticals, nearly anything can happen. Seven thousand people, including Palin and her husband, attended Kyle's memorial, which was held at Cowboy Stadium. At the time of this writing, Routh is awaiting trial for the two murders.

"Have You Killed Anyone?"

Killing others is morally reprehensible and a grievous sin. It's also criminal, but not in war. In no other setting are people trained to kill on sight, no warnings issued or questions asked. The rule of thumb is to shoot first, and deal with any moral uncertainties later. As Tony Dokoupil notes, however, the word *killing* "doesn't appear in training manuals, or surveys of soldiers returning from combat, and the effects of killing aren't something that the military screens for when people come home."[82]

Soldiers train to kill, but the actual act isn't discussed or even officially acknowledged, Dokoupil says. It's something that troops talk about among themselves, but among those higher up in the chain of command it's avoided. It's especially avoided in conversations with members of the public. When civilians meet active-duty troops, they tend to ask a number of questions that troops find annoying, but no question is more hated than, "Have you killed anyone?" What's really being asked, at least from the soldier's point of view, is, "Have you crossed the moral boundary that sanctifies life, thereby dirtying your soul?" It's the last thing any soldier wants to talk about and is the reason that many soldiers don't seek counseling. (Another question that veterans are asked frequently and avoid answering is, "What's it like over there?" How can they possibly explain what they have experienced to someone who hasn't gone to war recently? The horrors are unimaginable to those who haven't served. Similarly, veterans don't like it when someone says that wars are a waste of money or that soldiers are fighting for the rights to oil. What they hear is that, in the person's opinion, their best friend died for nothing.)

According to a 1994 study of PTSD among veterans of World War II, Korea, and Vietnam, the "responsibility for killing another human being is the single most pervasive, traumatic experience of war."[83] Shira Maguen, a research psychologist at the San Francisco VA Medical Center, agrees. In her work she has found that among Vietnam veterans, those who killed in combat are twice as likely to think about suicide as those who didn't kill. In later research, cited in *PTSD Research Quarterly*, Maguen and co-author Brett Litz, director of mental health care at a VA center in Boston, say that among returning Iraq veterans, "Taking another life was a significant predictor of PTSD symptoms, alcohol abuse, anger, and relationship problems."[84] The same is true, Maguen determined, for veterans of the first Gulf War.

Harry Holloway, an army psychiatrist, told *New Yorker* reporter Dan Baum that "as soon as we ask the question of how killing affects soldiers, we acknowledge we're causing harm, and that raises the question of whether the good we're accomplishing is worth the harm we're causing." He noted that there's a danger, too, should the military admit that there are psychiatric casualties. "If we get into this business of talking about killing people, we're going to pathologize an absolutely necessary experience."[85]

Killing isn't the only act that produces guilt, however. There is the guilt of failing to save a comrade, as well as the guilt of surviving when others don't. Dokoupil notes a study in which some veterans suffered more from the death of a friend in combat than they did from the death of a spouse, even when the friend died thirty years earlier and the spouse died in the previous six months.[86]

There is also the guilt of bearing witness to human suffering and being unable to do anything about it. Levi Derby joined the Army out of high school and served as a combat engineer in Afghanistan. Married with a young son, he was haunted by a singular wartime experience: He held out a bottle of water to a young Afghan girl, and when she came forward to take it she stepped on a land mine that had been left by the Russians when they invaded the country in the 1980s.[87] According to Derby's mother, in that moment her son felt that God wouldn't let him into heaven because it was his fault for failing to detect the land mine.[88] Five years after he came home, Derby hanged himself in his grandfather's garage, still distraught over that incident. He was twenty-five.

In a memory posting Derby's mother said, "The warm, sweet young man" who had enlisted in order to fight for his country came home "an empty shell." She ended the posting by saying, "In my heart my son still lives and in my arms the ache never leaves to hold him once more."[89]

Another kind of guilt results from crossing an imaginary boundary that conflicts with one's role or occupation. In *The Things They Cannot Say,* war correspondent Kevin Sites talks about walking away from an Iraqi soldier who was injured, but not gravely. Sites calls it "the most egregious thing I have ever done in my life." The man was one of five wounded insurgents who had been shot by U.S. Marines in a mosque. (At one time, the U.S. military exempted mosques and other religious sites from war. Then insurgents used this to their advantage, taking refuge in them after initiating attacks, and military policy changed.) After being treated by Navy corpsmen, the men were left in the mosque overnight, unguarded. The next morning a Marine lance corporal shot each of the men except the one insurgent, who hid under a blanket and feigned death. When Sites came upon the lone survivor, who was unarmed and wearing only a shirt and underpants, the man pleaded for help. Sites didn't offer it, and shortly thereafter the lance corporal discovered that the man was still alive and executed him while Sites bore witness to the murder through the viewfinder of his camera. The reason for the shootings is unclear, and in response to Sites's question the Marine said that he didn't know why he killed them.

Sites is a journalist, not a soldier, yet in a decade of covering wars around the world he has been a firsthand witness to killing, the same as any warrior. "I've seen the killing of human beings at nearly every point on the spectrum of our existence," he writes, "from small children to wrinkled octogenarians. I've watched killing from great distances, bombs dropped from the sky. I've watched killing within the distance of embrace, one man executing another. And these images, both as I captured them and as I contemplated them after, have changed me forever. They continue to define me and imbue me with a sense of importance and even swagger, while they also kill me slowly in the moments when I fully consider my complicity."

Feelings of guilt often depend on context. Studies show that Nazi soldiers who committed wartime atrocities didn't feel guilty about them because their actions were supported by German society, culture, and government. The same can't be said about U.S. soldiers who fought in Vietnam.[90] In fact, a major reason that Vietnam veterans lobbied for a national monument—the Vietnam Veterans Memorial in Washington, D.C.—was because it would have a redeeming effect on those who fought in the war. No doubt, when and if the United States concludes hostilities in the Persian Gulf, new monuments will be erected for the same purpose, to validate the sacrifices that individuals and families made in service to their country.

"Sweet Is Never as Sweet as It Was"

On his second day of active duty in Iraq, Staff Sergeant Georg-Andreas "Andrew" Pogany, a special ops interrogator, saw up close a dead Iraqi soldier whose body had been ripped apart by machine gun fire. Pogany had been a volunteer firefighter before he joined the Army, and he had seen damaged bodies pulled from car wrecks, but this was different. Afterward, Pogany had trouble breathing and vomited for hours. Later, he sought support from a chaplain and an Army psychologist. They said that what he was feeling was normal given the situation and filed perfunctory reports to that effect. The reports resulted in Pogany being the first soldier since Vietnam who was charged with cowardice, a crime that, in the military, is punishable by death. It was the fall of 2003, the fighting in Iraq was in its seventh month, the Bush Administration was trumpeting the patriotism of the troops, and Jessica Lynch, a nineteen-year-old Army supply clerk,

was being heralded as a heroine for surviving a rocket-propelled grenade attack on the Humvee she was riding in, after which she was
rescued following enemy capture. Lynch never considered herself a
heroine and, in fact, subsequently criticized stories that dramatized
her combat experience. Nevertheless, just as political and military
leaders spun her story into one that glorified the troops, Pogany's
story was spun in a way that singled him out for ridicule and scorn
that was no different from George Patton's treatment of injured
World War II soldiers. Although Pogany was later vindicated, retired
from the military, and today helps active-duty troops and veterans
connect with mental health services, his case sent a strong message
to others not to report similar reactions they had. Suck it up, hold it
in, and just keep moving was the unspoken mantra.

Numerous lawyers inside and outside the military also have discouraged troops from talking about their battlefield experiences,
but for a different reason. Lawyers are wary that soldiers might
incriminate themselves for war crimes. Moreover, given the way that
human minds work, these crimes could be imagined rather than real,
no matter how vividly a soldier describes them.

The challenges for members of the National Guard and military Reserves are even greater in many respects than they are for
active-duty troops. Many in the Guard and Reserves never expected
to be deployed when they enlisted, much less engage in actual fighting. Yet with an all-volunteer Army and recruiting efforts stalled,
the Guard and Reserves constitute 50 percent or more of our fighting force today. They receive much less training than active-duty
soldiers, but have the same expectations placed on them in terms of
waging war.

They face other challenges as well. Oftentimes they serve longer tours of duty, are given inferior equipment, and are assigned to
units where they know no one else. In addition, they don't live on
military bases, so neither they nor their families are able to draw
on the support of others who are experiencing similar deployments
and homecomings. They also are afraid of losing their civilian jobs
while they are deployed. Employers are legally required to hold
their positions open until they return; however, many members of
the National Guard and military Reserves own small businesses or
are self-employed. A further challenge is that during their military
service they are likely to see civilian contractors being paid three

times more money for doing many of the same tasks (except shoot-ing people).

As hard as it is for active-duty troops to adjust to the new nor-mal when they return to civilian life, it's even harder for people in the National Guard and Reserves. They can feel like they don't fit in either place, on the battlefield or at home. On the battlefield they assume the same risks as active-duty troops, but with less training and without the same sense of camaraderie, while at home they lack military support systems and are expected to resume their civilian lives immediately.

Bryan Ala joined the Kentucky Air National Guard at age eigh-teen to help pay for college. Two years later, in the summer of 2002, he was treated for depression. The following year he deployed to the Middle East as a medic at a military field hospital. His father, a Vietnam veteran, worried that serving abroad would aggravate his son's depression but didn't say anything because Bryan was an adult who could take care of himself. By 2004, however, his parents began observing troubling signs. Bryan binged on vitamins and nutritional supplements, became highly agitated while driving, and would hide whenever he thought he heard helicopters. In 2005, he was diagnosed with bipolar disorder and prescribed lithium but oftentimes didn't take it. After fighting with his girlfriend, he moved in with his par-ents and promised them that he wouldn't do anything rash. It was his mother who found his body, face down in a pool of blood in the family room, an antique rifle next to him.

"Life goes on after you lose a child," his father told a reporter in 2007, shortly after Bryan's death. "But sweet is never as sweet as it was. The sun's never as bright. I've got a hole in my heart that will never heal up."[91]

Colleen Rivas also has a hole in her heart. Her husband, Lieutenant Colonel Ray Rivas of the Army Reserves, killed himself in the parking lot of Brooke Army Medical Center in San Antonio, Texas, in 2009. Suffering from multiple concussions due to bomb blasts during deployments in Iraq, including one explosion that knocked him out temporarily, Rivas no longer was able to talk, rea-son, or remember clearly. When he was first hospitalized in San Antonio, he just sat in his room, attended to not only by medi-cal staff but by fellow soldiers who helped him bathe, dress, and eat.[92] After three years of therapy and medication, Rivas was able to go home, but his condition didn't improve. At age fifty-three, he was diagnosed with rapidly progressing Alzheimer's disease. The cumulative impact of his brain injuries was irreversible and taking its toll. Faced with the prospect of withering mental abilities and a probable move to an assisted living facility, he took his life outside the hospital where he had been treated.

Speaking of her husband and others who, like him, died by suicide following military service, Colleen Rivas said, "They had a life, they had a story." Rather than being mere statistics, easily lost or forgotten, "They were soldiers and they mattered. And they all left behind someone who loved them."[93]

Until 2006, the Army didn't track suicides of National Guard members. Once this practice began, the data were disturbing. When half your fighting force is comprised of the National Guard and Reserves, and these individuals are killing themselves at an alarming rate—even when they haven't deployed—something is seriously wrong. From 2007 to 2011, the state with the largest number of National Guard suicides was Oregon, with twenty. Close behind was Minnesota with eighteen. Included in the latter were a seventeen-year-old girl, nineteen-year-old youth, and thirty-eight-year-old man who supported himself by selling rides in a World War II–era tank.[94]

The Desire, a Plan, and a Hose

Jeff Lucey knew the rules. He and other drivers of U.S. convoys in Iraq had strict orders to run over anything that failed to get out of their way, including civilian vehicles, pedestrians, and children. The latter posed a significant problem because insurgents encouraged children to play in the road in order to slow down convoys and make U.S. troops more vulnerable to attack.[95] Convoy drivers like Lucey, a lance corporal in the Marine Reserves, were told to think of children and other obstacles as mere "bumps in the road," proceeding as if they weren't there.[96]

Lucey's convoy carried food, water, and ammunition, as well as Iraqi prisoners of war. The prisoners were bound and sometimes had bags over their heads. More often than not, they weren't given anything to eat or drink. The few prisoners who spoke English told their captors that they were forced to join the Iraqi army. If they refused, members of their family would be shot, one by one, until they changed their minds.[97] Whether this was true or not, Lucey couldn't forget it.

In July 2003, after five months in Iraq, Lucey returned to his parents' house in Belchertown, Massachusetts. He had memories and dreams of being chased, running through alleys, and shooting people. Nevertheless, before he was discharged he answered "no" when asked if he needed psychiatric help. Other Marines in his unit told him that if he answered "yes," he would undergo additional evaluations that would delay his homecoming.

Periodically, Lucey talked with his parents, sister, and girlfriend about the war, about some of the terrible things he was responsible for. "I have done so much immoral shit," he said, "that life is never going to seem the same. All I want is to erase [it], pretend it didn't happen."[98]

His unit participated in the initial invasion of Iraq in March 2003 and subsequently was in Nasiriyah when 1,000 Iraqis—many of them civilians—died in heavy fighting. He said he saw an Iraqi boy on the road, dead, holding an American flag. He also said that he saw Marines shoot elderly people as they tried to run away, and he was ordered to kill two Iraqi soldiers who were unarmed. A Marine investigation into the latter incident concluded that "there was no documented evidence to support that he [Lucey] had any engagement with the enemy, whatsoever."[99] That might be true; however, the same investigation determined that Lucey had "no interaction with prisoners of war," yet Lucey's father found a photo that his son had taken of Iraqi POWS he was transporting.[100]

Unable to sleep, beset by nightmares, and prone to vomiting, Lucey also suffered from hallucinations. He used the flashlight by his bed to check for camel spiders, a large arachnid found in the deserts of Iraq. He smoked marijuana to calm down, drank alcohol to pass out and sleep, and took various medications to try and still the monsters within. In between he snuck out of the house wearing full camouflage uniform. He also totaled two cars, emerging uninjured from both wrecks. At one point, says his mother, "His pain was so great that at twenty-three years of age, the Marine who had seen combat in Iraq asked his father one day if he could sit in his lap. For almost an hour, Jeff sat silently curled up as though he were a young boy."[101]

Jeff Lucey would never see twenty-four. His parents, not knowing what else to do, forced him to seek help at a VA hospital, in large part because he was making repeated references to suicide. There, Lucey told psychotherapists that he was considering three different ways of killing himself—by suffocation, overdose, and hanging. He also told them that he had bought a hose. Even so, he was discharged the next day to the care of his parents who were, according to the military, his "support system." Yet no one told Jeff's parents about the suicide methods he was considering or the fact that he had bought a hose.[102] Seventeen days later, his father found him hanging from a beam in the cellar of their home. The hose served as his noose. Nearby, in a box, Lucey had arranged photos of his parents, sisters, and girlfriend like a shrine. His pain had ended, but theirs was just beginning.

Making Warfare "Deceptively Cheap"

Each advance in weapons development and deployment throughout human history has been made with the same intended result—to kill the greatest number of adversaries while protecting the attacker's soldiers as much as possible. In the Civil War, combat was at close quarters with no helmets or armor. Muskets had limited range and accuracy, so soldiers charged an enemy's defensive lines and, in a few instances, dealt the fatal blow with rifle butts and bayonets. The effects of this type of fighting and massive bloodshed—unparalleled in our history—couldn't help but leave an indelible imprint on the minds of those involved. Union and Confederate troops who were lucky enough to survive the war weren't lucky enough to forget it. In diaries and letters they tried to describe what they had experienced, yet in many instances they were too overwhelmed to write more than a few words. The brutality was so great that it was unimaginable, beyond a person's ability to communicate it to others who weren't there. For those who were there, they didn't need to read about it; rather, they needed to escape it.

In World War I, machine guns and bolt-action rifles were used to inflict greater damage than the muskets and rifles used fifty years earlier. In addition, ineffective cannons were replaced by grenades, tanks, and poison gas. The result was that it was possible to kill enemy soldiers from a greater distance. No longer did troops need to engage in hand-to-hand combat or shoot others at close range as they had in the Civil War. In many instances enemy soldiers were far enough away that they could only be seen with binoculars, and sometimes not even then.

Twenty-five years later, with the start of World War II, new generations of machine guns and submachine guns had been developed that were more powerful than their predecessors. They could fire rounds faster, with greater accuracy, at longer distances. In addition, new weapons—rocket launchers, howitzers, and mortars—were added to the combatants' arsenals, and there were more varieties of armed vehicles. All were created to inflict maximum damage on the enemy with the least amount of risk to one's own troops. The culmination, of course, was the atomic bomb. On August 6, 1945, "Little Boy" was dropped on Hiroshima, and three days later "Fat Boy" was dropped on Nagasaki. Collectively, they killed more than 200,000 people, primarily civilians, and induced Japan's surrender. Since then, at least seven other countries have developed nuclear weapons (Russia, Britain, France, China, India, Pakistan, and North Korea), while Israel is assumed to have them but has never admitted it. Meanwhile, other nations such as Iran have been scrambling to procure a nuclear arsenal in order not to be at so great a disadvantage. As this is occurring, those countries with the capacity to build nuclear weapons are talking about the need to limit their proliferation through test ban treaties and disarmament.

Since World War II, and arguably earlier, the United States has had the most sophisticated military technology in the world. Largely because of a combined commitment of brainpower and resources, our military has been able to claim with ample justification that it is "the world's best killing machine."[103] While other countries play catch-up, we forge ahead, spending more money on defense than all of the other countries in the world combined.[104]

One of the newest and most ingenious weapons is the drone. It also may be the most insidious, as we are beginning to learn. Alternately referred to as unmanned aerial vehicles (UAVs) and unmanned aerial systems (UAS), drones vary in size from handheld models like the Draganflyer X6 that costs $40,000 to the Predator B, which is the size of a small plane—thirty-six feet in length with a wingspan of sixty-six feet—and costs $4 million.[105] Initially used in Iraq for surveillance purposes, many drones now carry Hellfire missiles that are launched remotely, by military personnel who are casually dressed and sitting in offices thousands of miles away. (In the United States, small, camera-equipped UAVs also are used by some police departments, border patrols, and a growing number of individuals and businesses. Amazon.com is testing drones to deliver customers' orders, and on the Riviera, paparazzi use drones to photograph celebrities in areas that are difficult to access otherwise.)

As noted by David Cole in the *New York Review,* "The drone allows CIA experts to kill someone halfway across the world by pushing a button, without exposing a single U.S. life to danger." Drones make warfare "deceptively cheap," Cole says, because ground troops aren't used, conventional bombing missions aren't needed, and it's possible for the military to engage in small-scale attacks that have the added convenience of an end run around the U.S. Constitution and United Nations charter where matters of waging war are concerned.[106]

Although President George W. Bush was the first to authorize drone strikes, President Obama has expanded their use dramatically. There were 43 drone strikes in Pakistan from 2004 to 2008, and more than ten times that number—447—in the first eleven months of 2012 alone.[107] Similarly, there was only one drone strike in Yemen in eight years under President Bush, and forty-six there in 2012.[108] In Afghanistan, the number of U.S. drone strikes increased from 294 in 2011 to 506 in 2012.[109] Today, more than one-third of the U.S. Air Force fleet is comprised of unmanned aircraft.[110]

United States drones have become so ubiquitous and annoying to villagers in the Middle East that they call them "wasps." Drones make war more palatable for the American public—our people aren't being killed or injured—as well as more removed. It helps, of course, that other countries are just developing the technology now, so U.S. residents are safe, at least for the time being. In all likelihood that will change in the near future, however, with drones becoming the focus of a new global arms race. Peter Singer, author of *Wired for War: The Robotics Revolution and Conflict in the 21st Century,* estimates that seventy-six other countries at present are either developing drones or are shopping for them.

Despite their promise as weapons that deliver deadly strikes with pinpoint accuracy and no risk to American troops, drones have drawbacks. For one thing, they aren't as precise as advertised. The *Huffington Post* estimates that in addition to the 2,500 military targets killed by drones in Pakistan, Yemen, and Somalia, 900 civilians have been killed since 2002 and more than 1,200 have been injured.[111]

The Bureau of Investigative Journalism puts the number of civilian casualties between 400 and 1,000, or about 1 civilian casualty per 3 combatants.[112] Any number is difficult to authenticate because traveling to the remote, tribal areas where most zone strikes occur is dangerous. Moreover, the Obama Administration counts all males of military age in a strike zone as enemy soldiers, so information released by the U.S. government regarding civilian casualties is problematic. Nevertheless, it's clear that there have been mistakes. In December 2013, an American drone in Yemen fired on a group of people that U.S. intelligence officers believed were Al Qaeda fighters. In fact, they were members of a wedding party. Twelve people—most, if not all, civilians—were killed and fifteen others were seriously injured.[113]

An even bigger concern, though, is the effect our drone program is having on individuals in other countries. "Understandably," says Cole, "the people of Pakistan, Yemen, and Somalia deeply resent the fact that the United States flies unarmed missiles over their heads and dispatches their countrymen to their death, apparently at will and without evident checks."[114]

Writing in the *New York Times*, Jo Becker and Scott Shane noted that "drones have replaced Guantanamo as the recruiting tool of choice for militants."[115] This sentiment is shared by Dennis Blair, former director of national intelligence. He believes that drones create so much resentment in countries where we deploy them that even instances of success, where high-level al-Qaeda leaders are killed, have negative repercussions because they generate sympathy for our enemies.[116]

The controversy regarding drones came to a head in 2011 when an American citizen named Anwar al-Awlaki was the deliberate target of a drone in Yemen. His execution without a trial or any kind of due process—a constitutional right in the United States for anyone accused of a crime, including treason—raised new questions about our use of drones in war. Currently, President Obama and higher-ups in the Pentagon and Central Intelligence Agency decide when and how drones are employed. They choose the targets and authorize the killings. Little information is provided after the fact unless administration officials choose to release it. Indeed, American media have come to depend as much on foreign sources when reporting drone attacks as on U.S. government spokespersons. While we might wish to believe differently, the practice is disturbingly analogous to a dictator's use of death squads to eliminate people he feels pose a threat to his rule. In the case of drone attacks, individuals are singled out and summarily executed with the only justification being a blanket claim that the target was a terrorist. Oftentimes this is true—but not always.

Incurring an Infinite Debt

No one has said it yet publicly—at least I haven't heard it—but another, presumed benefit of drones is that they reduce instances of posttraumatic stress, traumatic brain injury, and suicide in the U.S. military. Using drones to do our fighting means that American soldiers aren't exposed to combat situations. As a consequence, they are less likely to experience wartime trauma—being shot at, suffering injuries, losing buddies, and handling human remains. Drones make war almost antiseptic, so detached and impersonal that the horror on the ground—people being vaporized—is far away from the hearts and minds of those who push the launch buttons.

"War's new image as a sanitary, exact, efficient, and even economical enterprise in the public eye manufactures the impression that the carnage and despair of combat is fast becoming an anachronism," say Paulson and Krippner in *Haunted by Combat*. "Combat is thought to be conducted at a distance with remote controls and precision.... However, death and gore look the same in modern warfare, even if the medicine and prosthetics are more sophisticated."[117]

This is evident by the fact that drone pilots, as the operators are called, aren't exempt from stress. The environment in which they work is fast paced, and the risk of error is ever-present. According to a 2011 Pentagon report, nearly 30 percent suffer from burnout, and 17 percent are clinically depressed. Physically, their lives may not be in danger, but mentally they experience combat.[118]

Major Shauna Sperry is an Air Force psychologist who has worked in the drone program. She acknowledges that the concept of "moral injury" is an occupational risk among drone pilots, and that is the reason that she and a full-time chaplain each conduct thirty to forty formal counseling sessions per month with drone pilots, as well as regularly walk the halls where they work and talk with them informally.[119]

One reason that these drone operators experience a form of stress that isn't so different from that of soldiers on the ground—at least when it comes to killing—is because higher resolution surveillance videos are bringing the faces of individual enemy targets into clear view. An imaging system called ARGUS, developed by the Defense Advanced Research Projects Agency (DARPA), part of the Pentagon, can pick out a six-inch-long object from 20,000 feet in the air.[120] This technology makes it possible to zero in on people so closely that their facial features are easy to see, and their emotions—from rapture to fear—easy to discern. At this point the enemy becomes all too real, and the psychological consequences of initiating an action that causes the person's body to explode on a screen seconds later aren't much different than those of a Civil War soldier who fires his musket at another soldier only a few feet away. In both cases, there is a killing, and for the killer—though not the victim—it's done face to face.

"Looking another human being in the eye, making an independent decision to kill him, and watching as he dies due to your action combine to form one of the most basic, important, primal, and potentially traumatic occurrences of war," says Dave Grossman.[121]

The fact that the killer is far away from the scene, safe and secure in an air-conditioned bunker, doesn't mitigate that fact. With drones, distance no longer is as strong a protective factor.

Says Richard A. Gabriel, "Societies have always recognized that war changes men, that they are not the same after they return. That is why primitive societies often required soldiers to perform purification rites before allowing them to rejoin their communities. These rites often involved washing or other forms of ritual cleansing. Psychologically, these rituals provided soldiers with a way of ridding themselves of stress and the terrible guilt that always accompanies the sane after war. It was also a way of treating guilt by providing a mechanism through which fighting men could decompress and relive the terror without feeling weak or exposed. Finally, it was a way of telling the soldier that what he did was right and that the community for which he fought was grateful and that, above all, his community of sane and normal men welcomed him back."[122]

The time that soldiers spent coming home on ships from World War II served somewhat the same purpose. Troops had time to decompress with peers who shared the same experiences, and in so doing they received validation and support. There was no such mechanism of purification for soldiers in Vietnam, however. They left as they arrived—quickly and alone. The same is true for many veterans of Iraq and Afghanistan, at least the quickly part. Because they travel by air, most arrive home the same day that they depart from a war zone. Conversely, British troops fighting in the Falklands could have returned home by plane, but instead they were forced—deliberately—to cross the southern part of the Atlantic Ocean on Navy ships in order to have decompression time with other soldiers.

Today, the cleansing rites for U.S. troops consist primarily of ongoing praise and reassurance from peers and superiors that a soldier "did the right thing." It includes the awarding of badges and medals, which are meant to be worn proudly, as well as hometown ceremonies, parades, and monuments that honor the war effort. The intention is to distinguish wartime killing from peacetime murder, emphasizing the heroism and triumphs of soldiers rather than the dark, ugly things that they do and witness. What isn't acknowledged, though, as Kevin Sites points out, is that soldiers end up "killing a little of their own humanity every time they pull the trigger, even though they do so at our bidding."[123]

Jonathan Shay is a psychiatrist who worked for the VA in Boston for more than twenty years. He also has written extensively about the postwar experiences of Vietnam veterans, about their homecoming and about their battles with PTSD. He says, "When you put a gun in some kid's hands and send him off to war, you incur an infinite debt to him for what he has done to his soul."[124]

It's a debt that needs to be paid back, in full. Until we figure out how to do it, though, it will continue to mount.

"We know how to take the psychological safety catch off of human beings almost as easily as you would switch a weapon from 'safe' to 'fire,'" Dave Grossman says. Now, "We must understand where and what that psychological safety catch is, how it works, and how to put it back on."[125]

4

The Individual Is Blamed

*"It was hard for her to be aggressive
to prisoners. She thought we were
cruel to them."*

A RMY SPECIALIST ALYSSA PETERSON, FROM FLAGSTAFF, ARIZONA, was the third American woman killed in Iraq. She died on September 15, 2003, of a "non-hostile weapons discharge," according to official records.[1] One might ask: What does that mean? Army officials told the *Arizona Republic* that it could mean any number of things, "including Peterson's own weapon discharging, the weapon of another soldier discharging, or the accidental shooting of Peterson by an Iraqi civilian."[2] They didn't elaborate, nor did they indicate which of these scenarios occurred. Unspoken, but clearly implied, was that Peterson's death, while unfortunate, was inadvertent and unintentional.

Kevin Elston, who hosted a radio show in Flagstaff, was curious. He thought there had to be more to the story. Over the next two years, after making dozens of phone calls to military people that led nowhere, he filed a Freedom of Information Act request to access files on Peterson. The information he received was eye-opening.

Peterson was a devout Mormon who was particularly adept at learning languages. Before being sent on a Mormon mission to the Netherlands in the 1990s, she became fluent in Dutch. At Northern Arizona University, she received a degree in psychology with her education paid for by the Reserve Officers' Training Corps (ROTC). This meant that after graduating she had a military obligation to fulfill. Post-college, she studied Arabic at a military language school, then received training in interrogation techniques at Fort Huachuca, Arizona. Afterward she was sent to Tal Afar Air Base in Iraq to interrogate enemy prisoners and translate enemy documents. It wasn't what she expected. After taking part in just two interrogation sessions over her first three days, she asked to be transferred, objecting to the techniques that the military was using. This was seven months before the scandal broke at Abu Ghraib Prison in Baghdad where prisoners were tortured, raped, and murdered, and eleven U.S. soldiers ended up being court-martialed and sentenced to military prison for their actions. The same day that Peterson requested a transfer, she attended Army training on suicide prevention.

According to Elston, Army spokespersons refused to describe the techniques that Peterson objected to and said that the records pertaining to those techniques had been destroyed. In addition, Peterson kept a notebook that was found next to her body, but the contents had been blacked out. There was also a reference in the official report to a suicide note Peterson left, but when Elston filed another Freedom of Information Act request for a copy, he didn't receive it.

In the military's probe of Peterson's death, fellow soldiers noted her inability to separate personal feelings from professional responsibilities. According to the investigation, Peterson was "reprimanded" for showing "empathy" for the prisoners. "It was hard for her to be aggressive to prisoners/detainees," her first sergeant, James D. Hamilton, said. "She felt that we were cruel to them."[3]

Another soldier said, "We told her that you have to be able to turn on and off the interrogation mode, that you act differently towards the people we meet with outside of the detainee facility. She said that she did not know how to be two people; she...could not be one person in the cage and another outside the wire."[4] ("The cage" refers to the interrogation room; "outside the wire" means outside the military base.)

Army sergeant Kayla Williams was an interpreter who served with Peterson. Williams wasn't trained in interrogations, but she was forced to take part in a torture session anyway. In an interview with CNN, and subsequently in a book she wrote titled *Love My Rifle More Than You*, Williams described the physical, psychological, and sexual abuses that she witnessed. Among them were burning prisoners with cigarettes, hitting them in the face, blindfolding them, stripping them naked, then removing the blindfold and having them see her, whereupon Williams was "supposed to mock them and degrade their manhood."[5] In justifying such treatment, fellow soldiers told Williams that "the old rules no longer applied because this was a different world. This was a new kind of war."[6]

After she complained, Alyssa Peterson was reassigned to the gate at the air base. Her duties there included interviewing Iraqi workers and monitoring the behavior of Iraqi guards. It wasn't enough separation, however. What she had witnessed, and what she knew was going on, gnawed at her. Two weeks later she killed herself with her service rifle. She was twenty-seven.

"What are we as humans that we do this to each other?" Williams said after Peterson's death. "It made me question my humanity and the humanity of all Americans. It was difficult, and to this day I can no longer think I am a really good person and will do the right thing in the right situation."[7]

Williams said that she sat through the interrogations at the time but later told the noncommissioned officer (NCO) in charge that the United States might be violating the Geneva Conventions, and she wouldn't participate again. (The Geneva Conventions were established following World War II, ratified by nearly 200 countries, and define the humanitarian treatment of military and civilian prisoners during wartime. Their violation is subject to prosecution by the United Nations International Court of Justice.) The NCO agreed with her on both counts but—to her amazement—did nothing to stop what was going on. Williams said that she felt deeply conflicted about whether she should report the possible violations to someone higher up. And if so, who? Was it classified?[8]

In the end, she didn't take it further. Had a radio reporter not taken Alyssa Peterson's story further, either, her death would have been overlooked by everyone who didn't have a personal interest in it. In addition, her complaints about U.S. military interrogation tactics would be unknown, and the cause of her death—the Orwellian euphemism "non-hostile weapons discharge"—would have stood unchallenged.

Prior to the Civil War, suicide was widely condemned by white society for a variety of reasons, religious and moral. In newspaper accounts, it was described as "horrid," "a terrible deed," and "the most horrible of crimes."[9] The deceased was believed to suffer divine punishment, that is, eternal damnation. Families often buried victims privately and discretely, deliberately avoiding any reference to suicide in correspondence, funeral notices, and grave markers.

During and after the Civil War, though, suicide gained greater acceptance among whites. Shame gave way to sorrow, condemnation to regret. One reason for this was that many men at the end of the war, particularly men in the South, faced financial ruin. Their homes, farms, and other properties were lost or destroyed. Their slaves were now emancipated. They had enormous debt, whereas previously, in antebellum times, they not only had been self-sufficient but were, in fact, quite prosperous by the standards of the day. The turnabout was shocking and, for some, impossible to accept. Anything else was preferable—even death.

Women, too, came to consider suicide as an option, particularly war widows. According to Civil War historian Diane Miller Sommerville, the new dawn was for them a dark sunset. No longer safeguarded by their husbands and forced into new situations in which they had to take on roles that were alien to them, roles such as provider and protector, they suffered from the stress. In the later stages of the war, particularly in the South, where the majority of battles were fought and the heaviest losses occurred, women faced the added challenge of defending their homes and children from invaders. As a mother and a widow, should one fight or flee? Was it better to stay and try to save the homestead or abandon it, pack up children and essential items, and escape while it was still possible? And if one ran, where did she run to? For some, says Sommerville, the burden became so great that they suffered nervous breakdowns and ended up in asylums or resorting to suicide.

It wasn't long before news stories of suicide became common in the South.[10] According to one newspaper, "It is enough to make one wonder at human nature, to read daily accounts of *felo de se* occurring all over the land. It is the legacy of the war we suppose."[11]

Felo de se—literally a felon on himself—was the term used in English Law in the 1800s to describe suicide. At that time (and for many years later), killing oneself was considered a crime against society, therefore it was punishable. The punishment couldn't affect the victim, of course, since he or she already was dead, but it could affect his or her family. A jury ruling of *felo de se* authorized the confiscation of the deceased person's property, savings, and other possessions.[12] In this way it was supposed to act as a deterrent, although its value in this regard is dubious. Many people don't think of the punishment when they commit a crime. Moreover, if an individual is driven to suicide because of family conflict, depriving the family of assets might be an added incentive.

A more enlightened view emerged after the war when there was a social context for suicide. White society, especially in the South, had empathy for the deceased, as well as for his or her family. The death wasn't condoned, but neither was it denounced. There was a greater sense of understanding, of reluctant but resigned acceptance. A suicide death was unfortunate, but not altogether surprising given the circumstances of the day. Coroners, juries, and judges often spared families from potential pecuniary losses by declaring that the victim "was not of sound mind." This had the effect of removing blame and avoiding further hardship for kin. Newspaper accounts changed, too.[13] Instead of referring to a suicide death as a "horrid affair" or "terrible deed," as they had in the past, reports became matter of fact, with judgment reserved.[14]

It helped, no doubt, that some of the victims were well-known and revered, which mitigated potential criticism. Philip St. George Cocke, for instance, was one of the wealthiest plantation owners in Virginia. At the start of the war he owned 27,000 acres of land, had more than 600 slaves, and was worth $1 million—the equivalent of a billionaire today.[15] A graduate of the U.S. Military Academy at West Point, Cocke was appointed by Virginia's governor to command the state's militia. In doing so he organized the Confederate's response to John Brown's 1859 raid at Harpers Ferry. (Brown, three of his sons, and fifteen others attacked a federal arsenal in a misguided attempt to rally blacks to establish an antislavery republic in the South. Brown was captured, tried, convicted, and hanged, all with the approval of President James Buchanan. In the South, Brown generally is considered a fanatic and a lunatic, while many in the North consider him a martyr, although they disavow his use of violence.) Intensely proud,

Cocke felt that he wasn't sufficiently acknowledged for his role. "The perceived slights, on top of the strain of war, combined to take a toll on Cocke's psychological and physical health," says Sommerville, leaving him "a broken man."[16]

On December 26, 1861, at Belmead, his plantation overlooking the James River, Cocke shot himself. It's believed that he was the highest-ranking Confederate soldier to die by suicide. Left to grieve were his wife of twenty-seven years, four sons, and seven daughters.

James Lane also died by suicide. A lawyer like his father, who was a congressman from Indiana, Lane commanded two volunteer regiments in the Mexican-American War. Subsequently, he followed his father into politics and was elected lieutenant governor of Indiana, then to Congress as a Jacksonian Democrat. Rivals considered him ambitious, unscrupulous, and impulsive, yet also charismatic and a master at oratory. Instead of seeking a second term in Indiana, Lane moved to the Kansas Territory. When Kansas became a state, he was elected to the U.S. Senate as a Republican and became a strong supporter of President Abraham Lincoln. Not content to sit on the sidelines when the Civil War broke out, Lane led a brigade of 1,500 men—known as Lane's Brigade—in raids on pro-South towns in Missouri. Missouri, like Kansas, was a Union state, and Lane's unauthorized attacks incensed Union leaders. Rebuked, Lane was reassigned as Kansas's recruiting commissioner, whereupon he recruited the first African-American troops to fight in the war.

In 1865, Lane was reelected to the Senate. He was criticized by fellow Republicans for abandoning them after Lincoln's assassination, because he backed President Andrew Johnson's Reconstruction policies, including Johnson's veto of a civil rights bill. In addition, Lane was accused of financial improprieties concerning Indian contracts with the federal government. In 1866, he jumped from a carriage and shot himself in the head. According to reports, he was depressed and deranged.[17] Nevertheless, people in Kansas thought enough of him to name Lane County, the city of Lane, and Lane University in his honor. (Lane lived from 1814 to 1866. A different man, also named James Henry Lane, lived from 1833 to 1907 and was a Confederate general in the Civil War. After the war he was a college professor in Virginia and Alabama.)

According to David Silkenat, who studied the effects of suicide in North Carolina in particular, many of the state's wealthiest and most prominent citizens killed themselves, including at least thirty "well-to-do" farmers and planters, among them David Avera, the governor's son-in-law; Major W. W. Hampton, whose estate had been valued at $23,000 ($4.6 million today); Fendal Southerland, who owned "dozens of slaves"; and George Washington Wynn, who was worth $25,000 ($5 million today). The list also included "two dozen merchants and businessmen, nine doctors, five lawyers, three ministers, and three newspaper editors."[18] In addition, young men and women from prominent families killed themselves, including the son of a congressman, the sister of a senator, the daughter of a prominent doctor, and the son of a well-known minister. Silkenat notes that in one survey of nearly 500 suicide victims, fewer than 12 were "described as poor or coming from poor families."[19]

Another Union soldier who died by suicide was Joseph Aulenbach. According to newspaper accounts, he enlisted at age thirteen, then re-enlisted when his first tour of duty ended.[20] He was wounded in the Battle of Hatcher's Run near Petersburg, Virginia, nursed back to health, and spent several months in a Confederate prison before he was released. After the war he married and had six children but was forever tormented by his wartime experiences. Two decades after the war ended, at age thirty-eight, after eating dinner with his family, Aulenbach went down to his cellar and hanged himself. His father was the founder of Aulenbach Cemetery in Reading, Pennsylvania, and Joseph was buried there, in the cemetery that still bears his family's name.

When men of standing and privilege—wealthy farmers and businessmen—or their wives and mothers began dying by suicide, attitudes among whites changed. Greater emphasis was placed on the deceased's accomplishments and charitable acts than on how he or she died. The graphic descriptions of suicide that typically filled newspapers prior to the Civil War gave way to more balanced reporting in which the victim's life rather than his or her death became the focus. Negative judgments were replaced by expressions of consternation, sadness, and lament.[21]

"Death before Slavery!"

For blacks, it was exactly the opposite. In the antebellum South, slaves who died by suicide tended to be viewed as martyrs by their peers. There was a permissiveness toward suicide because it was seen as an acceptable response to human bondage. Moreover, it had elements of rebelliousness in it. By killing themselves, southern slaves were resisting the authority of their owners, exerting their autonomy in the only way that was available to them. Black newspapers often applauded their defiance.

"Death before slavery! George had tasted liberty!" proclaimed an 1843 newspaper article about a slave who tied the grindstone of a boat around his neck and jumped into a river to drown himself rather than return to his owner.[22]

"We have never known an instance where so much firmness was exhibited by any person as was by this negro," wrote another newspaper in admiration upon recounting a female slave's suicide by hanging. "The place from which she suspended herself was not high enough to prevent her feet from touching the floor; and it was only by drawing her legs up and remaining in that position that she succeeded in her determined purpose."[23]

In 1850, the black abolitionist newspaper *National Era* asserted that anyone who read newspapers "must know that suicide among slaves is not infrequent." The same year, *North Star*, Frederick Douglass's publication, estimated that "thousands of American slaves" had killed themselves.[24]

It wasn't lost on the black community that slave owners suffered in multiple ways when a slave resorted to suicide. First, the money that the owner had invested in purchasing and maintaining the slave was forfeited. Second, owners lost an important asset—the slave's labor. Third, the reputation of owners took a hit because a slave's suicide implied an owner's cruelty. Lastly, there was the fear that one suicide would lead other slaves to kill themselves, too.

The perception that slaves who took their lives were getting back at their owners for the many beatings they received created a problem for the owners. When a slave died by suicide, the owner had a dilemma to deal with. On one hand there was a need to make an example of the deceased, to mutilate the body in front of other slaves as a warning of what would happen if they chose to kill themselves. On the other hand, acknowledging the suicide could induce other slaves to follow suit, which would further diminish the owner's source of labor.

This isn't to say that suicides among slaves were commonplace before the war, or to suggest that they were celebrated. Rather, suicide was viewed as "a very last resort in the face of extreme stress."[25] Inasmuch as other slaves knew full well what it was like to be beaten by their owners, they understood the actions of the deceased while also mourning their deaths. After the war, however, many blacks in both the North and the South believed that the end of slavery opened new doors for them. Emancipation afforded blacks real opportunities for personal advancement, or so it was believed. Even though resentful whites blocked efforts by blacks to gain full citizenship and benefit from economic equality during the Reconstruction and later, a sense of optimism existed among blacks. This optimism united black communities and served as a buffer against the aftereffects of the war. The result, according to historian Joseph T. Glatthaar, was that blacks were protected from "the self-slaying epidemic" that white society experienced. It also meant that black suicides ceased to generate the same level of sympathy in the black community after the war as they did before it.[26]

Thus, attitudes toward suicide by whites and blacks flip-flopped. The prewar attitude of whites became the postwar attitude of blacks, while the prewar attitude of blacks became the postwar attitude of whites. The changes were rich in irony, and even richer in terms of social commentary. After the war, white society needed a way to explain the startling number of suicides, especially suicides by people of social standing. Financial losses served as an obvious answer, particularly for southerners whose fortunes, farms, and businesses were wiped out by the war. For those who weren't affected financially yet still killed themselves, other explanations were sought. Other than insanity or alcoholism, however, which sometimes were attributed as the cause of a person's suicide, no other reason was apparent.

The newfound compassion for whites who died by suicide resulted in a more sensitive treatment of the victims and their families. Newspaper accounts eulogized the deceased with words that were empathetic and largely free of bias. General Philip St. George Cocke, mentioned earlier, attained the same status in death that he would have had if he had been killed by enemy fire when the *Richmond Enquirer* proclaimed him "a martyr to his patriotism as if he had fallen in the field of battle." The explanation for his suicide was that he was "under the impulsion of a mental aberration that extinguished all responsibility."[27] In other words, it wasn't his fault that he killed himself; he was the victim of a psychological illness beyond his control. The *Richmond Daily Dispatch* explained another soldier's suicide in similar fashion by speculating that he probably was "tired of life and had concluded to try the realities of another world."[28]

Sommerville tells the story of John Mangham, who was a county ordinary in Georgia prior to the Civil War (ordinaries were county officials, primarily in the South, empowered to perform certain tasks such as issuing marriage licenses and settling various types of claims). When the war broke out, Mangham enlisted and subsequently was appointed a captain. After three years of fighting, he returned to his wife and four children. (Because he was an officer, Mangham could resign his post whenever he wanted and go home—an option that didn't exist for enlisted men.) Mangham also was reelected to his county position, but soon thereafter began exhibiting "manifestations of derangement." In the fall of 1864, he was institutionalized in an asylum. According to admission records, the cause of his condition was unknown, "unless it was the anxiety and excitement growing out of the state of the country."[29] As Sommerville notes, no mention was made of the three years he spent in battle.

In 1875, John M. Smith, a Union soldier, killed himself. His children subsequently filed a claim with the Pension Bureau alleging that Smith's death was the result of his wartime service. They said that he was never the same person mentally after he returned from battle and that his psychiatric problems contributed to both his divorce and his suicide. Neighbors supported the claim, but the Pension Bureau did not. It was rejected on the grounds that a "soldier's death from suicide in 1875 can in no way be attributed to his military service from which he was discharged in 1865. The alleged insanity is not shown by record, medical, or other competent evidence to have originated in the service."[30]

"What Happened, Michael?"

Only after the Vietnam War ended did the condition of posttraumatic stress take on a clinical name with psychiatric symptoms. For the first time it was added to the American Psychiatric Association's *Diagnostic and Statistical Manual of Mental Disorders*. It also was the subject of the *National Vietnam Veterans Readjustment Study*, commissioned by Congress and thousands of pages long. By 1980, soldiers with psychological problems finally had something they could point to that legitimized their suffering. They weren't making up phantom ailments; instead, their wounds were real, even if they weren't visible. This represented a significant victory for veterans.

It was counterbalanced, however, by the prevailing attitude that individuals rather than the war were to blame. Veterans diagnosed with PTSD were unable to deal with abnormal circumstances in a normal way, military leaders believed. They were mentally weak and therefore more vulnerable to trauma, even though they passed military tests that were designed to screen out those with psychological problems. The proof of their vulnerability was that under normal circumstances—meaning once they were away from the battlefront—they behaved abnormally, not the way most people behaved.

Inasmuch as little was known about PTSD in the immediate aftermath of Vietnam, many troops and their families didn't make a connection between a person's combat experiences and his or her behavior upon returning home. As stories grew of Vietnam veterans dealing with depression, nightmares, anxiety attacks, alcoholism, and social withdrawal, the military continued to fault the individual. The position of the Pentagon and the VA was that personal factors—relationship problems, legal issues, financial difficulties, and other readjustment challenges—were the reasons that veterans acted the way they did. There was no acknowledgment that fighting in a war had anything to do with it.

In a three-part series published by ePluribus Media titled *Blaming the Veteran: The Politics of Post Traumatic Stress Disorder*, the authors, one of whom was a retired Navy commander, describe the military's penchant for promoting the view "that the source of PTSD resides solely within the individual and not with the war itself. The soldiers hailed as heroic upon deployment find themselves, upon their return, portrayed as [having been] psychologically impaired *before* they went to war, morally weak, or untruthful, malingering veterans."[31]

Until recently, that position barely changed, for good reason. Blaming the individual absolved the military of responsibility. Only in the past few years, with rising numbers of veterans diagnosed with PTSD and corresponding increases in military suicides, has the issue taken root. Only now are people inside as well as outside the military beginning to concede that a problem exists. In some respects one might say that this is Saddam Hussein's legacy in the United States.

Hussein's invasion of Kuwait in August 1990 alarmed the world. President George H. W. Bush and Secretary of Defense Dick Cheney, in particular, felt threatened. Kuwait held 20 percent of the planet's oil reserves; moreover, it was only a hop, skip, and a jump away from the even richer oil fields of Saudi Arabia. When Hussein ignored a UN Security Council resolution to withdraw from Kuwait no later than mid-January 1991, Bush ordered the deployment of 500,000 U.S. troops—more than the number deployed at the height of the Vietnam War. Operation Desert Storm, led by General Norman Schwarzkopf, was quick and effective. By the end of February, Hussein was rebuffed and Kuwait was liberated, although not before Iraqi troops blew up Kuwaiti oil wells and dumped millions of gallons of crude oil into the Persian Gulf. By March, U.S. troops were coming home.

Hussein was defeated but not vanquished. That task was left to the next President Bush. Twelve years later, on March 20, 2003, after alleging that Hussein was responsible for 9/11 and hiding weapons of mass destruction (both proven later to be untrue), George W. Bush sent combat troops to Iraq. No doubt he expected another quick victory, and, in fact, on May 1, 2003, in a television address from the aircraft carrier *USS Abraham Lincoln*, Bush asserted that his administration's mission had been accomplished. The fact that nothing of consequence had changed—Hussein was still in power and U.S. soldiers were still fighting in Iraq—seemed to be of little concern.

The war in Iraq would produce tens of thousands of casualties— American troops, plus enemy soldiers and Iraqi civilians, killed and wounded. It also would produce casualties of a different kind— active-duty soldiers and recent war vets who killed themselves. In addition, it would lead to an increased number of U.S. troops in Afghanistan, where the real perpetrators of 9/11 were thought to be operating.

In 2003, the first year of the war in Iraq, seventy-nine active-duty soldiers died by suicide. Five of the deaths occurred in July. In response, the military sent a Mental Health Advisory Team to Iraq to assess the situation. The team concluded that soldiers were killing themselves for the same reasons that they killed themselves in the past, namely "insufficient or underdeveloped life coping skills."[32]

Specifically, the troops who died were unable to deal effectively with relationship problems, had legal or financial issues, or were abusing drugs or alcohol. Their deaths had nothing to do with their military service, the team said, even though each soldier had ready access to a firearm and all but one shot themselves. Subsequent Mental Health Advisory Team reports affirmed this conclusion.[33]

In January 2004, Army Specialist Jeremy Seeley returned from Iraq. Instead of going home, he checked into a motel, put a "Do not disturb" sign on the door, and swallowed poison. He was a third-generation warrior. His father had been a Marine in Vietnam, came home "different," and ultimately just disappeared. His grand-father served in World War II and was on the first Navy vessel on the scene after another Navy ship had been split in half by a Japanese torpedo. From the ship's deck he saw the bloated corpses of American sailors floating in the water. Following Jeremy's death at age twenty-eight, his grandfather said, "There's a time after you come back, you're disturbed."[34]

In March 2004, Chief Warrant Officer William Howell became the fifth Special Ops soldier—otherwise known as the Green Berets—in Iraq to kill himself.[35] Trained to be mentally and physi-cally tough, Howell shot himself three weeks after coming home. He was thirty-six and married with four children, and he had served in the military seventeen years. The Army denied any connection between his combat experience and his death but didn't investigate why a person of Howell's character would take his life. The Army also denied any connection between the antimalaria drug, Larium, that Howell had been taking and his suicide even though Larium's side effects include suicidal thinking, aggression, and delusions, according to the Food and Drug Administration.

Near the end, Howell's mood swings became impossible to predict. In the course of a few hours he would go from lovingly feeding his seven-month-old daughter to brandishing a handgun and threaten-ing violence. Among the military experiences that haunted him was when one of his twelve team members was killed by an IED. Also, Staff Sergeant Andrew Pogany was in Howell's unit, and Howell had to know what happened to Pogany when he sought help from a chap-lain and Army psychologist to deal with the horrors he witnessed. (As noted in the previous chapter, Pogany was the first soldier since Vietnam to be charged with "cowardly conduct as a result of fear."[36]

Although he eventually received an honorable discharge for medical reasons, it's likely that the military's treatment of him discouraged other soldiers with mental health problems, like Howell, from seeking help.)

A year later, in July 2005, a former Army captain, Stefanie Pelkey, testified before the House Committee on Veterans Affairs regarding the 2004 suicide of her husband, Captain Michael Pelkey. He showed symptoms of posttraumatic stress disorder—depression, hopelessness, nightmares, high blood pressure, severe chest pains—only the couple didn't know enough about PTSD, she said, to connect the dots. He slept with a loaded pistol under his pillow, which alarmed her because they had a two-year-old son, and oftentimes the captain woke up covered in sweat.

Michael Pelkey's life ended in the couple's living room. His wife was out, and his father found him—seemingly asleep in a favorite armchair. "His eyes were closed and his glasses rested on the edge of his nose," his wife recounted Pelkey's father telling her. In addition, there was a half-empty bottle of beer on the coffee table, and Michael's boots were placed neatly in front of the chair. Near the boots was the Sig Sauer 45 pistol that Pelkey bought in Germany. In Pelkey's chest was a hole so small that a person had to look hard to see it. The hole isn't what Pelkey's father saw, at least at first. Instead, he noticed that all of the color had disappeared from his son's face. "What happened, Michael?" he asked, but it was too late for Michael to answer.[37]

"He came home from the war with an injured mind," Stefanie Pelkey said in her testimony, and "died of wounds sustained in battle." For that reason she requested that his name be added to the Official Operation Iraqi Freedom Casualty of War list.[38] It wasn't.

"We Are a Family of Soldiers"

Pelkey, Howell, and Seeley were among the sixty-seven soldiers who killed themselves in 2004. This was a decrease from seventy-nine Army suicides in 2003. Military leaders said that renewed suicide prevention efforts were responsible for the decline. In 2005, however, the Army reported eighty-seven soldier suicides—the highest number since 1991, when, during the first Gulf War, there had been 102 suicides of active-duty soldiers.[39] Army Surgeon General

Kevin C. Kiley and others downplayed the increase, saying that they expected some variation from year to year. In addition, Kiley and Colonel Edward Crandell, who headed the Army's team of mental health experts, said that most suicides were the result of personal problems. Kiley and Crandell further asserted that troubled soldiers were receiving appropriate care.[40]

One of the 2005 victims was Major John Ruocco. He was a Marine Corps helicopter pilot who had made seventy-five combat missions in Iraq during a five-month deployment. Long suffering from depression, especially after four friends died in a midair helicopter collision during training in the 1990s, he considered mental health counseling but was ashamed of being depressed and unable to do his job, according to his wife, Kim.[41] In February, at age forty-one, he hanged himself in a hotel room near Camp Pendleton, California, shortly before being redeployed to Iraq. Following his death, Kim Ruocco, a long-time social worker, became involved with the Tragedy Assistance Program for Survivors (TAPS), a veterans support organization based in Arlington, Virginia. Today she is the national director of suicide education and outreach at TAPS.

Another casualty that year was twenty-year-old Private First Class Jason Scheuerman. His suicide note, nailed to his barracks closet, said, "Maybe finaly [*sic*] I can get some peace." The note showed up unannounced, in a government envelope, in his father's rural North Carolina mailbox more than a year after Jason's body was discovered in the closet, blood streaming from his mouth.[42]

Military service was in Jason's blood. His father, Chris, was a retired Army sergeant. His mother had served in the Army for a year, and one of his two brothers was in Afghanistan. Though grief stricken, they trusted the Army to investigate Jason's death and take appropriate action. Instead, each military document Chris received after his son's death brought more pain. In one document, a soldier whose name had been blacked out told investigators that Jason Scheuerman had put a rifle muzzle in his mouth more than once. "He said it was a joke," the soldier said. "He said he had thought about it before, but didn't have a plan to do it."[43] An Army chaplain said that Scheuerman's mood had "drastically changed" and recommended that his ammunition and rifle be removed and Scheuerman begin mental health counseling immediately. In addition, Scheuerman indicated on a mental health questionnaire that he had thoughts of killing himself, but denied it when talking with a psychologist. The psychologist concluded that Scheuerman didn't meet the criteria for a mental health disorder.

"The people that I trusted with the safety of my son killed him," Chris Scheuerman told reporters, "and that hurts beyond words because we are a family of soldiers."[44]

Suicides were highest in the Army because soldiers constituted a greater percentage of U.S. ground forces in the Gulf than Marines, sailors, or airmen. It wasn't just enlisted personnel who were killing themselves, however. The Department of Veterans Affairs determined that 29 percent of suicides from 2001 to the end of 2005 were by members of the National Guard, and 24 percent were by reservists. Together, Guard and Reserve members constituted more than half of all military suicides, yet at that time they comprised only 28 percent of U.S. military forces that were deployed in Iraq and Afghanistan[45] (today they comprise half).

Joshua Omvig was twenty-two years old, from Wyoming. In 2005, after an eleven-month tour in Iraq, he came home a week before Thanksgiving. He told family members that he thought that he had PTSD, and they believed it. He was depressed, suffered from flashbacks, frequently experienced nightmares, and said he felt "dead" since leaving Iraq.[46] His parents encouraged him to seek help, but he thought that would ruin his career. Three days before Christmas, and several weeks before he was scheduled to deploy again, he sat in his truck in his parents' driveway and shot himself.

In the aftermath of Omvig's death, Iowa congressman Leonard Boswell introduced a federal bill called the Joshua Omvig Veterans Suicide Prevention Act, which tasked the VA with setting up and monitoring a program to screen for suicide risk. The bill, which was approved by the House and the Senate and signed by President Bush, came too late to help the person it was named after, but other young men would be saved.

In 2006, the number of Army suicides jumped again, to 102, with at least 30 of them occurring in war zones. Whereas in 2001—prior to the second Gulf War—the suicide rate for soldiers was 9.1, the lowest since 1980 when the Army started counting, it rose to 12.8 in 2005, then to 17.5 in 2006. The 2006 rate was the highest recorded to that time.[47] It was just the beginning, though. As the war in Iraq continued and spilled over into Afghanistan, the number of military suicides kept climbing. Indeed, new records would be set each succeeding year, starting with 2007, when 121 soldiers killed themselves, a rate of 19.0.

One of the 2007 victims was Josh Barber. He enlisted in the Army in 1999 after receiving a high school equivalency degree and was assigned to a cooking school. A big man who loved food, he excelled at the fast-order grill work and at feeding other soldiers. In 2004, however, after the United States invaded Iraq, Barber was made a gunner in a combat unit because all cooking was done by contractors. That same year, a suicide bomber detonated explosives in a mess tent in Mosul, killing fourteen soldiers and eight civilians. Barber was present, unhurt but not unaffected.

Barber had no history of mental illness prior to enlisting. Manning a .50-caliber machine gun in combat is a lot different than whipping up eggs in a kitchen, though. After he rotated home to Fort Lewis, Barber had nightmares and flashbacks, suffered from significant mood swings, and drank heavily. In a health survey he said that he had seen U.S. and enemy soldiers killed and wounded, and he had fired his weapon in combat. He told his wife that he had killed an innocent Iraqi and, because of it, probably was doomed to hell.[48]

Although VA counselors diagnosed him with PTSD related to combat, in his Army records a diagnosis of depression is listed as "non-duty related," leading Barber to be washed out of the Reserves.[49] To get by, his wife worked fifty-two hours a week at two clerical jobs.

In August 2007, Barber dressed in battle fatigues and parked his Ford F-150 pickup truck outside the Madigan Army Medical Center at Fort Lewis. Next to him on the seat were 7 loaded guns and almost 1,000 rounds of ammunition, although he only seemed to have one target. He shot himself in the head, presumably intending to make a statement about the fact that the Army didn't help him. At least that's what his wife believes. Kelly Barber told a reporter that her husband killed himself at Fort Lewis "to prove a point: 'Here I am. I was a soldier. You guys didn't help me.'"

If Josh Barber thought that killing himself in front of the Fort Lewis medical center would receive attention, he was wrong, at least initially. A surveillance camera recorded his truck sitting in the parking lot for two days with his dead body inside before anyone noticed.

In a note to his wife, Barber wrote, "I love you. Please do not blame yourself. Sorry."[50] He was thirty-one.

It was near that time that Dr. S. Ward Cassells, the assistant secretary of defense for health affairs, said that the Army knew what the most common triggers were for military suicides—marital or relationship problems, abuse of drugs or alcohol, poor job performance, and feelings that they had failed on the battlefield. *Why* they resulted in soldiers killing themselves was a mystery, though, he said.[51]

Certainly the suicide of Captain Roselle M. Hoffmaster, an Army surgeon, seemed to be a mystery. In September 2007, roommates found her dead on her cot after she shot herself with a pistol. In the ensuing investigation, numerous colleagues as well as family members spoke of Hoffmaster's positive attitude. She was a top student at Smith College who enlisted in the Army to help pay for the costs of medical school. She volunteered to go to Iraq because she didn't have children and wanted to spare other physicians who did. She knew little about Army culture, however, according to the investigative report, and was overworked and unaccustomed to being reprimanded. Told by a supervisor that she needed to "toughen up," Hoffmaster confided in a female officer that she couldn't take it anymore and wanted to quit.[52] Near midnight the same day, she ended her life. According to the report, she had been depressed and prescribed Zoloft, but hadn't taken any pills from her most recent prescription. A civilian doctor who had been treating her for depression told investigators that there weren't any apparent problems with her marriage, and she never expressed thoughts of suicide.[53]

The suicides of four North Carolina National Guard members over the course of one year seemed like a mystery, too. Sergeant Jackie Blaylock joined the Army in 1999 when he was a teenager, after his high school girlfriend became pregnant. They decided to get married, and Blaylock told his father that he couldn't support his new wife "working at Fuddruckers."[54]

Twice during his eight-year commitment, Blaylock deployed to Iraq. The second time, in 2007, he was riding in a convoy late at night along a dark, dangerous highway when an IED exploded. Two soldiers—both good friends of Blaylock's—were killed. One of them had switched places with Blaylock during the ride, taking Blaylock's front gunner position and letting Blaylock ride in a rear Humvee. In the immediate aftermath, Blaylock curled into a fetal position and comrades wrapped him in a blanket as they drove him away from the scene. Later, Blaylock told people, "It was supposed to be me,"[55] meaning that he was the one who should have died. Instead, his friend who traded places with him was the casualty.

When Blaylock came home, he drank heavily, had nightmares of his two friends dying, and became estranged from his wife. He sought help from a VA medical center for "sleep problems," "excessive worry and anxiety," "recurrent thoughts of death," and other symptoms. He also screened positive for depression and answered "yes" to all four questions that are indicative of PTSD. According to his medical report, the counselor he saw focused on his need to stop smoking.[56]

In a second visit to the VA, Blaylock was assessed to be at "low" risk of suicide and "no" risk of imminent concern. Three days later he shot himself. A note found later in his car said, "I have failed myself....I have let those around me down."[57] He was twenty-six. A day after he died, the antidepressant and sleeping pills that had been prescribed for him arrived in the mail.

First Sergeant Jeff Wilson, like Blaylock, enlisted after high school and served multiple tours of duty in Iraq. He, too, witnessed the IED attack. At the time, he was standing alongside a disabled vehicle near the scene, shortly after being fired upon. He tried to warn the convoy that they were heading for a firefight when the roadside bomb exploded.

After he came home, Wilson coached Little League and volunteered for Special Olympics, but the war never went away. It was always with him. One day after Jackie Blaylock killed himself, Wilson reorganized the furniture in his home and painted his bathroom, with his mother's help. She didn't know until he had a seizure that he had overdosed on antidepressants. He died twenty-four hours after Blaylock and, like him, was twenty-six.

Wilson left behind an old guitar, the goggles and bandana he wore on missions, and the video camera he strapped to his M-16 rifle. He also left two paintings he had created when he was seventeen. The first featured a golden sunrise over a calm ocean with a lighthouse and cliffs. The second was dark with stormy skies, turbulent seas, and a rowboat carrying three figures—two gray phantoms and a soldier in green. His father told a reporter that Wilson painted the second one for his dad. "See? Two soldiers—ghosts," his father said. "And one still alive, paddling by himself."[58]

A third member of their unit, Wilson's commander, Roger Parker, attended Wilson's funeral and wake. At the time of the IED attack,

Parker was in a communications center, looking at a monitor that displayed the movements of convoys. When the GPS tracker in the truck that was hit suddenly stopped transmitting, Parker and others in the room became deathly quiet. They knew what had happened.

Parker dealt with the same psychological and emotional problems as Wilson and Blaylock, and eight months later he took the same way out, hanging himself at his home in Saluda, North Carolina.[59] He was forty-one.

The fourth member of the unit to kill himself, Specialist Skip Brinkley, also was a teenager when he joined the National Guard. He received numerous medals over ten years and two stints. After returning home in 2007, he and his fiancée bought a thirty-five-acre farm in rural North Carolina. Brinkley, who recently had changed his name from Larry Wayne Brucke, Jr., was considered "a perfect neighbor," according to a woman who lived nearby.[60] Nevertheless, in 2008, when police responded to a 911 hang-up at Brinkley's house, he shot a sheriff's deputy in the head and fired three shots at another officer's chest (the second officer survived because he was wearing a bullet-proof vest). After a five-day manhunt, Brinkley's body was found in a remote part of his farm, dead from a self-inflicted gunshot wound. He was thirty-two. The local sheriff said that Brinkley's motive for shooting the two policemen was unknown, but it's not a stretch to think that when someone is trained to be aggressive and suspect everyone, the sudden appearance of police on his doorstep can result in violence.

"Why Do the Numbers Keep Going Up?"

According to a *CBS News* investigation, there were nearly 2,200 suicides of active-duty soldiers between 1995 and 2007.[61] That statistic only begins to tell the story, though. When the number of veterans was added, the toll was much greater. CBS reported that there were 6,256 suicides in 45 states in 2007 of men and women who currently or formerly served in the military (data from 5 states weren't available). That equaled 120 per week and 17 every day. Veterans were twice as likely as non-vets to kill themselves, CBS concluded, with a suicide rate between 18.7 and 20.8 per 100,000, compared with a rate of 8.9 per 100,000 for other Americans. The age group with the highest rate was veterans ages twenty to twenty-four. They were two to four times more likely to kill themselves, with a suicide rate between 22.9 and 31.9 per 100,000 compared with 8.3 for non-veterans in that age group.[62]

In 2008, there were 121 Army suicides—an increase of more than 15 percent over 2007. In addition, the RAND Corporation announced the results of a large study indicating that 300,000 U.S. troops—about 20 percent of those deployed—were suffering from depression or posttraumatic stress as a result of serving in Iraq and Afghanistan.[63] Once again, the Army didn't have answers.

"Why do the numbers keep going up?" Army Secretary Pete Geren said in a Pentagon press conference early in 2009. "We cannot tell you."[64] Geren said that the Army was committed to doing everything it could to address the problem, but after hiring more mental health staff and implementing more suicide prevention trainings, he didn't know what else could be done.

Army Sergeant Coleman Bean was one of the 2008 suicides. Among the horrors he witnessed was a bus fire that burned twenty Iraqi civilians, mostly women and children. When he came home he couldn't sleep and began drinking heavily. His parents urged him to get help, but he resisted. Although he completed four years of active duty, he remained a member of the Army Reserves and, in 2007, deployed to Iraq again. His parents said he didn't have to go, that he could pack a suitcase and they would drive him from their home in New Jersey across the border into Canada. Bean replied, "That is not what we do. That is not who we are. And if I don't go, somebody is going to go for me."[65]

As soon as he came home, the sleeplessness and self-medicating with alcohol resumed. Already charged once with driving under the influence, Bean had a single-car accident while drunk and was taken to a nearby medical center. After being released and sent home in a cab, he broke open the locked case where he kept his gun and shot himself. Eleven months later, a member of his old platoon, Jacob Swanson, shot and killed his girlfriend in Mendocino, California, before killing himself. Swanson's mother said that her son continued to be haunted by his two tours of duty and had been diagnosed with PTSD.[66]

Another 2008 suicide was Scott Eiswert, a thirty-one-year-old member of the Tennessee National Guard. He deployed twice to Iraq, serving on road clearance missions that included seeing civilian casualties and body parts. In one instance, fellow soldiers were killed in a bombing while he was talking to them on a radio. After being honorably discharged in 2005, Eiswert exhibited symptoms of insomnia, irritability, anxiety, and depression and was prescribed medication. He applied for service-connected PTSD benefits, only to be turned down—three times. The last time, a VA doctor said that there was no "objective evidence" to verify stress. After Eiswert shot himself, the VA reversed its decision and said he was entitled to service-related disability for PTSD. The reversal was of little solace to Eiswert's widow and their three children.[67]

Although fewer Marines saw combat in Iraq or Afghanistan, the number of Marine suicides increased at rates consistent with those of the Army. In 2006, 25 Marines killed themselves, a rate of 12.9 per 100,000. In 2007, the number was 33 suicides—a rate of 16.5. In 2008, it was 41 suicides—a rate of 19.0.[68]

Military Rates versus Civilian Rates

For a long time, going back to Vietnam, military leaders claimed that the suicide rates of active-duty troops were consistent with the general population once demographic factors such as age and gender were considered. Nationally, men have a suicide rate that is three times higher than women, and men ages twenty to twenty-four are especially at risk. Since the majority of service members are males in this age group, one would expect their suicide rate to be higher than for the overall population, military officials said. As a result, the rate of suicides by active-duty troops wasn't surprising when looked at this way.

In 1987, in a study published in *JAMA*, the national Centers for Disease Control and Prevention reached a similar conclusion. CDC noted a small increase in suicide rates for veterans in the first five years after they left the service, but said that "the suicide rate among these veterans was not unusual" after that.[69]

More than two decades later, despite a dramatic increase in the number of military suicides, this thinking didn't change. Military leaders continued to claim that a soldier's service had no bearing on whether he or she died by suicide. Instead, factors such as women trouble, alcohol, and money problems were to blame. In 2009, Army General Peter Chiarelli said that in more than 70 percent of the cases there was one constant and that was a relationship problem.[70] A year later, Lieutenant General Eric Schoomaker, the Army surgeon general, reiterated the point, saying that "the one transcendent factor" associated with suicide "is fractured relationships of some sort."[71] Never mind that the relationship problem might be caused or exacerbated by one person's military service, or that the same person's depression, anxiety, social withdrawal, nightmares, alcohol use, aggression, or penchant for having a firearm nearby might be induced by his or her military training and experiences. Any causal connection was denied.

The proof of this, according to the military, was not just the fact that military and civilian suicide rates were comparable for males ages twenty to twenty-four, but that suicide might be less of a problem for young men in the service. The Armed Forces Health Surveillance Center issued a report in June 2012 that concluded, "When adjusted for age, rates of suicide are somewhat lower among active military members than civilians."[72] Implied was that instead of being a contributing factor, military service could be a buffer against suicide.

If true, that would be a significant conclusion. The report excluded from its calculations all National Guard and Reserve members, however, who have the highest suicide rates. The report explained this omission by saying that the dates when reservists started and ended active duty weren't available. Also excluded were troops who killed themselves after their military service ended—another convenient oversight. The report further noted that "suicide among military members is thought to be an impulsive act triggered by one or multiple stressors such as relationship breakups, legal/disciplinary problems, financial difficulties, or physical health problems."[73] Setting aside for the moment the fact that most experts now subscribe to psychologist Thomas Joiner's theory that impulsivity isn't a major factor in suicides, especially adult suicides, there is a flaw in the argument that people in the military are killing themselves less frequently than their peers in the civilian population. It assumes that there is no difference between the two groups other than the fact that one group serves in the military and the other doesn't. In reality, though, there is a major difference. Only healthy men are accepted in the military. Those who try to enlist but have serious medical or psychological problems are turned down.

Several psychiatrists, writing in the *New England Journal of Medicine*, noted that veterans weren't randomly selected from the general population. Instead, "veterans represent a highly selected group of healthy men from which those with serious medical or psychological problems are presumably excluded."[74] Given this, one would expect the suicide rate of vets to be lower than for civilians the same age, but this isn't the case, at least today. Current suicide rates in the military are much higher than in the civilian population, by themselves and among comparable demographic groups.

In the Army, the number of suicides doubled between 2004 and 2008,[75] and it increased another 15 percent in 2009, to 162, yet the number of soldiers who served remained constant. During this time, 45 percent of suicides by active-duty troops were eighteen to twenty-four years old. Overall, 69 percent had experienced combat (31 percent never deployed), and 54 percent were low-ranking soldiers, according to a study published in the journal *Injury Prevention*. In addition, soldiers who had been hospitalized for mental health problems had a suicide rate fifteen times higher than soldiers who hadn't been hospitalized, and for troops who received outpatient treatment for mental health issues, the suicide rate was nearly four times higher. The study, reported by the Army Public Health Command, noted that troops diagnosed with depression were eleven times more likely to kill themselves, and soldiers diagnosed with anxiety disorders were ten times more likely to take their lives.[76]

In a roundtable discussion with military reporters in August, 2009, President Barack Obama and Eric Shinseki, the secretary of Veterans Affairs, discussed a three-pronged approach to ending military suicides.[77] The first step was to reduce the time that troops spent in war zones without a break. To do that, Obama said, more troops would be recruited. The second step was to screen troops more aggressively and eliminate the stigma that exists when a person shows symptoms of PTSD. The president offered as an example renewed measures to deal with sexual assaults on females in the military. The third step was to make sure that mental health services were available. To that end, Secretary Shinseki noted that the number of mental health care providers in the VA had increased significantly.

"I think we have to remind ourselves," Shinseki said, "we're dealing with twenty-year-olds. Some of this is just the invincibility of youth.... We've got to work through that."

"There's no doubt we've had a change in attitude," Obama said. "Now translating a change in attitude at the top with transforming a massive agency with 288,000 employees...this is a big operation."[78]

Obama may have thought that the attitudes of those at the top had changed, but that was wishful thinking. More than two years later, in January 2012, Major General Dana Pittard, commander of the military base in Fort Bliss, Texas, said, "I have now come to the conclusion that suicide is an absolutely selfish act. I am personally fed up with soldiers who are choosing to take their own lives so that others can clean up their mess. Be an adult, act like an adult, and deal with your real-life problems like the rest of us."[79] Pittard retracted his statement after it became public, but the sentiment was still there.

Two months after Obama's roundtable discussion, General Chiarelli asserted that the situation was improving. Despite five consecutive years of a record number of suicides, Chiarelli said in a Pentagon news conference, "Our goal since the beginning has been to reduce the overall incidence of suicide, and I do believe we are finally beginning to see progress being made."[80]

In one respect Chiarelli was right. The number of suicides by active-duty soldiers declined slightly in 2010, from 162 to 156. When one included suicides by members of the Army National Guard and Army Reserves, however, who comprised a large part of America's fighting forces, it was a different story. The number nearly doubled, from 80 to 145, resulting in an overall increase for the Army of more than 24 percent, from 242 in 2009 to 301 in 2010.[81]

In trying to explain the increase among Guard members and reservists, Major General Raymond Carpenter, the acting director of the Army National Guard, said it wasn't a deployment problem because more than half the victims never deployed. He also discounted the impact of a troubled economy by noting that only 15 percent of the victims were jobless. He said that failed relationships were the most common factor.[82]

When the 2010 figures were released for the National Guard and Reserves, Chiarelli conceded that the Pentagon didn't know what was causing suicides among its troops. Each case was different.

A 2011 study conducted in partnership with the National Institute of Mental Health reported data on 900,000 soldiers who served in Iraq or Afghanistan between 2004 and 2008. All were active duty, not in the Army National Guard or Reserves. During that period the suicide rate more than doubled, from 10 per 100,000 to more than 20, with 389 deaths altogether.[83] Moreover, the rate increased for soldiers in all categories—those who were currently deployed, previously deployed, and never deployed. It was highest for those who were currently deployed, and three times higher for deployed women than women who never deployed, although the number of women who died by suicide during the time period—twenty-two, with eight deployed—represented a small sample.[84]

One of the women was Tina Priest. A twenty-one-year-old soldier from Austin, Texas, she killed herself in 2006. She had reported being raped by a fellow soldier at Fort Hood, and a chaplain who counseled her warned his superiors that she was a suicide risk. When an Army psychologist examined her, though, he said her condition "is stable with no risk management issues."[85] In typical military fashion, Priest was prescribed Zoloft (an antidepressant), Seroquel (an antipsychotic), and Ambien (a sleeping pill).[86] Two days later, and two weeks after the alleged rape, she shot herself. Subsequently, charges against her alleged rapist were dropped, and he pleaded guilty to lesser charges of being in the quarters of a soldier of the opposite sex.

"I gave my daughter to the Army for this country," her mother said, "and they let us down."[87]

Tina Priest wasn't married, and one of the buffers against suicide for troops who hadn't deployed, according to the study, was marriage. The study's authors theorized that married troops who weren't deployed engaged in less risky behavior. Once someone was in a war zone, however, marital status didn't make much difference. According to a different study, however, the marriages of enlisted women are nearly three times more likely to end in divorce than the marriages of enlisted men.[88]

The ethnic group with the highest suicide rate in all categories—deployed, formerly deployed, and never deployed—according to the NIMH study, was Asians. They comprised 3.5 percent of the Army, yet accounted for 9.5 percent of the suicides. Asians also had the highest rate of accidental deaths, regardless of deployment status. The report said that the reasons for this were unclear.[89]

As high as the rates are, both for military personnel and civilians, they would be even higher if suicides weren't underreported. When he was U.S. Surgeon General, David Thatcher noted in his 1999 national report on suicide, "Secrecy and silence diminish the accuracy and amount of information available about persons who have completed suicide."[90]

It doesn't help that the cause of someone's death can't always be determined with certainty. A person who drives off the road or into a tree may not leave skid marks, but whether he or she fell asleep at the wheel, swerved to avoid an animal, lost control of the vehicle, had a heart attack, or deliberately intended to die isn't obvious. Likewise in war, the difference between being brave and being foolhardy can be quite small. Exposing oneself to enemy fire in order to provide cover for others or to rescue someone who has been injured is courageous, but if it's done with disregard for one's own safety or, worse, with the intention of being shot, it constitutes a death wish.

Only 20 percent of suicide victims leave a note,[91] so coroners often have little to go on. Moreover, coroners frequently are pressured by family members to attribute questionable deaths to accidents rather than suicide, for reasons of stigma and also insurance (if a person is determined to have died by suicide within two years of a policy becoming effective, payment can be contested; beyond two years, life insurance is paid regardless of how the person died). In the absence of verifiable information, the official cause of death may be undetermined.

"It Was the War"

Since suicide is, for the most part, an individual act, there is a strong tendency to blame the individual. If he or she had just been tougher, stronger, more resilient, more hopeful, or had a better support system, the person would be alive today, or so the thinking goes.

In *Veterans on Trial*, Barry Schaller says that the prevailing attitude following World War II "was that psychiatric disability after the war was attributable to factors that predated the war rather than the war itself."[92] In other words, it wasn't exposure to combat that caused the problem, military officials believed; it was inherent weaknesses in the individual.

In Alyssa Peterson's case, which led off this chapter, it could be said that Kayla Williams probably witnessed many of the same interrogation tactics as Peterson, but Williams's experiences didn't drive her to suicide. Williams herself believes that there had to be more to Peterson's death than her military service, as traumatic as it was.

"I witnessed abuse," Williams said. "I felt uncomfortable with it, but I didn't kill myself."[93]

One can speculate on a variety of reasons for this. Perhaps the torture tactics Peterson observed were even more horrifying than those witnessed by Williams. Perhaps Peterson was more conflicted because she was an interrogator and Williams was not, meaning that Peterson was required to participate and be complicit in the torture while Williams's role was more passive. Perhaps because she was deeply religious, Peterson felt she no longer was a "good" person, that she was dead already, so her suicide merely confirmed it. No one knows. It's worth noting that while Alyssa Peterson reached her breaking point after two days, for Kayla Williams it was after one day.

Although the military investigation following Peterson's death concluded that she died by her own hand, most people—including members of Peterson's family—didn't question the version put forth by the military that Peterson's death was accidental. This isn't unusual. Families often lobby hard to have a loved one's cause of death declared an "Accident" or "Unknown"—anything to avoid the shame and stigma of suicide. With suicide comes judgment. With suicide comes unspoken accusations, not only of the deceased but of those closest to the person. As a spouse, parent, sibling, lover, or friend, one didn't do enough to keep the person alive. One didn't provide enough support, love, or friendship. One didn't see the clues, except in retrospect, that the person was contemplating suicide.

For years afterward, Penny Coleman believed that the suicide of her husband Daniel, who served in Vietnam, was her fault. "If only I had been kinder, more patient, listened better, noticed more, intervened faster," she says.[94]

It didn't matter that Daniel suffered from posttraumatic stress, that he "slept too much, drank too much, smoked marijuana too much," in Coleman's words.[95] PTSD wasn't a diagnosed illness at the time, so there was no one to consult about it. In addition, the aberrant behavior of a spouse generally isn't something that one shares with others; it's something one keeps locked up and hidden, unacknowledged and out of sight. When Daniel began making suicide attempts, they were hidden, too.

Coleman believed that because her husband died, she failed. Then stories started coming out about all of the suicides by Vietnam vets who experienced posttraumatic stress. These weren't isolated incidents; they represented an epidemic. In time, Coleman became convinced that the four-word eulogy spoken by Daniel's brother at the funeral service was true: "It was the war."

Ever since the Civil War, it has served the military well to lay the blame for a self-destroyed life on the individual rather than on his or her combat experiences. Citing character flaws and personal weaknesses is a way of absolving the military. Saying that each suicide is an isolated incident, brought about by a person's unique despair, shifts responsibility for it.

It's certainly in the military's best interests for families not to be too curious, to accept what they are told without questioning it. Then military officials don't have to disclose any additional information, including information that might portray the military in a negative light. Also, no one makes the connection between shooting at the enemy—a socially sanctioned act—and turning the barrel inward.

The problem with admitting a connection between wartime experiences and suicide, from the military's point of view, is that it undermines the country's ability to attack and defend. If the military admits that "normal" people can have psychological reactions to combat, reactions so severe that it leads them to take their lives long after they return home, then it negatively impacts recruitment efforts. Instead, the military places the blame on the individual, saying that whatever led him or her to resort to suicide was personal. It existed before the person deployed, and therefore it isn't war-related. The irony is that soldiers who go off to war are hailed as heroes, yet when they come back suffering from psychological trauma they are told that they are weak and that their mental health problems predate their combat service. In other words, they went off to war with strong minds and returned with fractured faculties, yet the dividing line between the two—their war experiences—didn't influence the change.

If the military takes full responsibility for all of the psychological casualties, the cost will be sky-high. According to the National Gulf War Resource Center, a twenty-four-year-old male soldier who has PTSD, is married with one child, and is unable to work because of his disability receives $2,400 per month from the VA for as long as he lives. Based on an average lifespan, and not adjusting for inflation, that totals more than $1.3 million.[96] That's just one soldier, and one family. And $2,400 per month isn't a lot for a family to live on in many areas of the United States, although it is tax free.

According to a 2013 analysis of federal payment records by the Associated Press, the U.S. government is continuing to make monthly payments to surviving relatives of veterans going all the way back to the Civil War. The compensation related to the Civil War and the 1898 Spanish-American War is minimal—as of March 2013, two children of Civil War veterans were receiving $876 per year each, and ten living relatives of those who fought in the Spanish-American War collectively received $50,000 per year. The Associated Press noted that the obligation increased to $20 million per year, however, for surviving relatives of World War I (which ended nearly a century ago), $5 billion per year for World War II, $2.8 billion per year for the Korean War, $22 billion per year for the Vietnam War, and $12 billion per year (so far) for the wars in Iraq and Afghanistan.[97] Since the number of new veterans who are filing for disabilities is increasing every day, the obligations for the wars in Iraq and Afghanistan will only go up.

"If history is any judge," the Associated Press report said, "the U.S. government will be paying for the Iraq and Afghanistan wars for the next century."[98]

Fearlessness, Not Fear

Among many members of the general public, the belief exits that suicide is an act of selfishness and/or weakness. By killing themselves, people are thinking only of themselves—not of the pain their deaths will cause loved ones. They also are taking "the easy way out," avoiding the need to deal with their problems. According to modern-day researchers, however, nothing could be further from the truth.

Many people who kill themselves believe that they are doing others a favor. They are relieving loved ones of the burden of caring about them, or they are sparing society from having to deal with the presence of a self-perceived murderer. Rather than being an act of selfishness, suicide is an act of sacrifice—at least in their eyes.

As for the perception that killing oneself is a sign of weakness, it's quite the opposite. "Suicide is not easy, painless, cowardly, selfish, vengeful, self-masterful, or rash," says Thomas Joiner in his book *Myths about Suicide*. Instead, Joiner says, "It's actually about fearlessness. You cannot do it unless you are fearless, and this is behavior that is learned."

By "learned," Joiner means that people develop the capacity to kill themselves through practice and repeated exposure to pain and death. This exposure may be experienced through various forms of risk-taking (driving fast, jumping from great heights, substance abuse), personal punishment (cutting, bulimia, anorexia), or previous suicide attempts. It also may be witnessed. Physicians and police officers have high rates of suicide because they are exposed to suffering on a regular basis, Joiner maintains. It doesn't take long before death seems neither unusual nor threatening to them. Added to this is the fact that doctors and cops have easy access to lethal means—drugs and firearms, respectively—and there are few obstacles in their way if they have the desire to kill themselves.

In this context, no occupation has greater exposure to death than that of soldier. Death is so commonplace, so much a part of a soldier's everyday world, that it's an overshadowing truth. Moreover, it occurs suddenly and unpredictably.

"In war, death becomes a megalithic presence, no longer somewhere in the future, but now," write Daryl S. Paulson and Stanley Krippner in *Haunted by Combat*. "It is greeting a sunrise and wondering if you will be alive to see the sunset. And, if you do survive to see it set, then you ask if you will be alive to see tomorrow's sunrise."[99]

Soldiers become inured to death. When combined with the fact that they carry a firearm at all times and have developed a mentality of focused aggression through training, the risk of suicide is high. Ninety-three percent of troops who deployed to a war zone and killed themselves later used a weapon to do it, rather than overdosing, hanging, jumping from a great height, or another means.[100]

Joiner's view, widely held by other experts in the field, doesn't absolve the individual of responsibility. It places suicide in a broader context, however. A variety of factors—physiological, psychological, emotional, social, and environmental—contribute to the problem. Ninety percent of suicide victims have a diagnosed mental disorder such as depression or schizophrenia, although not everyone who is mentally ill makes a suicide attempt. Roughly half of suicide victims drink to excess, although most alcoholics don't kill themselves. People who are mourning the death of a loved one—especially by suicide—are more likely to have suicidal thoughts, although not everyone who is grief stricken is a suicide risk.

To believe that all responsibility lies with the individual is a convenient way for others to wash their hands of the problem. While advocates for gun control cite research by the Centers for Disease Control and Prevention that having a loaded firearm in the house means that a suicide is five times more likely to occur, opponents say that guns aren't the problem—people are. While advocates for suicide deterrents point to research by the American Medical Association, Harvard School of Public Health, and others that prove suicide barriers save lives, opponents argue that all they do is cause suicidal people to resort to another lethal means—even though research shows that that isn't true in most instances. While advocates for mental health treatment advocate for therapy in combination with medication, often only the latter is prescribed because it's easier and cheaper—even though it doesn't always help.

In March 2014, the journal *JAMA Psychiatry* released the cumulative results of five years of studies conducted by military, government, and academic researchers. The new reports were welcome news for the Pentagon in multiple ways. First, they determined that most of the men and women in the Army with suicidal tendencies had them before they enlisted. Second, they said that service members whose risk of suicide was greatest had histories of impulsive anger, which worsened with the stresses of deployment but didn't start there. Third, they found that the Army's relaxation of standards for enlistment wasn't related to increased suicides among the troops. Lastly, they concluded that the risk of suicide in the military was similar to the risk of suicide in the general population.[101]

It was a familiar refrain: soldiers who ideate about or attempt suicide have a predisposition to killing themselves that is unrelated to their military service. Also, suicide rates in the military mirror those of the civilian population. The other findings—that the majority of suicidal soldiers have anger issues predating their enlistment and that the Army's looser standards, necessary to boost recruitment, aren't responsible for recent increases in military suicides—were a bonus, at least from the military's point of view. As for the studies' recommendations, they were equally predictable: improve the screening of new recruits and provide more training to troops in mental toughness as a preventative measure. In other words, keep doing what you're doing, just do it a little better.

Most of the troops whose stories are told in this book didn't exhibit suicidal tendencies prior to joining the military, according to family members. Most also didn't have histories of violent behavior, mood disorders, alcoholism, or substance abuse problems before they enlisted, again according to those closest to them. One could argue that in cases of suicide the warning signs were there and family members just missed them. Even if true, it means that people in the military missed them, too. Moreover, while suicidal behavior may be difficult to recognize, signs of drinking, drug use, and anger issues are not.

In terms of military suicide rates being comparable to civilian rates, information in the new studies is contradicted by other sources. For example, while these studies indicated that 14 percent of surveyed soldiers had had suicidal thoughts, 5 percent had made plans, and 2 percent had attempted suicide, the federal Substance Abuse and Mental Health Services Administration (SAMHSA), which funds the National Suicide Prevention Lifeline, Joshua Omvig Act projects, and other suicide prevention programs, reports that about 2.5 percent of the general population (8.4 million people) have suicidal thoughts, under 1 percent (2.2 million) make a plan, and 0.4 percent (1.1 million) make an attempt.[102] All of SAMHSA's numbers for civilians are five times lower than the military rates reported in the studies.

If one believes that suicide is a problem for individuals, not society, to deal with, then it is easy to ignore. When responsibility is thought to lie in the mind of the individual, there isn't a reason to hold institutions accountable. Yet sometimes a simple institutional change can have a profound impact on the suicide rate. For instance, until 2006, a disproportionately large number of men ages twenty to twenty-four in Israel were killing themselves. This is a high-risk age group anyway, but the problem was compounded by the fact that military service is mandated in Israel and virtually all young men serve in the military and have access to firearms. In 2006, however, a decision was made not to allow Israeli soldiers to take their weapons home with them on weekends. The result was that the suicide rate for men twenty to twenty-four dropped 40 percent almost overnight. Without access to lethal means when they were on leave, soldiers had a more difficult time killing themselves, even if they had the desire and the capacity to do so.[103]

Officially, the Army considers Ryan Alderman's 2008 death a suicide. Others don't believe it. During his one-year tour in Iraq, Alderman participated in some of the fiercest fighting, serving on 250 missions and being responsible for 16 kills, or so say soldiers at Fort Carson with whom he served (it's difficult to confirm these numbers). Still a teenager in Iraq, he didn't think he would be affected by post-combat stress because he "mostly had fun killing people and getting paid for it," according to his medical records. Reporters with Salon.com, who covered his death, note that "if that sounds monstrous, it is actually not unusual for war veterans to describe combat as simultaneously horrifying and thrilling."[104]

It also turned out not to be true. When he returned home, Alderman suffered from flashbacks, nightmares, panic attacks, emotional numbness, and many of the other symptoms of PTSD. Even so, doctors determined that his mental problems weren't evidence of posttraumatic stress and weren't related to his military service. Instead, they said he suffered from anxiety, bipolar, and personality disorders, alcohol abuse, and depression "NOS" (not otherwise specified). They prescribed so many different medications that it's possible—even probable—that he died from an accidental overdose rather than an intentional one.

Whatever the cause, Alderman received no help other than pills and no support from his superiors. When a friend escorted him to see his sergeant, the man dismissed Alderman by saying, "Everybody sees what you saw," as if it was an occupational hazard and Alderman had to deal with it like others in the service. Another sergeant told Alderman, "I wish you would go ahead and kill yourself. It would save us a lot of paperwork."

The latter sentiment speaks to an attitude that continues to exist in the military. According to the friend, "The Army treated Ryan as if he was the problem, not that he had a problem."[105]

"Thoughts in My Head"

If Alderman was perceived to be the problem, then other soldiers at Fort Carson, including Specialist Walter Padilla, Staff Sergeant First Class Kenneth Lehman, and Staff Sergeant Chad Barrett, were problems, too. They served in the Middle East as well, suffered from posttraumatic stress, and braved existing stigma in the Army by seeking mental health care. Also like Alderman, their treatment consisted of medication rather than counseling, and they ended up taking their lives.

Padilla, originally from Puerto Rico, came home to Colorado from Iraq in 2004, following an honorable discharge. He was a different person from the one who deployed, though, according to his friends—"more on edge," "constantly alert," and "moving in and out of depression."[106] One time while he was driving, he mistook the lights of a passing airplane for flashes of mortar and swerved across lanes of traffic to avoid being shot at. His marriage ended, he had trouble finding a job, and he couldn't keep up with payments on his house or car. Beset by nightmares as a result of manning a machine gun on a Bradley tank, Padilla was diagnosed with PTSD. He sought treatment and was prescribed a variety of antidepressants and painkillers, but he told family members and friends that medication wasn't helping, nor was talking with doctors, who couldn't understand his combat experiences. What he needed, he said, was to talk with someone who understood what it was like to kill. Anything else was a poor substitute. In 2007, Padilla considered going back to doctors and asking for better treatment. Instead, though, as the *New York Times* reported, "He withdrew to the shadows of his Colorado Springs home, pressed the muzzle of his Glock pistol to his temple, and pulled the trigger."[107] He was twenty-eight.

Kenneth Lehman, a Green Beret, deployed to the Middle East three times. In 2006, after returning to Fort Carson, he was thrown out of his all-terrain vehicle during a training exercise, landed on his head, and cracked his Kevlar helmet. The concussion he sustained resulted in memory loss, double vision, and headaches. He got lost walking around the base, even though he knew it well, forgot medical appointments, and had to turn his head sideways to read because of issues concerning his brain and vision. Nevertheless, a military physician noted that Lehman had only "minor cognitive problems" and could return to Iraq.[108]

Before he deployed again, however, Lehman overdosed—three times. The first time, his roommate found him unconscious on their couch and took him to a hospital. The second time followed an argument Lehman had with a former girlfriend. Both times Lehman maintained that he wasn't suicidal, and doctors believed him. The third time, in February 2008, in his barracks bathroom, Lehman anesthetized his body with an injection of Lidocaine, then used a surgical blade to cut his wrist. When paramedics arrived, they were too late. At age thirty-one the former Special Forces operative was dead.

Chad Barrett's third deployment in Iraq started on Christmas Day, 2007. According to his medical records, he was suffering from acute PTSD and had survived several explosions, including one that knocked him out.[109] When he came home, he experienced agonizing headaches and violent dreams. He also attempted suicide. Nevertheless, the Army cleared him for duty, and a psychiatrist determined that he had "no suicidal intent."[110] As *Salon* reported, "Along with his gear, Barrett packed up eight active prescriptions, including Klonopin for his anxiety and Ambien to help him sleep."[111]

When five fellow soldiers in Iraq were killed in an ambush, Barrett e-mailed his father that "really bad thoughts are running around my head. Part of me wishes one of those guys was me. I am goin[g] to try to talk to someone about sending me back home."[112]

His wife and parents urged Barrett to seek help, but he didn't receive the kind of help he needed. Five weeks later, he swallowed a lethal combination of sleeping pills and antidepressants. The envelope containing his suicide note was addressed, "THOUGHTS IN MY HEAD." The note itself was written on yellow legal paper and consisted of a list of one-line statements: "Lost," "Hopeless," "Anger," "Sadness, "Wanting to cry," "No reason or purpose in life," "Failed as a soldier," "Wanting to die," "Command will get rid of their problem soldier."[113]

The Army investigation into Barrett's death didn't examine how the military's health care system failed him. Instead, it placed the blame on Barrett himself, saying that if he had taken his medication in the prescribed dosage, he would still be alive.[114] It was the same old story: Barrett's suicide resulted from misuse of pills given to him by his doctors rather than from anything related to his combat experiences or subsequent mental health treatment. Apparently, it meant nothing that two of the drugs prescribed for him—Clonzepam and Topiramate—included warnings that suicide was a possible adverse reaction.

Barrett killed himself on the same day that Kenneth Lehman killed himself, February 2, 2008. Barrett was thirty-five, Lehman thirty-one. Two other soldiers killed themselves on the same day, this time March 21, 2012. Their lives and deaths were the subject of a lengthy article in *Time* magazine.

Ian Morrison was an Air Force captain and pilot of an Apache helicopter. Nicknamed "Captain Brad Pitt" by his buddies because of his good looks, he flew seventy missions in Iraq over nine months. He never engaged the enemy in direct combat, but his base was hit often by incoming mortars, and on at least one occasion Morrison was nearly struck. When he returned home to his wife in Texas, he sought help six times for depression, anxiety, and inability to sleep. The first time, after waiting three hours, Morrison was told by a doctor that he couldn't be seen because he was a pilot and needed to go to a flight surgeon. The flight surgeon merely prescribed sleeping pills that didn't help, so Morrison went to another clinic. There he was told that the wait would be two and a half hours. Because he was busy, he left. The last time he called Military OneSource,[115] a military hotline that promises "immediate help 24-7." Morrison was on hold for more than forty-five minutes, at one point texting his wife in aggravation, "STILL on hold."[116]

Morrison's wife, Rebecca, was a graduate student in counseling. She knew that her husband needed more help than he was receiving. She also knew to ask him directly about suicide. When she did, he disavowed having any suicidal intentions. "He looked me right in the face and said, 'Absolutely not—no way—I don't feel like that at all. All I want to do is figure out how to stop this anxiety.' "[117]

Two hours after his text message, Morrison called Rebecca, but she was in class and didn't answer. When she came home, she found him dead on the floor in their bedroom, the victim of a self-inflicted gunshot to his neck. He was in full uniform and didn't leave a note.[118]

Morrison's death represented more than the loss of one service member, as tragic as that was. It also represented the loss of a valuable military asset. His West Point education cost $400,000, and his pilot training cost $700,000.[119]

Michael McCaddon's military training was expensive, too. He enlisted in the Army at age seventeen, following in the footsteps of his father and stepfather, both of whom served in bomb disposal units. McCaddon was trained to dismantle bombs as well, and his team was one of the first to arrive on the scene in the aftermath of the Oklahoma City bombing in 1995. Smart, motivated, and ambitious, he applied to the military's medical school in Maryland and was accepted. He also met, married, and had three children with his wife, Leslie. McCaddon completed medical school, but the stress of a family, school, the military, and his past experiences left him depressed and suicidal. Leslie begged him to get help, but he wouldn't consider it. It would end his career, he said.

That left her with two choices: hope that somehow he would pull through, that his dark moods would lift on their own, almost like the removal of a spell, or seek help for him. She chose the latter, acknowledging that it was "the scariest thing I've ever done."[120] Specifically, she made an appointment with McCaddon's commander to talk about her husband's condition. When she arrived, she was ushered into a room where a colonel and several other officers were seated. She had barely started talking when the colonel interrupted her and summoned McCaddon. She tried to stay composed as she expressed concerns, in her husband's presence, about his mental state and how it was affecting their family. McCaddon's superiors countenanced help for him but didn't order it. When the session was over, McCaddon bolted from the room, livid with his wife. She broke down in tears, knowing that her attempt to save their marriage had the opposite effect. On her way out, the colonel remarked, "This doesn't sound like an Army issue to me. It sounds like a family issue." He told her not to worry. "My first marriage was a wreck, too," he said.[121]

The fact that military officials have a tendency to cite relationship problems as the explanation for a service member's suicide is troubling to those whose loved ones take their lives. It's the age-old problem of casting aspersions on the victim rather than the true culprit.

"I'm not as quick to blame the Army as the Army is to blame me," said Leslie McCaddon after her husband ended his life. "The message I get from the Army is that our marital problems caused Mike to kill himself. But they never ask why there were marriage problems to begin with."[122]

The Dark Side of Nationalism

*"We're the future leaders of America.
It's our duty to serve."*

W HEN TERRORISTS ATTACKED ON SEPTEMBER 11, 2001, PHILLIP Kent was a student in the University of South Carolina's Reserve Officers' Training Corps program. He planned to spend his career in the Army, which was why he joined the ROTC. He was proud of his military training and eager to put it to use. On that same day, 9/11, he told a reporter who interviewed him, "We're the future leaders of America, so it's our duty first and foremost to serve our country."[1]

In November 2003, Kent arrived in Iraq as a second lieutenant. He spent the next five months there as a platoon leader in a military police (MP) battalion assigned to guard inmates at Tikrit Prison, north of Baghdad. The prison was overcrowded, holding more than two hundred prisoners when it was built to house eighty. In addition, American soldiers received no guidance or instruction in how to run the prison. Problems were so rampant that several months before Kent arrived the *Wall Street Journal* reported on the lack of order and controls at the prison.[2] On top of this, the manhunt for Saddam Hussein, Iraq's dictator, was at its peak, and Tikrit was considered a probable place for him to be hiding because it was Hussein's birth-place. American intelligence sources focused on the area, and soldiers were ordered to conduct frequent searches and raids in an attempt to capture him. Eventually, Hussein's former bodyguard, who was being held at the prison, succumbed to "high-pressure interrogation" and disclosed Hussein's location, which turned out to be nearby.[3]

Between guarding prisoners without any operating procedures and participating in an intense manhunt whose smallest develop-ment was world news, the stress and pressures on MPs in Tikrit was great. When Kent returned home three months later, his mother barely recognized him. He weighed ninety pounds.

"It's screaming at me when he gets off the bus," she told a local TV news station. "He is not well. He's stressed, he's on edge, he's just a bundle of nerves."[4]

Kent couldn't sleep and had no interest in sports or music, two of his major passions prior to being deployed. In addition, his high anxiety and stress levels strained his marriage, and his life really began to fall apart.

Despite his physical condition, which doctors diagnosed as a form of dysentery that subsequently turned into bulimia, and his depres-sion, which had led him to start talking about suicide, Kent was returned to active duty. His mother sought help from an Army chap-lain, and two months later Kent was hospitalized for posttraumatic stress. He was kept only three days, however, then released. Without follow-up care, he turned to drinking. Several months later, after he was arrested but not charged following a fight with his wife, Kent was given an early and honorable discharge. It did nothing to assuage his shattered dreams. A year later, at age twenty-six, he shot himself.

In doing research on Civil War suicides, history professor Diane Miller Sommerville concluded that soldiers on both sides believed that courage was a core tenet of manhood, and their concept of courage meant not acknowledging fear. "By the 20th century, cour-age is actually knowing that you are scared but are managing it," Sommerville says. "The 19th century soldier had not realized that."[5]

Henry Fleming, "the youth" in Stephen Crane's 1895 novel *The Red Badge of Courage*, embodies this ideal. A vainglorious hero in his mind, he worries that when the real fighting comes he will flee. When in fact this happens, the disparity between his imagined and real selves haunts him. Only when he acquires his own "red badge of courage"—that is, a battle wound—is the uncertainty about his true stock as a man seemingly answered.

It wasn't an option, Sommerville says, for Civil War soldiers to act on their fears. Death was preferable to being labeled a coward because that label would haunt a soldier and his loved ones long after he went to his grave. The dilemma for many young soldiers was what to do. They didn't want to fight, but they couldn't go home and endure a lifetime of humiliation and ridicule. One way out, she says, was suicide.

"Death by one's own hands," says Sommerville, "assured a solder that he, not the chaotic, uncertain, and unpredictable conditions on the battlefield, would determine his fate. And importantly, he could control, to a degree, his posthumous reputation by eliminating the possibility of what many soldiers feared; a cowardly display on the battlefield." In killing themselves, Sommerville says, "soldiers acted on the precept, 'death before dishonor.' "[6]

It's the way out that John Crittenden Coleman chose. He was the grandson of a Kentucky senator and twenty-six years old when he cut his throat while he was stationed in Florida. Sommerville notes that no explanation was given for his death other than to say that he had been "under a state of mental derangement."[7]

Suicide was the option, too, of Captain Christopher Fisher. A man of prominence, Fisher left his post and shot himself as he was riding home. According to Sommerville, "Suicide permitted the young captain to escape the taint of cowardice that surely would have followed him had he lived, just as it spared him the pain of facing loved ones as a man who had failed the battlefield test."[8]

As noted in earlier chapters, men rushed to enlist during the Civil War out of a sense of patriotism if they joined the Union, or in defense of the values they shared with fellow Confederates. The brutality of the war and the widespread carnage and destruction it produced quickly changed many men's minds, however. It was hard to believe that the fighting was justified when the result was killing on a scale no one had ever witnessed before. Still, in the aftermath of the war, the general feeling on both sides was that it had been worth it, despite all of the bloodshed. For people in the North, the Union had been preserved and slavery abolished. For people in the South, the war had produced a valiant effort to maintain a way of life that most southerners believed in, even if the cause turned out to be a losing one.

In 1895, Oliver Wendell Holmes, Jr. delivered a Memorial Day speech to the graduating class at Harvard. It was thirty years after the Civil War had ended, with no major conflicts taking place in the interim. Holmes was fifty-five at the time, a Massachusetts judge, and his speech was titled "A Soldier's Faith." President Theodore Roosevelt admired the speech so much that it influenced his decision to nominate Holmes to the U.S. Supreme Court seven years later, where Holmes served for thirty years.

Holmes knew well the consequences of war. After one particularly bloody battle he noted in his diary, "The dead of both sides lay piled in the trenches 5 or 6 deep—wounded often writhing under the superincumbent dead."⁹ At the Battle of Antietam, Holmes was so seriously wounded that his death seemed imminent. Three decades later, however, Holmes looked back on the war not as a bloodbath but as a necessity. "War, when you are at it, is horrible and dull," he said to the new college graduates. "It is only when time has passed that you see that its message was divine."¹⁰

Holmes continued, "As long as man dwells upon the globe, his destiny is battle, and he has to take the chances of war.…It is not vain for us to tell the new generation what we learned in our day, and what we still believe. That the joy of life is living, is to put out all one's powers as far as they will go; to ride boldly at what is in front of you, be it fence or enemy, to pray, not for comfort, but for combat; to keep the soldier's faith against the doubts of civil life, more besetting and harder to overcome than all the misgivings of the battlefield.…We have shared the incommunicable experience of war; we have felt, we still feel, the passion of life at its top."¹¹

In other words, war is unavoidable at times, but don't worry. The result can be sublime and virtuous. It's this romantic rendering that has proven to be so seductive.

"Suicide in the Trenches"

One of the British soldiers who fought in World War I was Siegfried Sassoon. Largely unknown in the United States, Sassoon was highly decorated for bravery. His claim to fame, though, or notoriety— depending on one's point of view—was his writing. In poetry and prose, while the war was being fought and afterward, he denounced the fighting. His reputation on the battlefield aided his credibility, as did his personal friendships with well-known writers of the day—Robert Graves, Wilfred Owen, Bertrand Russell, and E. M. Forster. It also spared him from prison.

Despite his Germanic sounding first name, Sassoon had no German ancestry. Rather, he was named by his mother, who came from a well-known family of British sculptors and was a fan of Wagner operas. Shortly after England declared war, and six months before his younger brother was killed at Gallipoli, Sassoon was commissioned into the British army and sent to the front in France. There he earned the nickname "Mad Jack" after numerous courageous acts, including rescues of wounded soldiers while being exposed to enemy fire.[12] His heroism masked a growing depression over the horrors that he and other soldiers were witnessing, however, and after a convalescent leave he refused to return to duty. Instead, in 1917, he sent a letter to his commanding officer that was forwarded to the press and read in Parliament. Titled "Finished with the War: A Soldier's Declaration," the letter condemned the government's military motives.

"I believe that this war, upon which I entered as a war of defense and liberation, has now become a war of aggression and conquest," Sassoon wrote. "I have seen and endured the suffering of the troops, and I can no longer be a party to prolong these sufferings for ends which I believe to be evil and unjust."[13]

Sassoon sought to bring the war home to people who were far from the fighting, people who were not exposed to the horrors that soldiers witnessed. In this way he aimed "to destroy the callous complacency with which the majority of those at home regard the continuance of sufferings which they do not share, and which they have not sufficient imagination to realize."[14]

The letter caused an uproar and exposed Sassoon to a potential court martial. Fortunately for him, government leaders were reluctant to prosecute a war hero. With strong urging from Robert Graves, they took a different tact. Sassoon was diagnosed with "shell shock" and sent to a war hospital in Scotland for treatment. He returned to active duty in 1918, but not before he threw the ribbon from his Military Cross medal into a river. A short time later he was wounded, promoted, and spent the rest of the war in England.

Sassoon died in 1967 at age eighty. In 1985, he was one of sixteen Great War poets commemorated in the Poet's Corner at Westminster Abbey. The words on his inscription, written by friend and fellow poet Wilfred Owen, who died in World War I, were fitting: "My subject is War, and the pity of War. The Poetry is in the pity." The following Sassoon poem is titled "Suicide in the Trenches":

> I knew a simple soldier boy
> Who grinned at life in empty joy.
> Slept soundly through the lonesome dark,
> And whistled early with the lark.
> In winter trenches, cowed and glum,
> With crumps and lice and lack of rum,
> He put a bullet through his brain.
> No one spoke of him again.
> You smug-faced crowds with kindling eye
> Who cheer when soldier lads march by,
> Sneak home and pray you'll never know
> The hell where youth and laughter go.[15]

It's a refrain that many soldiers identify with, for who else other than someone who has trained for battle and participated in combat can truly understand the monstrosity of war? To leave fresh-faced for the front and return home—if one is lucky enough to survive the fighting—a grizzled, cynical, and empty man isn't something that people who lack the experience can fully comprehend. It's not just the physical hardships that are so challenging; psychological trauma exerts a toll as well.

For the first three years of World War I, the United States was an interested but passive observer. President Woodrow Wilson's renominating slogan in 1916 was, "He Kept Us Out of War." Even after an American merchant ship carrying wheat to England was torpedoed by a German U-boat in January 1915, after an American tanker was sunk in May 1915, after the British ocean liner *Lusitania*, carrying 1,900 passengers, went down six days later due to enemy fire, and after another American merchant ship was sunk off the coast of Scotland, Wilson tried to avoid joining the battle. At the same time, behind the scenes, he was preparing for it. After five more American commercial and passenger ships were sunk, he no longer had a choice. Wilson's request to Congress in April 1917 to declare war on Germany was met with wild applause, despite his admonition that "it is a fearful thing to lead this great, peaceful people into war, into the most terrible and disastrous of all wars." Afterward he told an aide, "My message today was a message of death for our young men. How strange it seems to applaud that."[16]

One of the few dissenting voices was George W. Norris, a Republican senator from Nebraska. He maintained that the United States was declaring war to further its financial interests, not advance its principles. "We have the cold-blooded proposition," he said, "that war brings prosperity." Financial institutions "see only dollars coming to them through the handling of stocks and bonds that will be necessary in case of war," Norris said, not the "human suffering and sacrifice of human life."[17]

The fears of Wilson and Norris proved well-founded. More than 100,000 U.S. troops died in the war, many of them buried thousands of miles from home and loved ones. An additional 300,000 men were left disabled, with 50,000 still hospitalized for psychiatric reasons twenty years after the war ended.[18]

In 1936, Major General Smedley Butler said, "On a tour of this country, I have visited eighteen governmental hospitals for veterans. In them are a total of 50,000 destroyed men...men who were the pick of the nation eighteen years ago. Boys with a normal viewpoint were taken out of the fields and offices and factories and classrooms and put into the ranks. They were remolded; they were made over; they were made to 'about face'; to regard murder as the order of the day. They were put shoulder to shoulder and, through mass psychology, they were entirely changed. We used them for a couple of years and trained them to think nothing at all about killing or being killed. Then, suddenly, we discharged them and told them to make another 'about face'! We didn't need them anymore."[19]

At the time, Butler was the most decorated Marine in U.S. history. He served in the Philippines, China, Central America, and the Caribbean during the early 1900s, and commanded a military base in France during World War I. He received the Medal of Honor twice— one of only nineteen men to do so—as well as other distinguished service medals in a thirty-four-year career. In retirement, however, he became an outspoken critic of war, having seen what it does to young men.

A Flag, a Photo, and Immortality

The ultimate symbol of nationalism is a country's flag. It's flown proudly not only by the military but also by individual citizens as an act of patriotism. People pledge allegiance to it, national anthems are sung to it, and soldiers vow to defend it. In contrast, when individuals denounce a country's actions, particularly in instances of war, they burn the flag. Literally and figuratively, it's the most incendiary thing they can do.

If there is one image that personifies Americans' feelings of pride, determination, and superiority in World War II, it's a photo taken in 1945 by Joe Rosenthal of six Marines raising the U.S. flag at the top of Mount Suribachi on the island of Iwo Jima. Many Americans today may not know the importance of the moment, but the image is burned into our national consciousness nonetheless, both from Rosenthal's photo and from the sculpture of it outside Arlington National Cemetery. In *Flags of Our Fathers*, James Bradley says that the image of his father, John Bradley, and five other Marines raising the flag on Iwo Jima "transported many thousands of anxious, grieving, and war-weary Americans into a radiant state of mind: a kind of sacred realm where faith, patriotism, mythic history, and the simple capacity to hope intermingled."[20]

Iwo Jima is a small, rocky island in the Pacific Ocean that had great strategic value. Controlled by Japan, the island, with its radar equipment, was the last line of defense in a warning system to alert the Japanese of U.S. air attacks. Capturing the island was considered an essential precursor to an Allied invasion of the Japanese island of Okinawa, and the month-long battle between U.S. and Japanese forces was intense. American soldiers numbering 80,000, fighting above ground, sought to eradicate 20,000 Japanese soldiers who were hidden in 1,500 manmade caverns connected by 16 miles of tunnels. When the battle ended, U.S. forces had secured the island, but at a considerable cost. Nearly 7,000 Marines had died, 19,000 others were wounded, and nearly all of the Japanese soldiers had been killed.[21]

Three of the six Marines who raised the flag on Iwo Jima died in the battle. One of the three survivors was Ira Hayes, a Pima Native American. Hayes was trained as a paratrooper who had the code name Chief Falling Cloud. When the Marine Corps disbanded paratrooper units in 1944, Hayes was transferred to another division. It was one of the first Marine divisions to land on Iwo Jima, and Hayes ended up being among the men who were ordered to plant a large American flag on the mountaintop as a signal that the Allies were taking charge. Their act was immortalized in Rosenthal's photo, to Hayes's regret. Unusually shy and intensely private, he couldn't lead a normal civilian life after the war. Letters poured in for him, reporters wanted to interview him, and people would drive through the reservation where he lived looking for him.[22] He and the two other survivors were asked to play themselves in the 1949 John Wayne movie, *Sands of Iwo Jima*, and Hayes reluctantly agreed. They also were honored five years later as war heroes by President Dwight D. Eisenhower.

Meanwhile, Hayes's life was unraveling. According to Bradley, whose book became the basis for a Clint Eastwood movie of the same name, Hayes suffered from posttraumatic stress. He was arrested more than fifty times for public drunkenness, and at one point explained his alcoholism by saying that he was "cracking up thinking about all of those other guys who were better than me not coming back, much less to the White House."[23]

A year after the ceremony with Eisenhower, the thirty-two-year-old Hayes was found dead early one morning near an abandoned adobe hut on the Gila River reservation. He had been drinking and playing cards in a bar and was lying in his own blood and vomit. According to the coroner, death was accidental, caused by overexposure—the weather was frigid—and alcohol consumption.[24]

As for the other two surviving flag bearers, John Bradley, a medic, was forever after haunted by a fellow Marine's death at Iwo Jima. "We could choose a buddy to go with," Bradley told his son one of the few times he ever talked about his wartime experiences. "My buddy was a guy from Milwaukee [Ralph Ignatowski]. We were pinned down in one area. Someone else fell injured and I ran to help out, and when I came back my buddy was gone. I couldn't figure out where he was. I could see all around, but he wasn't there. And nobody knew where he was. A few days later someone yelled that they'd found him. They called me over because I was a corpsman. The Japanese had pulled him underground and tortured him.... It was terrible. I've tried hard to forget all this."[25]

When Ignatowski was found, his eyes, ears, fingernails, and tongue had been removed. He had been stabbed multiple times with a bayonet, his teeth had been smashed, his arms broken, and the back of his head smashed in. As if that wasn't enough, his penis had been stuffed in his mouth.[26]

Corpsmen tend to bear greater witness to the physical atrocities of war than other soldiers. Their job, after all, is to provide emergency medical treatment to those who are injured in combat. According to James Bradley, his father's "entire mission on Iwo was to hop from blown face to severed arm, doing what he could under heavy fire to minimize the damage, stanch the flow, ease the agony."[27]

With so much fighting and so many casualties, John Bradley was in constant demand. There was no escaping the horror.

"The corpsmen remembered," James Bradley says. "And their memories ruled the night."

After the war, John Bradley refused to talk to reporters, and he consented to only one public interview for the rest of his life. Assailed by nightmares, he said he wished that "there had never been a flag on top of that pole."[28] He told his children that he was a false hero, and the true heroes were the men who had died.[29]

The other survivor among the six flag bearers, Rene Gagnon, ended up in the photo by accident. There were communication problems between the top and bottom of the mountain, and he was ordered to take up a radio battery. When he arrived, the five other men were straining to plant the flag because the pipe to which it was attached was heavy. Like all good Marines, Gagnon instinctively lent a hand.

After the war Gagnon drank heavily and held a succession of menial jobs from which he was often fired. According to his son, he was tormented by the knowledge that he had been immortalized for doing something quite ordinary, not at all courageous. The rest of his life was an emotional roller coaster, one minute living like a celebrity with parades and reporters and autograph seekers, and the next minute being ignored by everyone. "It was stop-and-go hero-ism," his son said.[30] Rene Gagnon died in 1979 at age fifty-four from a heart attack.

At least he lived longer than Gaspar T. Pelletier, who also served on Iwo Jima. In 1948, Pelletier drove his red Jeep to the middle of the Golden Gate Bridge and jumped. He was thirty-nine. Six months earlier, another World War II veteran, Philip H. Sheridan III, also jumped from the Golden Gate Bridge. He was the grandson of Civil

War general Philip H. Sheridan and had flown seventy-six combat missions over Europe as a B-26 pilot. Despite being happily married, by all accounts, to a Santa Barbara debutante, and living in a quiet resort area in northern California, Pelletier was suffering from war neuroses, according to his mother. He was en route to a VA hospital when he parked his wife's convertible coupe near the bridge. On the car's seat he left a note addressed "To whom it may concern," instructing whomever found the note to call Sheridan's neighbor, a woman named Mrs. Williams, and "ask her to go up the hill and break the news to my wife."[31] Sheridan was thirty-one.

A Dictator's Preoccupation with Suicide

When Iwo Jima fell in March 1945, the outcome of World War II no longer was in doubt. A month later, Mussolini was caught and publicly hung, ending Italy's fight, and it was only a matter of time before Japan was finished as well. American troops who searched through caverns on Iwo Jima found the bodies of hundreds of dead Japanese soldiers. With surrender imminent, they had killed themselves by holding grenades to their stomachs and pulling the pin.

In Germany, Nazi leaders prepared for the end by carrying potassium cyanide capsules. They were aware of Mussolini's unheroic death and wanted to avoid similar ignominy. When Adolf Hitler and his top two officers, Heinrich Himmler and Joseph Goebbels, killed themselves, dozens of other party members followed suit, including the ministers of justice and education, as well as Hitler's official successor as Reich chancellor. Fifty-three army generals, fourteen Luftwaffe generals, eleven admirals, eight regional party leaders, and seven police chiefs also took their lives.[32] Hitler's mistress, Eva Braun, whom he had married just a few hours earlier in his bunker, plus Goebbels's six children, also swallowed cyanide capsules. (Goebbels and his wife didn't resort to poison; instead, Goebbels ordered a SS guard to shoot both of them.) Commander-in-Chief Hermann Göring killed himself later, the night before he was scheduled to be executed for war crimes.

Nazi leaders encouraged German citizens to take their lives as well, promulgating fear of what would happen to them once the Russians invaded. Government officials said that German men would be tortured and murdered while German women would be raped, then killed. It wasn't an idle threat. In *The Last Battle*, Cornelius Ryan estimated that 100,000 babies were born in Berlin after World War II as a result of rapes.[33]

In April 1945, with the fall of Berlin looming, Hitler Youth passed out poison pills to members of the audience at the last performance of the Berlin Philharmonic. Not coincidentally, the orchestra played Wagner's climatic opera *Götterdämmerung* ("Twilight of the Gods")—a Hitler favorite—which ends when the heroine kills herself.[34] As Christian Goeschel notes in his book, *Suicide in Nazi Germany*, Hitler and other Nazis believed that the state was the final arbiter of life and death, not the individual. Thus, it was in keeping for the state to provide the means to suicide when the demise of Germany was certain.[35] As a farewell gift, Hitler allegedly gave cyanide pills to his secretaries.[36] (Until the end of the war, Nazi leadership considered suicide an act of resignation or surrender and didn't condone it—with one exception. When people whom the state thought were eugenically unfit and ill killed themselves, their deaths were welcomed. Hitler was so interested in suicide that Goebbels was charged with giving him frequent data on suicides, written in big letters with a special typewriter so that Hitler, who was myopic, could read it.)

There were 3,881 recorded suicides in Berlin in April 1945, 20 times the number in March.[37] "For a brief period in the spring of 1945," Goeschel writes, "when the Third Reich came to its end, suicide lost its status as a taboo and became a routine phenomenon."[38]

In the last days of battle, Japanese civilians were urged to kill themselves, too. Emperor Hirohito and commanders of the Red Army said it was more honorable than submitting to the enemy—not surprising, since from the days of the samurai, death in Japanese military culture has been viewed as preferable to the shame of capture. Now, with Japanese war efforts failing, citizens were promised a special place in the afterlife equal to those of soldiers who died in combat. The military supplied the means by distributing grenades, even though they were in short supply because of the war, and thousands of people complied or were massacred. The result was a dark stain that several Japanese leaders today have tried to airbrush from the country's history books.[39]

The dark stain for future editions of American history comes from all of the suicides that have occurred as a result of U.S. war efforts, particularly in recent years. Every segment of our armed forces is affected by it, from active-duty men and women to our growing number of veterans, from troops who have never deployed to our most-decorated combat warriors, from those who are at the bottom of the military hierarchy to commanders near the top. No one is immune.

An element of the wars in Iraq and Afghanistan that is unique for American soldiers is that their duties have been expanded from previous wars. Firing their weapons and claiming valuable real estate once held by the enemy—regions, cities, and streets—no longer is their sole or primary duty, even though it constitutes nearly all of their training. In 2005, when General David Petraeus took charge of military operations in the Middle East at the behest of President George W. Bush, he advocated a new role for soldiers. It was a role that he had articulated previously in a textbook he wrote on counterinsurgency titled *Field Manual 3–24*. According to the manual, "To confine soldiers to purely military functions while urgent and vital tasks have to be done, and nobody else is available to undertake them, would be senseless. The soldier must then be prepared to become . . . a social worker, a civil engineer, a schoolteacher, a nurse, a boy scout."[40]

Under Petraeus, a variety of tasks not normally associated with military duty—directing traffic, running prisons, building schools, maintaining public utilities, and establishing local judicial systems—became the responsibility of U.S. service members. It's a totally different use of troops than in previous wars. It means that current troops assume many roles for which they haven't been trained, while also receiving less guidance in fulfilling them. Overall strategies continue to be dictated from the top, but implementing these strategies—working out the details—falls on people much farther down the line. When something goes wrong—as invariably it does—it's lower-level people who are blamed. They are the ones who take the fall for everything from prisoner abuses to warlord payouts, from civilian raids gone bad to millions of dollars that can't be accounted for. It doesn't matter that their behavior—including the use of torture—is known and condoned by superiors. An argument can be made that the lack of direction is intentional; it insulates higher-ups from military or congressional investigations.

"I Am Sullied—No More"

At the same time that today's troops take on responsibilities they haven't assumed in the past, some traditional military jobs have been shifted to the private sector. Among the most common outsourced jobs are mess hall cooks, base guards, and mechanics. As of January 2012, there were more than 113,000 employees of defense contractors in Afghanistan, compared with 90,000 U.S. troops.[41]

Outsourcing these jobs to civilian companies places nonmilitary personnel in harm's way. During the first four years of fighting in Iraq and Afghanistan, through June 2007, more than 1,000 U.S. contractors were killed and many others physically injured or psychologically damaged.[42] In 2011, at least 430 employees of U.S. contractors were killed in Afghanistan, compared with 418 U.S. soldiers.[43] In all likelihood, the number of contractor deaths is higher since American companies aren't obligated to report publicly the deaths and injuries of their employees, and oftentimes don't. Similarly, there are no public reports of suicides by employees of private companies who returned from war zones.

One contractor who killed himself was Dale McIntosh of Glendale, Arizona. He served five years in the Marines, part of the time in Special Ops. His service ended shortly before the second Gulf War started, and because he never saw action, he felt unfulfilled, likening it to an athlete who trains hard but never gets in a game. He signed on to do private security work, spending six months in Afghanistan, five months in Iraq, two months in Bosnia, and another two months in Iraq, all in 2004 and 2005. The work was dangerous, but also thrilling, providing the adrenaline rush that he missed out on by never experiencing combat. It was lucrative as well, paying up to $25,000 per month.

McIntosh survived firefights, ambushes, IEDs, snipers, and other hazards of war. He also fired a weapon and saw friends die. Once home, he went to college, earning a degree in finance and enrolling in graduate school. At times he seemed to be doing well, according to his father, a Vietnam veteran, and brother, an anesthesiologist. Other times, though, he was angry and paranoid, despairing and suicidal. Family members couldn't get him to relinquish the gun he slept with or the firearms he kept in a closet. They also couldn't convince him to seek help. Shortly before he shot himself he told his brother, "I don't want to die. I just want the pain to stop."[44] He was taking medication for PTSD, which seemed to be helping, but he also took an anxiety medication that made him more disoriented.

"We are a civilian society," his brother told a reporter afterward. "Most people haven't done this [dealt with someone traumatized by war] so there is no understanding of what they've been through, no support network. It's like these cute pit bulls they put in a ring to fight and maim and then they expect them to interact with kids. It doesn't work."[45] McIntosh was thirty-five when he died.

Another contractor who killed himself was Wade Dill. A Marine Corps veteran, he quit his private-sector job with a local pest company to take a job as an exterminator in Iraq. The financial benefit was too great not to. KRB Inc. (formerly Kellogg Brown & Root), a Department of Defense contractor in northern California, hired Dill at a salary of almost $11,000 per month—more than double his former salary—to trap and kill rodents and feral animals. The high wages would enable Dill and his, wife, Barb to pay off their mortgage, start a college fund for their daughter, and put money away for retirement, he reasoned. What he didn't know was that he would be exposed to frequent mortar fire, and his responsibilities in regard to hazardous waste removal included having to clean up the splattered remains of a soldier who shot himself in the head.

Of the latter, Dill said that night over the phone to his wife, "The smell, the smell. I can't get rid of it."[46] He sobbed uncontrollably.

Barb had never heard him cry before. Marines don't cry.

When Dill came home, she almost didn't recognize him. He had lost weight, there were heavy bags under his eyes, and he was often angry, lashing out at the two people he loved most—his wife of seventeen years (they were high school sweethearts) and his daughter, age sixteen. At one point, in a fit of anger, he ripped the wiring out of their TV and appliances, smashed mirrors, and destroyed the cushions on their couches. His wife encouraged him to get help, but instead he sought the company of his 9-mm handgun. In a hotel room, he wrote a suicide note to Barb, left a picture for his daughter with the words, "I did exist and I loved you,"[47] then shot himself. The year was 2006; he was forty-seven.

After Dill died, his widow applied for compensation benefits, available through the Defense Base Act. This act requires defense companies to buy highly specialized and expensive workers' compensation insurance for employees in war zones. The insurance covers death and injury, except in cases of suicide—unless the suicide victim is determined to have been mentally incapacitated at the time of his or her death. Survivors of civilian contracts can receive up to $63,000 per year for life if their loved one's death is related to his or her contract work. In Wade Dill's case, the military's insurance company, AIG, contested Barb Dill's claim and hired a psychiatrist who said that Dill killed himself because of depression and marital problems that were unrelated to his experiences in Iraq. In 2011, the Department of Labor ruled in Barb Dill's favor. It was small consolation.

"I believe that if he had never gone over there, he would still be here today," she says. "He left behind a lot of pain and two ruined lives. I never dreamed I would be without him and my daughter without a father."[48]

The privatization of military support functions by major Defense contractors such as Academi (formerly known as Blackwater) hasn't accomplished what it was intended to do—reduce the cost of war. In books such as *Corporate Warriors: The Rise of the Privatized Military Industry*, by P. W. Singer, and *Shadow Force*, by David Isenberg, the dramatic increase from millions to billions of dollars being spent on independent contractors is laid out, along with the fact that there has been relatively little accountability. Moreover, the shift has resulted in numerous illegal acts by contract employees, everything from fraud to rape to murder.[49] At least one officer was so disgusted and ashamed by the abuses he witnessed that he killed himself.

At the time of his death in June 2005, Ted S. Westhusing was the highest-ranking officer to die in Iraq. Age forty-four and married with children, he volunteered for service at a time when he could have remained comfortably ensconced at West Point as a full professor. Instead, Westhusing had a history of leading by example. He was a star basketball player in high school in Oklahoma, a devout Catholic who served as an officer in a fellowship of Christian athletes, West Point's honor captain his senior year, and—post graduation—a platoon leader and division operations officer in the Army.

Westhusing walked the talk, which is why he volunteered. Once he was in Iraq, though, serving as a colonel, he became dismayed. As a scholar, he specialized in military ethics. His doctoral dissertation was on the meaning of honor. He believed West Point's honor code—"A cadet will not lie, cheat, steal, or tolerate those who do"—with every fiber of his being and followed it rigorously. Soon after he deployed, however, he learned that others didn't operate with the same high standards. In particular, he was appalled by the corrupt practices of U.S. military contractors. In e-mails to his family he said that the values he held dear—duty, honor, and country—had been supplanted by greed. Private companies were cheating the U.S. government out of millions of dollars and violating human rights as well, he said, all in the name of profits. It was in direct contradiction to what he taught and how he lived.

Westhusing reported the abuses to higher-ups, but nothing changed. Whether his superiors had more important things to worry about, no latitude to hold outside contractors responsible, or orders from the top to look the other way, the problems continued.

"I didn't volunteer to support corrupt, money-grubbing contractors," Westhusing wrote in a note to two generals, Joseph Fil and David Petraeus. "I came to serve honorably, and feel dishonored. . . . I cannot live this way."[50]

Westhusing shot himself with his service pistol in his military base trailer in Baghdad. Inside his trailer, found after his death, was the note to the generals. In addition to apologizing to his wife and children, Westhusing told Fil and Petraeus, "I am sullied—no more."

"The Wizard Said My Job Sucks"

At one time, Michael Baker was the highest-ranking civilian in the U.S. military, reporting to Colin Powell. A trauma surgeon who teaches and consults for the Department of Defense, Baker was a rear admiral in the Navy at the same time that he was chief of surgery at a large hospital in the San Francisco Bay Area. He oversaw all medical services in Korea during the Korean War and in recent years completed several tours as a trauma surgeon mentor at Landstuhl Regional Medical Center in Germany, where all U.S. casualties from Iraq, Afghanistan, and Africa are treated after they are stabilized and before they are flown home.

Baker is a staunch defender of the troops. At the same time, he has seen firsthand the physical horrors wrought by combat and the corresponding cost of medical care for the wounded, which rarely is included in the final tally of a war's expenses. Baker is well aware, too, of the psychological toll of war—another hidden cost. The problem isn't limited to victims and their families, he says. It includes a group of people that most members of the public don't think about—military recruiters.

The Department of Defense spends more than $4 billion per year on the recruitment of new troops. This figure includes $1.5 billion for advertising and the maintenance of stations around the country that are staffed by more than 20,000 recruiters.[51] Much of the money is used to convince teenagers to enlist. Nearly 60 percent of America's active-duty soldiers and reservists signed up when they were teens. Those who are under eighteen require parental consent and may not have graduated from high school, but oftentimes this isn't a problem. They are seduced by pitches that emphasize service to country and personal-growth opportunities,[52] and either lobby for a signature or, in some instances, forge it.

In selling military service, the Pentagon is able to recruit new troops without needing to resort to a draft. It doesn't mean that the people who are doing the recruiting have it easy, though.

"Recruiters know what they're sending these kids into," Baker told me. "Even if recruits survive the war physically, they may not survive it mentally."

Nils Aron Andersson is one of at least sixteen Army recruiters who have killed themselves since 2000. He enlisted in 2002, three years after graduating from high school. In 2003, he was deployed to Iraq to fight in the initial U.S. invasion. It was the first time he had ever been abroad, and he earned a Bronze Star for saving two other soldiers during a firefight. He also told his former girlfriend that he had kicked in more than 1,000 doors in raids to root out insurgents, yet "most of the time it was the wrong place. There would be terrified old people and little kids sitting there."[53]

Back in the United States, Andersson was transferred to the Houston Recruiting Battalion, where he worked long hours trying to sell the virtues of military service to prospective recruits. The challenge of encouraging young people to enlist in a high-risk career proved too much for him, however. He was criticized repeatedly for failing to meet the goal of signing two new recruits each month and passed over for promotions. When he stuck a gun in his mouth, he was taken to a psychiatrist in San Antonio for three days of testing and counseling. The psychiatrist concluded that Andersson was "clinically depressed but no immediate danger to himself," and referred him to another psychiatrist in Houston.[54] Andersson didn't see the Houston psychiatrist until two months later, on March 5, 2007.

That was a busy day for the twenty-five-year-old Army recruiter. At 8:30 a.m., in a brief civil ceremony, Andersson married a woman he barely knew, who like him suffered from depression. Then he saw the psychiatrist, telling a friend immediately afterward, "The wizard said I need to get out of the Army and my job sucks. I could have told her that."[55]

Following dinner, Andersson and his new wife of twelve hours got into an argument. Andersson said he was going to stay with a friend that night, but he didn't make it. Instead, shortly after midnight, he locked himself in the cab of his new pickup truck and shot himself in the mouth with the same .22-caliber pistol that he had put in his mouth five months earlier. The Army never confiscated it. The following day, his new wife, an investment banker, purchased a handgun from a local sporting goods store. She put on Andersson's fatigue jacket and dog tags, pointed the loaded gun at her head, and pulled the trigger. It was one day after her husband had shot himself, and two days after their wedding.

A Broken Contract

Nick Rodriguez didn't need to be recruited. He came from a long line of soldiers going back generations, all the way to the Civil War. At age twenty-one, he joined the Marines, feeling that by enlisting he was honoring both his family and his country. In 2010, after completing basic training in San Diego—3,000 miles from his home in Pennsylvania—Rodriguez deployed to Afghanistan. To the relief of his mother and stepfather, he wasn't exposed to any combat, at least at first. Instead, he told them that it was boring, that his unit wasn't doing anything. Afterward, his calls came less frequently, and he was more guarded when he talked, while his parents were reluctant to ask him questions about his experiences. Their only concern was that he return unharmed, and in 2011 when he came back to Camp Pendleton they were grateful.

Then they started seeing cracks. He was "jumpy," "on guard," had headaches, and couldn't sleep. He started drinking a lot and bought a gun. At a New Year's Eve party, he hit the ground when the first firework went off. Visiting his parents, he happened to be outside early one morning when someone drove by and threw an object at their house. Rodriguez sprinted after the vehicle and leaped on the hood. The woman inside was terrified—she was just delivering morning newspapers.[56]

Two months later, Rodriguez was dead. When his parents were notified—two Marines in uniform knocked on their door—they were told that Rodriguez was found in a bathroom on the base at Camp Pendleton, San Diego, with a gunshot wound in his chest. That is all the Marines said. Later, Rodriguez's parents learned that he had killed himself with the .357 Magnum that he had purchased. They also learned from other military personnel the details of one particularly traumatic incident. Rodriguez was on patrol when he encountered a twelve-year-old Afghan boy with an AK-47 assault rifle. In the same instant that he thought about his young nephews and nieces at home, he thought about the safety of himself and other members of his unit. Instinctively, he fired his own weapon, ending the threat—and also the boy's life.[57]

When Rodriguez came back from Afghanistan, he didn't seek help. His parents didn't know anything about PTSD or moral injuries so they couldn't connect the dots. Only in retrospect did they see the red flags leading to his death. Meanwhile, the Marine Corps investigated Rodriguez's case and reached a conclusion that absolved the military of any blame. According to the report, Rodriguez "received an adequate amount of suicide-awareness training not only from his chain of command, but through the battalion chaplain's warrior transitioning training both in Afghanistan and upon his return to the United States."[58]

Rodriguez's mother wrote the funeral notice for her twenty-four-year-old son. The published piece said he "died peacefully," but she didn't write that. Probably, she thinks, the funeral home added it, a fact that bothered her later. "Everybody who knows how Nick died," she said, "knows it wasn't peacefully."[59]

As a nation, we make a social contract with our troops. They surrender some of their freedoms, including the right to make individual decisions and be in charge of their own destinies. They submit to the authority of the military, as it is communicated to them by their commanders, in order to protect and defend the rights of all Americans. In return, they receive training, equipment, health care, subsidized housing, educational opportunities, and shopping privileges that many people in this country don't have. When they leave the military they still have access to these benefits, as well as others—financial assistance, employment counseling, peer support, vacation clubs, family services, life insurance, a military pension, and special cemeteries. It may seem like a fair deal; certainly those who enlist seem to think so.

The benefits are only part of the reason that people join, however. A major incentive is that they believe military service is honorable. They believe what the country's leaders tell them about the necessity of preparing for and engaging in war. They believe that fighting for the rights of all Americans is the highest calling one can have.

Military service, by its very nature, epitomizes nationalism. A country's culture and interests are exalted over the culture and interests of other nations, with troops defending them to their deaths. Uniforms are worn with pride, and ribbons, badges, and patches are added to note distinction, commitment, and heroism.

Yet this defense has a price, and it's paid not only on the battlefield but at home, and not just in the immediate aftermath of war but in the decades that follow. This price consists of psychiatric and physical casualties. Sometimes these casualties—particularly psychiatric ones—end in suicide. When this happens, they represent a broken contract. Soldiers, sailors, airmen, and Marines have honored their side of it, abdicating basic rights to the authority of the government in order to serve the nation. The nation hasn't held up its side of the deal, however.

"Every person that I served with wanted to contribute to our country," says Iraq veteran Kevin Powers. Each one "felt that it was something that they could do on behalf of fellow citizens."[60]

Alan McLean certainly felt that way, and he paid for it dearly. A second lieutenant in the Marines in Vietnam, he received a Purple Heart and Bronze Star after a land mine blew off his legs. After the war, he became the rector at an Episcopal church in Wenatchee, Washington, a small farming community. McLean was an early supporter of the war in Iraq and Afghanistan, and his sermons, says Ilona Meagher in *Moving a Nation to Care*, expressed the need for people "to have faith in the government's mission."[61] As the war progressed, however, McLean's own faith wavered. He experienced more flashbacks of his time in combat, and new nightmares and panic attacks.

With war casualties climbing, and the American public seemingly oblivious to the toll, he delivered a new sermon in opposition to the war. He also wrote a letter to his family apologizing for what he was about to do. On February 11, 2005, he shot himself in his office at the church.

"I underestimated the power of the war to take his life," his daughter said later. "Though my dad's been in Wenatchee, the war in Iraq killed him."[62]

As a nine-year-old boy, Ken Dennis insisted that his family fly the American flag when the first Gulf War began. Thirteen years later, Dennis was a corporal in the Marines, among the first to arrive in Iraq in 2003 following previous assignments in Pakistan, Somalia, Djibouti, and Afghanistan. He was a rifleman who was trained in special operations and antiterrorist activities. Returning home, he told his father, "You know, Dad, it's really very hard—very, very hard—to see a man's face and kill him."

Dennis rented an apartment in a quiet neighborhood in Renton, Washington. Eight months removed from a combat zone, he was found by a friend, dead in the bathtub. He was twenty-three. His suicide, like all suicides of young men and women, cut short a life of promise and transferred his pain to those who loved him.

"Everybody Deals with War Differently"

Today, in America's all-volunteer military, the sense of nationalism among current troops remains strong—at least at the outset. New recruits, like Phillip Kent, whose story led off this chapter, are motivated by 9/11 and subsequent terrorist attacks. They feel compelled to uphold the ideals of the country the same way that troops did during the Civil War, World War I, and World War II. This makes their subsequent deaths by suicide all the more tragic.

When young people go off to war, they don't expect to be changed. They expect to return home more or less the same person who left— more disciplined perhaps, more mature, physically tougher and with new skills, but otherwise no different. Yet it's the rare person who comes home unaffected. The horrors that troops witness and participate in can't be easily forgotten. The act of killing people and seeing others killed is so outside the norm of civilian life that it's incomprehensible to those who aren't part of it. Returning soldiers don't want to talk about these horrors for multiple reasons: They don't want to relive them, they don't want to expose their actions to negative judgments, and they don't want to admit any psychological weaknesses because that isn't what soldiers do. At the same time, they can't escape them. Untreated, the effects of a service member's post-traumatic stress—depression, flashbacks, nightmares, irritability, alcoholism, and drug use—can lead to self-destruction.

No study has proven this, but the risk of suicide may be greatest for those whose sense of nationalism is strongest. These troops are the ones who often end up most disillusioned, who experience the greatest disparity between their ideals at the time that they enlisted and their subsequent military service. This isn't to suggest that having a lower regard for one's country serves as a buffer against psychological trauma or suicide. Rather, when you believe strongly in something and have that belief shattered, the psychological impact tends to be magnified.

One can argue that in previous wars, when the United States conscripted troops, draftees didn't feel the same way as those who enlisted voluntarily. Draftees didn't want to fight and weren't enticed into military service by the potential benefits. Instead, there were two reasons that they joined. Either they were shamed into it by feelings of manhood and fears of being labeled a coward (as in the cases of the Civil War and world wars) or they couldn't avoid it; it was either enlist, flee the country, or go to jail (which was the case with Vietnam). Except for Vietnam, however, which has its own unique set of circumstances, draftees haven't had a low opinion of the military or of the war in which the country was engaged. Quite the opposite. Soldiers were respected and held in high regard, and the causes for which they were fighting were revered and widely supported.

When Patrick Gibbs, Jr., of Davenport, Iowa, enlisted in the Army in the fall of 2005, he was seventeen. He hadn't graduated from high school, being a class cut-up who was expelled—"politely," according to his father, a former police officer and one-time mayor of the city.[63] Gibbs passed the high school equivalency exam, then completed basic training in Georgia. Afterward, he was assigned to an infantry unit at Fort Lewis in Washington. Four months later, he was in a sniper school in Germany and also had gotten married. It was a lot of change for anyone, especially a teenager. The changes continued when he became a father, then when he deployed to Iraq in June 2007.

At that point his young marriage began to fall apart, and he started experiencing battle as an Army sniper, which is different from the way that other soldiers engage in combat. While most soldiers let loose a hail of bullets that quickly becomes part of a larger firefight, indistinguishable from the whole, a sniper peers through a scope at a single target, pulls the trigger, and watches the target fall. If the target happens to be a woman or young child who may be strapped with explosives or clutching a grenade, the psychological impact of killing the person is increased exponentially.

For Gibbs, the war took a personal turn when his closest friend and mentor, a twenty-nine-year-old Iowa native and Army Ranger who was serving his fifth deployment, was killed. The man led a six-person team into a building in Sinsil, Iraq, that was suspected of being a safe house for insurgents. The building was booby-trapped, and all six soldiers died in the explosion.

After nineteen months in a war zone, diagnosed with PTSD, and going through a divorce, Gibbs tried to kill himself by overdosing on medication. He was sent to Landstuhl to receive psychiatric care. While he was in Germany he met a twenty-one-year-old medic named Savannah Huelsman, who was in the Ohio National Guard. They developed a relationship that continued after Gibbs was discharged. They got engaged, lived together in Mason, Ohio, and had a son. Still, Gibbs was on edge all the time, unable to sleep. At one point, Mason police found him walking city streets late at night calling out the names of former comrades in Iraq who had been killed.[64] A subsequent suicide attempt, the result of swallowing a full bottle of pills, resulted in Gibbs receiving a new prescription for antidepressants, as if the solution to his problems lay in additional medication.

In January 2010, Gibbs and Huelsman, along with their infant son, visited Gibbs's parents. While others were watching TV or slept, Gibbs hanged himself with an extension cord in the basement. He was twenty-two. Like most suicides, his death left those who loved him asking questions that wouldn't be answered. Chief among the latter was why the Army didn't do more before and after Gibbs was discharged. Even if he never sought help—a common occurrence given the military's warrior mentality—his case should have been followed up after he was released from the hospital. Whether, in fact, he did seek help isn't known to his family, mainly because military spokespersons cite confidentiality laws in refusing to disclose information specific to an individual. What is known is that Gibbs fell through the cracks, which, when it comes to military suicides, are more like large fissures.

After his death, Huelsman remained in the Reserves and, in fact, was redeployed to Afghanistan in 2011. When a reporter asked her before she left if she had any reservations, she paused.

"I do," she said. "I understand that everybody deals with war differently," then her voice trailed off. She was lonely, confused, and trying to understand why Gibbs killed himself when they were in the process of starting a new life together. Then she collected herself and said, "This is what I signed up for. I think everybody who is willing and able should serve their country."[65]

Clay Hunt believed it, too. He enlisted in the Marines in 2005, and like Patrick Gibbs, Jr., he ended up training as a sniper. Hunt's life changed forever, he told *60 Minutes* correspondent Byron Pitts, in 2007, a month into his first tour in Iraq.[66] That was when his bunkmate was killed by an IED. Three weeks later, another close friend died in an ambush. Shortly thereafter a sniper's bullet struck him in the wrist, and he was evacuated to Germany, then California.

Being separated from his unit was demoralizing, and Hunt committed himself to healing quickly and rejoining them. The following year, he deployed to Afghanistan where two other good friends were killed. By this time, Hunt was questioning the war's purpose. In addition, he was dealing with survivor's guilt, PTSD, and the breakup of his marriage. Still, he didn't seem like a candidate for suicide. On one arm he had tattooed a quote from J. R. R. Tolkien's *Lord of the Rings*: "Not all those who wander are lost."[67] He didn't hide the fact that he needed help, and even appeared in one of the military's public service campaigns aimed at preventing suicides.

After he was discharged in 2009, Hunt felt a sense of purpose by volunteering with several nonprofit causes, including one comprised of veterans who helped earthquake victims in Haiti and Chile. In his last few months, he moved back to Houston, took medication for his PTSD, got a job with a construction company, rented an apartment, began dating, and thought about reenlisting. By all accounts he was focused on the future. Unfortunately, he couldn't forget the past.

He confessed to his parents that he had thought more than once about killing himself, but would never do it for a simple reason.

"I love you guys too much, and I just don't want you to have to go through that."[68]

Nevertheless, he continued to be tormented, believing that he should have died in Iraq with his buddies. On March 31, 2011, a Thursday, Hunt didn't show up for work, nor did he answer his phone. Maintenance workers broke into his apartment and found his dead body. He was twenty-eight and had shot himself.

More than 1,100 people filled the church in Houston for Hunt's memorial service. Jake Wood, a fellow Marine and Hunt's best friend, who organized the relief efforts in Haiti and Chile, gave the eulogy. "He thought the world was supposed to be a better place than it is," said Wood. "He lived every day of his life thinking, perhaps naively, that his efforts could make the world be what he thought it should be."[69]

"Fiddler's Green" wasn't read at the service. It rarely is when a soldier dies by suicide.

Fiddler's Green is the shady green meadow where—mythically—infantry soldiers go after they are killed in battle. It derives from a ballad of the same name, by an anonymous writer, that first appeared in the *U.S. Cavalry Manual* in 1923. In Fiddler's Green "the souls of all dead troopers" are buried "halfway to hell," and a fiddler plays continuously. The ballad is often recited at memorial services for deceased soldiers. It ends by saying that if "hostiles come to get your scalp, just empty your canteen, and put your pistol to your head, and go to Fiddler's Green." The inference at the time, with World War I recently concluded, was that if death was unavoidable, it was better to kill yourself than give the enemy that satisfaction. Today, in the wake of so many suicides by active-duty soldiers and veterans, it takes on a different meaning. Today, "the hostiles who come to get your scalp" may be inner demons, with the act of suicide a way to quiet them and end one's pain. That's not the kind of death that lends itself favorably to myth, however. Moreover, the words, if they were recited, would provide more pain than comfort to family members whose loved one died by suicide. Until someone comes up with a new version of "Fiddler's Green," one that respectfully acknowledges the dark recesses of the mind and the travels of a troubled soul, silence is preferable.

The Challenges Coming Home

"He really left us a long time ago."

T RAVIS TWIGGS WAS A HIGHLY TRAINED AND DECORATED MARINE. He enlisted in 1993 and deployed five times—four times in Iraq and once in Afghanistan. Nicknamed "Tebeaux" as a boy ("handsome little man" in Cajun—Twiggs was from New Orleans), he was a weapons expert, martial arts instructor, and "one of the best combat trackers alive,"[1] according to Mike Tucker, a former Marine who went on patrol with Twiggs and wrote about him in a book titled *Ronin*. Tracking was a skill that Twiggs acquired in his youth, according to his wife, who had known him since childhood.

"When we played hide and seek, you had to be on Tebeaux's team or you'd get the bejeezus scared out of you,"[2] Kellee Twiggs told William Finnegan, a writer for the *New Yorker* whose lengthy article about Twiggs appeared in September 2008.

In 2006, after Twiggs returned home following his third tour of duty in Iraq, he was transferred to the Marine Corps Warfighting Laboratory at Quantico, Virginia. It wasn't his choice, but commanders believed that his extensive combat experience would be helpful in assessing new weapons. Far away from the war and his platoon, however, Twiggs started going into a tailspin. Without the distraction and adrenaline rush of battle, he began drinking. He also thought obsessively about Iraq. In particular, he grieved the loss of two corporals in his platoon. Aged twenty-three and twenty-five, they officially died "from an indirect fire explosion." In reality, they were going to the bathroom when a mortar blew up their latrine. Twiggs was the first person on the scene, but there was nothing he could do. One man succumbed as soon as Twiggs arrived, and the other man died later that night, in a hospital. Twiggs had personally trained both Marines and felt responsible for their deaths.

In January 2008, Twiggs caused a minor brouhaha when he wrote about dealing with posttraumatic stress in an article that appeared in the *Marine Corps Gazette*. Titled "PTSD: The War Within," the article acknowledged the emotional problems Twiggs had developed, while emphasizing his ability to recover from them. Returning home after each tour of duty, he found the readjustment more and more difficult, he wrote. Despite loving his wife (her name was tattooed in multiple places on his body) and their two young daughters, he was irritable, "paranoid for no reason," he said, and couldn't sleep. He spent hours in front of an upstairs window, peering out, looking for insurgents. Whenever he heard a car driving up the gravel road to his house, the crunching sound of tires approximated the sound of machine-gun fire, and he would throw himself on the floor. He stashed loaded guns everywhere, including between the mattress and box springs of his bed. He also kept thinking about the two Marines who died.

"I cannot describe what a leader feels when he does not bring everyone home," he wrote. "To make matters worse, I arrived at the welcome home site to find that these two Marines' families were waiting to greet me as well. I remember thinking, 'Why are they here?' From then on my life began to spiral downward."[3]

When he arrived back in the United States after his third tour of duty in Iraq, Twiggs was taken to Bethesda Naval Hospital "for detoxification and to stabilize my vitals." While he was there, he was anything but a model patient. "I was experiencing psychosis where I would fight my way through the hallways and clear rooms as if I were back in theater," he said. "The hospital police would have to be called in to secure me."[4] After a two-week stay, he was released and prescribed twelve different daily medications. He also got into three automobile accidents.

The medications—fourteen to nineteen pills per day—had a negative effect. "I was experiencing visual and audible hallucinations that I firmly believe were a direct result of being overmedicated," Twiggs said. "I slept covered in sweat every night and constantly shook uncontrollably."[5]

His recovery consisted of therapy, reduced medication, and a new deployment. "I was going back to the fight," he wrote, "back to shared adversity, where the tempo is high and adrenaline pulses through our veins like hot blood." He confessed that his PTSD wasn't gone entirely, but "life with my family is wonderful again," and, with his wife's blessing (she was reluctant but knew she couldn't talk him out of it), he was returning to Iraq.[6]

After the *Marine Corps Gazette* article appeared, Twiggs became a poster child for conquering PTSD. He even met the president, George W. Bush, at the White House. Rather than shake Bush's hand, Twiggs gave him a bear hug and said, "Sir, I've served over there many times, and I would serve for you anytime." Bush, in turn, had his photo taken with Twiggs and signed it, "To the Family of Staff Sergeant Travis Twiggs, USMC, with respect and appreciation."[7]

Three weeks later, however, in May 2008, Twiggs went absent without leave and tried to drive his Toyota sedan over the edge of the Grand Canyon. His older brother, who idolized him, was in the passenger seat. The car got caught on a small fir tree just below the rim, 5,000 feet above the canyon floor. The two brothers left it hanging there, donned backpacks, and set out on foot. A National Park Service ranger made a wanted poster using the photo of Twiggs and Bush. He noted that it was the first time in making a poster that he had had to crop out a president.

Twiggs and his brother stole a tourist's Dodge Caliber hatchback at gunpoint, then dropped in unannounced on an uncle in Texas. The uncle urged them to turn themselves in at Fort Hood—just up the road. As a war hero, Twiggs would be treated leniently. Twiggs said they would, but they didn't. Instead, they headed east, where they encountered a routine Border Patrol inspection. Officers motioned Travis to pull over, but he had other ideas. He gunned the engine and led police on a one-hundred-mile-per-hour chase across the Sonoran Desert.

"Did Travis believe that he was back in Iraq?" Finnegan wrote. "He might have. The whapping of chopper blades, the hostile vehicles, the heat of the chase—the adrenaline rush had to be familiar."[8]

When the stolen car's tires blew out, the chase was over, but Twiggs had one more play. Police approached cautiously because Travis had waved a gun out the window. Warriors don't like to be captured, though. Before officers reached the car they heard shots, then silence. Travis, age thirty-six, had killed his brother, then himself.

Months later, Kellee Twiggs told Finnegan that she still couldn't understand it. "Tebeaux would never hurt anybody," she said. "I just don't get that. I'm having a real hard time with it. I can't believe he would leave me, can't believe he would leave us, leave our girls." She paused, then said, "But he really left us a long time ago. He tried to come back. But he couldn't. That was not my husband out there."[9]

After the Civil War, tens of thousands of families mourned the dead, tended to the wounded, and tried to find reasons to go on despite historic casualties. Meanwhile, "Broken soldiers returned home burdened with combat stress," says historian Diane Miller Sommerville, "as well as the herculean task of rebuilding themselves, their families, and the region."[10]

One Ohio soldier, William H. Younts, arrived in his hometown while a church service was going on. When people noticed him, the service ended immediately, and there was a rush to greet him. Within seconds, though, he found that his mind had wandered and all could he think about were those who weren't returning. He wrote in his memoirs that he became preoccupied with "some comrade who, unlike me, was not permitted to return home to his family, but his body lay moldering in some cemetery in the south, or his bones lay bleaching on some battlefield, far from home and friends."[11]

On top of the horrors witnessed, the grieving and the loss, there were new economic and social realities to contend with, especially in the South. Many Confederate soldiers returned from the war to find their homes destroyed, their farms ruined, and their slaves emancipated. They faced enormous debts with no prospects for relief. Federal pensions weren't available to them because they had fought against the Union, and they had to rely on state entitlements programs, which were smaller and provided more modest benefits.

Those in the North had it somewhat easier. Federal pensions for disabled veterans had been approved following the American Revolution, and they were expanded one hundred years later, after the Civil War, to include all Union veterans and their dependents. At the same time, it was almost impossible for Union soldiers who suffered from psychological trauma to receive financial support. Unless they could prove the existence of their condition to the government's satisfaction, which was unlikely given the absence of clinical diagnoses at that time, they didn't have a case. Additionally, no one was lobbying on their behalf, and they had no political power. Even though one-third of the federal budget in 1891 went to military pensions, and more money eventually was paid out in pensions than the $8 billion that was spent on the war itself,[12] no consideration was given to those who risked their lives and suffered psychologically as a result.

"Those who had been psychically damaged," says Penny Coleman in *Flashback*, "whose wounds did not show, who were least able to advocate for themselves, were afforded the least support and compassion."[13]

It wouldn't be any different in subsequent wars. Whether it was World War I, World War II, the Korean War, Vietnam, or the first Gulf War, returning soldiers who carried within them the invisible wounds of battle were, for the most part, ignored. Either the country was too busy celebrating the victories, or too eager to look past the losses, or too absorbed in individual matters to pay much attention to the psychological consequences of those who did the fighting. All anyone cared about was that the war was over.

Although the Civil War produced the most American casualties of any war in U.S. history, and World War I was, for the brief period of two decades, the deadliest global conflict ever, neither came close to matching World War II in terms of human destructiveness. United States causalities were high—300,000 killed and 700,000 wounded—but that was nowhere near as high as the 7.5 million Russian soldiers who were killed, or the 3.5 German soldiers, 2.2 million Chinese soldiers, or 1.2 million Japanese soldiers. Every country that participated in the war was worse off at the end than at the beginning—except for the United States. Unlike Germany, Italy, and Japan, which had surrendered; France, which had been conquered; England, which had been heavily damaged; and Russia, which in addition to soldier deaths had suffered massive civilian casualties (an estimated 22 million), the United States was more powerful than ever. In many respects, this country emerged from the war as the world's top superpower. Our armies had proven to be the strongest, repelling fascist forces and ensuring democracy. Our technology was the most advanced, as demonstrated by the development and deployment of nuclear weapons. Our economy was robust, with the G.I. Bill affording new opportunities and new benefits in education and housing for veterans, as well as new prosperity for the country overall.

All was not rosy, however. In the months following the armistice, there were ugly remnants of the war to deal with, starting with the horror that was revealed when U.S. troops went into Nazi concentration camps and found that more than six million Jews had been gassed or shot, along with millions of Slavs and Eastern Europeans. Then there was the national debate over whether President Harry S Truman was justified in ordering nuclear bombings of Hiroshima and Nagasaki to expedite the end of hostilities (a debate that continues today). There also was the shame of interring thousands of Japanese American citizens due to the belief that they would aid the enemy (a smaller number of Germans and Italians living here were ostracized as well). Finally, there was a growing fear of communism that resulted in the witch-hunt hearings of Wisconsin senator Joseph McCarthy, who initially alleged that there were communists in the U.S. government, then expanded the scope to include other sectors of American society. In 1951, at the height of the hysteria, Julius and Ethel Rosenberg, American citizens, were accused of passing atomic secrets to the Soviet Union and sentenced to death. Following their execution in 1953, new information and testimony came to light indicating that any secrets they may have provided had little or no value, adding further to the country's collective sense of guilt.

Still, it was a time of peace, and for that everyone was grateful. Well, almost everyone. There were those families whose loved ones didn't make it home, who ended up buried close to where they fell, in distant cemeteries. There were the thousands of soldiers, too, who returned in tatters, missing limbs or suffering other serious and permanent physical injuries. Finally, there were the troops—tens of thousands of them—who came back emotionally and mentally scarred. As with the men who were physically damaged, the war would leave them changed and—in many cases—unable to recapture the sense of normalcy that existed before they went off to fight. It was a new world, and although many rejoiced because of it, behind the doors of many homes were the dark secrets that families kept hidden about the lasting despair of their one-time war hero.

At least they were considered heroes. That wouldn't be the case in Vietnam.

Marking off the Days

The point system that Albert Glass developed in the Korean War to measure the frequency, duration, and intensity of a service member's exposure to trauma was dusted off and employed in Vietnam, but with a twist. Soldiers, sailors, and airmen were told before they even deployed that they would be returning home in twelve months, Marines in thirteen months. The date of expected return from overseas, or DEROS as the policy came to be called, was intended to relieve much of the anxiety of troops who were deployed by giving them a fixed date that they and their families could count on as the extent of their service commitment. It didn't matter where the person was when the date was reached, or what his unit was doing. After twelve months, his tour of duty was over. In this way, military leaders believed that they could limit the psychological damage caused by fighting in a war. Unfortunately, the policy had the opposite effect.

With DEROS, soldiers came to be self-focused, and all of the benefits that accrued from being part of a unit—before and after the war—disappeared. Serving in Vietnam became a matter of biding one's time, holding on as best one could until the magic day arrived. Troops were separated after basic training and shipped to different locations. When a soldier arrived in his new unit, he was an unknown quantity. Other soldiers distrusted him because his lack of experience threatened the survival of the group. This ended up isolating new recruits and making them feel alone. Then, after a recruit settled in, he began ticking off the days until his time was up. The closer he got to his departure date, the more likely he was to avoid new transfers in order to ensure that he made it home alive.

In *The Things They Cannot Say*, war photographer and journalist Kevin Sites describes the practice of one infantryman in Vietnam. Army Specialist Joe Caley drew an outline of Ohio, his home state, on the liner inside his helmet. Then he divided it into 365 squares. After each passing day, he marked an "X" in one of the squares until his one-year tour of duty was finished and he could return home.[14]

The result was that there was no bonding with other members of one's unit, and no opportunity or real reason to develop trust.

A person served his time, then came home, in many instances not even bothering to say goodbye to those he served with. Why should he? In all likelihood he would never see them again. There is a reason that Vietnam veterans, unlike veterans of other wars, rarely have reunions. They weren't close to anyone.

The same reason contributed, at least in part, to a high desertion rate. Roughly 25 percent of soldiers in Vietnam went AWOL (absent without leave) for a week or more.[15] They had much less allegiance to members of their unit than soldiers before them. Moreover, they had less reason to stay, given the inherent dysfunction of the unit, their growing resentment of military officers who were inexperienced and assigned to new commands willy-nilly, and increasing concerns over the reasons they were fighting in the first place.

African-American soldiers in particular were struck by the position they were in. Not only were they dying at a higher rate than soldiers of other ethnicities—in the early years of the war, blacks comprised 10 percent of U.S. troops and suffered 20 percent of the casualties[16]—but they were supposed to risk their lives to preserve the freedom of people in another country when they themselves were denied basic rights at home. As boxer Muhammad Ali said in 1967 after he refused to be inducted, "They want me to go to Vietnam to shoot some black folks that never lynched me, never called me nigger, never assassinated my leaders."[17]

Twelve months later, it would be Dr. Martin Luther King, Jr. who was assassinated (by a white man, James Earl Ray, who had never been convicted of a violent crime before, wasn't considered smart enough to have planned the shooting on his own, and didn't espouse a hatred of blacks but, like Lee Harvey Oswald, is considered by most historians to have been the lone assassin). Before then, though, King's public comments about the war echoed those of Ali. For King, the country was "taking the young black men who had been crippled by our society and sending them 8,000 miles away to guarantee liberties in Southeast Asia which they had not found in Southwest Georgia and East Harlem." The result, King said, was that "we have been repeatedly faced with the cruel irony of watching Negro boys and white boys on TV screens as they kill and die together for a nation that has been unable to seat them together in the same schools."[18]

The one thing that soldiers of all races shared was that they not only arrived in Vietnam alone, but if they survived they often left the country alone. Pulled out of their unit after exactly one year, leaving other soldiers to carry on without them, they boarded an airplane—sometimes a commercial flight—that was filled with strangers. There they sat silently, eyes staring ahead, numbed by the quick transition from the battlefield to the home front. Around them, oblivious to the war and what it meant, people laughed and chatted light-heartedly about vacations they were taking, business trips they were on, the latest celebrity mishaps, new electronic gadgets, fashion trends, sporting events, TV shows, movies, and other topics that seemed surreal to troops who had been ducking bullets every day. Whereas it usually took weeks for World War II soldiers to come home because they traveled on troop ships with other soldiers and crossed oceans, a soldier in Vietnam was home within twenty-four hours. He had no time to decompress, to begin processing his war experiences before seeing loved ones, much less anyone to talk to who would understand, be sympathetic, and not judge. In what seemed like the blink of an eye, he went from a hot, muggy environment that was filled with loud noises, intense drama, and constant danger to the temperature-controlled cabin of an airplane, the calm, unhurried conversations of those around him, and the comfort of an upholstered seat. By the time the war ended, the United States had dropped seven million tons of bombs on Vietnam—more than were dropped on Europe and Asia by all sides combined in World War II.[19] Soldiers were expected to adjust naturally from a world of napalm and body counts to the domestic tranquility of civilian life.

When they arrived home, there were no crowds to greet them, no media flashbulbs going off, and no parades. There also were no debriefings, few instructions, and a scarcity of services. In the whole country, only two VA hospitals were equipped to deal with psychiatric casualties of the war.[20] Patients who sought help, if they were lucky enough to be seen, were much more likely to be prescribed medications than counseled. In addition, soldiers who were discharged without any record of mental or physical disabilities weren't eligible to be treated at VA hospitals prior to 1980. That was the year that posttraumatic stress was included for the first time in the American Psychiatric Association's *Diagnostic and Statistical Manual of Mental Disorders*. In addition, if a veteran developed symptoms more than a year after being discharged, his condition was considered unrelated to the war,[21] which proved convenient for the military as well as cost effective. Fewer than 1 percent of American soldiers were considered psychiatric casualties while they were in Vietnam, a far smaller number than the 43 percent from World War II.[22] The low rate was attributed to having psychiatrists in the field (though never more than twenty),[23] as well as making aggressive use of anti-anxiety drugs and tranquilizers. What wasn't acknowledged was the rampant use of illegal drugs—primarily marijuana and heroin, which troops could procure easily and cheaply—which led to a whole new array of problems that would play out decades later.

Many of these problems weren't dealt with by mental health professionals in hospitals or clinics; rather, they were dealt with by judges and juries in courtrooms after criminal charges had been filed. According to the *National Vietnam Veterans Readjustment Study*, by 1988 roughly 480,000 veterans had some form of PTSD, although only 55,000 (under 12 percent) had filed a claim.[24] One-quarter of the male Vietnam veterans with PTSD had engaged in thirteen or more violent acts in the previous year, compared with 3.5 violent acts for Vietnam vets who didn't have PTSD. Among the former, half had been arrested or jailed at least once, 84,000 had been arrested multiple times, and 26,000 had been convicted of a felony.[25] Of the 71,000 inmates in federal prisons at the time, 10,000 were veterans—14 percent, even though vets comprised a smaller percentage of the population. Moreover, that number didn't include the thousands of veterans who were currently behind bars in state prisons. Sixteen years later, that number would be 127,500.[26]

Inasmuch as military training and combat foster violent, aggressive acts, and the more aggression a soldier displays in military performance the more he or she is rewarded,[27] it's not surprising that problems ensue when troops return home. According to two University of Virginia professors, writing in the *Indiana Law Journal* about crimes of veterans returning from Iraq and Afghanistan, "Soldiers are conditioned to survive harsh, threatening, and violent environments. They are taught to attack an enemy target dispassionately, quickly, and without hesitation."[28] Says Barry L. Levin in "Defense of the Vietnam Veteran with Post-Traumatic Stress Disorder," soldiers learn to suppress normal instincts such as fleeing from a threat because that undermines the effective functioning of a military unit.[29] Instead, they confront it immediately and aggressively in order to protect themselves and others in their unit.

This kind of behavior, necessary in combat, rarely has a place side the battlefield, however. Yet it can't be turned off easily. When one is preoccupied solely with completing a mission, on accomplishing military objectives without regard for the human suffering that might result, adjusting to civilian life isn't easy. Not only does stateside domesticity lack the same concrete and focused objectives, but civilians rarely encounter life-threatening situations, and an absence of constant threats can be boring to someone who has grown accustomed to them. That's one of the main reasons that some soldiers who complete a tour of duty re-up for another one—they miss the action-charged moments of combat.

The hyperalertness required of troops in Iraq and Afghanistan, combined with the increased speed of modern warfare, leave soldiers in a constant state of heightened emotion. There is an adrenaline rush all the time that soldiers get used to. Coming home, they can have problems adjusting to the slower tempo of civilian life. A forty-hour work week, governed by the clock, is far different than eighteen-hour days, seven days a week. Many veterans attempt to duplicate the adrenaline rush they experienced in combat by driving fast and taking up hobbies like motorcycle racing. Two years after the first Gulf War, the death rate for returning troops was 9.4 percent higher than for others in the military, and they were 148 percent more likely than civilians to be killed on motorcycles.[30] Ilona Meager reported in *Moving a Nation to Care* that at least 150 Marines died in off-duty accidents in 2006 alone.[31]

BATTLEMIND

John Madden, the former coach and announcer, says that if a man plays in just one National Football League game, his body may never be the same, and if he plays one season, his body definitely will never be the same. The athletes are so big, so strong, and so fast that their violent collisions exact a permanent toll. Fans don't always understand this since, in the comfort of our homes, we aren't privy to the full bone-crushing sound. We see big hits on our TV screens, and sometimes even hear them, but the sound is muted from our being so far away. It isn't anywhere near as loud or as brutal as it is on the field.

In much the same way, if a person has trained for war, his or her mind may never be quite the same, and if the person has engaged in combat, he or she almost certainly isn't the same person mentally after that. This is something that often eludes family members and friends when a soldier returns from combat. Like the collisions in a football game, the impact of war can't be fully sensed by people who are distant from it. Without evidence of physical injuries, it's easy to believe that a person survived largely unscathed. In *Thank You for Your Service*, David Finkel describes the red eyes of a combat veteran staring at himself in a mirror at home and taking inventory. "Two eyes, two ears, two arms, two legs, two hands, two feet. Nothing missing. Symmetrical as ever."[32] Yet the veteran, Adam Schumann, came back from Afghanistan with PTSD and thoughts of killing himself (he is now receiving psychiatric treatment).

At a minimum, many veterans have a higher level of anxiety than non-vets. If someone approaches them unknowingly from behind, they tend to react violently, without thinking. This is as true for Vietnam veterans, who last fought forty years ago, as it is for veterans of wars in Iraq and Afghanistan today. Most vets warn other people of their startle reflex in order to avoid striking someone unintentionally. Best-case, soldiers adjust once they are stateside, usually with the support of family members, and often with the assistance of counseling. Worst-case, they experience a never ending succession of sleepless nights and guilt-ridden days, a nightmare existence that results in marriage problems, alcoholism, prolonged depression, hallucinations, violent outbursts, slurred speech, facial tremors, body shakes, and thoughts of suicide.

"Time spent in a war zone changes people," write Laurie B. Slone and Matthew J. Friedman in *After the War Zone*. "There are many who feel the pain of no longer fitting in, the despair of no longer knowing their loved ones, or the incongruity of not being the same people they used to be."

Being shot at, shooting others, witnessing death and destruction, and surviving harsh living conditions take a toll on many service members. Physically, wartime experiences often lead to sleep problems, upset stomachs, trouble eating, rapid heartbeat, and lack of exercise. Any existing health problems tend to be exacerbated. In addition, abuse of drugs and alcohol, excess smoking, and flashbacks are common. Mentally and emotionally, a person is often angry and irritable, easily upset or annoyed, and unable to feel happy or hopeful. He or she distrusts others, is withdrawn and asocial, and exhibits controlling and overprotective behaviors. In addition, the person may feel rejected because others don't seem to understand what he or she has been through, or believe that exposure to war has changed him or her so much that others naturally are repulsed.

Whereas before the war a person may have been outgoing and fun loving, the life of the party, now he or she is aloof and sullen, ill tempered and difficult to please. No longer eager to have friends over for dinner or go to other peoples' homes, the person doesn't want to see anyone, even family members, preferring instead to spend hours alone playing video games, watching war movies, and consuming alcoholic beverages. (According to the NPD Group, which tracks sales of various products, five of the ten top-selling video games of 2011 had war-related themes, including number one—*Call of Duty: Modern Warfare 3*—which edged out *Madden NFL 12*. Similarly, seven of the twenty most popular computer games in 2011 focused on combat scenarios.) Attempts by others to engage in conversation are met with mumbled words. Attempts to coerce someone out of the house to attend a child's school play or sports activities are met with silent stares. The last thing a returning soldier wants is to be in the company of strangers, especially when they ask about his or her battlefield experiences. There is no way that a veteran can describe them in the context of everyday life at home. The second-to-last thing a soldier wants is to hear people moan about the price of eggs or other items. After months of immersion in a war zone, exposed constantly to destruction and death, soldiers have little patience for complaints that are petty by comparison.

The act of war requires individuals to behave in ways they never would in other circumstances. "Actions that would be criminal in civilian life become acceptable—even required—in military life," says Judge Barry R. Schaller in *Veterans on Trial*. However, "Upon return to civilian life, those actions become criminal again."[33]

Newsweek reporter Tony Dokoupil describes it similarly. He says that U.S. troops today "shuttle between two worlds; ours, where thou shalt not kill is chiseled into everyday life, and another, where thou better kill, be killed, or suffer the shame of not trying."[34]

War challenges a person's beliefs, and if he or she is religious, the result is either a stronger connection to one's chosen faith or breaking that connection. There is a reason that people say "faith is found or lost in a foxhole." A person's spirituality may offer the hope needed to survive the atrocities of war, or it may cause someone to question how a loving God can permit such atrocities to occur. Either way, what one sees and does on a battlefield isn't something he or she is eager to talk about, especially with family members and friends who can't possibly understand the situation. Only fellow soldiers know what war is like. This is why the closest relationships many soldiers have after they come home are with other members of their military unit. High levels of trust and a strong sense of camaraderie develop among individuals who fight side by side, and their shared experiences tend to carry over when the fighting ends to form the only social interactions a soldier is interested in. Talking with war buddies is a way to protect loved ones from knowing about a soldier's actions while protecting soldiers from negative judgments that loved ones might make.

For these and other reasons, war not only changes those who serve, but it also changes those who love them. Spouses and children who wait for soldiers to come home are the ones who not only bear witness to what can be a difficult and painful reintegration process but also share it fully. Many troops who return from a war zone exhibit behavior that is disruptive to families—being on edge, hyperalert, secretive, and overprotective. Outbursts of anger, needed to survive in combat, damage relationships with loved ones and friends when home. Driving aggressively, at high speed, with the expectation that everyone else is supposed to move out of the way and let you pass, likewise is necessary when deployed in a war zone, but a source of problems in civilian life. A constant state of alertness, required on the battlefield, creates stress and tension at home, as does overprotective behavior such as getting a guard dog, putting up security lights, or having weapons in the house. A soldier's need for control and safety can be irritating at best and frightening at worst to other members of his or her family. It doesn't translate well in the structure of most households where there is latitude in following rules and performing tasks. In the military there is no freedom of choice; commands are issued and followed.

Prior to seeing combat, soldiers go through intensive training and preparation. In contrast, there is little or no training or preparation for coming home. Yet rebuilding the intimacy one had with his or her spouse and children takes time and effort. It doesn't happen overnight, as much as everyone might like it to. Instead, there are adjustments for all.

BATTLEMIND is the acronym for a training program that is used by the Army to help soldiers readjust to life at home. Created by a team of people at the Walter Reed Army Institute of Research, led by Colonel Carl Castro, it focuses on the differences between succeeding and surviving in a war zone and reintegrating smoothly once someone is stateside. The more that soldiers and families understand BATTLEMIND, the fewer problems they will experience upon return, or so the thinking goes.

"B" stands for buddies, the only people who truly understand what a soldier experiences, the only people he or she can count on. Once home, soldiers are likely to miss their buddies dearly, and socialize with them whenever possible. This is a normal reaction to being separated from individuals with whom one has bonded deeply, yet it can result in family members feeling excluded if wartime relationships end up supplanting relationships with loved ones.

"A" is for accountability and the notion that in the military every service member is responsible for his or her equipment, gear, weapons, actions, and the well-being of fellow soldiers. Once home, however, problems can develop if someone else touches or interferes with a soldier's belongings, or if a soldier feels that no one else cares enough to see that a job is done right. Moreover, the strict chain of command that is required in the military, which soldiers have been trained to follow, doesn't work in most family settings, resulting in discord.

The first "T" stands for targeted aggression, an integral part of military training. Soldiers learn early on to be forceful and act immediately in situations where one's survival hangs in the balance. When it's a matter of kill or be killed, a soldier can't hesitate. The same behavior at home, however, can result in overreactions to minor incidents, heated arguments, and incidents of domestic violence. Soldiers who are constantly on edge and unable to calm down, who routinely snap at their partners and at their children, increase the stress levels of everyone around them.

The second "T" stands for tactical awareness. Soldiers must be hyperalert every minute, ready to respond instantly to any threat. Such vigilance is what keeps soldiers alive, but it has negative consequences when they come home. Although spouses and children have, out of necessity, assumed greater responsibility and exercised more independence in the absence of a service member, when that person returns, he or she tends to be overprotective. Living in constant fear and being unable to control one's environment can cause someone to want to take extra measures to safeguard those at home. This may mean not allowing children to play outside or wives to leave the house unaccompanied. It also can mean making frequent perimeter checks to ensure that all doors and windows are locked and no one can break in. In addition, a person might feel the need to keep a watchful eye on all rooftops—even in a quiet, residential area—because of the threat of snipers.

"L" is for lethally armed, a virtual requirement in a war zone. Soldiers are trained to consider their weapons as their best friends and to carry them at all times. They break down and reassemble weapons constantly to ensure that they can operate them under any conditions and that their weapons remain fully functional. Once home, a soldier may continue this habit. Moreover, he or she may feel vulnerable without a loaded firearm, and insist on always having one within reach. This creates a dangerous situation, especially when the holder has a short temper and is trained to be aggressive.

"E" stands for emotional control, another essential part of military training. In combat, mental toughness is valued, and soldiers learn to project stoic faces that don't betray any feelings. In particular, hiding one's fears is important because it means showing no weaknesses. The same emotional control on display to family members, however, makes a soldier seem withdrawn, uncaring, and detached. This is especially true for soldiers who were outgoing and talkative before the war and now, upon returning home, are thought to be numb and unwilling to connect with anyone other than service buddies.

"M" stands for mission security, that is, being careful to talk about a mission only with those who need to know. Obviously, there are practical reasons for mission security in the context of war, because leaked information can result in tactical failure and unit deaths. In the context of a family, though, a soldier's unwillingness to talk about things that happened while he or she was deployed can be interpreted by loved ones as secretiveness and a lack of trust. A soldier believes that he or she needs to safeguard information while family members are trying to understand the person's wartime experiences.

"I" is for individual responsibility, including both responsibility for a soldier's things, duties, and life, and responsibility for the lives of others. A consequence of the latter is that virtually every combat unit includes soldiers who are wounded or killed in action. With each wound or fatality survivors have guilty feelings that they failed to protect their buddies. A consequence of the former is that soldiers often think that they should be able to handle their problems themselves. As a result, they are reluctant to seek help or rely on others.

"N" stands for nondefensive driving, which is the type of driving that occurs in Iraq and Afghanistan. To avoid improvised explosive devises, vehicle-born IEDs, and crossfire, soldiers must drive fast and erratically and keep to the center of the road. Drivers of all nonmilitary vehicles not only are expected to yield but also to pull over to the side and stop until soldiers have passed. Such aggressive behavior is essential for the survival of American military personnel in theater, yet it is contrary to the rules governing driving in the United States. It scares passengers and makes family members afraid to be in the car, as well as results in traffic tickets, incidents of road rage, and accidents.

"D" stands for discipline, as integral to military life as training. If soldiers are to work together to accomplish goals and survive in combat, they must follow orders. This is why the military is so hierarchical. Someone gives an order that others at a lower rank are expected to obey without question. Ignoring the order and taking matters into one's own hands can threaten the mission and the group, as well as result in a court martial. At home, however, rigid discipline can be counterproductive. In most families, rules are discussed and decisions are shared—at least among parents, and sometimes among children, too. At a minimum, communication is two-way.

BATTLEMIND is just one program, but the basic concepts are incorporated into all efforts by military branches to ease the adjustment of soldiers and their families following deployment. When service members and their loved ones are aware of the mindset needed by soldiers to engage in combat, and how this mindset runs contrary to civilian life, reintegration becomes smoother. Not smooth, but smoother.

"Death before Dishonor"

Some soldiers, however, never adjust. No matter how hard they try, or how strong their support system is, they can't outrun the demons that haunt them.

Douglas Barber was in the Army Reserves when he deployed to Iraq in 2003 with the Ohio National Guard. He served seven months, primarily as a truck driver carrying supplies between Baghdad Airport and a military base in Balad. The base was large and had been hit so many times by enemy fire that troops referred to it as Mortaritaville. Returning home, Barber seemed sad to his friends. He was diagnosed with PTSD and given medication, but remained depressed.

"All is not okay or right," he wrote, "for those of us who return home alive and supposedly well. What looks like normalcy and readjustment is only an illusion....Some soldiers come home missing limbs and other parts of their bodies. Still others will live with permanent scars from horrific events that no one other than those who served will ever understand."[35]

He also blogged about his difficulty "coping with an everyday routine," having "a short fuse," and the stress of being on guard all the time. He wrote about soldiers being "trained to be killers" and wondering, going to bed at night, if "you will be sent home in a flag-draped coffin because a mortar round went off on your sleeping area."[36]

Early in 2006, Barber changed the message on his answering machine. "If you're looking for Doug," he said, "I'm checking out of this world. I'll see you on the other side."[37]

He then called the police, grabbed his shotgun, and stood on his porch, waiting for officers to arrive. Apparently his intention was to initiate suicide-by-cop, an all-too-common phenomenon in which a suicidal person—invariably male—baits the police into killing him. In this instance, the officers who responded tried to talk Barber down. When it became clear that they weren't going to shoot, Barber turned the gun on himself and pulled the trigger. He was thirty-seven.

Levi Fogg joined the Army Reserve in 2009. When he was four years old, his curiosity got the best of him, and he threw gasoline on a still-smoldering charcoal grill, suffering serious burns to his stomach and one leg. For years afterward, he attended camps in Ohio and Colorado for burn victims, first as a camper, then as a counselor. He planned to become a firefighter, and the Reserves seemed to provide him with the opportunity to learn new skills and also earn money for college. Then reality set in. He learned that he was going to be sent to Afghanistan to fight in a war he didn't believe in. Diagnosed with depression, he received counseling and medication, neither of which improved his spirits. Before deployment, he went AWOL from his unit, bought a gun from a local sporting goods store, and left an unfinished letter. In the letter he said, "I have a hard time living day-to-day life," and that going AWOL meant that the Army would "dishonorably discharge me, forever putting a black mark on my life and future careers."[38]

In the early hours of the morning, before sunrise, Fogg sat alone in the front row of InfoCision Stadium on the University of Akron campus. The stadium was dark; no one else was around. Fogg wore his formal Army Reserve uniform, the jacket and slacks pressed, his shoes shined. The following day was his twenty-third birthday, but he wouldn't live to see it. When crews arrived at around 11 a.m. to prepare the stadium for a football game, they found Fogg's body, shot with the pistol he had bought the day before. On his Facebook page Fogg had written, "Death before Dishonor."[39]

The military called Fogg's mother afterward, but she had only one thing to say. "You killed my son." Then she hung up.[40]

Jeremy Gibson, from Chattanooga, Tennessee, was in the Air Force and among the service members who accompanied President George W. Bush on a trip to Peru and Colin Powell to Paris. He also covered the Republican National Convention and, one Thanksgiving, helped guard the Bush family. Every time he was TDY (Temporary Duty), he brought his wife back a snow globe—a silly gift perhaps, but one that marked his return home.[41]

At Hurlburt Field in Okaloosa County, Florida, the Air Force base where he was stationed, Gibson was an "explosive ordnance disposal technician"—part of a bomb squad responsible for defusing or otherwise rendering safe various kinds of explosive devices. On some missions he didn't wear a bomb suit because the explosives were so powerful that a suit wouldn't make any difference. If the bomb detonated, he would be killed regardless of how much protective clothing he had on.

Despite the dangers inherent in his work, Gibson didn't die from a bomb, or from enemy fire. He died instead by his own hand. In 2010, he dialed 911, then walked into his backyard and shot himself, without displaying any signs of suicide, according to his wife. With his death at age thirty-one Gibson became another casualty of war, although his name isn't on any memorial wall. His widow winces every time she has to say how he died, knowing that some people will sit in judgment.[42]

Base Trouble

Joint Base Lewis-McChord is the largest military base on the West Coast. Located nine miles from Tacoma, Washington, it's a training and mobilization center that grew out of recommendations made by the 2005 Base Realignment and Closure Commission. The commission was tasked with determining which military bases should be closed or merged in an effort to cut costs. Five years later, in February 2010, U.S. Army base Fort Lewis, named after explorer Meriwether Lewis (himself a victim of suicide), and McChord Air Force Base, named in honor of Army Air Corps Colonel William McChord, were joined. According to the official Lewis-McChord Facebook site (yes, even military bases have Facebook sites these days), the base supports 42,000 active service members, 15,000 civilian workers, 56,000 family members who live on and off the base, and 30,000 retired military personnel who live within 50 miles. Altogether, that's more than 140,000 people—equivalent to a mid-sized metropolitan area such as Portland, Las Vegas, Sacramento, or Salt Lake City.

Lewis-McChord has been in the news a lot in recent years, and not in ways that the military prefers. In 2005, the *Seattle Weekly* reported that there had been seven homicides and three suicides in western Washington involving current or veteran Iraq War troops based at Lewis-McChord. Of the three service members who died by suicide, one did so after killing his wife, another after killing his girlfriend. "No one can say if the killing can be directly connected to the psychological effects of war," the paper said. "But most involve a risk factor distinctive to the military—armed men trained to kill—and some killers carry the invisible scars of war."[43]

In 2010, the armed services' publication *Stars and Stripes* called Lewis-McChord "the most troubled base in the military," and it hasn't improved noticeably since then. In 2011, there were twelve soldier suicides at the base, up from nine in 2009 and the same number in 2010. That's only the beginning, though.

In March 2012, a thirty-eight-year-old Army sergeant, Robert Bales, who had been stationed at what is now Lewis-McChord for ten years, was charged with killing sixteen civilians in two Afghan villages, including nine children. The father of two, Bales had served three previous deployments in Iraq, where he suffered head and foot injuries, before being deployed to Afghanistan. He also had been awarded the Army's medal for good conduct three times. In 2013, in a trial at Lewis-McChord, Bales pleaded guilty to all sixteen murders in order to avoid the death penalty. In front of Afghan villagers who traveled nearly 7,000 miles to testify against him, he was sentenced to life in prison without the possibility of parole by a six-member military jury.[44]

Also in March 2012, in Gilroy, California, a twenty-seven-year-old Iraq war veteran, Abel Gutierrez (born Hector Aguilar), shot to death his eleven-year-old sister and fifty-two-year-old mother before turning the gun on himself. An Army specialist who had trained at Lewis-McChord, Gutierrez served in Iraq, then served a second tour with the National Guard in Kuwait. Family members and neighbors described him as quiet and respectful prior to enlistment, and totally changed after returning home. He would sleep with firearms, talk to walls, and spend endless hours watching war movies on his computer. Although the Gutierrez family pleaded for help just two weeks before the murder-suicide, and despite a police recommendation to the local VA office to treat Gutierrez for possible posttraumatic stress disorder, there was no follow up.

Two months earlier, on New Year's Day 2012, a twenty-four-year-old Iraq war veteran, Benjamin Barnes, formerly stationed at Lewis-McChord, shot and killed a Mount Rainer National Park ranger. The night before, Barnes shot four people at a New Year's Eve party in Seattle. He fled to Mount Rainier, where he had camped and fished before. When he was stopped by an unarmed female park ranger, he shot and killed her. A day later, Barnes's dead body was found in a creek, a victim of drowning and hypothermia. Nearby lay a handgun and a rifle.

As the *Los Angeles Times* reported in 2011, "Over the last two years, an Iraq veteran pleaded guilty to assault after being accused of waterboarding his seven-year-old foster son in the bathtub. Another was accused of pouring lighting fluid over his wife and setting her on fire. One [veteran] was charged with torturing his four-year-old daughter for refusing to say her ABCs."[45] All were trained and stationed at Lewis-McChord.

So was a sergeant who killed his wife and hid her body in a storage bin; a soldier who kidnapped two women, shocked one with jumper cables that were attached to a car battery, and sexually assaulted both of them; and a thirty-eight-year-old combat medic named David Stewart who crashed his car after a high-speed chase with police. Stewart shot himself before officers could stop him. In his car was his wife, who also had been shot and killed. His five-year-old son was found dead in his home as well.

Army Specialist Leslie Frederick, Jr., served fifteen months in Iraq. Although his regiment wasn't trained in urban peacekeeping, they did the best they could. They confiscated weapons, repaired roads and sewers, built schools, provided humanitarian relief in the form of food and clothing, and closed down an operation that was printing counterfeit money. Frederick's tour of duty and those of his unit were supposed to end after twelve months, but they were extended another three months. To people on the outside, three months might not seem like much, but extended tours of any length can be devastating for troops and their families. Birthdays and anniversaries are missed, jobs and school are pushed back, and children and spouses are crushed. In Frederick's case, the extension was compounded by two other factors: His marriage was ending and his unit, upon return, was transferred from Fort Polk, Louisiana, to Fort Lewis, Washington.

It was at Fort Lewis that Frederick became one of the first soldiers to receive the new Combat Action Badge. The award recognizes troops who engage the enemy during combat, a distinction that, it seems, many soldiers would earn, although Army Chief of Staff Peter J. Shoomaker, who flew from Washington, D.C., specifically to present the award, said that it "will go down in history as a very, very esteemed representation of the Warrior Ethos, of what being a soldier and a warrior stands for."

A week after the award ceremony, Frederick's divorce became final. Four days later, he shot himself. He was twenty-two.

Lewis-McChord is in U.S. senator Patty Murray's district. The four-term congresswoman chairs the Senate's Committee on Veterans' Affairs, and in 2012 her office began actively investigating problems at the base as well as at military hospitals across the country. In particular, she was concerned that cost considerations were resulting in fewer diagnoses of posttraumatic stress disorder than actually existed. As an example, she cited disclosures at Madigan Army Medical Center on Joint Base Lewis-McChord that more than 40 percent of 690 patients who had been diagnosed with PTSD had those diagnoses reversed by medical screeners. Soldiers who are diagnosed with PTSD are eligible for more financial benefits, so there is a cost incentive to undercount them. Murray voiced her concerns in a Senate Defense Appropriations subcommittee hearing when she questioned Army Surgeon General and Lieutenant General Patricia Horoho. Horoho, herself a former commander at Madigan Medical Center, said that the Army was investigating the issue but used the same diagnostic tool for PTSD as the other military branches.

The problems aren't limited to Lewis-McChord. Nearly every base has problems, the majority stemming from troops who return from deployments with mental health issues that the military lacks the resources to treat.

Army Sergeant Douglas McHale was one of twenty-two suicides at Fort Hood, Texas, in 2010. He had served two combat tours in Iraq, was diagnosed with PTSD and severe depression, and had started to drink heavily. In addition, his marriage was falling apart. After leaving the base without permission and being brought back by police, he tried to kill himself in his barracks. Doctors at Fort Hood told him that they didn't have enough people to treat everyone, so they sent him to a psychiatric hospital 150 miles away. Whatever treatment he received there didn't help. A month later, he sent his mother a text message saying that he was sorry and that he hoped she, the rest of the family, and God would forgive him. Alarmed, his mother drove ninety minutes from her home to Fort Hood, but she arrived too late. According to the police report, her son exited the base, walked into a local restaurant, went into the bathroom, locked the door, and shot himself in the head with a newly purchased gun. He was twenty-six.

Four of the 2010 suicides at Fort Hood occurred within days of each other. All were combat veterans. One—Sergeant Michael Franklin, age thirty-one—murdered his wife before killing himself, leaving their two young children orphans. Another—Armando G. "Mando" Aguilar, Jr., age twenty-six—shot himself at a gas station following a high-speed chase with police officers. In Iraq, a good friend in his unit, Private Eugene Kanakole, shot himself in a latrine.[46] Ironically, the .45-caliber handgun that Aguilar used had been taken from another soldier who was stopped from killing himself.[47]

Although there is no indication that the four knew each other, when suicides are clustered it raises the issue of suicide contagion, which is when one person's death leads to instances of copycat behavior. Sometimes referred to as the Werther effect after the hero of German writer Johann Wolfgang von Goethe's novel *The Sorrows of Young Werther*, who kills himself following a failed romance, whereupon other young men follow suit, it results when people know about a suicide and feel compelled to imitate it. The initial victim may be a celebrity whose death is widely reported, or someone whose suicide is a source of local knowledge. Either way, it results in a succession of other suicides in a school or a community.

Twenty-nine-year-old Sergeant Timothy Rinella, forty-three-year-old Sergeant First Class Eugene Giger, and thirty-nine-year-old Master Sergeant Baldemar Gonzalez also were among those who killed themselves at Fort Hood in 2010. Rinella spent more than half of his eight-year marriage abroad, missing the birth of his son. Giger served three tours in Iraq in six years and was going through a divorce. Gonzalez was taking five separate drugs for PTSD, according to his wife, and killed himself after dropping off their daughter at a high school football game.[48]

As of 2010, about 25 percent of all troops stationed at Fort Hood had been in counseling during the previous year, with 4,000 soldiers in therapy sessions every month. Still, the need was so great that nearly 600 additional soldiers a month were being sent to private clinics in the area.[49]

A Nurse's Advice and a Soldier's Insistence

In 1789, President George Washington said, "The willingness with which our young people are likely to serve in any war, no matter how justified, shall be directly proportional to how they perceive the veterans of earlier wars were treated and appreciated by their nation."[50]

Judging by that standard, the United States is failing. Stories abound of vets who have waited hours at VA facilities without being seen, then leaving in disgust. One of them was Jesse Huff, age twenty-seven, of Dayton, Ohio. An infantryman in Iraq, he was injured in a ground blast that crippled his back and left him depressed. In 2010, when he sought treatment at the VA medical center in Dayton, he waited nearly five hours in the emergency room, in considerable pain. Not knowing how much longer he might have to wait, Huff retrieved his military assault rifle, stood at the entrance to the building in his Army fatigues, and shot himself on the front steps, near the foot of a Civil War statue. Inside the van he drove to get there, police found a bottle of Oxycodone with Huff's name on it (Oxycodone often is prescribed to treat severe pain). After Huff killed himself, bomb squad technicians blew apart the backpack he carried as a precaution in case he planted explosives there.[51] He hadn't.

Don Woodward served in Iraq for five months. It wasn't a long time as far as deployments go, but it was long enough. He killed three Iraqis and saw his own lieutenant killed. When he came home to Pennsylvania, he was sullen, withdrawn, and couldn't sleep. He enrolled in college but dropped out after one semester. He tried to reconcile with his wife but ended up pushing her and others away. When family members suggested that he seek counseling, he resisted. It was only after he set his truck on fire and got inside of it, attempting to kill himself before his wife stopped him, that he scheduled an appointment with the Lebanon VA Medical Center. The appointment was a month away, however. Before he could be counseled, Woodward hiked one of his favorite trails and shot himself. His body was found by a group of students. He was twenty-three.

One of the biggest barriers to treatment is the backlog of unprocessed claims in the VA's fifty-eight regional offices. Disabled vets of all generations and wars are victims of it. At the start of 2013 there were nearly 850,000 unprocessed claims, of which more than 550,000 had been pending more than 125 days. Among those without a pension, waiting for his disability claim to be processed, was the former Navy SEAL credited with killing Osama bin Laden.

According to the VA, the average wait time in 2013 for a veteran to receive disability compensation and other benefits was 273 days. A review of internal VA documents by the nonprofit Center for Investigative Reporting found that it was actually two months longer than that, however, ranging from 316 to 327 days. Moreover, in large cities it was double—642 days in New York, 619 days in Los Angeles, and 618 days in Oakland, which serves northern and central California.[52]

As of 2007, fewer than 10 percent of the 2.7 million disabled veterans in the United States were considered fully disabled by the VA and thus eligible to receive the maximum monthly benefit amount—$2,393, tax free. Nearly half received benefits below $338 per month.[53] They were the lucky ones. Many veterans weren't receiving any benefits at all, despite applying for them.

In 2013, 34 percent of claims applications to the VA were denied, according to Ndidi Mojay in the VA's Office of Public and Inter-governmental Affairs. That number is a little misleading, however. "The fact that a claim is denied does not necessarily mean that the veteran is not receiving benefits," she told me. "Over half of the V.A.'s current claims inventory are claims from veterans already receiving benefits."[54]

In FY2013, the VA provided $53.6 billion in disability compensation to 3.6 million veterans. While that sounds like a lot—and in many respects it is—it works out to an average of $1,500 per claimant per month. In many parts of the country, that amount won't cover a family's rent, much less other expenses. A record 1.17 million claims were filed in 2013, with a high of 129,000 in September.

One reason for the increase is that the VA—to its credit—added exposure to Agent Orange to the list of diseases eligible for benefits, which has resulted in many Vietnam vets filing new claims. The major reason, though, is because of the growing number of veterans. Within the next five years, a million current service members are expected to leave the military, at which time many of them will file claims.

The surging number of claims is only part of the problem, though. Additional challenges derive from the fact that new claims tend to be multifaceted and increasingly complex, requiring more time to assess and make determinations. Whether an illness or injury claimed by a veteran is, in fact, real is only the beginning. Claims workers have to decide if it's the result of a person's military service or is uncon-nected. Was a traumatic brain injury caused by an IED or the result of a concussion from playing high school football? Did a chronic back problem start when a soldier was thrown out of a military Humvee or when the person was in a traffic accident at home? How long is an individual's postwar diagnosis of PTSD relevant—three months, a year, longer?

On top of this, if a claim is approved, workers have to quantify the severity somehow with little or no guidance. Does that brain injury, bad back, or PTSD merit 100 percent disability, 50 percent, or 10 per-cent? The difference can be $1,000 or more in the monthly amount that a veteran receives. Collectively, it adds up to billions for the VA.

Eric Shinseki became U.S. secretary of Veterans Affairs in 2009. A retired four-star general who previously served as Army chief of staff, Shinseki was born on the Hawaiian island of Kauai a year after the Japanese attack on Pearl Harbor. His Japanese grandparents emigrated at the turn of the century from Hiroshima, and because the United States was at war with Japan, Shinseki was classified at birth as an enemy alien. Despite this, and the fact that Japanese Americans had been sent to internment camps during World War II, Shinseki was drawn to military service. He went to West Point, then served two tours in Vietnam. When he retired in 2003 after thirty-eight years in the military, he was the highest-ranking Asian in U.S. military history. An experience he had in Vietnam in 1970, though, defined his life thereafter. He tripped on a land mine, and half his right foot was blown off. Airlifted to an Army evacuation hospital in Da Nang for emergency surgery, he was told by a nurse there that Army doctors would want to amputate his whole foot for various stated reasons. The real reason, though, she said, was that the Army didn't have a prosthetic for half a foot, and it would be easiest to amputate his whole foot. He would have to fight to keep his ankle, she said. Shinseki did fight, angering an Army orthopedic surgeon who, as a colonel, outranked Shinseki, then a captain. In the end, Shinseki got his way, but only because he was insistent and informed. As he told a reporter later, the nurse "gave me choices no one else was willing to give me, and it has made all the difference in how I have been able to live my life."[55]

Since taking charge of the VA, Shinseki was applauded by many people who note that it was his decision to expand eligibility benefits to include Vietnam veterans who were exposed to Agent Orange, even though that meant 250,000 additional cases for the VA to review, make determinations, and provide compensation when warranted. Another 500,000 claims were added when Shinseki approved benefits for combat vets who have been diagnosed with PTSD. And, since March 2013, the VA had—by its account—reduced the waiting list by 34 percent, putting the department on track, Shinseki said, to eliminate the backlog altogether by 2015 with an accuracy rate of 98 percent.[56]

It sounded good, but it was only a start. According to information that the VA provided to me, there were 676,000 claims pending as of February 2014. Of this number, 397,000 had been pending more than 125 days, and the average amount of time to process a claim had declined only slightly, to 265 days. On the plus side, claims accuracy increased to 96 percent for the three months ending in February 2014, according to the VA's Mojay.[57]

Today, the VA has 335,000 employees, making it larger than any governmental department other than Defense. Its budget has increased 40 percent since President Obama took office, to $140 billion.[58] Even so, things continue to move slowly. At the same time that he announced a 34 percent reduction in the backlog of disability claims, Secretary Shinseki told reporters that the VA was easing back temporarily on its use of mandatory overtime—which contributed significantly to the reduction—because workers were burning out.[59]

"Invincibility Is a Curse"

The Travis Twiggs case, which led off this chapter, contains nearly all of the elements described previously in this book. From an early age, Twiggs lived by a code of masculinity that enabled him to excel in war but also have difficulty adjusting to life away from his unit and combat. He was trained to kill, did kill, and witnessed the deaths of others, and in so doing developed a fearlessness of death that is essential to taking one's life. He was diagnosed with PTSD but received treatment that emphasized medication rather than therapy. He took pride in his military service, yet it led him to drink, engage in high-risk behavior, commit criminal acts, and ultimately kill himself after killing his brother. No one attempted to attribute his death to a personal failing, but only because it was hard to find one. His marriage was solid, he loved his two daughters, he didn't have any legal or financial problems, and he had served with distinction in the Marines for fifteen years. Still, he was a casualty of war the same as if he had died by an enemy bullet or bomb.

So was Justin Eldridge. The thirty-one-year-old father of four shot himself October 28, 2013. He was a Marine for eight and a half years and served in a motor transport unit in Afghanistan. In 2008, following depression, dramatic mood swings, and continued suffering resulting from a traumatic brain injury he incurred during the war that, for a long time, wasn't diagnosed, he retired from the military. Unable to work, he was a stay-at-home dad whose wife stayed home, too, because he needed as much care as their children. While he abused alcohol and drugs, and alternately was plagued by insomnia and nightmares, his wife sought help for him from the VA. It took an appeal to their local congressman and the Connecticut state attorney general before Eldridge was seen, however. For a while the treatment he received seemed to make a difference. Then it didn't. In one of his last postings on Facebook, made only twelve hours before he killed himself, Eldridge referred to the challenge of living with severe PTSD. "Invincibility isn't a gift," he wrote. "It's a curse."[60]

It's a curse that Mike Little of Indiana knows well. In 2007, as he was getting ready to deploy to Iraq with the Naval Reserves, Little learned that his childhood mentor, a man who was in the National Guard and had inspired Little to join the military, killed himself. Two years later, before Little deployed to Afghanistan, another friend in the military died by suicide. Then during the year that Little was away, three more military friends killed themselves. Just as he got home near the end of 2010, Little learned that a sixth friend who was in the military had taken his life.

It didn't end there. The seventh casualty was someone everyone on the base turned to for support, a soldier who had been in combat, dealt with stress, and wasn't judgmental. Little told a reporter afterward, "I remember worrying that maybe we were all dumping too much on him, but he was probably the nicest guy I've ever known."[61] The eighth suicide was a high school teacher in Yonkers who was in the Naval Reserve, like Little, and served with him in Afghanistan. The day before she killed herself she posted on Facebook how excited she was to take her two daughters, named Kennedy and Reagan—two presidents who were shot—to cheerleading camp. The next day she was dead at age thirty-eight, survived by her daughters, husband, brother, and grandmother.[62]

Since 2007, Little has battled his own suicidal thoughts, as well as depression and other risk factors. What troubles him most is the prospect of other military suicides. After learning of a ninth suicide, this one not of a service member but of the father of a friend in the Reserves, Little told *Stars and Stripes*, "I've got a buddy who's headed to Afghanistan [now], and I'm worried about how he'll come back, and whether he could be next."[63]

"We refurbish tanks after time in combat," wrote Nicholas D. Kristof in the *New York Times*, "but don't much help men and women exorcise the demons of war. Presidents commit troops to distant battlefields, but don't commit enough dollars to veterans' services afterward. We enlist soldiers to protect us, but when they come home we don't protect them."[64]

It's time for that to change.

The Road to Answers

*"Becomes much excited. Supposes he is in
battle; gives commands."*

N EWELL GLEASON WAS A SUCCESSFUL CIVIL ENGINEER WHEN HE
was commissioned in 1862 at age thirty-eight to lead a Union
regiment. His unit participated in heavy fighting at Chattanooga that
year, as well as a year later at Chickamauga. In the latter battle, nearly
half of his 366 men were killed or wounded. Gleason's commanding
officer said of Chickamauga that Gleason demonstrated "coolness and
great promptness" and that his bravery helped avert what would have
been an even greater defeat.[1] Gleason's men, however, had a different
view. After the battle and the large number of casualties, they said
that he was "nervous and excitable," easily rattled.[2] Nevertheless, he
was promoted to brevet brigadier general and assigned to General
William T. Sherman's Atlanta campaign.

Sherman's march across the South, starting in Mississippi and
ending in Georgia, emphasized total destruction, with everything
of value taken or ruined. When the army left Atlanta, much of the
city was in flames. In Savannah, after bisecting the South, Sherman
remarked to President Abraham Lincoln, "We have devoured the
land.... To realize what war is, one should follow in our tracks."[3]

During his time with Sherman, Gleason's psychological condition grew worse—much worse. When the Union Army reached South Carolina, there was a strong feeling among the troops that Gleason had become deranged. At one point he told his men not to leave a live thing in the state and ordered them to shoot several hogs that had crossed the road in front of them. This may have been in keeping with Sherman's dictum, but it was unlike Gleason's usual line of conduct.[4] At other times Gleason would cry like a child, then soon thereafter laugh loudly for no apparent reason. According to historian Eric T. Dean, Jr., Gleason's health was "shattered by his experience in the army," and he suffered from "complete mental prostration."[5]

When the war ended, a fellow soldier brought Gleason home to Indiana, separate from Gleason's men. The soldier, who was a physician, had to sedate Gleason along the way because Gleason was so agitated.

Once home, Gleason tried to resume his civil engineering practice. He had difficulty concentrating and completing tasks, however. In 1874, following a three-day manic-depressive episode, he was taken to the Indiana State Hospital of the Insane outside Indianapolis. There, staff wrote on his record, "Becomes much excited. Supposes he is in battle; gives commands."[6]

Over time his condition seemed to improve, and he was released, although he continued to be tormented. A doctor who was treating Gleason said that the one-time general was depressed and "filled with dreams that seemed to make sleep exhaustive rather than refreshing."[7] At some point every night, Gleason would wake up and roam about the house, unable to rest.

In July 1886, Gleason and his wife visited another couple. Gleason told the couple that he had no willpower and couldn't make even simple decisions anymore. When he and his wife returned home, Gleason was, if anything, more despondent. His wife stayed up with him most of the night, applying cold compresses to try and soothe him, but they had little effect. At 4 a.m., after dozing off, she awoke with a start to find him missing from their bed. When she went to look for him, he was standing at the top of the stairs leading to their cellar. He shouted for her to leave, then pitched forward, head first. The coroner attributed his suicide to insanity, while a physician concluded that Gleason's condition had been "induced by disorders and hardships incurred in the U.S. Military Service."[8] Neither determination provided much comfort to his widow, whose claim for a pension was rejected.

Gleason's death at age sixty-one occurred twenty-one years after the Civil War ended.

During the Civil War it was common for soldiers who developed psychiatric problems to be given brief rest and sedatives with the expectation that they would return to service shortly thereafter. If their condition didn't improve, it was believed that they were either malingering or insane. The cure for malingering was a return to the front, preceded by the same threat of death and dishonor as for desertion. Regarding insanity, there was no known cure, and people were remanded to asylums where, presumably, they would live the rest of their days.

The same thinking carried over to the start of World War I. Shell-shocked soldiers remained near the front and received what in later wars would be referred to as "three hots and a cot"—several hot meals and a good night's rest. The restorative power of this treatment, it was believed, in combination with positive encouragement from a psychiatrist, was sufficient to boost a soldier's morale and hasten his return to active duty.

Leading up to, during, and following subsequent wars, additional strategies were tried. In World War II, pre-enlistment screening was implemented with minimal success, while Walter Freeman's ice-pick lobotomies after the war were ineffective and grotesque. In the Korean War, there was Albert Glass's point system designed to measure quantitatively a soldier's exposure to trauma and trigger his release from service. In Vietnam there was DEROS, a soldier's date of expected return from overseas. It was intended to improve on Glass's point system but instead had the opposite effect. Unit cohesion was undermined, and soldiers felt isolated, alone, and on the clock, focusing primarily on counting down the days until they could go home.

By the time the first Gulf War started, much had been learned from previous wars about the psychological stress of combat. Even so, little changed. Men and women continued to be trained in conventional tactics, soldiers were neither encouraged nor supported in seeking help for mental health problems, and only token efforts were made to determine why there was a rising number of suicides by active-duty troops.

In 2011, the Center for New American Security, an independent, nonpartisan research institute in Washington, D.C., issued a study titled "Losing the Battle: The Challenge of Military Suicide." It focused on a number of problem areas, including: 1) military transfers, which disrupt unit cohesion and complicate mental health care because patients often are reluctant to begin treatment anew; 2) mental health screenings, which don't elicit accurate information because troops know that any admissions may affect their careers and delay homecomings; 3) privacy issues, which prevent commanders from accessing confidential medical information about their troops, even though they are in the best position to help; 4) substance abuse and prescription medications, which contribute to more than a quarter of Army suicides and nearly half of all accidental or undetermined Army deaths, according to the report; 5) infrequent interactions of unit leaders with National Guard members and reservists, which limit their ability to help subordinates who are struggling with mental health issues; and 6) legal restrictions, which preclude commanders from asking troops about privately owned weapons despite the fact that easy access to firearms increases the risk of suicide. (In the Department of Defense's "Suicide Event Report" for calendar year 2010, privately owned weapons were used in 48 percent of military suicides in 2010. Military-issued weapons were used in another 14 percent, while non-weapons such as pills or rope constituted the balance. According to the 2011 National Defense Authorization Act, the Department of Defense cannot "collect or record any information relating to the otherwise lawful acquisition, possession, ownership, carrying, or other use of a privately-owned weapon by a member of the Armed Forces or civilian employee of the Department of Defense,"[9] unless the individual lives on a military base. Military leaders can talk with a service member who lives off-base about privately owned weapons if the person appears to be a suicide risk, but if the person denies it, the conversation ends.) The study also highlighted the importance of reducing the stigma associated with mental health care, as well as the need for more accurate and comprehensive data to determine the true number of veterans who end up dying by suicide.[10]

General Peter Chiarelli, the Army's top commander in charge of suicide prevention at the time, didn't care for the title of the report or its implication that too little was being done. He said he didn't believe that the military was losing the battle because progress was being made in understanding military suicides.[11] "The question you have to ask yourself," he told reporters after the report was issued, "and this is the number that no one can prove, what would it [the military suicide rate] have been if we had not focused the efforts we focused on it?"[12]

Jan Kemp, the suicide prevention coordinator for the VA, had a somewhat different take. She said, "As long as any vet or service member dies by suicide, we are in fact losing the battle. But we've made huge strides toward winning the war."[13]

In November 2011, Colonel John Bradley, head of the psychiatric department at Walter Reed Army Medical Center in Washington, D.C., and the National Naval Medical Center in Bethesda, Maryland, told *Medscape Medical News* that "the suicide rate among armed services personnel is the highest it has ever been," primarily due to "the operational tempo in the wars in Iraq and Afghanistan."[14] Operational tempo, he explained, is the number of times that a soldier gears up for combat, is deployed, and then comes home. He noted that current practices of repeated deployments are different than in World War II, Vietnam, or the first Gulf War. In World War II, soldiers didn't come home until the war was over. In Vietnam, most soldiers deployed for only one year. In Operation Desert Storm, troops went for the duration, but it was relatively short. Bradley acknowledged that the current practice of sending people repeatedly "does place extraordinary strain on our force" but said that the key is to develop a culture where seeking help is encouraged. He used the analogy of a military vehicle. If a Humvee idles roughly, soldiers don't keep driving it until the engine blows, he said. Instead, they get it fixed. In the same way, a soldier with mental health issues needs to be cared for so that a suicide doesn't result.[15]

This is easier said than done. Even General Chiarelli came to the conclusion that current efforts weren't enough and the military was, indeed, losing the battle when it came to suicide.

"I'll tell you point-blank," Chiarelli told a *New York Magazine* reporter, "though I've avoided this conclusion for two years: Where we're really seeing the increase in suicide is in the population that never would have contemplated suicide, but with successive deployments, or a single deployment, or an event in a deployment, they go into this danger area."[16]

Today, it's not unusual for troops to be deployed to war zones four times or more. While one might assume that each subsequent deployment is easier to deal with, in fact it can be harder. For one thing, there may be lingering issues from previous separations and reunions that haven't been addressed adequately. Every deployment is stressful for troops and their loved ones, but when a new deployment occurs before families have had a chance to resolve past differences, issues tend to fester, increase in magnitude, and result in nonmilitary spouses giving up on the relationship.

Then there is the fact that each deployment is different. Soldiers may return to different units and end up being thrust into relationships that are new to them. This is especially true for reservists. A combat unit is analogous to a family with members depending on one another for physical protection and emotional support. With each new deployment, it's as if the family is reconstituted. Soldiers may be sent to new parts of the world as well, including different countries, where they have no familiarity with native cultures or languages.

Multiple deployments extract a toll. Soldiers must transition back and forth from the cohesion and discipline of a combat unit to the insulation and relative lack of order in a family. They must shift between a life that is based on accountability and tactical awareness to one where responsibilities are defused and decisions—such as what kind of food to buy—seem inconsequential. In theater they have a purpose and orders to follow. At home they are often aimless. They practice targeted aggression in a war zone, then have to learn to let perceived slights go when they are stateside, then become confrontational again when deployed, and tactful again when home. They have to be in control of their emotions when engaged in combat, yet at home are expected to be open, caring, and willing to make small talk in the company of family members and friends. The more deployments a soldier has, the more times he or she makes the transition. Each transition is marked by a relatively quick turnaround, a plane flight either to the front or from it that offers little opportunity to adjust.

According to one poll, three-fourths of troops in Iraq served multiple tours.[17] One of them was Sergeant Jared Hagemann. An Army Ranger, he was married and the father of two young sons. According to the Army, he deployed six times, but his wife, Ashley, says it was eight. Hagemann enlisted out of high school in 2004 because of 9/11. In 2011, after six or eight tours already, he received notice that he would deploy again, this time to Afghanistan. It was the final straw.

"My husband would drink himself senseless before and after his deployments," Ashley told a reporter. "He would drink before a deployment to numb himself from what he was about to do, and he would drink after a deployment to forget what he had just done."[18]

With each deployment, Hagemann was promised that it would be the last one. Instead, there was always one more.

Haunted by nightmares, diagnosed with posttraumatic stress, and seeking help without receiving it, other than medication, Hagemann shot himself in June 2011 in a training area of Joint Base Lewis-McChord. He was twenty-five. Before his death, Ashley said that he told her that there was no way any God could forgive him for what he had done, and that he was going to hell.[19] Unable to live with himself, he believed that others shouldn't have to live with him, either.

One positive development occurred in July 2011, when the White House reversed its long-standing policy regarding condolence letters. Up to that point, presidential letters were sent to the families of service members who were killed in action, but not to those who took their own lives. The justification for this had been that any recognition of suicides would encourage more of them, a decision that angered many families who believed that their loved one's death should be acknowledged. In announcing the change, President Obama said that instead of encouraging suicides, the new policy might prevent them by reducing the stigma associated with mental health problems and urging service members to get help.[20]

"This issue is emotional, painful, and complicated," Obama said, "but these Americans served our nation bravely. They didn't die because they were weak."[21]

The new policy is far from perfect, however. It applies only to troops who kill themselves in war zones. Suicides occurring on foreign bases that aren't in combat areas, or in the United States, continue to be unacknowledged. Since 80 percent of suicides by active-duty troops occur in the United States,[22] and nearly all suicides by veterans are outside combat zones, some people consider the new policy to be less a reversal and more a clarification about which suicides merit condolences from the president and which ones don't.[23]

In addition, the new policy was applied only to future military suicides, not past ones. White House officials claimed that it would be too time-consuming to track down families whose loved ones killed themselves prior to the policy change.

That meant the family of James Keenan didn't receive a letter. Keenan served two tours of duty in Iraq. In his first tour, his roommate died in a car bomb explosion. Three weeks later, in Mosul, Keenan's platoon was ambushed while on patrol, and Keenan, the gunner in the last of four vehicles, provided cover during the firefight until the vehicles were out of the kill zone. This included shooting two enemy combatants who were only five feet away.[24] In his second tour, Keenan was a guard at Camp Cropper, the prison where Saddam Hussein was taken following his capture.

Keenan, age thirty-three, was a decorated member of the Army National Guard and the father of a seven-year-old son. He shot himself in his New Hampshire apartment one week before the new policy went into effect. His girlfriend told police that he was "despondent" and having "war-related nightmares."[25] The police report noted that Keenan had gone to the Manchester VA two days before he died and was prescribed medication for depression and panic attacks. Keenan's father said that his son changed after Mosul. "He never left that," Robert Keenan said. "He lived that every day."[26]

A New Concept: Posttraumatic Growth

According to Defense secretary Leon Panetta, who retired from the position in 2013, preventing military suicides is the most frustrating challenge he experienced.[27] According to Army general Peter Chiarelli, who retired in 2012 and now heads a nonprofit organization called One Mind, which studies mental illness and brain injuries, reducing suicides was the most difficult test he encountered in his forty-one years of military service.[28] According to Lloyd J. Austin III, a four-star Army general who in March 2013 took charge of Central Command, leading all military operations in the Middle East, suicide is the toughest enemy he has faced in his thirty-seven-year military career.[29]

Despite the large and growing number of suicides, military leaders maintain that there are signs of hope. The most obvious one is that many soldiers who are diagnosed and treated properly for PTSD are able to lead relatively normal lives after combat ends. In some respects they may even be stronger mentally than they were prior to their military service because they have developed effective coping tools to deal with adversity and stress. A 1980 study of aviators who had been prisoners of war in Vietnam found that 61 percent believed that the experience benefited them psychologically. They said that their religious convictions were stronger, they appreciated others more, and they derived more enjoyment from life. Those who suffered the worst during captivity had the greatest change.[30] A follow-up study in 2005 affirmed the initial results.[31] Senator John McCain, who was a POW in Vietnam for five years, said later, "I don't recommend the treatment, but I know that I'm a better person for having experienced it."[32]

Other American POWs in Vietnam have reported in various studies that they, too, benefited from the experience. They said that they are more patient now, more optimistic, have better insight into themselves, and get along better with others. "Overall," according to Eric T. Dean, Jr., in *Shook Over Hell*, "These former POWs have testified that they experienced personal growth and felt that they had acquired wisdom as a result of their wartime experiences. Remarkably, these attitudes were positively related to the harshness of the treatment these men endured in captivity."[33]

This phenomenon is being referred to as "posttraumatic growth" and is a focus of new research on treating PTSD. At the heart of it is a belief that what helps most is having a positive attitude. Being optimistic in the aftermath of an event—even if it is cataclysmic—enables people to survive it mentally. Not only that but optimism can be learned, or at least nurtured, so the thinking goes. Part of the resiliency training that soldiers undergo today is learning how to reframe negative experiences. For example, when U.S. soldiers go into native villages, they may be pelted with rocks and spit at because they weren't invited and have waged a war that has resulted in civilian casualties. Yet there also may be a smaller number of instances where American troops are welcomed into peoples' homes and offered food and drink. Remembering and appreciating these moments of kindness and hospitality can help soldiers get through other situations that could be demoralizing.

Army flight surgeon and Brigadier General Rhonda Cornum, now retired, advocated strenuously for resiliency training for all soldiers.

She became a prisoner in the first Gulf War after the Black Hawk helicopter in which she was flying, on a rescue mission, was shot down in the desert. Five crew members died in the crash. Cornum survived, but both of her arms were broken and she was captured by enemy soldiers.

In her book *She Went to War*, Cornum says, "In any dangerous situation, I always try to imagine the worst thing that could happen to me. Then whatever does happen to me has to be better, or at least no worse."[34] In the case of her helicopter crash, she says, "I was badly injured, but I knew I'd heal eventually. The crash had been so devastating that I should have died then, and I regarded every minute I was alive as a gift."[35]

During her eight days in captivity, Cornum believes that she could have been killed at any time. The fact that she wasn't proved to be good-enough luck for her. "Be thankful you are still alive," she told herself, "and focus on staying alive."[36]

To that end, she sang out loud for hours, songs that she loved, including her favorite, which reminded her of her husband, who also was in the service. She prayed too, but not to ask God to do anything else for her. She felt that He had already done enough by keeping her alive.

When Cornum returned home, instead of telling anguished stories of her crash and capture, she talked about the pluses of her POW experience. She had greater empathy for her patients after she had been a patient herself. She felt closer to her family and gained confidence in herself as a leader.[37] These lessons led her to advocate for and eventually develop, with psychology professor Martin Seligman of the University of Pennsylvania, the Army's Comprehensive Soldier Fitness program. This program teaches soldiers to judge events not as good or bad but as neutral from which positive outcomes can be gleaned.

As with most ideas, there are skeptics. Whether someone feels mentally stronger depends to a large extent on that person's perspective, which isn't always accurate. It's not uncommon for people to try and make sense of a senseless tragedy by reaching for some silver lining in the experience, to seek something positive from it even if it's a stretch. In viewing the person, family members and friends may not think that he or she has changed at all, or that the change is subtle and not nearly as dramatic as the person makes it out to be.

Even if a person's life is improved significantly in some way, it can be difficult to measure the change objectively, much less apply it to others.

Beyond that, it's hard to see how killing people and seeing others killed—the most traumatic combat experiences—facilitates personal growth. Yet even here it's possible to neutralize judgment of a negative experience in order to achieve a positive outcome. Instead of thinking, "I can never forget the horrors of war," it's more constructive to think, "I might not be able to forget the horrors of war, but I won't allow them to stop me from getting on with my life." Instead of saying, "I'm responsible for the deaths of innocent civilians," say, "Terrible things happen in war, and warfare itself is responsible for civilian deaths. A part of me died, too." Instead of feeling guilty because "I survived and my buddies didn't," feel grateful to have survived and vow "to honor my dead comrades by the way I live my life."[38]

Reframing past experiences in order to see them in a different light is a common psychological approach. In this instance, the Army has committed $125 million over five years to implement a plan to foster posttraumatic growth.[39]

"You Are Specialist Kyle Norton..."

Meanwhile, military leaders continue to encourage soldiers to seek help. Each branch of the armed forces today—Army, Navy, Air Force, and Marines—has implemented suicide prevention programs. The VA has hired suicide prevention coordinators for each of its hospitals in the country, set up more than 300 centers where veterans can receive special counseling, and implemented new screening tools and treatment procedures. The VA also partnered with the National Suicide Prevention Lifeline to answer crisis calls and electronic chats from suicidal vets 24 hours a day, 365 days a year. Since the Veterans Crisis Line was launched in July 2007, through February 2014, a total of 1,059,961 calls and 143,840 chats were handled, with 34,668 rescues initiated (that is, police intervention due to a veteran's imminent risk of suicide).[40]

It's all helping some, but more is needed. Some of the focus is on getting two massive bureaucracies—the Department of Defense and the Department of Veterans Affairs—to coordinate better. While the former oversees health care and other services for active-duty troops and the latter does the same thing for people after they leave the military, each has tended to operate in silos when it comes to suicide prevention.

"You've got two bureaucracies that have basically developed their own approach to dealing with these systems," Panetta told members of Congress in July 2012 regarding military suicides, "and they get familiar with them. That's what they use. They resist change. They resist coordination."[41]

This is true inside each department as well. In a 2011 study that was commissioned by the Department of Defense, titled *The War Within: Preventing Suicide in the U.S. Military*, researchers with the National Defense Research Institute, part of the RAND Center for Military Health Policy Research, found that each of the branches of the armed forces had created its own suicide prevention strategies, programs, and tools. The report lauded these efforts while barely noting that having multiple and overlapping programs within each branch makes it confusing for service members seeking help and presents too many variables to conduct a meaningful assessment. The impact of one program can't be separated from the impact of other programs. In addition, the report didn't call into question the lack of collaboration among branches or acknowledge that few attempts were made to share information or incorporate best practices from another branch.

These inefficiencies were highlighted in a 2012 report issued by the Institute of Medicine, a nonprofit, nonpartisan organization formed under the charter of the National Academy of Sciences. The report noted that while both the Department of Defense and the VA operate numerous programs for troops and veterans with posttraumatic stress, only about half of those diagnosed with PTSD actually get treatment. Moreover, neither department was tracking which treatments were being used or how well they worked in the long term.[42] In other words, no one knew whether any of the programs were effective or not. (The Institute of Medicine, which advises the government, plans to release a second report that will have more specific information regarding the number of active-duty troops and veterans who have PTSD, the cost of their treatments, and the outcomes.)

The RAND team identified twelve separate suicide prevention initiatives in the Army, eleven in the Marines, nine in the Navy, and three in the Air Force. The Army initiatives have names like Strong Bonds, ACE (Ask, Care, Escort), Resiliency Training, Warrior Adventure Quest, RESPECT-Mil (Re-Engineering Systems of Primary Care Treatment in the Military), CSF (Comprehensive Soldier Fitness), and ASIST (Applied Suicide Intervention Skills Training, developed by a Canadian company named Living Works). The Marine initiatives include OSCAR (Operational Stress Control and Readiness), Command-Level Suicide Prevention, and Are You Listening? Some of the Navy initiatives are OSC (Operational Stress Control), Returning Warriors Workshops, and Reserve Psychological Health Outreach Program. By contrast, the Air Force initiatives, with the exception of Landing Gear, are free of contrived names and acronyms. Perhaps it's coincidental that the Air Force has the best overall record among the U.S. Armed Forces when it comes to suicide prevention. The fact that the Air Force has only three initiatives, however, of which one is targeted to mental health clinical staff who assess and manage suicide risk, may be a reason that it has had more success than other branches of the military when it comes to suicide prevention.

Despite the challenges, military officials assert that communication and collaboration between the Pentagon and the VA is improving. In November 2011, the Defense Suicide Prevention Office was established. Peter Gutierrez, a clinical research psychologist with the VA in Denver, told me that the office is holding monthly conference calls involving representatives from all branches of the U.S. Armed Forces, the VA, and the National Institute of Mental Health to discuss the latest developments in suicide prevention, including epidemiological research and data collection, clinical trials, and creative uses of technology. When I asked Gutierrez whether the push was coming from the top down or the bottom up in terms of dealing with the problem, he said it was coming from both places, that anyone in the system can make recommendations, which are reviewed and implemented when they make sense and are doable. He added that while it's difficult for departments as large as Defense and the VA to initiate change, likening it to altering the direction of an aircraft carrier, it's not impossible.

Gutierrez is co-chair of the Military Suicide Research Consortium, along with Thomas Joiner of Florida State University. MSRC, as it's called, was founded in 2010 with a five-year grant from the

Department of Defense to sync military and civilian efforts in a multidisciplinary approach to suicide prevention. In particular, the consortium conducts research on risk assessment and treatment as they pertain to military suicides. The goal is to identify quickly those individuals who are at risk for suicide, treat them effectively, and thereby prevent suicide attempts. The $30 million grant expires in September 2015, and a renewal grant request for another five years of funding is pending.

One of the MSRC-affiliated research projects is being led by Rebecca Bernert at Stanford University. Bernert, a clinical psychologist who studied under Joiner, is examining sleep deprivation and the use of cognitive therapy in treating insomnia. There is a strong correlation between the amount of sleep a person gets and his or her predilection for suicide. The less sleep—a common occurrence in war zones, especially today—the greater the likelihood of a suicide attempt.

Many service members have trouble sleeping, in part because they are troubled by nightmares. The treatment, Bernert tells me, can be as little as four individual or group sessions, with the focus on re-scripting bad dreams. This doesn't mean turning bad dreams into good dreams; instead, it means that patients learn to engage in pleasant imagery that serves to replace the recurrent, disturbing visions they have, making it possible to sleep restfully rather than fitfully.

One benefit of Bernert's research is that people returning from war often feel more comfortable talking with psychologists and therapists about insomnia than about traumatic events. There is less stigma if a person admits to a physical problem rather than a mental one. This makes it easier for researchers like Bernert to recruit willing subjects for their studies. At the same time, many people who suffer from insomnia, meaning that they have experienced at least one month of chronic sleep loss that has caused problems for them at work, at home, or in important relationships, have no military background. Doctors have known for a long time that sleep problems and mood disorders tend to go hand in hand, but it has only been in recent years that sleep therapy has started to be seen as an aid for depression, with the two ailments treated simultaneously.

According to Dr. Andrew Krystal, who is in charge of a research project at Duke University, sleep is "this huge, still unexplored frontier of psychiatry." He says, "We treat during the day, and make little effort to find out what's happening at night."[43]

Other research, also part of the Military Suicide Research Consortium, is under way at Harvard University's Laboratory for Clinical and Development Research. There the director, Matthew K. Nock, a clinical psychologist, and his team are administering a variety of tests to people who have a history of suicidal behavior. Nock's goal is to develop a bona fide way to measure a person's suicide risk in real time. He told a *New York Times* reporter in 2013 that he envisions one day being able to transmit daily tests to a service member's phone, the results of which could then be used to determine whether the soldier's current mindset puts him or her more at risk for suicide. With that information, doctors could see in the moment what patients are thinking and intervene before the risk escalates into a suicide attempt.[44]

In 2011, a different kind of project began with the opening of a $52 million "warrior transition" barracks at Lewis-McChord's Madigan Army Medical Center. There, 400 or more soldiers who are physically injured or mentally stressed can spend time decompressing and recovering from various traumas. Military officials assert that this program is helping to reduce the number of mental health problems, as is the Army's Comprehensive Soldier Fitness program, which aims to ensure soldiers' health both before they go to war and after they come back. Colonel Michael Brobeck, a commander at Lewis-McChord, explains the CSF program this way: "We teach them about patience, about maturity, about how it's okay to have issues because everybody has issues."[45]

While that is well and good, if someone is unable to absorb this kind of training, the implication exists that he or she didn't try hard enough, that the individual rather than his or her military experiences is to blame for any psychological problems. As Penny Coleman notes, " 'Posttraumatic growth' has become the new standard to fail by."[46]

Moreover, the challenge remains of getting soldiers to seek help. Ashley Hagemann went up the chain of command at Lewis-McChord, all the way to the top, seeking help for her husband, who was often drunk and violent, she said, and threatened suicide multiple times. Nobody would listen, though.

Most of the strategies in place today to prevent military suicides are targeted primarily to active-duty troops. VA hospitals, clinics, and other resources such as the Veteran's Crisis Line are available to everyone who has served, now or in the past, but the emphasis of most military programs is on current warriors. Not only are they the ones whose suicides receive the majority of media attention, but their deaths are more closely tied to their military service and, therefore, present the biggest public relations problem. Veterans who die by suicide years after they left the military don't generate the same level of interest, and there isn't the same close connection between their service and their death.

One example of this emphasis on present-day soldiers is cutting-edge video game technology that the military is commissioning. As Corey Mead describes it in his book, *War Play: Video Games and the Future of Armed Conflict*, the technology presents high-stress, noncombat situations that address psychological and emotional issues faced by troops. Real actors are used, the games are shot on location, and each game—which lasts two to three hours—has more than eighty moments when the player has to make a decision that affects the outcome, resulting in more than 1,000 variations. The first game, *Saving Sergeant Pabletti*, developed by a company called WILL Interactive in Maryland, was mainly concerned with sexual harassment. A more recent game developed by the same company, called *Beyond the Front*, focuses on suicide prevention. Mead describes it this way:

"You are Specialist Kyle Norton, a nineteen-year-old Midwesterner whose life has begun to spiral downward following a tour as a bomb-disposal technician in Iraq. Already beset by financial difficulties, you receive a surprise e-mail from your fiancée, who announces that she has become pregnant by another man. Still reeling from the news, you learn that your best friend has just been killed in an ambush. As these scenarios unfold, questions appear on your video screen, prompting you to decide whether, as Norton, you should seek help for these issues. Depending on your responses, Norton either becomes suicidal or begins to heal."[47]

Military officials were so pleased with *Beyond the Front* that they began requiring every active-duty service member in the Army and Army Reserve to play it. Subsequent games such as *The War Inside*, *The Home Front*, and *The Mission to Heal* have been designed by WILL with multiple perspectives built in so that players can assume different characters, including a soldier with PTSD, a sergeant who is trying to encourage troops to seek mental health services, and a social worker who is experiencing compassion fatigue. Future games, Mead says, will deal with the effects on family members when troops return home.

It's an intriguing idea, and like other projects that are currently underway, it could make a difference. At the same time, it's not enough. The steps that each branch of the military has implemented to date have achieved varying levels of success in reducing and preventing suicides; however, even the most ardent supporters admit that the situation isn't improving much. Large numbers of soldiers—past and present—continue to take their lives. For this to end, additional steps are needed.

Step 1: Pursue Perfection

In 2001, the Behavioral Health Services division of the Henry Ford Health System in Detroit implemented what many people considered to be a radical depression care program. Its main purpose was to eliminate suicides by patients. Not reduce the number of patient suicides, but eliminate them altogether.

The Henry Ford Health System is a health maintenance organization (HMO), meaning that patients are covered by private health insurance. The system's Behavioral Health Services division consists of two hospitals, ten clinics, and more than five hundred employees. Prior to 2001, the division had a suicide rate of 89 per 100,000 patients, which is 7 times higher than the national average, although it's lower than the estimated suicide rate of patients with an active mood disorder.[48] Still, it wasn't nearly good enough for Dr. C. Edward Coffey, chief executive officer of Behavioral Health Services. Coffey rounded up every employee in the division—including janitorial and cleaning staff—to brainstorm ways that patient suicides could be reduced. Among the initial conversations was what constituted an acceptable goal. Was it enough to cut the HMO's suicide rate in half? To the national level? More?

Coffey notes today that if 99.9 percent accuracy is good enough, then 12 babies in this country will be given to the wrong parents every day, 18,000 pieces of U.S. mail will be mishandled every hour, and 2 million tax records will be lost every year by the Internal Revenue Service.[49] One Henry Ford employee said that even a single suicide was unacceptable if it was your child, and that helped set the target: zero. In other words, the goal was perfection, not a single suicide among any of the system's thousands of patients.

Perfection is rarely achieved, which is why it usually isn't established as a goal. People think it's unrealistic to aim so high or worry that participants will be discouraged if they see progress but still fall short. In fact, though, according to Coffey, the result has been just the opposite. Employees have been energized by the goal. They have committed to it, so much so that it has affected the whole system.

"Pursuing perfection is no longer a project or initiative for our team," Coffey says, "but a principle driving force embedded in the fabric of our clinical care."[50]

After setting the goal, the Behavioral Health Services division began strategizing ways to achieve it. The first step was to establish a consumer advisory panel that would help design the program. They were the people for whom the program was targeted, therefore they would have a considerable say in how it was conceived. Then came the program itself. It was decided that every patient would be assessed for suicide risk, regardless of the reason that he or she was admitted, with specific interventions crafted for each of three risk levels. Next, every employee who had patient contact would take a course in suicide prevention and be required to score 100 percent on a course test—perfection—or retake it. Finally, protocols would be devised to remove weapons from patients' homes, psychotherapists would receive additional training, services would be made available to members of a patient's family, and multiple means would be developed for patients to access help and information (three were created: e-mail consultations with physicians, drop-in medication appointments, and same-day medical appointments).

The results after eight years were reported in *JAMA*.[51] In the first four years of the depression care program, suicides among Henry Ford patients dropped 75 percent, to 22 per 100,000. It was a good start, but only that. By 2010, when *JAMA* covered the story, Henry Ford had gone two and a half years without a single suicide among its patient population. The commitment to perfection from the top down and from the bottom up had resulted in unparalleled success.

"The encouraging results of the initiative suggest that this care model can be highly effective for achieving and sustaining breakthrough quality improvement in mental health care," Coffey said.

There is every reason to think that the same commitment by the military would achieve dramatic results, at least among active-duty troops. These troops are in the system now and their activities are being monitored every day so there are plenty of opportunities for assessment and treatment. Even one suicide is unacceptable if that person is your father, mother, husband, wife, partner, sibling, child, or friend. By adopting the mindset of zero as a target, rather than an arbitrary number or striving for a rate that is consistent with the general population, the military can begin working to achieve the same kind of breakthrough that Henry Ford has achieved. It won't be easy, but for too long military officials have offered lip service to change. Despite throwing millions of dollars at the problem—far more than is devoted to preventing civilian suicides—the Pentagon and VA have relatively little to show for it. The time has come for officials to demonstrate a genuine willingness to end military suicides. Not reduce them, but end them. Pursuing perfection is essential to the process.

Step 2: Assume Everyone Needs Help

One of the ironies of battle is that the bravest soldiers, by virtue of their willingness to place themselves in the most dangerous situations, tend to be exposed to the most trauma. This, in turn, makes them more likely to develop psychological problems. At the same time, anyone can develop these problems; no one is immune. Being tough has nothing to do with it. The challenge is that for people in the military, who are used to taking care of themselves, seeking help is contrary to how they operate. Just as it is considered "unmanly" for infantry soldiers to complain about fatigue or blisters, so is it considered a sign of weakness for troops in any branch of the military to need mental health services.

According to a 2004 study published in the *New England Journal of Medicine*, only 23 to 40 percent of soldiers returning from Iraq and Afghanistan who admitted that they suffered from mental health problems said that they sought care. For the majority, fear and stigma—fear of hurting their image and ruining their military careers, and stigma from being labeled mentally unfit—were too strong.[52]

Things haven't changed significantly in recent years. The existing code of military conduct emphasizes physical and mental toughness, and the admission by any individual soldier that he or she has lost heart or mind has negative repercussions. For this reason, the military must operate under the assumption that *all* troops, when they return home, are dealing with some form of posttraumatic stress. In many cases it's less severe than diagnosable PTSD, but it's rarely absent altogether. In a study of psychiatric stress among Allied troops who landed in Normandy during World War II, Roy L. Swank and Walter E. Marchand determined that after two months of continuous combat, 98 percent of surviving soldiers had psychiatric problems of some kind. The 2 percent who didn't had "aggressive psychopathic personalities."[53]

Just as all patients in Henry Ford Behavioral Health Services are assessed for suicide, so should every service member be evaluated for suicidal risk. Instead of leaving it up to individuals to come forward on their own, the military should initiate treatment measures for all who serve—particularly members of the National Guard and Reserves, who often are less prepared than active-duty troops to deal with traumatic situations and receive the least support. Evaluations should focus less on written questionnaires and more on extensive, mandatory, one-on-one mental and physical examinations. These evaluations shouldn't be limited to the service member, either; family members should be interviewed as well (separately and confidentially). In addition, the evaluations should be conducted every three months for three years following deployment in order to identify delayed responses to combat.

Today, when a soldier's tour of duty ends, he or she usually is required to spend time—several days or up to a week—at a special demobilization center before returning home. In addition to filling out paperwork, updating records, returning equipment, having any medical needs addressed, receiving information about military benefits and services, and being briefed by commanders, soldiers complete a Post Deployment Health Assessment, or PDHA. This two-page questionnaire assesses a person's physical and mental well-being and aims to identify and help those individuals who may be suffering from posttraumatic stress and other war-related problems but either don't know it or are reluctant to admit it. Toward the end of the assessment, troops are asked questions such as, "Did you see anyone wounded, killed, or dead during this deployment? If so, was it a fellow soldier, an enemy soldier, or a civilian (mark all that apply)." "Did you ever feel that you were in great danger of being killed?" "Over the last two weeks, how often have you been bothered by any of the following problems: little interest or pleasure in doing things; feeling down, depressed, or hopeless; thoughts that you would be better off dead?" "Are you currently interested in receiving help for a stress, emotional, alcohol, or family problem?"[54]

The assessment is done just before a soldier comes home, however, and the only thing that service members want to do at this time is see their families. Thus, there is a tendency to answer questions quickly and mindlessly. Moreover, if soldiers admit to any problems, they believe—with sufficient justification—that it could delay their homecoming.

In *Lethal Warriors*, David Philipps describes the PDHA answers of a soldier named Kenneth Eastridge. Eastridge enlisted in the Army at age nineteen and returned from Iraq in July 2007 at age twenty-four. According to Philipps, in Iraq Eastridge "had watched his favorite sergeant die. He had been through multiple bomb blasts. He had shot and killed an estimated twenty people. He had helped bag mutilated and dismembered bodies. He had nightmares. He avoided crowds. He felt numb and detached." Yet Eastridge answered "no" to every question on the PDHA, saying that he hadn't been in combat and hadn't ever fired his weapon. Today, Eastridge is serving a ten-year prison term after being convicted of being an accessory in the December 2007 murder of Kevin Shields, a fellow soldier in Colorado Springs, by another Fort Carson service member.

According to a 2008 study, troops are two to four times more likely to report depression, PTSD, suicidal thoughts, and interest in receiving care when they complete an anonymous survey than when then they fill out the PDHA.[55] On the plus side, as a result of the 2010 National Defense Authorization Act, medical and behavioral health professionals are now required to conduct PDHA evaluations individually and face-to-face.[56] Previously, written questionnaires were distributed to groups of soldiers who completed them in the presence of their peers.

The limited usefulness of the PDHA led the military to implement a follow-up screening called Post Deployment Health Re-Assessment (PDHRA). Administered three to six months after a soldier returns home, it assesses the person's mental health at that time with the assumption that he or she will answer more truthfully than the first time.

The VA's National Center for PTSD developed a simple and sensible PTSD screen to be used by doctors in primary care settings. Soldiers are asked if, in their lives, they have ever had an experience that was so frightening, horrible, or upsetting that, in the past month, they: 1) had nightmares about it or thought about it when they didn't want to; 2) tried hard not to think about it or went out of their way to avoid situations that reminded them of it; 3) were constantly on guard, watchful, or easily startled; or 4) felt numb or detached from others, activities, or their surroundings. A "yes" answer to any of the questions doesn't confirm a diagnosis of PTSD, but it indicates some probability.

Not every soldier needs treatment. Many are able to adjust to civilian life on their own. Every soldier needs help of some kind, though, to process feelings about his or her wartime experiences. By assuming that this is the case, and assessing each service member for suicide rather than expecting those in need to come forward on their own, the military can reduce the stigma associated with seeking help and keep more troops from killing themselves.

Step 3: Do More to Eliminate Stigma

Retired Major General Mark Graham knows about the stigma of suicide firsthand. In 2007, Graham assumed command of Fort Carson in Colorado, one of the largest and, at the time, most troubled military bases in the country. In addition to 21,000 troops and 5,000 civilian employees, nearly 200,000 members of the National Guard and Reserves train at Fort Carson—basically all Guard members and reservists west of the Mississippi. Before Graham arrived, nine soldiers at the base had been involved in fourteen homicides. In his first fifteen months on the job, there were nine suicides.

Graham almost didn't make it to Fort Carson. After thirty years in the Army, during which time he served in Desert Storm and had a primary role in the military's response in New Orleans following Hurricane Katrina, he was emotionally devastated. Within eight months, both of his sons were dead. In June 2003, his youngest son,

Kevin, age twenty-one, died by suicide after being in ROTC and planning to be an Army doctor. Then his other son, Jeff, twenty-four, a second lieutenant in the Army, was killed in February 2004 by an IED in Iraq.

Graham thought seriously about leaving the service, but decided to tough it out. For one thing, that is what soldiers do. For another thing, it was his way of honoring both sons. Lastly, by helping other military families deal with tragedies, he felt like he would be helping himself.

What struck Graham and his wife, Carol, was that Jeff was treated as a war hero for dying in Iraq while Kevin's death was largely ignored. They noted that the parents of sons and daughters who are killed in combat receive a gold star and oftentimes are invited to meet with dignitaries, including the president, but there is no equivalent for parents of service members who die by suicide.

"They were fighting different enemies," Graham said of Kevin and Jeff, "but both were really, really great sons. It wasn't like we had one bad son or one good son."[57]

Kevin was a top student in his ROTC class at the University of Kentucky. Unbeknownst to most people, though, including his parents, he was battling depression. He saw a doctor and was prescribed Prozac but didn't want to take it, afraid it would jeopardize his ROTC scholarship and future Army career. When he failed to show up for a round of golf with Jeff, Jeff called their sister, who shared an off-campus apartment with Kevin. She found him hanging in his bedroom.

As for Jeff, after he graduated from the University of Kentucky and arrived for basic training at Fort Knox, he was told that he could stay there rather than deploy to Iraq. He wouldn't hear of it. "The only thing worse than being at war," he said to his fiancée, "was being a soldier and not being at war."[58]

While on foot patrol in Kalidiyah, outside Fallujah, Jeff Graham stopped his platoon when he saw something suspicious on the guardrail of a bridge. As he grabbed a radio to alert others, the bomb exploded, killing him and another soldier. When she read on the Internet that two soldiers died in Kalidiyah, Carol Graham had a premonition that one was her son. A short time later, she and her husband were driving to a funeral home for the second time in under than a year.

It was at a stoplight on the way back that Graham decided not to retire. He told his wife, "The loss of the boys can either be the whole book of our lives, or it can be two tragic chapters."[59]

Six weeks into his command at Fort Carson, General Graham implemented a new program called Warrior and Family Community Partnership. The program encourages soldiers to get help by connecting them with services and resources. He also started mobile teams of behavioral health specialists to counsel troops before they deploy and after they return. In addition, he mandated that all soldiers on the base receive full military funerals regardless of how they die (the practice at many bases is to have smaller "remembrance ceremonies" for soldiers who die by suicide). The latter proved controversial, but Graham held his ground. A first step in overcoming the stigma of suicide is breaking the silence that surrounds it.

"If a soldier dies by suicide, some people think he wasn't killed by the enemy," Graham said. "But I always tell people that we can never know what they were going through or what kinds of things they were fighting."[60]

In 2007, six soldiers at Fort Carson killed themselves. With each death, Graham felt as if his son Kevin had died again. He told his assistant to clear his calendar so that he could attend each memorial service, which no other commanding officer there had done. He also made sure to personally extend his condolences to grieving family members.[61]

Initially, Graham's well-publicized efforts seemed to have little effect as 2008 set a new record for suicides at the base. Then they declined marginally in 2009 and dropped in half in 2010.

Graham retired in 2012. Since then, he and Carol have been active in local and national suicide prevention efforts. They also established the Jeffrey C. and Kevin A. Graham Memorial Fund at the University of Kentucky. The fund supports activities that aim to prevent school-site suicides, including orienting parents and students to depression and related suicide warning signs. It's all about getting help for people as quickly as possible, the Grahams say.

Prior to Kevin's suicide, General Graham didn't make a practice of hugging people; hugs aren't part of traditional military conduct. Today, though, whenever he meets a father whose child died in combat or by suicide, Graham gives him a hug.

"Men grieve differently," he explains. "But I still remember someone hugging me after Jeff's death and just whispering, 'Let me take a little bit of that pain off of you.' "[62]

According to its website, the Center for a New American Security (CNAS) is "an independent, nonpartisan, and nonprofit organization that develops strong, pragmatic, and principled national security and defense policies." In a 2011 study on military suicides, CNAS found that 43 percent of troops who killed themselves didn't seek help from the military in the month prior to their deaths. This was actually an improvement over 2008, CNAS said, when 60 percent of troops who killed themselves didn't seek help a month before their deaths, and 2009, when the number was 54 percent. Still, CNAS concluded, "The stigmatization of mental health care remains an issue."[63]

In May 2012, Defense Secretary Panetta sent a letter to military commanders stating that "suicide prevention is a leadership responsibility." He said, "Commanders and supervisors cannot tolerate any actions that belittle, haze, humiliate, or ostracize any individual, especially those who require or are responsibly seeking professional services."[64]

As well-intentioned as that sounds, putting it into practice represents a significant challenge. In many parts of the world, including America today, people are used to seeking care for physical injuries and sicknesses, but not for psychological ones. A major reason for this is because psychological injuries aren't visible. We can't see them so they are more difficult to diagnose, assess, and treat. Oftentimes their existence is questioned. As Penny Coleman writes in *Flashback*, "Bullets and bombs are destructive to human beings in fairly predictable and immediately apparent ways. Terror and horror work more mysteriously, but the psychic wounds they inflict are no less real or incapacitating. Such wounds are more difficult to see, to categorize, to measure. They have been less well understood and so have been more vulnerable to prejudice and superstition."[65]

A physician I know, Neil Fruman, has a traveling road show that he uses to demonstrate the effects of aging. He has people put on a special pair of glasses that simulate cataracts. He gives people ear plugs that make it harder to hear. He straps on knee braces that make it difficult to walk. It only takes a few minutes with these encumbrances for people who aren't elderly to appreciate the physical challenges that seniors face. There is no corollary for mental illness, though. Someone who is schizophrenic and also self-aware—a rare combination—can say that he or she hears so many voices it's as if the person is watching dozens of TV channels simultaneously, and we understand that intuitively, but we don't really accept it. It's outside our realm of experience.

Psychiatrist Jonathan Shay writes in *Odysseus in America: Combat Trauma and the Trials of Homecoming* that those who suffer from PTSD carry "the burden of sacrifice for the rest of us as surely as the amputees, the burned, the blind, and the paralyzed carry them."[66]

Concrete steps must be taken to de-stigmatize posttraumatic stress. After the Vietnam War, PTSD was added as a mental illness in the American Psychiatric Association's *Diagnostic and Statistical Manual of Mental Disorders*. Debate has ensued ever since, however, about whether it should remain, primarily because combat trauma is different from other types of trauma, and there is no consensus on treatment.

In many respects PTSD is a mental injury rather than a mental illness. Just as every soldier is susceptible to physical injuries, so is he or she susceptible to mental injuries. If viewed this way, with more compassion and understanding, and without judgment, soldiers and their families will be better served. Even brave, strong men and women can be victims of emotional suffering—it doesn't make them less brave or less strong.

Admittedly, mental illness and suicide can't be de-stigmatized overnight. Moreover, it's not the military's responsibility alone to do it. Nevertheless, there are steps the military can take. In addition to receiving appropriate diagnoses and treatment for PTSD, troops need to see that military careers aren't threatened by it. Soldiers with PTSD who are able to manage it should be considered for promotions the same as soldiers who recover from physical wounds. Moreover, when a soldier recovering from PTSD is promoted, his or her ability to overcome a mental injury should be recognized publicly so that it serves as a model and inspiration for others, just as overcoming a serious physical injury can provide hope and encouragement for people with similar disabilities. Also, if the practice is to award Purple Hearts whenever a soldier suffers a serious physical injury, then Purple Hearts should be awarded to those who suffer serious mental health injuries, too. Finally, presidential letters of condolence should be sent to the families of all soldiers who die by suicide, regardless of when or where their deaths occur. The current practice of sending letters only in cases in which the person was in active service and died overseas in a war zone is unacceptable. Families grieve the death of loved ones regardless of the circumstances, and military acknowledgment ought to follow suit.

Many soldiers with PTSD are receiving treatment in primary care settings today. Physicians and mental health professionals work together under one roof to provide integrated services. Physicians receive training in assessing behavioral health care needs, then hand off patients to clinicians for therapy. This raises the question of why we have a separate medical system in the United States for veterans. An obvious answer is that many vets have special needs different from those of the general population, and they have earned the right to subsidized care by virtue of their military service. At the same time, if VA hospitals and clinics are unable to meet these needs because of inefficiencies, understaffing, or other reasons, then it makes sense for veterans to be able to access care from nonmilitary venues. Certainly they aren't precluded from doing this now, but it means having—and paying for—additional coverage. Veterans groups have lobbied hard for the rights they have, and giving up a major one, as would be required if vets didn't have access to a separate medical system, is unlikely. Nevertheless, if there was one health care system in the United States that was available to all, the end result might be that vets received better care. In addition, civilians who live in areas that are underserved by public and private hospitals now, but have medical facilities for veterans, might be better served, too.

Prior to 1990, Congress considered closing down the whole VA health care system and giving veterans vouchers to use at private facilities because of substandard treatment at VA hospitals. Over the next fifteen years, however, changes were implemented that resulted in improved care, greater consumer satisfaction, and a 2006 award from Harvard University for "Innovations in American Government."[67] Today, though, the red tape involved in getting appointments and the wait time before a veteran is able to see a health care worker leave much to be desired. Moreover, the onslaught of new patients is taxing the VA far beyond its current capacity, despite the fact that the department operates the largest integrated health care system in the country. It's time to at least consider the possibility of a different system of care.

Step 4: Emphasize Connectedness

In World War II, U.S. troops were told that they were fighting to defend freedom and democracy against fascism. This didn't prove to be strong enough motivation, however, even when combined with messages of Nazi evil. According to former Army ranger Dave Grossman, "Numerous studies have concluded that men in combat are usually motivated to fight *not* by ideology or hate or fear, but by group pressures and processes involving 1) regard for their comrades, 2) respect for their leaders, 3) concern for their own reputations with both, and 4) an urge to contribute to the success of the group."[68] According to Herbert Spiegel, a psychiatrist and front-line doctor, what enabled World War II U.S. soldiers "to attack and attack and attack, week after week in mud, rain, dust, and heat...lay not in any negative drive but in a positive one. It was love more than hate that propelled these men. This love was manifested in a number of ways: in regard to their comrades who shared the same dangers; in respect for their platoon leader or company commander who led them well and supported them with everything he had; in concern for their reputation with their leaders; and in the urge to contribute to the success of their group."[69]

Firsthand accounts of soldiers, past and present, confirm this. As much as they may have felt that they were fighting for their lives, or fighting for their country, or fighting for a set of ideals, when it came down to it the prevailing reason was because they were fighting out of a sense of camaraderie and shared affection for the soldiers around them. Rather than being motivated by negative feelings toward the enemy, they were motivated primarily by positive feelings toward one another, of wanting to protect and save their brothers in arms. Assuming this is true, and there is no good reason to doubt it, the challenge becomes one of determining how this bond can be reinforced and group loyalty can be sustained in order to prevent a soldier from breaking down.

Before going there, it's important to reiterate that training people to fight in wars—teaching them how to fire various weapons and surmount the morality of killing other human beings—has inherent and largely unavoidable consequences. Moreover, these consequences are directly related to the elevated risk of suicide among troops.

"Repeated exposure to military training as well as to violence, aggression, and death dulls one's fear of death and increases tolerance for pain," say the authors of "Losing the Battle," the 2011 report issued by CNAS. "The very experience of being in the military erodes this protective factor, even for service members who have not deployed or experienced combat, in part because service members experience pain and discomfort from the beginning of their training. By removing some of the protective factors of suicide, therefore, military service, especially during wartime, may predispose an individual toward suicide."[70]

Another 2011 study, this one published in *Suicide and Life-Threatening Behavior*,[71] came to the same conclusion, with a slight twist. It said that exposure to combat not only increases an individual's tolerance of pain but also increases his or her sense of fearlessness about death. The greater the exposure, the more likely a person is to acquire the capacity for suicide, according to the study. Whereas military service, until recently, may have been a protective factor against suicide, with rates lower than the general population,[72] this isn't true anymore.

The study referenced and affirmed the conclusion of a 2007 Institute of Medicine committee that "there is sufficient evidence supporting the relationship between deployment to a war zone and suicide in the years after deployment."[73] While combat exposure varies in numerous ways, the new study said, including the frequency and degree of violence, the proximity of combatants to one another, and a person's level of participation, violent combat events "are more strongly associated with the capability for suicide than other combat events marked by less aggression." At the same time, the study conceded "that *all* forms of combat exposure predict higher levels of capability, based on previous research. Even military personnel without combat experience report less fear of death and have a greater ability to tolerate pain than civilians."[74] The conclusion reached by the authors was that "the very qualities that characterize the optimal combatant (i.e. fearlessness about death, high tolerance for pain, competency in using firearms), and the very experiences that the combatants are trained to endure (i.e. violence and exposure to death), are the same qualities that increase the capability for lethal self-injury."[75]

Because these factors are unalterable, the authors recommended that the military's suicide prevention efforts focus on reducing the desire of individuals to kill themselves rather than their capacity to do so. The way to achieve this, they said, is to strengthen a soldier's social connectedness and sense of purpose, which serve as protective factors against suicide. When people feel socially connected and believe that life is meaningful, suicidal intent declines. Conversely, when people are isolated and feel hopeless or a burden to others, they lose sight of other options besides suicide. Once someone has developed the desire to die, has the means such as a firearm or pills, and already has developed the capacity to pull the trigger or overdose, the risk becomes high.

The strong connection to other soldiers in one's unit—lacking in the Vietnam War but present in virtually every other war in which the United States has engaged—not only needs to be recognized but enhanced. Soldiers who train together should deploy together. When they come home, they should come home together, and if they deploy again it should be as members of the same unit. In recent years this has become the case more often, but there are numerous exceptions.

The most effective programs that aim to reduce youth suicides focus on the role of friends. If a suicidal youth confides in anyone, it's most likely to be a friend. So as a young person, what do you do when your best friend tells you that he or she is feeling suicidal, but makes you promise not to tell anyone? You don't want to see your friend get hurt, but you also don't want to divulge his or her confidences. Programs that focus on preventing youth suicides refer to this as "the deadly secret" and teach youths to disclose it to a trusted adult, even if it means that the friend feels betrayed. What may seem like an act of disloyalty can be the gift of a lifetime.

It's not so different in the military. If a soldier is suicidal and tells anyone, most likely it will be a fellow soldier. Alternatively, if a soldier doesn't tell anyone but there are warning signs, these signs most likely will be observed by someone in his or her unit. That person needs to insist that the soldier seek help immediately and also let him or her know that the appropriate person—unit commander, local chaplain, military psychologist—must be informed as well. Seeking help isn't a sign of weakness; it's a sign of strength, of knowing what one's limitations are, and the military needs to do all it can to emphasize this. Just as good conduct medals and combat awards are bestowed on troops, so should commendations be given when soldiers refer others for help when needed. It's part of developing a strong, healthy team.

Another way to emphasize connectedness, specifically as it applies to treating moral injuries, already is starting to take root. This is the practice of soldiers seeking forgiveness—real or imagined—from victims. Clinicians work with soldiers to write letters to those who died or to have imaginary conversations with them. From a soldier's point of view, the only people who can offer forgiveness are dead. Even so, providing context and expressing remorse after the fact can be therapeutic. So can soldier-to-soldier listening groups such as those operated by chapters of Soldier's Heart.

In "Atonement," *New Yorker* reporter Dexter Filkins describes the meeting of a former Marine named Lu Lobello and an Iraqi mother and daughter nearly a decade after Lobello and fellow Marines shot up the three civilian cars in which the mother, daughter, and other members of the Kachadoorian family were riding. All three drivers—the father and two sons—were killed, and the daughter, a young girl at the time, was bleeding from shrapnel wounds in her shoulder. For years afterward, Lobello was haunted by memories of the day. He punched walls, broke things, and couldn't sleep. At one point, Filkins says, "Lobello ran into the parking lot of his apartment building in his underwear, clutching his AR-15, preparing to shoot a man he believed had been following him."[76] Eventually, Lobello was diagnosed with PTSD and prescribed medication, but it didn't help. Only when he was able to connect with the two surviving members of the Kachadoorian family—mother and daughter, now living in southern California, as was Lobello—who agreed to meet him and offered him forgiveness, did he feel absolved.

Step 5: Expedite Treatment and Claims

The most effective treatments to date for PTSD are Cognitive Processing Therapy (CPT) and Exposure Therapy (ET). Both involve changing the way a person thinks and acts, particularly in regard to his or her perception of the world as being dangerous, believing that he or she is powerless or inadequate, and feeling guilty for outcomes that couldn't have been prevented. In CPT, a person writes about his or her war zone trauma, then works with the therapist to reexamine and eventually restructure the narrative to reflect more accurately the experience. For instance, the driver of a convoy may feel responsible for a comrade's death because he or she didn't do enough to evade enemy crossfire. Upon being challenged by the therapist, however, the driver comes to realize that he or she did everything humanly possible, and the friend's death, while tragic, couldn't be averted. In Exposure Therapy, a person reimagines a traumatic event multiple times in a safe environment, gradually gaining control of his or her fears and disconnecting the memory from the distress associated with it. Both therapies consist of ten to twelve sessions, on average. By the end, a person's memories are less painful and less scary. He or she may still have negative reactions when these memories resurface, but they won't dominate his or her life.

The challenge for many vets is receiving treatment in the first place. Despite the addition of hundreds of new employees with mental health backgrounds, the Department of Veterans Affairs has been unable to keep up with the exploding demand for services. Much of this is due to the growing number of new veterans returning from Iraq and Afghanistan, many of whom are dealing with the mental and physical effects of their recent military service. Not only are they flooding VA hospitals and clinics, but they tend to have multiple needs that can't be treated quickly or easily.

Veterans shouldn't have to wait a year or more for their claims to be processed. Hiring additional claims processors hasn't seemed to help much, nor has the four-year rollout of a $537 million computer system. Regarding the latter, VA officials say that once the system is fully implemented, it will eliminate the department's reliance on paper records. As of spring 2013, however, 97 percent of all veterans' claims continued to be on paper.[77] Moreover, files had become so thick that claims workers continually asked veterans to resend documents because the initial documents couldn't be found. Compounding the problem, until December 2012 there was a points system that rewarded workers for sending determination letters to veterans but didn't value time spent collecting information and reviewing a claims file. Incentives favored the processing of cases with less complexity; thus, the claims of veterans with multiple war injuries or missing paperwork languished.

The VA has a large mandate. There are twenty-two million veterans in this country, and the VA is responsible for providing medical and mental health services to every vet who is enrolled in the Veterans Health Administration (VHA), as well as processing disability claims, home loans, the G.I. Bill (for education subsidies), and death benefits through the Veterans Benefits Administration (VBA). In total, the VA operates 1,700 sites across the country, including 152 hospitals and 131 cemeteries (other sites include clinics, regional loan centers, and vet centers).

Tommy Sowers, assistant secretary for public and governmental affairs at the VA and an Iraq war veteran, notes that 236,000 veterans and eligible family members have health care appointments every day through the VHA, making it the largest integrated health care system in country. That number is equivalent to seeing every active-duty member of the Marine Corps and the Coast Guard daily. In addition, the VA processes monthly payments (referred to as "grants") to more than 3.6 million veterans.[78]

While the VA has a lot to manage, it also has considerable resources—more than 335,000 employees (one for every twenty-five veterans who are enrolled) and a budget of $140 billion. Regardless of the challenges, the process has to be speeded up significantly. It's easy to question the VA's sense of urgency when VA secretary Eric Shinseki told the U.S. Senate Committee on Veterans' Affairs in April 2013 that the problem would be fixed by 2015. Given the enormity of the challenge, though, that might be optimistic. Meanwhile, veterans are feeling the effects, especially as they have their homes foreclosed on and their cars repossessed, and they and their families are forced to soup kitchens, food pantries, and homeless shelters in order to survive. The unemployment rate for veterans continues to be considerably higher than for civilians—10.0 compared with 7.3 as of August 2013.[79]

In December 2012, Francis Guilfoyle drove his 1985 Toyota sedan to the VA campus in Menlo Park, California, retrieved a stepladder and rope from the car, threw the rope over the limb of a tree, and hanged himself. He was fifty-five years old and homeless. A year earlier another veteran, Lisa Silberstein of Hamden, Connecticut, killed herself after applying for benefits and being put on hold. She suffered from posttraumatic stress as a result of serving in Bosnia and being exposed to multiple horrors, one of which was a mess hall fire in which friends of hers died. In December 2011, at age thirty-seven, depressed, unable to hold a job, and feeling—in her sister's words—"worthless," Silberstein killed herself—still waiting for compensation that never arrived.

Many veterans who served their country with pride now feel abandoned. The biggest impediment for them in transitioning to civilian life is receiving health care and compensation for injuries they suffered that are related to their military service. Both must be provided sooner rather than later. If nothing else, first-time claims should be handled before second-, third-, and fourth-time claims, as Joe Stein suggested in a *Time* magazine article, and veterans claiming 100 percent disability should have their cases reviewed before those with 20 percent disabilities.[80] Currently, half of the backlog is the result of veterans who have reapplied either because their initial claims were denied or because they are seeking increased benefits because their condition worsened.[81]

Everything Else

The 2011 RAND report, referenced earlier, notes six practices that are critical to preventing military suicides. They are: 1) raise awareness of the problem and promote self-care (including reducing known risk factors such as alcohol abuse); 2) identify individuals at high risk by screening for stress, depression, and mental illness; 3) facilitate access to quality behavioral health care and reduce barriers to service; 4) provide quality behavioral health care through methods that have proven to be effective empirically; 5) restrict access to lethal means (difficult in the military, but not impossible); and 6) respond appropriately after a suicide occurs (that is, communicate information to family members, fellow soldiers, and the media in ways that are respectful but don't glorify suicide or lead to imitative behavior).

These recommendations are worth adopting but by themselves are inadequate. In addition to the five steps I noted previously, and the RAND recommendations, five other steps are needed.

First, the number of combat deployments should be reduced, as well as the length of each deployment. No one should be sent to a war zone four or five times, and a year or more is too long for someone to serve in a state of constant readiness and hyperalertness. British soldiers in World War I received four days of rest after about twelve days of combat. In the United States, World War I soldiers saw up to eighty days of combat in a row. It's only in the twenty-first century, with the size of our military fixed and too small for the wars we are fighting, that soldiers go back again and again, each time being exposed to continuous combat over many months. Reducing the number of deployments isn't the sole answer, since a number of suicide victims among active-duty soldiers and reservists never deploy, but it will help.

Second, predeployment training needs to be adjusted to take into account the way wars today are waged and the changing role of our military in current conflicts. Soldiers dealing with an asymmetrical battlefield, combatants who dress like civilians, and an enemy that commits random and anonymous acts of violence without a central command need to be able to handle these situations. Whether it's resiliency training, the placement of mental health professionals in war zones, more skill-building among troops to provide mental health assistance, or another option, it can't be ignored. The fact that today's soldiers are called on to provide urban peacekeeping services—repairing roads, fixing sewer systems, building schools, policing streets, and distributing food and clothing— that aren't related to traditional military training also needs to be acknowledged. In addition, when soldiers are put in charge of prisons, they need more training and better direction. They shouldn't be left to fend for themselves, making up rules as they go along.

Third, as much training as troops receive in how to prepare for war, that much training and more needs to be provided at the back end, when they return from combat. Surmounting the moral compunction against killing people requires intensive, near-psychotic immersion in a new mindset, and breaking that mindset when one's military tour of duty ends is no quick and easy feat. The only other people in this country who are socially sanctioned to kill—under specific circumstances—are police officers, and most of them are trained to deal with the psychological consequences of firing their weapons. No such training exists for returning vets. If this lack of training isn't addressed, feelings of guilt, remorse, and unworthiness can haunt a soldier forever. Symptoms can be treated, in part, with medication, but in many instances psychotherapeutic counseling is required.

For too long, the military's answer to psychiatric problems has been to issue a cocktail of antidepressants. In 2010, one-third of Army soldiers were on prescription medications, and 76,500 troops—nearly half—were taking painkillers.[82]

In 2011, Jennifer Senior wrote in *New York Magazine*, "Walk into any of the larger battalion-aid stations in Iraq or Afghanistan today and you'll find Prozac, Paxil, and Zoloft to fight depression, as well as Wellbutrin, Celexa, and Effexor. You'll see Valium to relax muscles (but also for sleep and combat stress) as well as Klonopin, Ativan, Restoril, and Xanax. There's Adderall and Ritalin for ADD and Haldol and Risperdal to treat psychosis; there's Seroquel, at subtherapeutic doses, for sleep, along with Ambien and Lunesta. Sleep, of course, is a huge issue in any war. But in this one, there are enough Red Bulls and Rip Its in the chow halls to light up the city of Kabul, and soldiers often line their pockets with them before missions, creating a cycle where they use caffeine to power up and sleep meds to power down."[83] (According to a 2012 poll by the *Military Times*, women are twice as likely as men to be prescribed psychiatric medication. Antidepressants like Prozac, Paxil, and Zoloft are the most commonly prescribed drugs for both genders, followed by sleep aids such as Ambien and Lunesta.) Many veterans share their medications—especially sleeping pills—with each other, compounding the problem.

Prescribing medication is quick, easy, and relatively cheap, which is why it's common in the military. Oftentimes it leads to more problems than remedies, however. When Ryan Alderman, whose death is described earlier in this book, was discharged from the military hospital at Fort Carson, Colorado, in 2008, doctors had prescribed for him a medicine cabinet full of drugs—Neurotin to prevent seizures (800 milligrams three times per day), Ultram for pain relief (100 milligrams three times per day), Geodon for bipolar disorder (a total of 100 milligrams per day), Clonodine to lower blood pressure (0.1 milligrams three times per day), Remeron for depression (60 milligrams once per day), and Prozac (10 milligrams twice per day). On occasion, Alderman also took Xanax to reduce anxiety, and morphine for pain relief.[84] The Army maintains that Alderman died by suicide, although family members and friends believe that he accidentally overdosed. They say that what he needed was counseling, not so many pills.

Fourth, it's important that supportive services—everything from meaningful employment and affordable housing to help navigating a maze of resources and dealing with anger management issues—are available to veterans. Educational opportunities, substance abuse treatment, child care, loan programs, and legal assistance are just a few of the myriad needs that veterans have, yet even in instances where the military provides these services, information about them can be hard to come by, and the services may be insufficient given the demand.

Last but not least, for the benefit of women who serve, it's essential that all branches of the military adopt an attitude of zero tolerance when it comes to sexual harassment. Too often today, perpetrators go unpunished, and women—who are the primary victims—are made to suffer in silence. This isn't acceptable and shouldn't be condoned. When the person in charge of a program that aims to prevent military sexual assault is himself accused of sexual assault, as Air Force Lieutenant Colonel Jeffrey Krusinski was in May 2013, something is seriously wrong (until his arrest, Krusinski headed the Air Force Sexual Assault Prevention and Response unit). Allowing investigations to be handled by independent military prosecutors rather than the commander in charge seems so obvious that one wonders why it hasn't been standard practice. One also wonders why commanders, to this point, have had the authority to reverse convictions, potentially rendering the outcomes of any proceedings meaningless.

In "Why Soldiers Rape," Helen Benedict recommends that the military make a greater effort to promote and honor female troops, teach everyone that rape is torture and a war crime, expel men who attack female comrades, ban pornography, and stop admitting soldiers who have a history of sexual or domestic violence.[85] These recommendations are made with the intent of showing more regard for women and lessening the abuse that they receive from fellow soldiers. All are worth implementing as a way of reducing suicides by female service members.

Each of the ten steps I have noted, in addition to the RAND recommendations, has a price. In many instances it's significant, and collectively it's astronomical. That price can't stop us from considering these actions, though. Indeed, the sum has to be included in the overall cost of preparing for and waging war. If nothing else, it should give us serious pause before we commit our military forces in the future.

Other Considerations

The long-term cost of fighting the current war in the Middle East goes beyond the psychiatric costs, as large as those are, and the cost of providing medical care to troops with physical injuries that can require ongoing and sometimes life-long treatment. There are homicides by service members and vets, often precipitated, at least in part, by their combat experiences. There are instances of domestic violence caused or exacerbated by a veteran's learned aggression and acquired irritability. There are motor vehicle accidents that result when the driving habits of troops, necessary to survive in war zones, continue on roads at home. And, too, there are the costs borne by our criminal justice system when returning veterans with PTSD are tried for committing crimes, as well as the cumulative effect of these crimes on society in general and a veteran's family in particular.

As Ann Jones reports in *They Were Soldiers*, when the first troops returned to Fort Bragg, North Carolina, from Afghanistan in 2002, there was a rash of murder-suicides. On June 11, Sergeant First Class Rigoberto Nieves shot his wife, then himself. Two weeks later, Master Sergeant William Wright strangled his wife, buried her in the woods, and hanged himself in jail after he was arrested. Two weeks after that, Sergeant First Class Brandon Floyd killed his wife, then himself. In between, Sergeant Cedric Ramon Griffin stabbed his estranged wife fifty times and set her house trailer on fire with their two daughters, ages six and two, inside (the girls escaped and survived).[86]

Stephen Sherwood came home from the war in 2005 a changed man. In Iraq, a rocket attack had killed everyone in his unit while he was on leave. He removed the American flag that was in front of his house and scraped the bumper sticker that expressed support for the troops off his car. Then he and his wife of seven years started arguing, and she admitted that she had had an affair while he was deployed. A short time later, he shot her five times in the face and neck with a pistol, then killed himself with a shotgun. Their young daughter was at a neighbor's house at the time and wasn't harmed. Afterward, police found a newspaper clipping in Sherwood's pocket that said 30 percent of troops returning from Iraq have mental health problems.[87] Sherwood was thirty-five years old when he died and was considered an "outstanding soldier" by Army officials at Fort Carson, where he was stationed.[88] His wife was thirty.

Anthony Marquez also was based at Fort Carson. In 2006, after serving in Iraq, he got into a heated argument with a nineteen-year-old pot dealer who supplied him with weed. The dealer didn't back down, even after Marquez pulled a gun and threatened him. Suddenly Marquez fired two shots, known in the military as a "double tap," into the victim's chest. Then, to the stunned disbelief of others who were present, Marquez calmly collected the two shell casings and his marijuana and left. He didn't even mention the murder to his girl-friend that night when they went out, and he surrendered without incident to police the next day.[89]

"When someone grabs you or something in Iraq, you're going to light 'em up," Marquez said afterward. "It probably won't even be that hard because it's not like it's your first time." He added, "I should not have had a gun. I was on way too much medication. But when he rushed me, I just reacted. If that was a military training exercise, I would have passed."[90]

It wasn't a military exercise, though, and Marquez, who joined the Army at age eighteen, had become addicted to painkillers fol-lowing a friendly-fire injury in Iraq. Only twenty-one at the time of the murder, he pled guilty and is serving a thirty-year prison term. "The Army had spent over a year preparing Marquez for war," David Philipps writes in *Lethal Warriors*. "They didn't spend more than a day preparing him for peace."[91]

According to a 2008 report in the *New York Times*, more than 120 veterans of Iraq and Afghanistan who had psychiatric prob-lems related to the war had been charged with homicide. One-third of the victims were spouses, girlfriends, children, or other rela-tives, one-quarter were fellow soldiers, and the rest were strangers. Thirteen of the veterans killed themselves afterward. The *Times* article noted that the Department of Defense only tracks crimes that pertain to its bases, and no entity—not the VA, Justice Department, or Federal Bureau of Investigation—tracks crimes that veterans com-mit after they become civilians.[92] As a result, the actual number of murders committed by veterans is undoubtedly higher.

One of the murders in 2008 was of a nineteen-year-old aspiring actress. Army Ranger John Needham, age twenty-six, was charged with killing her. In so doing he joined a group of at least thirteen current or former soldiers stationed at Fort Carson in Colorado—Marquez and Sherwood included—to be convicted or accused of murder in the previous four years. The majority of them were in a battalion that called itself the Lethal Warriors.

Prior to the war, Needham was an easygoing surfer who grew up on the beaches of southern California. In 2006, he told his father, a Vietnam War veteran, that he wanted to enlist. His father tried to talk him out of it, but Needham, twenty-three, felt called to duty. Already in good shape, he started his own training regimen, adding forty pounds of muscle to his six-foot-two frame. As David Philipps reports in *Lethal Warriors*, when Needham arrived at Fort Carson that August, his sergeant had the new recruits wrestle each other in a sand pit to establish a pecking order. Needham emerged on top.[93]

Despite his training, Needham wasn't prepared for the horrors he witnessed during his deployment in Iraq. In one instance, an innocent boy riding on a bicycle was shot without cause. When Needham tried to render assistance, he was told to "let him bleed out."[94] In another instance, an Iraqi man who had been wounded in a firefight lay next to what looked to Needham to be a "drop weapon." ("Drop weapons" are confiscated Iraqi rifles that platoons stash in their Humvees. "If we killed someone who was unarmed," a soldier told Philipps, "we would drop the AK next to the body for the pictures to prove his guilt."[95]) Noting that the man was still alive, a sergeant came by and shot him twice.

Needham received two Purple Hearts for injuries received in combat and three medals for heroism. In 2007, he notified military leaders of war crimes he witnessed being committed by U.S. troops, supporting his allegations with atrocity photos. According to an Army document that was suggestive of an investigation, which CBS News obtained, the "offense of War Crimes did not occur." It was impossible for CBS to determine whether the document was an actual investigation or merely the report of one because much of it was redacted, and 111 pages were withheld.[96]

After coming home, Needham claimed that he was suffering from posttraumatic stress. He only received a 10 percent rating for PTSD, however, which effectively denied him one-on-one treatment. In the meantime, he spent the money he had saved up in the Army on a sleek, powerful new car and, two weeks later, in a drunken stupor, totaled it, nearly killing himself. Shortly thereafter he started dating Jacqwelyn Villagomez, who had the looks of a model and the build of an anorexic (at five-foot-seven, she weighed only ninety-five pounds). After they broke up, Villagomez wouldn't leave the townhouse they shared, even though Needham had started seeing another woman.

Villagomez and Needham had a fight, during which Villagomez's beautiful face was beaten badly and she was possibly strangled. An hour later she was pronounced dead at a local hospital. Phillips notes that "homicide detectives searched his [Needham's] room for some kind of weapon because they did not believe that John could do so much damage with just his fists."[97]

During an outside investigation into the charges against Needham, a tape recording was uncovered in which a psychologist admitted to being pressured to make diagnoses that lowered or eliminated the benefits that a soldier like Needham might receive for mental health care. According to reporter Michael De Yoanna, who received an Edward R. Murrow award for investigative journalism in 2011 and covered the Needham case, the tape recording had no effect on the military's finding.

"The Army, investigating internally and quietly," De Yoanna said, "absolved itself of any wrongdoing."[98]

John Needham died in February 2010 while he was free on a $1 million bond, ending the need for a trial. A coroner ruled that the cause of death was opiate intoxication; however, the manner of death wasn't determined, leading to speculation that Needham could have overdosed on medication (he was recovering from back surgery and taking painkillers) or deliberately killed himself. Either way, he became another sad statistic.

So, too, did a thirty-six-year-old Navy sailor living in San Diego military housing who was accused of homicide. In December 2011, the sailor, Sekai Southern, killed his twenty-six-year-old wife, who also was in the Navy, then himself. The couple's eighteen-month-old boy was unharmed in his playpen, and their five-year-old girl was at day care.

Another murder-suicide occurred on New Year's Day, 2012. John Robert Reeves, a twenty-five-year-old Navy fighter pilot at Miramar Air Station, where parts of the movie *Top Gun* were filmed, killed a fellow Navy fighter pilot and two friends before shooting himself in the head. No reason for the murders was made public, although a subsequent toxicology report found that Reeves had twice the legal limit of alcohol in his system.

A month later, in Daytona Beach, Florida, another soldier shot his wife, then himself. Jason Pemberton, twenty-eight, had been a sniper in the U.S. Army. After serving three tours in Iraq, receiving three Purple Hearts and a Bronze Star, he was discharged following a back injury that he suffered when his parachute opened incorrectly. Diagnosed with PTSD, and living with a woman he had married recently, he was going to school to become a motorcycle mechanic when he killed himself and his young bride. In summarizing what happened, the Daytona Beach police chief said, "It's a horrific tragedy. You have a twenty-five-year-old woman who never set foot in Iraq, yet she is a casualty of the war. Clearly, the staff sergeant had issues as a lot of returning veterans do."[99]

Military officials tend to think otherwise. After the 2008 spate of murders by service members at Fort Carson, a commander at the base told the *Los Angeles Times*, "Anybody that does crimes of that nature, it goes deeper and farther back than anything in the U.S. Army.... Nothing here has trained them to do what they are charged with."[100]

It's true that some soldiers who commit violent crimes have psychopathic tendencies that predate their military experiences. Saying that they all do, though, is a stretch. Moreover, if these tendencies existed prior to enlistment, why didn't they show up in military screenings?

In terms of domestic violence, the majority of incidences go unreported, both inside and outside the military. A number of factors—fear, dependency, shame, religious beliefs, and self-blame—lead victims to remain silent and oftentimes stay in abusive relationships. Even when victims come forward seeking legal and physical protection, they may not receive it. The wife of Sergeant William Edwards pressed charges after he beat her, and she obtained a restraining order against him. He was confined to his base (Fort Hood), yet left repeatedly without consequence. After skipping an anger management class, he left the base again, drove to his wife's house, shot her, then killed himself.

Army Specialist Rico L. Rawls, Jr. killed his wife in April 2012 while their one-year-old daughter slept in another room. Then he led police on a high-speed chase that started in Tennessee and ended in Georgia. Rawls, who served two tours in Iraq and was stationed at Fort Campbell, Kentucky, shot himself after police used spike sticks to stop his vehicle.

In *Veterans on Trial: The Coming Court Battles over PTSD*, retired judge Barry R. Schaller writes about the frequent stress placed on marriages when a spouse returns home following deployment. It's a big change for both people and can result in discord and violence.

"When the seeds of marital unrest are combined with the diminished capacity of both spouses to readjust to the relationship and to solve all the problems that exist," Schaller says, "the volatile situation may escalate to the point of combustion."[101]

One study that assessed the quality of life and stresses among spouses of Army soldiers determined that the average military family relocates every 3.3 years. Many of these families are large (42 percent have three or more children), the spouses are uneducated (21 percent lack high school diplomas), and the mothers are young (the average median age is 26.5). In addition, 87 percent have husbands who have deployed previously, with the average separation exceeding seven months.[102] It's a lot for anyone to deal with, posing more challenges than most civilian families face.

Among the effects of deployment is a soldier's aggressive driving habits when he or she comes home. One mother, who appeared on camera in the HBO documentary *Wartorn 1865–2010* following the suicide of her military son, noted that he accumulated $12,000 worth of speeding tickets prior to his death. Another veteran, Marine sergeant Bart Ryan of Stockton, California, who returned in 2005 after eight months of combat in Iraq, had a string of auto accidents and drug arrests that he considered deeply humiliating. In one accident he totaled a car. In another, he nearly killed himself on a motorcycle. In a third accident he was arrested for driving on the wrong side of the road. Twice Ryan sought outpatient help from the VA, only to be turned away because of understaffing. He ended up hanging himself in a jail cell after he couldn't post $5,000 bail following a drug arrest.

According to an unpublished study by the VA, reported in 2013 by the *Washington Post*, male veterans of the wars in Iraq and Afghanistan have a 76 percent higher rate of dying in a vehicle crash than civilians, and female veterans have a rate that is 43 percent higher. Racing through intersections, tailgating, straddling lanes, not conceding the right of way, and swerving on bridges are common habits in war zones. Many soldiers are reluctant to wear seat belts because they get in the way of a quick escape. In addition, after being in combat, veterans are more likely than civilians to engage in drunk driving and thrill seeking, which increase the risk of an accident. The risk is greatest in the immediate months after a soldier comes home, as well as among troops with frequent deployments, according to the *Post*.[103]

Lawrence Adler, a retired VA psychiatrist in Colorado, once described a patient with two habits: driving with a loaded gun on the seat next to him and avoiding traffic jams by veering into the wrong lane. The paradox, said Adler, was that this kind of behavior, extremely dangerous at home, was necessary for survival in a war zone. "What do I tell him—that we can get him on medication and relaxed?" Adler said. "If this patient stops acting like that, he'll be in grave danger once he goes back."[104]

A Final Word

Despite all of the money that has been spent to this point fighting terrorists in the Middle East, all of the lives that have been lost there and at home, and all of the families who now are mourning the deaths of service members and civilians, the situation hasn't improved. Judging by news accounts, the world isn't any safer, American interests are no more secure, and none of the hatred aimed at the United States has quelled. America and Americans remain vilified in many parts of the Arab world, and terrorists have no problem finding new recruits.

Nothing really changed in Korea when the Korean War ended, either. The same political morass, North versus South, remained and, in fact, continues to this day. A similar argument can be made regarding Vietnam, and it's not a stretch to think that the result of years of fighting in Iraq and Afghanistan will be no different. Saddam Hussein, Osama bin Laden, and numerous other evildoers are dead, but the fighting goes on, the number of casualties—military and civilian—keeps growing, and uncertainty continues as to the outcome and future stability of the region.

What has changed is even more alarming, however. Additional billions of dollars have been spent on homeland security. Civil liberties have been restricted. Fear of terrorist attacks is ever-present. Suspected insurgents remain incarcerated at Guantanamo Bay, Cuba, without trial, years after their capture. In addition, the number of suicides by active-duty service members and veterans has reached levels that would have been unthinkable a generation ago.

The obvious solution to ending military suicides is not to wage war. If troops aren't trained to kill, don't kill, and aren't continually placed in situations where they see others killed or seriously injured, much if not all of the trauma associated with war will be eliminated. Feelings of fear, anxiety, guilt, and remorse will be diminished or dispelled altogether.

An early reviewer interpreted the above comment to mean that I intend this book as a platform for advocating against war. Not true. I intend this book as a platform for helping all of us understand the true impact of war, which goes well beyond battlefield deaths, physical destruction, and monetary outlays, as significant as they are.

Suggesting that people and countries stop fighting with each other is unrealistic. Whether it is empire building or self-defense, dreams of greater dominance or fears of losing autonomy, individuals and nations employ violence as a way to protect their interests and weaken or destroy their adversaries. This doesn't mean that war is the right answer, but it's the one humans resort to when diplomacy fails—or, in some instances, before diplomacy is seriously tried. If my message was that all of us need to set aside our differences and just get along, few readers would be inclined to pick up this book.

What is realistic and should be demanded of political leaders who choose to go to war is to comprehend and disclose the true cost. Too often, it seems, the effects aren't fully considered. It isn't lost on those in power that a president's approval rating goes up when he declares war. A perceived threat is presented to the American public with dire consequences if it isn't met head on. Our commander-in-chief looks tough, invincible, and fully in charge when he says that there is no other option but to stand up to the bully who threatens us, or defend those who are defenseless, or protect our own best interests, be they access to natural resources, a region's stability, or our military position. Yes, the lives of young men and women will be endangered, and a few, regrettably, may be lost, but they and their families love our country so much that they are willing to accept this risk. They just need our support.

The talking points are uniform, regardless of the speaker's political party or affiliation, because they never change. Questions of economic costs are pushed aside with vague, undocumented numbers that are presented in a way that minimizes the short-term impact while ignoring long-term consequences altogether. In many instances, the cost isn't factored into the national budget because that would balloon the deficit, which no one wants to defend. Instead, it's tracked separately or, in some instances, isn't tracked at all, leading to abuses for which no one is held accountable.

Little if any thought is given—or so it appears—to the many victims of wars who aren't killed, particularly active-duty troops, reservists, and veterans who suffer long-lasting psychological injuries. These injuries are what lead them to contemplate suicide and, in more than a few instances, to plan, attempt, and complete it.

It's not enough for all of us to be horrified and saddened by each new account of a soldier's death at his or her own hand. As a nation, we must accept some measure of responsibility for these suicides, and commit to ending them. Our troops and their families deserve no less.

Afterword

Shortly after I submitted the final draft of this manuscript and it went into production, three events occurred. The first was front-page news for a day and disappeared within the week. The second received almost no attention, at most appearing one time on an inner page of print publications and going unreported by electronic media. The third produced disbelief, outrage, and a lot of finger pointing, but its lasting impact is unknown at this time. All three events are relevant to the subject of this book.

First, on April 2, 2014, a thirty-four-year-old soldier named Ivan Lopez killed three of his peers and wounded sixteen others before shooting himself at Fort Hood in Texas. Lopez served four months in Iraq in 2011 and was being treated for depression, posttraumatic stress, and insomnia. In the immediate aftermath, Lieutenant General Mark Milley, the commander at Fort Hood, said, "We have very strong evidence that he [Lopez] had a medical history that indicates an unstable psychiatric or psychological condition.... We believe that is the fundamental underlying casual factor here."[1] Army Secretary John McHugh told Congress, however, that when a psychiatrist examined Lopez a month earlier, "There was no indication on the record of that examination that there was any sign of likely violence, either to himself or to others, no suicidal ideation."[2]

Subsequently, General Milley said that Lopez's mental health condition didn't influence his actions; rather, an argument that Lopez had with one or more soldiers at the base precipitated the attack.[3]

The true reason, or reasons, behind Lopez's deadly rampage may never be known. Suicide is complex behavior, and murder-suicides are especially complex, as Thomas Joiner notes in his book *The Perversion of Virtue: Understanding Murder-Suicide*. Nevertheless, this latest example of criminal shootings at U.S. military bases (since 2008 there have been at least nine such incidents) offers another example of how the military goes about dealing with the actions of veterans that end in their suicides.

To recap: The initial reason offered by military officials as to why Lopez killed three soldiers and wounded others then shot himself was because Lopez was mentally unstable. This raises the question of whether Lopez was mentally unstable before he enlisted. If so, why didn't military screening identify his condition and weed him out? Why was he accepted, trained, and deployed? Moreover, before he joined the Army in 2009, Lopez had been in the National Guard for ten years. Why weren't his psychological problems apparent during this service? On the contrary, Puerto Rico National Guard Command Sergeant Major Nelson Bigas, who served with Lopez for seventeen months, said he was "one of the best soldiers we had in our infantry."[4] Bigas said that Lopez worked hard, was a leader within his team, and "never showed any signs of distress."[5]

If Lopez's mental health problems developed after he enlisted, then the questions are even more difficult for the military to answer. Why did they develop, and why wasn't military treatment effective in dealing with them? More ominously, McClatchy Newspapers reporter James Rosen asked, "Have the Iraq and Afghanistan wars created American-grown human time bombs with mental and physical wounds that the military and veterans' health care systems can't adequately track or treat?"[6]

To avoid answering questions like this, military officials had to backtrack from their original position. It was still important to distance the military from bearing any responsibility for what happened, but a new approach was needed. Thus, General Milley said, "We believe that the immediate precipitating factor was more likely an escalating argument in his unit area."[7] According to the Associated Press, General Milley "declined to discuss the cause of the argument but said investigators believe Lopez made no effort to target specific soldiers."[8] In other words, Lopez was so mad about something that he went out and purchased a non-military .45-caliber semiautomatic pistol from a store called Guns Galore,[9] then began firing it indiscriminately before killing himself—unpredictable behavior that indicated the workings of an irrational and demented mind.

A few days later, the story was modified. In the new rendition, Lopez was upset because of an argument that originated when his request for leave to attend his mother's funeral in November 2013 was delayed. His mother, an emergency room nurse in his native Puerto Rico, died suddenly of a heart attack, and it took five days for Lopez's leave request to be approved. Meanwhile, the family postponed the wake until Lopez could attend. Recently, when Lopez went to Fort Hood's personnel office to pick up another leave form, he was told to come back later.[10] His bitterness from his earlier experience surfaced, which led to some sort of verbal altercation, although the specifics haven't been made public. Since then, military officials said that one of the soldiers who was killed was involved in the dispute, but they haven't said in what way. When asked, General Milley told the media, "I don't have details on that."[11]

Military leaders did make a point of noting that Lopez's initial request for twenty-four-hour leave had been extended to two days, as if this compensated for the five days it took to process the request. They also said that Lopez never participated in combat but did receive resiliency training. Both points served the military's purpose. By saying that there was nothing in Lopez's military records to indicate that he saw battle, the Army could deny any connection between it and Lopez's subsequent rampage. And saying that Lopez received resiliency training was a way of absolving the military from responsibility by implying that the Army did all that it could to prepare him for his stint in Iraq.

As other stories in this book show, many soldiers who have been exposed to battlefield situations don't admit it. Doing so delays homecomings and opens them up to additional questions that they don't want to answer. Whether Lopez engaged in combat is uncertain, although he told family members that he sustained a brain injury in Iraq and suffered from PTSD.[12] Neither has been confirmed by the Pentagon, which only acknowledges that Lopez was a truck driver.[13] Inasmuch as driving convoys is one of the most dangerous assignments in the Middle East, it's safe to assume that Lopez thought he was in combat, whether he was fired on or not. According to the *Christian Science Monitor*, Lopez made Facebook posts from Iraq in which he described "hours of agony" and fear driving convoys.[14]

As for the resiliency training, a spokeswoman for the program told the *Los Angeles Times* that Lopez attended classes at Fort Hood and probably at Fort Bliss in El Paso as well, where he was stationed previously. "But we don't know the quality of his training," Becky Farmer said. "Not all instructors are created equally."[15] In other words, the Army could vouch for the training, but not for the trainers, even though the trainers were hired and, presumably, vetted by the Army.

Training is the military's answer to everything. When problems arise, the military's solution is to provide more training. Training is relatively simple, and cheap besides. In contrast, making deep-seeded changes in policies, procedures, attitudes, and culture requires much greater effort and commitment.

Lopez, his wife, and young daughter moved into an apartment in Killeen—adjacent to Fort Hood—a week before his deadly spree. One neighbor told CNN, "He seemed pretty fine, happy." Another said of Lopez and his wife, "They would smile whenever they'd see someone."[16] In his hometown of Guayanilla, Puerto Rico, Lopez was thought of highly—"an extraordinary human being," according to the mayor, Edgardo Arlequin, who directed the school band where Lopez was a percussionist.[17] When Lopez's wife first heard of the shooting on TV, she feared for her husband's safety. Then when reports identified the shooter as Lopez, she became hysterical, according to neighbors.[18]

A week later, there was no further information, and the same was true a month after that. It was just another sad story of a soldier's suicide, in this instance preceded by three murders, all of which quickly became old news. In recounting it, I don't excuse in any way Lopez's violent acts, which have torn apart multiple families, including his own. Instead, my point is that the military bears some of the responsibility. Placing all the blame on Lopez isn't appropriate. If Lopez had psychological problems before he joined the Army, then he shouldn't have been admitted. If these problems developed afterward, while he was in the service and, particularly, following deployment, then military leaders need to explain why they developed, why they weren't treated, or why treatment failed. Without this kind of examination, similar incidents are more likely in the future.

The second event, the one that received scant attention, was a Pentagon report released on April 25, 2014 that provided final data on suicides among active-duty troops in 2013. According to the report, there was a 15 percent reduction in suicides among current service members, offering hope that the military's prevention programs were working and a decade of escalating suicide rates was ending. Among the four military branches, the total number of suicides dropped from 343 in 2012 to 289 in 2013. Army suicides decreased from 185 to 151, Navy suicides from 59 to 44, Air Force suicides from 51 to 49, and Marine suicides from 48 to 45. The report noted that most of the victims were young and white, killed themselves with a nonmilitary firearm, and experienced the seemingly obligatory "family or relationship stress."[19] Military leaders were hesitant to conclude that success had been achieved in the battle against suicide, but they expressed optimism. The Navy's officer in charge of suicide prevention and resilience programs, Rear Admiral Sean Buck, said, "I think we've changed the cultural mindset—that it's okay for a sailor or a soldier or an airman or a Marine to come forward and ask for help."[20]

As in the past, however, the Department of Defense focused on active-duty troops, not members of the National Guard and Reserves. In 2013, a total of 152 Army National Guard members and reservists killed themselves. Not only was this an 8 percent increase over the 2012 number of 140, but it also exceeded the number of suicides among active-duty soldiers in 2013 (151).[21] In other words, more members of the Army National Guard and Reserves killed themselves than Army soldiers who weren't guardsmen or reservists. Granted, the total number of active-duty troops, guardsmen, and reservists who died by suicide in 2013 was still 8 percent lower than in 2012, which is encouraging. It also means, though, that the risk of suicide among National Guard and Reserve members continues to climb, with no turnaround in sight.

The third event was shocking news from the VA in Phoenix that forty veterans died while waiting to receive health care. In addition, there were allegations that top-level administrators in Phoenix not only knew about but also approved methods designed to hide the fact that veterans experienced long waits—up to twenty-one months—before they could get an appointment to see a doctor. Subsequently, there were charges that employees received bonuses if they provided timely care, implying that there were financial incentives for them to lie about it, and indications that records in Phoenix were being shredded in order to destroy evidence of manipulated wait times.

When the VA inspector general's office looked into the matter, it found that 1,700 veterans who were waiting to see a doctor at the Phoenix VA were never scheduled for an appointment or were placed on a list and hadn't been seen yet. They were "at risk of being lost or forgotten," the report concluded. The internal investigation also determined that seventeen veterans died as a result of delayed care in Phoenix, although two weeks later that number was revised to thirty-five.[22]

One casualty who may or may not have been part of the official count was Daniel Somers. He was in the National Guard and served in Iraq. In 2008, a year after his second deployment ended, he sought treatment from the Phoenix VA for PTSD. According to his parents, the VA referred him to a Department of Defense hospital because he was active duty and not a veteran. The Department of Defense referred him back to the VA because of his reserve status. Ultimately, the Phoenix VA agreed to provide care, but the care—mainly medication—didn't help. In 2013, Somers killed himself.

In a suicide note to his wife and family, Somers said, "You will perhaps be sad for a time, but over time you will forget and begin to carry on. Far better that than to inflict my growing misery upon you for years and decades to come, dragging you down with me. It is because I love you that I can not do this to you. You will come to see that it is a far better thing as one day after another passes during which you do not have to worry about me or even give me a second thought. You will find that your world is better without me."[23]

Somers went on to describe the "screaming agony in every nerve ending in my body," which he said was "nothing short of torture. . . . My mind is a wasteland, filled with visions of incredible horror, unceasing depression, and crippling anxiety, even with all of the medications the doctors dare give me. Simple things that everyone else takes for granted are nearly impossible for me. I can not laugh or cry. I can barely leave the house. I derive no pleasure from any activity. Everything simply comes down to passing time until I can sleep again. Now, to sleep forever seems to be the most merciful thing."[24]

In 2004–2005, Somers was part of an intelligence unit that interrogated insurgents and suspected terrorists in Iraq. According to Gawker, which published his suicide note with permission from his wife and family, Somers also participated in more than 400 combat missions, operating a machine gun in the turret of a Humvee. In 2006–2007, he ran the Northern Iraq Intelligence Center in Mosul.

"The fact is that any kind of ordinary life is an insult to those who died at my hand," he wrote. "How can I possibly go around like everyone else while the widows and orphans I created continue to struggle? If they could see me sitting here in suburbia, in my comfortable home...they would be outraged, and rightfully so. ...Is it any wonder that the latest figures show 22 veterans killing themselves each day? That is more veterans than children killed at Sandy Hook, *every single day.*"[25]

Somers blamed the government for turning him into a "sociopath"—his word. He also blamed the VA for abandoning him when he came home suffering. "I am left with basically nothing," he said. "Too trapped in a war to be at peace, too damaged to be at war." He was thirty when he died.

In the wake of the scandal in Phoenix, Eric Shinseki, secretary of the VA, publicly denounced the actions of administrators there and vowed to implement immediate changes. It was too little, too late, however. In an election year, members of Congress in both parties voiced their displeasure with his leadership and called for his resignation, as did the American Legion, the nation's largest veterans group. When it came, it was tinged with regret. Shinseki had served admirably in the military for nearly fifty years, including the last five years as head of the VA, and he clearly was blindsided by the duplicity of some VA health care leaders. Nevertheless, the situation was untenable, and he had to go.

It's still untenable and isn't likely to be resolved by the time this book is published. The problems are too deep-seeded. Moreover, with a new secretary there will be a learning curve that results in additional delays in fixing the system.

No wonder the nation's veterans feel mistreated and distrustful of the VA. They served their country loyally, risking life, limb, and mind to protect and defend us all, yet when it comes to protecting and defending them, we as a country are failing. This can't change soon enough.

Appendix A
About Suicide

Here is a simple question, the answer to which surprises most people: Are there more homicides or suicides in the United States?

The majority of Americans assume that there are more homicides. After all, stories of murder fill our daily news and are dramatized in countless TV shows and movies. By comparison, suicides seem to occur much less frequently. In fact, though, it's the reverse. More than twice as many people kill themselves every year in the United States than are murdered. In 2010, the latest year for which statistics are available, 38,364 Americans died by suicide (one every 14 minutes), while 16,259 were murdered (one every 32 minutes). In 2009, there were 36,909 suicides and 16,799 homicides.[1] That's a ratio of 2.3 suicides to every 1 homicide. Another way to look at it is that the same number of people who were killed in the 9/11 terrorist attacks now die by their own hand in America *every month*.

From the viewpoint of the media, suicide is newsworthy only under unusual conditions—a celebrity is involved, the method is unusual, there are multiple suicides at one time, or a person kills others before turning the gun on himself. (The male pronoun is used here deliberately. Women rarely murder others before killing themselves.) This is why suicides aren't reported more often. As for portrayals of suicide, by age 18 the average TV viewer in the United

States will see 800 suicides depicted in various shows and movies. During that same period of time, he or she will see 40,000 murders depicted.[2] When the former comprises only 2 percent of your viewing experience, it's easy to think that suicides are relatively rare—certainly not as common as homicides.

One way to understand this is to compare the list of famous people who have been murdered with those who died by suicide. Except for assassinations of political leaders, the shootings of several musical performers (John Lennon, Mexican-American singer Selena, and hip-hop artists 2Pac and Biggie), and the death of zoologist Dian Fossey, one is hard-pressed to name anyone famous who has been slain. Actress Natalie Wood died under mysterious circumstances, as did activist Karen Silkwood, and teamster president Jimmy Hoffa disappeared, but their deaths have never been confirmed as homicides. As for actress Sharon Tate, her fame today rests more on the circumstances surrounding her death than on accomplishments while she was alive. The same is even more true for child model JonBenet Ramsey.

In contrast, the list of well-known suicide victims is long, even omitting political leaders such as Adolf Hitler and Roman emperor Nero. It includes Ernest Hemingway, Sigmund Freud, Marilyn Monroe, Vincent Van Gogh, Bruno Bettelheim, Abbie Hoffman, Diane Arbus, Jack London, Hunter Thompson, Meriwether Lewis, Kurt Cobain, Jerzy Kosinski, David Foster Wallace, Sylvia Plath, Virginia Woolf, Iris Chang, Richard Brautigan, Anne Sexton, Michael Dorris, Margaux Hemingway, Mark Rothko, Cleopatra, Hart Crane, Spalding Gray, Alan Turing, Robin Williams, and Stefan Zweig. George Eastman of Eastman Kodak; Ray Raymond, who founded Victoria's Secret; and Rudolf Diesel, who invented the diesel engine, also died by suicide. So, too, did Yasunari Kawabata, who won the 1968 Nobel Prize for Literature, homeless advocate Mitch Snyder, singer Phil Ochs, actress Jean Seberg, one-time Superman George Reeves, former Senate majority leader William Knowland, former secretary of defense James Forrestal, All-Pro football players Junior Seau and Jim Tyrer, Olympic beach volleyball medalist Mike Whitmarsh, Olympic freestyle skiing medalist Jeret Peterson, ladies pro golfer Erica Blasberg, Cy Young Award winner Mike Flanagan, Yankees pitcher Hideki Irabu, and Angels pitcher Donnie Moore. The latter shot himself three years after giving up the winning home run in game five of the 1986 American League Championship Series when he was one strike away from clinching the team's first-ever pennant—a fact many Angels fans didn't forgive or forget.

Two of Bing Crosby's sons died by suicide. So, too, did the sons of Danielle Steel, Tony Dungy, Marie Osmond, Pierre Salinger, and Judy Collins; the daughters of Winston Churchill, Marlon Brando, Art Linkletter, and Burt Bacharach and Angie Dickinson; the mothers of Drew Brees and Jane and Peter Fonda; the fathers of Ted Turner, Archie Manning, and Chesley Sullenberger; the spouses of Robert F. Kennedy, Jr., Bill Bixby, and Isadora Duncan; the longtime girlfriend of Mick Jagger; the sisters of David Sedaris and Charlotte Rampling; the half-sister of Julia Roberts; the brother of Anderson Cooper (who was the younger son of Gloria Vanderbilt); and Mariette Hartley's father, uncle, and cousin.

In 2002, Enron vice chairman J. Clifford Baxter took his life shortly after the company's financial schemes became public. In 2008, French investment fund manager Thierry de la Villehuchet died by suicide after learning that all of the money he encouraged clients to invest with Bernard Madoff was lost. David Kellerman, the chief financial officer of Freddie Mac, killed himself in 2009 after the insurance giant reported billions of dollars of bad loans. Aaron Swartz, one of the co-founders of Reddit, an Internet news service, died by suicide in 2013 at age twenty-six after he was charged with hacking into and illegally downloading articles from a database at the Massachusetts Institute of Technology.

According to the federal Substance Abuse and Mental Health Services Administration (SAMHSA), more than 1.1 million Americans attempt suicide each year. More than 2.2 million Americans make a suicide plan. More than 8.4 million Americans have serious thoughts of suicide.[3]

One might think that seeing a doctor makes a difference in terms of lessening the risk, but statistics don't bear this out. More than three-quarters of the people who die by suicide have visited their primary care physician within the past year, and nearly half have seen their doctor within the past month.[4]

The percentages are equally high for military service members. According to the National Center for Telehealth and Technology, 45 percent of troops who die by suicide have visited an outpatient medical clinic in the previous month, and 73 percent of troops who suffer from a self-inflicted injury—usually a suicide attempt—sought medical care in the previous thirty days.[5]

The most dangerous time for someone who has been admitted to a psychiatric hospital following a suicide attempt is immediately after the person is discharged. One study determined that for men, the risk is 102 times greater in the first week following discharge while for women it's 256 times greater.[6] A reason for this is the mistaken belief that when the person is discharged, medical staff have dealt with the problem so loved ones can relax. In fact, it's the opposite. Regardless of whether the person received proper care in the moment, he or she is still at high risk. Hospitalization has bought time, which is important, but the danger remains. Loved ones need to operate with heightened awareness of the problem and increased urgency in seeking longer-term treatment for the individual.

Overall, there are an estimated 650,000 emergency department visits per year in the United States resulting from suicide attempts. The cost of medical treatment is $3 billion annually.[7]

To an outside observer, the reason that a person dies by suicide may seem straightforward. A relationship ends, a loved one dies, a job is lost, a test is failed, a financial catastrophe occurs. This is too simplistic, however. The great majority of people in these situations never attempt suicide, much less complete it. Even people who are diagnosed with a fatal illness, whose life expectancy is shortened and whose last days may be filled with physical pain, have suicide rates in keeping with people the same age who aren't dealing with the same prognosis. Similarly, many individuals who are in the highest-risk groups—isolated seniors, mentally ill adults, Native American and homosexual youths, active-duty soldiers and veterans—never make an attempt.

The scientific study of suicide goes back a little more than 100 years. French sociologist Emile Durkheim published the first empirical study in 1897. He attributed suicide to a variety of factors having to do with how socially connected a person is. Individuals who are married, have children, are employed, and practice a religion where followers are close-knit, such as Judaism, interact more with others, Durkheim maintained, and for that reason they attempt suicide less often. Marriage, parenthood, a job, and shared spiritual beliefs all act as buffers against suicide. Conversely, being single, without children, unemployed, and lacking the support that a person's community of faith may provide increases the risk.

Following Durkheim, the study of suicide was taken up by mental health professionals, some of whom owe their reputations to the pioneering work they did analyzing why people kill themselves. Karl Menninger, Edwin Shneidman, and Aaron T. Beck moved away from social causes to focus on psychological issues. It was Shneidman who coined the phrase "psychache" to refer to the emotional duress that a suicidal person is experiencing. Others examined feelings of helplessness, hopelessness, and depression as they pertained to suicide.

In recent years the study of suicide—suicidology, another word that Shneidman coined—has taken a physical turn. Researchers are beginning to note potential links between chromosomal genes and suicidal behavior. If verified, these studies may help prove that a predisposition to suicide exists among some people—no doubt welcome news to loved ones since it will lessen feelings of anger, guilt, and shame that accompany a death by suicide. Other studies indicate that decreased levels of serotonin, a neurotransmitter in the brain, probably play a factor. Serotonin is associated with feelings of well-being and happiness, and there is good reason to believe that lowered amounts bring on feelings of depression. (Drugs such as Prozac, Paxil, and Zoloft increase serotonin levels, which is why they are often prescribed for depressed patients.)

Today, all of these factors—social, mental, and physical—are considered integral to understanding suicide. So, too, is the ability to kill oneself, as researcher Thomas Joiner's work is proving. It isn't enough that people want to die; they have to develop the capacity to make a suicidal attempt. After all, surmounting the self-preservation instinct that humans are born with isn't easy. According to Joiner, it requires repeated exposure to pain and suffering, directly or indirectly. In this way, a person becomes habituated to death, and fearless of it.

While suicidal behavior is complex, thoughts of suicide often result from problems that seem unfixable. Gambling losses, legal issues, relationship problems, academic failures, mental disorders, unemployment, substance abuse, grief, and feelings of being a burden to loved ones can contribute to insurmountable feelings of despair—but not for everyone. Some people are able to manage these challenges, while others can't, and that is more difficult to explain. Just as two people may experience the same horrific event, yet only one of them develops PTSD, so can two people experience similar setbacks, yet only one of them resorts to suicide. Is it because the other one has stronger coping skills and is more resilient? Few, if any, of us could withstand the tragedies faced by Job in the Bible, whose livestock, servants, and ten children die and who is made to suffer from horrible skin sores (all to prove his faith in God), but most of us, at various times, have had to bear our own heavy burdens. If they don't push us over the edge, is it because we are able to find a bright side somewhere, to hold onto something positive even in the midst of an overwhelming loss? And if we can find something, why can't others?

People don't kill themselves because they want to die. They kill themselves because they want their pain to end—whether it's physical, mental, or emotional pain—and suicide seems like the only way this will happen. In most cases there are other options, but the person can't see them because his or her judgment is impaired.

In talking with someone who is suicidal, counselors don't eliminate that option, they don't take suicide off the table. Not only would it be naive and unrealistic, but the thought of suicide for some people is comforting rather than scary. They don't want to lose it. While everything else may seem out of their control, they still have the power to determine their fate. They and they alone can decide whether to persevere or give up. What counselors do is acknowledge that suicide is an option, but emphasize that it's not the only option. The goal is to push suicide farther down the list. It may not disappear altogether, but in time and with support, the person may find reasons to live.

It doesn't help that suicide as a subject is taboo in our society. People are afraid to talk about it. One reason that it's taboo is because of the mistaken belief that talking about suicide will plant the idea in someone's mind when it wasn't there before. We don't have the same fear in regard to other problems—drug use, alcoholism, smoking, domestic violence, homophobia, and unsafe sex, for example—but we do when it comes to suicide. Yet anyone who has counseled clinically depressed people will tell you that the person was thinking about suicide long before the clinician—or anyone else—first mentioned it. Once it's mentioned, the person often feels relieved, as if he or she has been given permission to talk about it, but not until then.

The stigma of suicide prevents many people who need help from seeking it. Instead, they hide their thoughts, ashamed to have them and unwilling to let others know, especially loved ones who, they believe, won't be able to deal with them effectively, and will sit in judgment besides. Even the language commonly used to refer to suicide is inappropriate. For instance, the phrase "committed suicide" implies that suicide is illegal when it's not. No one says that a person "committed cancer." Instead, he or she died by cancer, and someone who kills themselves should be referred to in the same way, as dying from suicide. Similarly, it's inappropriate to call someone's death "a successful suicide" or say that the person "failed" in his or her suicide attempt, because suicide shouldn't be a goal. The correct phrase for a suicide death is "a completed suicide."

The situation is improving slightly. Suicide is starting to come out of the shadows, but it has a long way to go before real progress is made. Suicide today is where HIV/AIDS and breast cancer were twenty years ago. In the past two decades, considerable resources in the form of funding, research, and support services have been directed to these two diseases, with notable success. Detection and screening are much better now, as is treatment.

While there has been a committed effort to combat HIV/AIDS and breast cancer, to apply our knowledge, technology, and compassion in order to eliminate unnecessary suffering, the same can't be said about suicide. As a nation, we still fear suicide rather than want to conquer it.

Suicidal thinking isn't easy to identify, either in the military or outside it. At the same time, it's not that difficult to detect once a person knows what to look for, once he or she learns common warning signs:

- Talking about suicide or making statements revealing a desire to die.
- Drastic changes in behavior (withdrawal, apathy, moodiness).
- Losing interest in hobbies and in personal appearance.
- Ongoing depression (chronic crying, sleeplessness, loss of appetite, feelings of hopelessness).
- Worsening academic or job performance; sudden failure to complete assignments.
- Lack of interest in activities and surroundings (dropping out of sports and clubs).

- Settling affairs (giving away prized possessions).
- Increased irritability or aggressiveness.
- Remarks suggesting profound unhappiness, despair, or feelings of worthlessness.
- Self-destructive behavior (taking unnecessary risks or increased drug or alcohol use).

There is a myth that people who talk about suicide won't really do it. This is wrong. Before attempting suicide, many individuals make direct statements about their intention to end their lives or less direct comments about how they might as well be dead or that their family and friends will be better off without them. Any reference to suicide should be taken seriously. People who have tried to kill themselves before are especially at risk, even if their previous attempts seemed half-hearted or more designed to gain attention than inflict self-harm. Unless they are helped, they may try again, and the next time could be fatal.

Several years ago, the American Foundation for Suicide Prevention sponsored a magazine ad. The ad featured a good-looking young man in a white T-shirt sitting on a park bench. Printed on his T-shirt, in large, black letters, were the words "I'm suicidal." Underneath the photo was the headline, "If only it was that easy to identify." The point of the ad was that suicide isn't easy to identify, primarily because as a subject it's stigmatized.

If someone says that he or she is contemplating suicide or shows signs of being suicidal, the best way to help is to talk with the person about it. There are no magic words; there is only the willingness of family members, friends, and mental health professionals to discuss suicide openly and honestly. As scary as that might seem, it shows the person that others care.

Ask questions about how the person feels. "You seem really down. Is there a reason?" Ask questions about suicide itself. "Do you know how you'd do it?" Determine whether the person has the means to carry out a plan, such as access to a gun or pills. The more specific the plan, the higher the risk. Also, be aware that anniversaries—of a birth, a death, a marriage, a divorce—can be triggers.

In asking questions and assessing intent, it's important to avoid false promises and comments that, unintentionally, add to a person's dark mood. For example, saying that a lover probably will return or that someone's depression will go away may serve to lift someone's spirits temporarily but ultimately can result in an even harder fall if the promise doesn't materialize. In the same way, telling someone, "You're better off than most people; you should appreciate how lucky you are," only increases feelings of guilt and makes the suicidal person feel worse.

Many suicidal people have given up hope, believing that they can't be helped. Most likely, though, things will improve for them at some point if they are able to hang on. Just as good times don't last forever, bad times don't last forever, either.

It's up to others to see that suicidal people get the help they need. Specific resources are listed in Appendix B.

Appendix B
Resources

Suicide Prevention

National Suicide Prevention Lifeline (NSPL): A toll-free phone number, 800-273-TALK (8255), and chat service that anyone who is suicidal can contact day or night to receive free, immediate counseling and support. The service is supported by the VA and SAMHSA, and callers can press "1" to connect to special resources for veterans. Calls to 800-SUICIDE (784-2433) also are routed here. In addition, NSPL operates a twenty-four-hour Spanish-language suicide hotline (888-628-9454) and has an extensive website. www. suicidepreventionlifeline.org

American Association of Suicidology (AAS): A research institute whose website features facts and statistics, multimedia resources, and information for family members and friends of suicide victims, as well as for suicide attempt survivors. AAS also certifies crisis centers across the United States, qualifying them to handle calls from the NSPL. www.suicidology.org

American Foundation for Suicide Prevention (AFSP): A non-profit agency with a website that has facts and figures, research findings, public policy and advocacy information, and education and training materials. AFSP also organizes "Out of the Darkness" walkathons throughout the United States whose aim—in addition to raising money for the organization—is to promote suicide awareness. www.afsp.org

Defense Suicide Prevention Office (DSPO): A new entity with authority for all suicide prevention programs, policies, and surveillance activities within the Department of Defense. DSPO oversees the strategic development, implementation, centralization, standardization, communication, and evaluation of efforts by the Army, Air Force, Marine Corps, Navy, National Guard, and Coast Guard to reduce suicides by active-duty service members. www.suicideoutreach.org

Suicide Prevention Resource Center (SPRC): An education and training center whose website has information on assessing and managing suicide risk, a library of resource materials and online trainings, and a listing of school and tribal communities that receive special funding for suicide prevention from SAMHSA. SPRC also maintains a best practices registry that recognizes agencies whose suicide prevention programs are considered to be models in the field. www.sprc.org

All Armed Forces

U.S. Department of Defense: www.defense.gov

Armed Forces Crossroads: A source of information on deployment, employment, education, financial assistance, health care, and relocation. www.afcrossroads.com

Battlemind: A website with information to help troops and their families deal with the stress of deployment. www.battlemind.org

Department of Defense Deployment Health Clinical Center: The official website of the military health system for active-duty service members. www.health.mil

Deployment Health and Family Readiness Library: A website for troops who are deploying and their families. http://deployment healthlibrary.fhp.osd.mil

Military OneSource: A toll-free, twenty-four-hour phone number (800-342-9647) that active-duty troops, their families, and veterans can call for help and information. www.militaryonesource. com

Military.com: A website that connects troops, their families, and veterans with a variety of benefits. www.military.com

National Guard Family Program: A source of information about benefits, resources, and programs for National Guard members and their families. www.guardfamily.org

Reserve Affairs: A resource for members of the Reserves regarding services and benefits relative to family readiness in the event someone deploys. www.defenselink.mil/ra

Air Force

U.S. Air Force: www.af.mil
U.S. Air National Guard: www.ang.af.mil
U.S. Air Force Reserve Command: www.afrc.af.mil

Army

U.S. Army: www.army.mil
U.S. Army Reserves: www.armyreserves.com
U.S. Army National Guard: www.arng.army.mil
Army MWR: A source of information for soldiers and their families concerning morale, welfare, and recreation. www.armymwr.com

Marine Corps

U.S. Marines Corps: www.usmc.mil
U.S. Marine Corps Forces Reserve: www.marforres.marines.mil
Marine Corps Community Services: A source of information on Marine and family programs, recreation resources, and retirement. www.usmc-mccs.org

Navy

U.S. Navy: www.navy.mil
U.S. Navy Reserve: www.navyreserve.com

Coast Guard

U.S. Coast Guard: www.uscg.mil
U.S. Coast Guard Reserves: www.uscg.mil/reserve

Veterans

U.S. Department of Veterans Affairs: 800-827-1000; www.va.gov
Veterans Benefits Administration: www.vba.va.gov
Veterans Health Administration: www.va.gov/health
My Health eVet: A portal for veterans and their families to access health-related information. www.myhealth.va.gov
Vet Centers: A nationwide network of more than 300 places where veterans and their families can receive counseling and other services. www.vetcenter.va.gov
Veterans and Families Coming Home: A nonprofit organization that helps veterans transition to civilian life and assists their families to support their homecoming. www.veteransandfamilies.org

General/Other

211: A free, national, three-digit phone number, answered by a variety of community-based organizations, that provides information about all kinds of local health and social services available daily and following a disaster to anyone in need. www.211.org
Give an Hour: A nonprofit organization with a national network of mental health professionals who offer one hour per week of free counseling for troops and their families. www.giveanhour.org
Healthfinder.gov: A website with health information sponsored by the U.S. Department of Health and Human Services. www.health finder.gov
National Alliance on Mental Illness (NAMI): An organization of mental health consumers and family members with local chapters across the United States and a veterans' resource center. www. nami.org
Patriot Guard Riders (PGR): An affiliated group of motorcycle riders across the country that honors fallen veterans by attending their funeral services, after being invited by the family, as well as participates in events for returning or wounded troops. www. patriotguard.org
Soldier's Heart: A nonprofit organization that helps families and communities support healing veterans. www.soldiersheart.net
Tragedy Assistance Program for Survivors (TAPS): A bereavement service for families of troops who are killed. www.taps.org

Wounded Warrior Project: A nonprofit organization that helps men and women in the military who have been severely injured during battles in Iraq, Afghanistan, and elsewhere in the world. www.woundedwarriorproject.org

Research

Centers for Disease Control and Prevention (CDC): A federal agency, under the Department of Health and Human Services, responsible for protecting the public health and safety of U.S. citizens through disease control and injury prevention. In addition to providing information that aims to improve Americans' health, the CDC engages in research projects and maintains extensive databases on suicide, other types of morbidity, disease, and injury. www.cdc.gov

Mental Illness Research, Education, and Clinical Centers (MIRECC): Ten VA research centers, most affiliated with an academic institution, that study the causes and treatments of mental disorders. The focus of each center is different; for example, the New England MIRECC studies dual diagnosis (veterans who have both a mental illness and addiction problems), while the Desert Pacific MIRECC studies chronic mental health disorders such as schizophrenia. The Rocky Mountain MIRECC, in partnership with the University of Colorado School of Medicine, focuses on reducing suicide among veterans. www.mirecc.va.gov/visn19

National Center for PTSD: A research and education institute that is focused on understanding, preventing, and treating posttraumatic stress disorder. It is one of the ten VA Mental Illness Research, Education, and Clinical Centers. www.ptsd.va.gov

Appendix C
Glossary

Acronyms are common in the military. Wherever possible, I have tried to avoid their use. Listed here are terms that appear in this book.

ASIST: Applied Suicide Intervention Skills Training: A training program in suicide prevention endorsed by SAMHSA, the National Suicide Prevention Lifeline, and various military branches.

CBT: Cognitive Behavioral Therapy: A form of therapy in which accurate, positive thoughts replace negative and faulty thinking.

CDC: Centers for Disease Control and Prevention: A federal agency that conducts research and maintains extensive data on health-related factors in the United States.

CPT: Cognitive Processing Therapy: A form of therapy in which one or more traumatic events are processed through written narratives and restructured assessment.

CSF: Comprehensive Soldier Fitness: An Army program that focuses on resiliency training for current soldiers.

DEROS: Date of Expected Return from Overseas: The date that a service member's tour of duty ended during the Vietnam War.

DoD: Department of Defense: All active-duty branches of the U.S. Armed Forces—Army, Navy, Air Force, Marine Corps, National Guard, Reserves, and Coast Guard.

DSM: *Diagnostic and Statistical Manual of Mental Disorders*: A comprehensive guide to all kinds of psychiatric conditions, with definitions, symptoms, and recommended treatments, published by the American Psychiatric Association. The fifth and most recent edition was released in May 2013.

Dwell time: The Army name for the period of reintegration following a soldier's return home from deployment.

Flashback: An unwanted memory that seems real.

FOB: Forward Operating Base: A military base in an unfriendly area that is secure and is used to support tactical operations.

Forming: The process by which someone learns what it means to be a Marine.

IED: Improvised Explosive Device: A bomb, often buried in trash on the side of the road.

In country: In a foreign land.

In theater: In a combat zone.

JAG: Judge Advocate General: The military branch that deals with justice and law. Duties include providing legal counsel to commanders and prosecuting court-martial cases.

MHC: Medical Holding Company: A facility for active-duty soldiers who can't return to full duty yet, often because they are recovering from an injury.

MREs: Meals Ready to Eat: Packaged food that doesn't require cooking and has a long shelf life. Soldiers joke that the initials stand for Meals Rejected by Ethiopia.

NCO: Noncommissioned officer.

NG: National Guard: Military reserves whose service is controlled by state government, but who can be called on to serve in time of war or natural disaster by the federal government.

NSPL: National Suicide Prevention Lifeline: A toll-free telephone number (800-273-TALK) that is answered twenty-four hours a day by certified crisis centers. Anyone who is feeling suicidal can call for free phone counseling and support; veterans can press "1" for special assistance.

OEF: Operation Enduring Freedom: The name for current military operations in Afghanistan.

OIF: Operation Iraqi Freedom: The name for military operations in Iraq before September 2010.

OND: Operation New Dawn: The name for the U.S. presence in Iraq since September 2010.

Outside the wire: Leaving the safety of an enclosed military base.

PDHA: Post Deployment Health Assessment: An evaluation of a service member who returns from a war zone to determine whether he or she has any physical or mental health issues.

PDHRA: Post Deployment Health Re-Assessment: Similar to a PDHA except that it's done three to six months later.

PE: Prolonged Exposure therapy: A form of therapy in which a traumatic event is relived in a therapeutic setting and feelings about it are examined.

PIE: Proximity, Immediacy, Expectancy: The model developed in World War I to provide front-line treatment for troops with psychiatric problems. Sometimes an "S" is added at the end for Simplicity.

POW: Prisoner of War: A combatant who is captured and imprisoned by the enemy.

PTSD: Posttraumatic Stress Disorder: A clinical condition that results from exposure to one or more horrific events and life-threatening situations.

RPG: Rocket-Propelled Grenade: A grenade launched via rocket.

SAMHSA: Substance Abuse and Mental Health Services Administration: A branch of the federal government, under the U.S. Department of Health and Human Services, focused on treating and preventing substance abuse problems and mental illness. Federally funded suicide prevention programs fall under SAMHSA's purview.

Sandbox: The colloquial term for Iraq.

Taking the pack off: Leaving combat mentally and physically.

TBI: Traumatic Brain Injury: An internal head injury oftentimes resulting from artillery explosions in which a helmet offers no protection.

VA: U.S. Department of Veterans Affairs, until 1989 known as the Veterans Administration.

VBA: Veterans Benefit Administration: The source of death, disability, and other benefits provided to veterans by the VA.

VBIED: Vehicle-Born Improvised Explosive Device: A bomb that is attached to a moving vehicle.

VHA: Veterans Health Administration: The system of hospitals and clinics operated by the VA that provides medical care and mental health services to veterans.

Notes

History is the transformation of tumultuous conquerors into silent footnotes.

    —*Paul Eldridge*

Preface

1. Ronald H. Cole, *Operation Urgent Fury.*
2. "The Unfinished War: A Decade since Desert Storm," CNN.com, Gulf War Facts, 2001.
3. "The Military-Civilian Gap: Fewer Family Connections."
4. Laurie B. Slone and Matthew J. Friedman, *After the War Zone: A Practical Guide for Returning Troops and Their Families,* 205–6.
5. National Priorities Project, www.costofwar.com.

Chapter 1

1. Letter of Angelo Crapsey to Laroy Lyman, March 1, 1862.
2. Letter of Crapsey to Lyman, May 22, 1861.
3. Letter of Crapsey to Lyman, May 22, 1861.

4. Letter of Crapsey to Lyman, May 22, 1861.

5. Letter of Crapsey to his father, June 5, 1863.

6. Letter of Crapsey to Lyman, October 10, 1861.

7. Letter of Crapsey to Lyman, January 4, 1862, describing the Battle of Dranesville.

8. Letter of Crapsey to Lyman, March 1, 1862.

9. Letter of Crapsey to Lyman, March 1, 1862.

10. Letter of Crapsey to Lyman, September 30, 1862.

11. Letter of Crapsey to Lyman, September 30, 1862.

12. Letter of Crapsey to Lyman, September 30, 1862.

13. Letter of Crapsey to Frank Sibley, September 7, 1863.

14. Dennis W. Brandt, in notes accompanying the HBO documentary *Wartorn, 1865–2010*.

15. Deposition of Charles H. Robbins in pension hearing of Angelo Crapsey, January 18, 1893.

16. Drew Gilpin Faust, *This Republic of Suffering*, 4.

17. Dennis W. Brandt, "Angelo Crapsey (Subject Feature)," http://www.hbo.com/documentaries/wartorn-1861-2010#/documentaries/wartorn-1861-2010/article/angelo-crapsey-subject-feature-.html.

18. Dennis W. Brandt, *Pathway to Hell*, 146.

19. Brandt, "Angelo Crapsey (Subject Feature)."

20. Brandt, *Pathway to Hell*, 150.

21. Department of Defense Personnel and Military Casualty Statistics, "Casualty Summary by Reason, October 7, 2001 through August 18, 2007," Defense Manpower Data Center.

22. David Philipps, *Lethal Warriors*, 11.

23. Sherr, "Coming Home."

24. "Suicide Rate for Veterans Twice That of Other Americans."

25. Andrew E. Kramer, "A New Hotel, Where the Stay Used to Be Mandatory."

26. Greg Mitchell, "She Survived Iraq—Then Shot Herself at Home."

27. Eric Coker, "Historian Focuses on Civil War Suicides."

28. David Silkenat, *Moments of Despair: Suicide, Divorce, and Debt in Civil War Era North Carolina*, 9.

29. Diane Miller Sommerville, "A Burden Too Heavy to Bear," *Civil War History*.

30. Richard A. Gabriel, *No More Heroes: Madness and Psychiatry at War*, 42.

31. Sommerville, "A Burden Too Heavy to Bear," *Civil War History*.

32. R. Gregory Lande, "Felo De Se."

33. Lande, "Felo De Se."

34. Lande, "Felo De Se," 157.

35. Brandt, "Angelo Crapsey (Subject Feature)."

36. Doris Lessing, *A Small Personal Voice*, 92.

37. Ben Shephard, *A War of Nerves*, 169.

38. Aaron Glantz, "Suicide Rates Soar among WWII Vets, Records Show."

39. Penny Coleman, *Flashback*, 130.

40. Coleman, *Flashback*, 143.

41. *Agent Orange Review* 2, no. 2, June 1983, 1.

42. Coleman, *Flashback*, 144.

43. P. J. Crane et al., "Mortality of Vietnam Veterans," *The Veteran Cohort Study: A Report of the 1996 Retrospective Cohort Study of Australian Vietnam Veterans*, 1997.

44. Australian Institute of Health and Welfare, *Morbidity of Vietnam Veterans: Suicide in Vietnam Veterans' Children (Supplementary Report 1)*, 2000.

45. Norman Hearst, Thomas B. Neuman, and Stephen P. Hulley, "Delayed Effects of the Military Draft on Mortality," 620–24.

46. Jacob D. Lindy, *Vietnam: A Casebook*, xvi.

47. Anderson, "Vietnam Legacy: Veteran's Suicide Toll May Top War Casualties."

48. "The War That Has No Ending," 44–47.

49. "Vietnam 101."

50. "CBS Reports: The Wall Within."

51. Lindy, *Vietnam*, xvi.

52. Chuck Dean, *Nam Vet: Making Peace with Your Past*, 36.

53. U.S. Centers for Disease Control and Prevention, http://www.cdc.gov/nceh/veterans/pdfs/volumeiv/psychologicalandneuropsychologicalevaluation2_5.pdf.

54. George Howe Colt, *November of the Soul: The Enigma of Suicide*, 244, citing data from the World Health Organization.

55. Paul Elias, "Court Orders Mental Health Overhaul."

56. Greg Jaffe, "VA Study Finds More Veterans Committing Suicide."

57. Janet E. Kemp, "Suicide Rates in VHA Patients through 2011 with Comparisons with Other Americans and Other Veterans through 2010."

58. Michael Kelley, "The U.S. Government Is Failing Miserably at Helping Veterans," quoting Phil Stewart of Reuters.

59. "Tragic Iraq War Veteran, 25, Shoots Himself Dead in Front of Father in Family's Backyard after Battle with PTSD."

60. Anthony Swofford, " 'We Pretend the Vets Don't Even Exist.' "

61. Coleman, *Flashback*, 146.

62. Mark S. Kaplan, Nathalie Huguet, Bentson H. McFarland, and Jason T. Newsom, "Suicide among Male Veterans: A Prospective Population-Based Study, July 2007."

63. Kristen Moulton, "U. Study: Combat Puts Soldiers at High Suicide, PTSD Risk."

64. Eric T. Dean, Jr., *Shook Over Hell*, 212.

65. Baldor, "This Is What It's Like to Be an Army Woman in Combat."

66. Armed Forces Health Surveillance Center, "Deaths by Suicide while on Active Duty, Active and Reserve Components, U.S. Armed Forces, 1988–2011."

67. News 21 Staff, "Back Home: VA System Ill-Prepared for Residual Effects of War."

68. Helen Benedict, "Why Soldiers Rape."

69. Rachel Natelson and Sandra S. Park, "Exposing the Ugly Details of the Military Sexual Violence Epidemic."

70. Anne G. Sadler et al., "Factors Associated with Women's Risk of Rape in the Military Environment," *American Journal of Industrial Medicine* 43 (2003): 262–73.

71. Paulson and Krippner, *Haunted by Combat*, 152.

72. Moulton and Peterson, "Nineteen Veterans, Service Members Sue over Military Sexual Assault."

73. Bentson H. McFarland, Mark S. Kaplan, and Nathalie Huguet, "Datapoints: Self-Inflicted Deaths among Women with U.S. Military Service: A Hidden Epidemic?"

74. Spiegel, "Study: Female Vets Especially Vulnerable to Suicide."

75. Elisabeth Bumiller and Thom Shanker, "Pentagon Is Set to Lift Combat Ban for Women."

76. Julia Savacool, "Rising Suicide Rates among Female Veterans Show How Deep the Emotional Wounds Can Be."
77. Paulson and Krippner, *Haunted by Combat*, 138.
78. News21 Staff, "Back Home."
79. News21 Staff, "Back Home."
80. News21 Staff, "Back Home."
81. "The Veteran Experience: Profile of Differences by Era," Care for the Troops, http://www.careforthetroops.org.
82. Mark Thompson, "Is the U.S. Army Losing Its War on Suicide?"
83. Jennifer Senior, "The Prozac, Paxil, Zoloft, Wellbutrin, Celexa, Effexor, Valium, Klonopin, Ativan, Restoril, Xanax, Adderall, Ritalin, Haldol, Risperdal, Seroquel, Ambien, Lunesta, Elavil, Trazodone War."
84. Senior, "The Prozac, Paxil . . . War."
85. Paulson and Krippner, *Haunted by Combat*, 88.
86. Charles W. Hoge and Carl A. Castro et al., "Combat Duty in Iraq and Afghanistan, Mental Health Problems, and Barriers to Care."
87. Dexter Filkins, "Atonement."
88. Kevin Sites, *The Things They Cannot Say*, 213.
89. Laurie B. Slone and Matthew J. Friedman, *After the War Zone*, 102.
90. J. John Mann, Alan Apter, Jose Bertolote, et al., "Suicide Prevention Strategies: A Systematic Review."
91. Thompson, "Is the U.S. Army Losing Its War on Suicide?"

Chapter 2

1. Penny Coleman, *Flashback*, 38–39.
2. Coleman, *Flashback*, 42.
3. Coleman, *Flashback*, 41.
4. Coleman, *Flashback*.
5. Coleman, *Flashback*.
6. Coleman, *Flashback*, 149.
7. R. Gregory Lande, *Madness, Malingering, & Malfeasance*, 178.
8. Lande, *Madness, Malingering, & Malfeasance*, 176–77.
9. Richard J. McNally, "Psychiatric Disorder and Suicide in the Military, Then and Now: Commentary on Frueh and Smith," 776–78.

10. Eric T. Dean, Jr., *Shook Over Hell*, 126–27.

11. Dean, *Shook Over Hell*, 127.

12. Dean, *Shook Over Hell*.

13. Lande, *Madness, Malingering, & Malfeasance*, 36.

14. B. Christopher Frueh and Jeffrey A. Smith, "Suicide, Alcoholism, and Psychiatric Illness among Union Forces during the U.S. Civil War," 773.

15. Judith Pizzaro, Roxane Cohen Silver, and JoAnn Prouse, "Physical and Mental Costs of Traumatic War Experience among Civil War Veterans," *Archives of General Psychiatry* 63 (2006): 193–200.

16. Dean, *Shook Over Hell*, 158.

17. Dean, *Shook Over Hell*, 123–24.

18. Lande, *Madness, Malingering, & Malfeasance*, 195.

19. Lande, *Madness, Malingering, & Malfeasance*, 195.

20. Coleman, *Flashback*, 25.

21. Joseph T. Glatthaar, *Forged in Battle*, 237–43.

22. Dean, *Shook Over Hell*, 29.

23. Dean, *Shook Over Hell*, 30.

24. Denis Winter, *Death's Men*, 129.

25. Ben Shephard, *A War of Nerves*, 22.

26. Coleman, *Flashback*, 32.

27. Dean, *Shook Over Hell*, 30–31.

28. Charles S. Myers. *Shell Shock in France, 1914–1918*, 90.

29. Nicholas L. Rock, James W. Stokes, et al., *Textbook of Military Medicine: War Psychiatry*, chapter 7, "U.S. Army Combat Psychiatry," 154.

30. Rock, Stokes, et al., "U.S. Army Combat Psychiatry," 155.

31. Philip Gibbs, *Now It Can Be Told*, 175.

32. George Thomas Kurian, ed., *A Historical Guide to the United States Government*, 489.

33. Coleman, *Flashback*, 45.

34. Dean, *Shook Over Hell*, 39.

35. Shephard, *War of Nerves*, 144.

36. Kenneth C. Davis, *Don't Know Much about History*, 249.

37. Ilona Meagher, *Moving a Nation to Care*, 17.

38. Roger J. Spiller, "Shellshock," *American Heritage* Magazine, May/June 1990, 3.

39. Shephard, *War of Nerves*, 201.

40. Dean, *Shook Over Hell*, 35.

41. Shephard, *War of Nerves*, 217.
42. Coleman, *Flashback*, 53.
43. Charles M. Province, *The Unknown Patton*, 94.
44. Anna Mulrine, "Sgt. Bales and Multiple Tours of Duty: How Many Is Too Many?"
45. Coleman, *Flashback*, 53.
46. Department of Veterans Affairs, Office of Facilities Management, "70 Years of VA History," April 2001.
47. Shephard, *War of Nerves*, 217.
48. Robert Youngson and Ian Schott, "Brief History of the Lobotomy," adapted from *Medical Blunders* (1998).
49. Coleman, *Flashback*, 55.
50. Shephard, *War of Nerves*, 337.
51. Richard Gabriel, *Painful Field*, 27–28.
52. Barry R. Schaller, *Veterans on Trial*, 65.
53. David Shields and Shane Salerno, *Salinger*, 158.
54. Schaller, *Veterans on Trial*, 65.
55. Gabriel, *Painful Field*, 26–27.
56. *Let There be Light* (dir. John Huston), 1946.
57. Kenneth Turan, "John Huston's 'Let There Be Light' Online."
58. Turan, "John Huston's 'Let There Be Light' Online," 277.
59. Appel and Beebe, "Preventive Psychiatry: An Epidemiological Approach," 1470.
60. Archibald and Tuddenham, "Persistent Stress Reaction after Combat: A 20-Year Follow-up," 475–81.
61. Shephard, *War of Nerves*, 330.
62. Major Timothy P. Hayes, Jr., "Post-Traumatic Stress Disorder on Trial," 69.
63. Jo Knox and David H. Price, "Healing America's Warriors: Vet Centers and the Social Contract."
64. William "Wild Bill" Guarnere and Edward "Babe" Heffron, with Robyn Post, *Brothers in Battle, Best of Friends*, xxiii.
65. Guarnere, Heffron, and Post, *Brothers in Battle*, 238.
66. Scott Wilson, "Obama: Korean War Is 'Forgotten Victory.' "
67. Wilson, "Obama: Korean War Is 'Forgotten Victory.' "
68. Wilson, "Obama: Korean War Is 'Forgotten Victory.' "
69. Dwight D. Eisenhower, farewell address to the nation, delivered on television July 17, 1961.

70. Public Papers of the Presidents, Dwight D. Eisenhower, 1960, 1,035–1,040.
71. Schaller, *Veterans on Trial*, 71.
72. Hayes, "Post-Traumatic Stress Disorder on Trial," 76.
73. Coleman, *Flashback*, 56,
74. Jim Goodwin, "The Etiology of Combat-Related, Posttraumatic Stress Disorders," *Posttraumatic Stress Disorders of the Vietnam Veteran*, ed. Tom Williams, 6.
75. Ilona Meagher, *Moving a Nation to Care*, 18–19.
76. Spiller, "Shellshock."
77. John Whiteclay Chambers II, *The Oxford Companion to American Military History*, 181.
78. Davis, *Don't Know Much about History*, 382.
79. MacPherson, "McNamara's 'Moron Corps.' "
80. Laurie B. Slone and Matthew J. Friedman, *After the War Zone*, 20.
81. Gerald Linderman, *Embattled Courage*, 36.
82. Diane Miller Sommerville, "A Burden Too Heavy to Bear," *Civil War History*.
83. Lawrence M. Baskir and William A. Strauss, *Chance and Circumstance: The Draft, the War and the Vietnam Generation*, 8–10.
84. Richard A. Kulka et al., *Trauma and the Vietnam War Generation: Report of the Findings from the National Vietnam Veterans Readjustment Study*, xxvii.
85. Davidson, "Post-Traumatic Stress Disorder: A Controversial Defense for Veterans of a Controversial War," 415.
86. Coleman, *Flashback*, 163, citing an Army study published in October 2004 in the *New England Journal of Medicine*.
87. Coleman, *Flashback*, 58–60.
88. Coleman, *Flashback*, 61–63.
89. Coleman, *Flashback*, 124.
90. Dempsey, "Man's Wife Sensed Crisis Was Brewing."
91. Dempsey, "Man's Wife Sensed Crisis Was Brewing."
92. Kulka et al., *Trauma and the Vietnam War Generation*, xxvii
93. Dean, *Shook Over Hell*, 15–16.

94. Shephard, *War of Nerves*, 392.

95. Shephard, *War of Nerves*.

96. Samuel P. Menefree, *The "Vietnam Syndrome" Defense: A "G.I. Bill of Criminal Rights"? Army Law*, February 1985, 1 (quoting the Charlie Daniels Band, "Still in Saigon," on Windows [Epic Records, 1982]).

97. Mulrine, "Sgt. Bales and Multiple Tours of Duty."

98. Shephard, *War of Nerves*, 364.

99. Herb Kutchins and Stuart A. Kirk, *Making Us Crazy: DSM: The Psychiatric Bible and the Creation of Mental Illness*, 124.

100. Schaller, *Veterans on Trial*, 10.

101. Hans Pols, "Waking Up to Shell Shock: Psychiatry in the U.S. Military during World War II," *Endeavour* 30 (December 2006).

102. Slone and Friedman, *After the War Zone*, 155.

103. Karl Marlantes, *What It Is Like to Go to War*, 47.

104. Terri Tanielian, Lisa H. Jaycox, et al. *Invisible Wounds of War: Psychological and Cognitive Injuries, Their Consequences, and Services to Assist Recovery*, xi, 3–6.

105. Thomas L. Hafemeister and Nicole A. Stockey, "Last Stand? The Criminal Responsibility of War Veterans Returning from Iraq and Afghanistan with Post-Traumatic Stress Disorder," 90n12.

106. "Report on VA Facility Specific Operation Enduring Freedom (OEF), Operation Iraqi Freedom (OIF), and Operation New Dawn (OND) Veterans Coded with Potential PTSD," Epidemiology Program, Post-Deployment Health Group, Office of Public Health, Veterans Health Administration, Department of Veterans Affairs, September 2012.

107. Reno, "Nearly 30% of Vets Treated by V.A. Have PTSD."

108. Kristen Moulton, "U. Study: Combat Puts Soldiers at High Suicide, PTSD Risk."

109. Moulton, "U. Study."

110. Leon E. Panetta, speech delivered June 22, 2012, in Washington, D.C.

111. Michael P. Atkinson et al., "A Dynamic Model for Post-Traumatic Stress Disorder among U.S. Troops in

Operation Iraqi Freedom," *Management Science* 55 (September 2009).

112. Mark Thompson, "Is the U.S. Army Losing Its War on Suicide?"

113. Jim Rendon, "Post-Traumatic Stress's Surprisingly Positive Flip Side."

114. Mark Benjamin. "The V.A.'s Bad Review."

115. *Daily Mail Reporter*, "Tragic Iraq War Veteran, 25, Shoots Himself Dead in Front of Father in Family's Backyard after Battle with PTSD."

116. *Daily Mail Reporter*, "Tragic Iraq War Veteran."

117. Greg Jaffe, "Marine's Suicide Is Only Start of Family's Struggle."

118. Jaffe, "Marine's Suicide."

119. Jaffe, "Marine's Suicide."

120. Jaffe, "Marine's Suicide."

Chapter 3

1. Amy Goodman, "The War and Peace Report," *Democracy Now*, May 28, 2012.

2. Murphy, "A Base 'on the Brink,' as Is the Community."

3. Nina Shapiro, "Derrick Kirkland, Iraq War Veteran, Hung Himself after Being Mocked by Superiors, Say Lewis-McChord Soldiers."

4. Shapiro, "Derrick Kirkland, Soldier Who Hung Himself, Was Deemed a 'Low-Moderate Risk' after Attempting Suicide Three Times Before."

5. Murphy, "A Military Base 'on the Brink.'"

6. Goodman, "The War and Peace Report."

7. Goodman, "The War and Peace Report."

8. Darroch Greer, "County Civil War Casualties, Week-by-Week, for the Abraham Lincoln Presidential Library and Museum," BRC Imagination Arts, 2005.

9. Robert S. Robertson, *Diary of the War*, 182.

10. Bertram Wyatt-Brown. *Southern Honor: Ethics and Behavior in the Old South*, 35.

11. Nancy Cott, ed., *No Small Courage: A History of Women in the United States*, 279.

12. Drew Gilpin Faust, *This Republic of Suffering*, 55.
13. Faust, *This Republic of Suffering*, 69.
14. David T. Hedrick and Gordon Barry, Jr. *I'm Surrounded by Methodists: Diary of John H. W. Stuckenberg, Chaplain of the 145th Pennsylvania Volunteer Infantry*, 44.
15. *I'm Surrounded by Methodists*, 58.
16. *I'm Surrounded by Methodists*, 60.
17. Ambrose Bierce, "A Tough Tussle," *The Civil War Short Stories of Ambrose Bierce*, 39.
18. Faust, *This Republic of Suffering*, 199.
19. Faust, *This Republic of Suffering*, 196.
20. Faust, *This Republic of Suffering*, 196.
21. David Silkenat, *Moments of Despair*, 55.
22. Faust. *This Republic of Suffering*, 121.
23. *New York Times*, October 20, 1862.
24. Penny Coleman, *Flashback*, 24.
25. Faust, *This Republic of Suffering*, 102.
26. Faust, *This Republic of Suffering*, xii, 149.
27. Guy Gugliotta, "New Estimate Raises Civil War Death Toll."
28. Gugliotta, "New Estimate Raises Civil War Death Toll."
29. Silkenat, *Moments of Despair*, 8.
30. Faust, *This Republic of Suffering*, xvi.
31. Faust, *This Republic of Suffering*, 4.
32. Faust, *This Republic of Suffering*, 4.
33. Megan A. Perrin et al., "Differences in PTSD Prevalence and Associated Risk Factors among World Trade Center Disaster Rescue and Recovery Workers."
34. Eric T. Dean, Jr., *Shook Over Hell*, 78.
35. Kate Cumming, *The Journal of Kate Cumming; A Confederate Nurse, 1862–1865*, ed. Richard Harwell, 5–6.
36. Cumming, *The Journal of Kate Cumming*.
37. John G. Perry, *Letters from a Surgeon of the Civil* War, ed. Martha Derby Perry, 175.
38. Charles T. Quintard, *Doctor Quintard, Chaplain C.S.A. and Second Bishop of Tennessee: Being His Story of the War*, ed. A. H. Noll, 60–61.
39. Faust, *This Republic of Suffering*, 32.
40. Dave Grossman, *On Killing*, 23.
41. Grossman, *On Killing*, 24–25.

42. Grossman, *On Killing*, 10.
43. Faust, *This Republic of Suffering*, 41.
44. Grossman, *On Killing*, 123.
45. "Wings of Valor: The Lost Battalion in the Argonne Forest," http://www.homeofheroes.com/wings/part1/3_lostbattalion.html.
46. Parrish, "Florence Native Commanded Famed Lost Battalion."
47. The Great War Society, "Charles Whittlesey: Commander of the Lost Battalion" (2000), http://www.worldwar1.com/dbc/whitt.htm.
48. Great War Society, "Charles Whittlesey."
49. Kenneth C. Davis, *Don't Know Much about History*, 248.
50. Davis, *Don't Know Much about History*, 248.
51. Grossman, *On Killing*, 12.
52. Grossman, *On Killing*, 58.
53. BBC News, "Hiroshima Bomb Pilot Dies Aged 92."
54. BBC News, "Hiroshima Bomb Pilot Dies Aged 92."
55. S. L. A. Marshall, *Men against Fire: The Problem of Battle Command in Future War*, 54.
56. Grossman, *On Killing*, 36.
57. Dave Grossman, *On Killing*, 12.
58. Dave Grossman, *On Killing*, 12.
59. Dave Grossman, *On Killing*, 31.
60. Dave Grossman, *On Killing*, 31.
61. Charles Duhigg, " 'Enemy Contact, Kill 'em, kill 'em.' "
62. Coleman, *Flashback*, 160.
63. Peter Davis, *Hearts and Minds*, 1974.
64. Peter G. Bourne, "From Boot Camp to My Lai," *Crimes of War*, 464.
65. Ben Shephard, *A War of Nerves*, 233.
66. Kilner, "Military Leaders' Obligation to Justify Killing in War."
67. E. B. Riker-Coleman, "Reflection and Reform: Professionalism and Ethics in the U.S. Army Officer Corps, 1968–1975 (Ph.D. diss., University of North Carolina, 1997), www.unc/edu/ffichaos1/reform.pdf, 31.
68. Nick Turse, *Kill Anything That Moves: The Real American War in Vietnam*, 246.

69. George C. Herring, " 'Cold Blood': LBJ's Conduct of Limited War in Vietnam," *An American Dilemma: Vietnam 1964–1973*, by Dennis E. Showalter and John G. Albert, 1993, 64.

70. Barbara Mikkelson and David Mikkelson, "M-16," Urban Legends Reference Pages, Snopes.com, July 7, 2002, www.snopes.com/military/m16.asp.

71. Coleman, *Flashback*, 84.

72. Tony Dokoupil, "Moral Injury."

73. Freedman, "Tending to Veterans' Afflictions of the Soul."

74. Grossman, *On Killing*, 268–69.

75. Daryl S. Paulson and Stanley Krippner, *Haunted by Combat*, 93.

76. Paulson and Krippner, *Haunted by Combat*, 93.

77. Paulson and Krippner, *Haunted by Combat*, 94.

78. Paulson and Krippner, *Haunted by Combat*, 101.

79. Chris Kyle, Scott McEwen, and Jim DeFelice, *American Sniper: The Autobiography of the Most Lethal Sniper in U.S. Military History*, 4.

80. Nicholas D. Schmidle, "In the Crosshairs."

81. Schmidle, "In the Crosshairs."

82. Schmidle, "In the Crosshairs."

83. Christopher Hayes, "The Good War on Terror."

84. Shira Maguen and Brett Litz, "Moral Injury in Veterans of War."

85. Baum, "The Price of Valor."

86. Dokoupil. "Moral Injury."

87. Moni Basu, "Why Suicide Rate among Veterans May Be More Than 22 a Day."

88. "Levi Derby," http://www.fallenheroesproject.org/united-states/levi-derby/.

89. "Levi Derby."

90. Shephard, *War of Nerves*, 371–2.

91. Ungar, "Suicide Takes Growing Toll among Military, Veterans."

92. Barbara Starr, "Behind the Scenes: Triumph and Tragedy for Two Wounded Soldiers."

93. "Report: Texas Vets Dying Young at Alarming Rate."

94. Mark Brunswick, "Battle on Home Front Is Guard's Most Perilous."

95. Coleman, *Flashback*, 2.
96. Ilona Meagher, *Moving a Nation to Care*, 110.
97. Christopher Buchanan, "A Reporter's Journey," *Frontline*, March 1, 2005.
98. John Judis, "An American Suicide: What War Did to Jeffrey Lucey."
99. Judis, "An American Suicide."
100. Judis, "An American Suicide."
101. "Parents Mourn Son's Suicide after Returning from Iraq Duty: 'He's a Casualty of War but He'll Never Be Known as That,'" *Democracy Now*, August 11, 2004.
102. Ann Jones, *They Were Soldiers*, 100.
103. Dokoupil, "Moral Injury."
104. Jill Lepore, "The Force."
105. Gary Martin and Viveca Novak, "U.S. Fast-Tracks Widespread Use of Drones."
106. David Cole, "Obama and Terror: The Hovering Questions," 34.
107. Lev Grossman, "Rise of the Drones."
108. Bergen, "Drone Wars."
109. Kim Gamel, "U.N.: Drone Strikes in Afghanistan Climb."
110. Grossman, "Rise of the Drones."
111. Wood, "Obama Drone War 'Kill Chain' Imposes Heavy Burden at Home."
112. David Remnick, "Going the Distance: On and Off the Road with Barack Obama."
113. Remnick, "Going the Distance."
114. Cole, "Obama and Terror," 34.
115. Cole, "Obama and Terror," 34.
116. Cole, "Obama and Terror," 34.
117. Paulson and Krippner, *Haunted by Combat*, xx.
118. Grossman, "Rise of the Drones."
119. Wood, "Obama Drone War 'Kill Chain' Imposes Heavy Burden at Home."
120. Grossman, "Rise of the Drones."
121. Grossman, *On Killing*, 31.
122. Richard A. Gabriel, *No More Heroes: Madness and Psychiatry in War*, 155–56.
123. Kevin Sites, *The Things They Cannot Say*, xxxii.

124. Sites, *The Things They Cannot Say*, 57.
125. Grossman, *On Killing*, 336.

Chapter 4

1. Amy Goodman, "Soldier Killed Herself after Objecting to Interrogation Techniques Being Used on Iraqi Prisoners."
2. Goodman, "Soldier Killed Herself after Objecting."
3. Greg Mitchell, "A Suicide in Iraq—Part II."
4. Larry Hendricks, "Flag Soldier Died Deeply Conflicted."
5. Mitchell, "A Suicide in Iraq—Part II."
6. Mitchell, "A Suicide in Iraq—Part II."
7. Mitchell, "A Suicide in Iraq—Part II."
8. Mitchell, "A Suicide in Iraq—Part II."
9. David Silkenat, *Moments of Despair*, 11.
10. Silkenat, *Moments of Despair*, 9.
11. Silkenat, *Moments of Despair*, 38.
12. R. Gregory Lande, "Felo De Se: Soldier Suicides in America's Civil War."
13. Silkenat, *Moments of Despair*, 25.
14. Silkenat, *Moments of Despair*, 11.
15. *Encyclopedia Virginia*, Virginia Foundation for the Humanities.
16. Diane Miller Sommerville, "A Burden Too Heavy to Bear," *New York Times*.
17. Territorial Kansas Online, 1854–1861, www.territorialkansasonline.org.
18. Silkenat, *Moments of Despair*, 32.
19. Silkenat, *Moments of Despair*, 33.
20. Darrin Youker, "Did Lingering Pain Cause Suicide of Civil War Vet?"
21. Silkenat, *Moments of Despair*, 25.
22. "An Enslaved Man's Noble Suicide."
23. "What Has the North to Do with Slavery?"
24. Mark Schantz, *Awaiting the Heavenly Country*, 143.
25. National Humanities Center, "Suicide among Slaves."
26. Joseph T. Glatthaar, *Forged in Battled: The Civil War Alliance of Black Soldiers and White Officers*, 237–243.

27. Sommerville, "A Burden Too Heavy to Bear," *New York Times*.
28. Sommerville, "A Burden Too Heavy to Bear," *New York Times*.
29. Diane Miller Sommerville, "A Burden Too Heavy to Bear," *Civil War History*.
30. Eric T. Dean, Jr., *Shook Over Hell*, 148
31. Ilona Meagher. *Moving a Nation to Care*, 65–66.
32. Operation Iraqi Freedom Mental Health Advisory Team, *Annex D: Review of Soldier Suicides*, Falls Church, Virginia, U.S. Army Surgeon General, 2003.
33. Penny Coleman, "Military Suicides: Those We Might Yet Save."
34. Scott Calvert, "A soldier's grim homecoming."
35. Mark Benjamin, "Seventh Iraq War Veteran Kills Himself."
36. Lynda Hurst, "Troops in Iraq on Suicide Watch."
37. Pelkey, "In His Boots."
38. Statement of Stefanie E. Pelkey before the Committee on Veterans Affairs, House of Representatives, July 25, 2005, http://veterans.house.gov/hearings/schedule109/jul05/7-27-05f/spelkey.html.
39. Kristin Roberts, "U.S. Army Suicides Hit Highest Rate since Gulf War."
40. Chedekel and Kauffman, "Army's Suicide Struggles Continue: 2006 Rate of Self-Inflicted Deaths in Iraq Could Exceed Record Set in 2005."
41. Rebecca Ruiz, "Memorial Day 2012: Honoring Service Members Who Died by Suicide."
42. "Father Says Military Support System Failed Suicidal Soldier."
43. "Father Says Military Support System Failed Suicidal Soldier."
44. "Father Says Military Support System Failed Suicidal Soldier.".
45. Kimberly Hefling, "Iraq War Vets' Suicide Rates Analyzed."
46. "Joshua Omvig Veterans Suicide Prevention Act of 2007."
47. Pauline Jelinek, "Army's Efforts Fail to Quell Suicide Rate."
48. Gregg Zoroya, "Army Suicides Rise as Time Spent in Combat Increases."
49. Zoroya, "Army Suicides Rise as Time Spent in Combat Increases."
50. Zoroya, "Army Suicides Rise as Time Spent in Combat Increases."
51. Lizette Alvarez, "Army and Agency Will Study Rising Suicide Rate among Soldiers."

52. Fred Contrada, "Army Report Released to Newspaper Says Smith College Graduate Shot Herself in Iraq."

53. Contrada, "Army Report Released to Newspaper Says Smith College Graduate Shot Herself in Iraq."

54. Erica Goode, "After Combat, Victims of an Inner War."

55. Goode, "After Combat, Victims of an Inner War."

56. Goode, "After Combat, Victims of an Inner War."

57. Goode, "After Combat, Victims of an Inner War."

58. Goode, "After Combat, Victims of an Inner War."

59. Konrad Marshall, "In Their Minds It's Never Gonna Go Away. The War Is Still There."

60. Hannah Mitchell, "Caldwell Killing Suspect Known as Peaceable."

61. Armen Keteyian, "Suicide Epidemic among Veterans."

62. Keteyian, "Suicide Epidemic among Veterans."

63. Terri Tanielian, Lisa H. Jaycox, et al, "Invisible Wounds: Mental Health and Cognitive Care Needs of America's Returning Veterans."

64. Jelinek, "Suicides May Top Combat Deaths, Army Says."

65. Mark Mueller and Tomas Dinges, "Military Suicides: Army Sgt. Coleman Bean's Downward Spiral Ends with Gunfire."

66. Mueller and Dinges, "Military Suicides."

67. Kristin M. Hall, "Suit Claims VA Negligent In Suicide."

68. "Bid to Limit Marine Suicides," *Los Angeles Times*, February 27, 2009.

69. Coleen A. Boyle, Pierre Decoufle et al. "Post Service Mortality among Vietnam Veterans," U.S. Department of Health and Human Services, Public Health Service, Centers for Disease Control, February 1987, 257: 790–95.

70. Blake Farmer, "Record High Army Suicides Prompt Action."

71. Mark Thompson, "Is the U.S. Army Losing Its War on Suicide?"

72. Armed Forces Health Surveillance Center, "Deaths by Suicide while on Active Duty, Active and Reserve Components, U.S. Armed Forces, 1998–2011."

73. Armed Forces Health Surveillance Center, "Deaths by Suicide while on Active Duty."

74. Hearst et al. "Correspondence," 506–7.

75. "Suicide in the Armed Forces."

76. Steven Reinberg, "U.S. Army Suicides Rising Sharply, Study Finds."
77. "Partial Transcript of President Obama's Roundtable with Military Reporters."
78. "Partial Transcript of President Obama's Roundtable with Military Reporters."
79. Feeney, "The Military Suicide Epidemic."
80. Pauline Jelinek, "Glint of Hope on Suicide Rate."
81. Michael Hoffman, "Guard, Reserve Suicide Rate Sees Big Spike."
82. Nancy A. Youssef, "Suicides Soared in 2010 for Army Reserve, National Guard."
83. Aaron Levin, "Army Gets Closer to Pinpointing Soldiers at Risk for Suicide."
84. Gregg Zoroya, "Female Soldiers' Suicide Rate Triples When at War."
85. Marty Toohey, "Did Army Do Enough to Prevent Soldier's Death?"
86. Chedekel and Kauffman, "Army's Suicide Struggles Continue."
87. Chedekel and Kauffman, "Army's Suicide Struggles Continue."
88. Julia Savacool. "Rising Suicide Rates among Female Veterans Show How Deep the Emotional Wounds Can Be."
89. "Army STARRS Preliminary Data Reveal Some Potential Predictive Factors for Suicide," National Institute of Mental Health, March 22, 2011, http://www.nimh.gov/science-news/2011/army-starrs-preliminary-date-reveal-some-potential-predictive-factors-for-suicide.shtml.
90. David Satcher, "The Surgeon General's Call to Action to Prevent Suicide," U.S. Public Health Services, 1999, http://profiles.nlm.nih.gov/ps/access/NNBBBH.pdf.
91. George Howe Colt, *November of the Soul: The Enigma of Suicide*, 239.
92. Barry R. Schaller, *Veterans on Trial*, 68.
93. Mitchell, "A Suicide in Iraq—Part II."
94. Coleman, "Military Suicides."
95. Coleman, "Military Suicides."
96. Stephen L. Robinson, "Hidden Toll of the War in Iraq," 8.
97. "Costs of U.S. Wars Linger for Over 100 Years."
98. "Costs of U.S. Wars Linger for Over 100 Years."

99. Daryl S. Paulson and Stanley Krippner, *Haunted by Combat*, 138.

100. Thompson, "Is the U.S. Army Losing Its War on Suicide?"

101. Benedict Carey, "Suicidal Tendencies Are Evident before Deployment, Study Finds."

102. Pamela Hyde, "Suicide: The Challenges and Opportunities behind the Public Health Problem."

103. Lubin, Werbeloff, et al., "Decrease in Suicide Rates after a Change of Policy Reducing Access to Firearms in Adolescents."

104. Mark Benjamin and Michael De Yoanna, "Kill Yourself. Save Us the Paperwork."

105. Benjamin and De Yoanna, "Kill Yourself. Save Us the Paperwork."

106. Michael De Yoanna, "Vet's War Continued at Home."

107. Dan Frosch, "Fighting the Terror of Battles That Rage in Soldiers' Heads."

108. Michael De Yoanna and Mark Benjamin, "Mark Waltz, Kenneth Lehman, Chad Barrett."

109. Michael De Yoanna, "Despite PTSD, Fallen Soldier Was Determined to Return to Iraq."

110. Benjamin and De Yoanna, "Mark Waltz, Kenneth Lehman, Chad Barrett."

111. Benjamin and De Yoanna, "Mark Waltz, Kenneth Lehman, Chad Barrett."

112. Benjamin and De Yoanna, "Mark Waltz, Kenneth Lehman, Chad Barrett."

113. Benjamin and De Yoanna, "Mark Waltz, Kenneth Lehman, Chad Barrett."

114. Benjamin and De Yoanna, "Mark Waltz, Kenneth Lehman, Chad Barrett."

115. David Martin, "Army Suicide Widows: Too Little, Too Late."

116. Nancy Gibbs and Mark Thompson, "The War on Suicide?"

117. Gibbs and Thompson, "The War on Suicide?"

118. Gibbs and Thompson, "The War on Suicide?"

119. Gibbs and Thompson, "The War on Suicide?"

120. Gibbs and Thompson, "The War on Suicide?"

121. Gibbs and Thompson, "The War on Suicide?"

122. Gibbs and Thompson, "The War on Suicide?"

Chapter 5

1. Conger, "Shockwave."
2. Bravin, "Army Report Omitted Prison Details."
3. Ilona Meagher, *Moving a Nation to Care*, 36.
4. Angie Goff, "Soldier's Recent Suicide Many Not Have Been Isolated Incident."
5. Eric Coker, "Historian Focuses on Civil War Suicides," Discovere, Binghamton University, http://discovere.binghamton.edu/faculty-spotlights/sommerville-3571.html, February 15, 2011.
6. Diane Miller Sommerville, "A Burden Too Heavy to Bear," *Civil War History*.
7. *Daily Picayune* (New Orleans), September 1, 1861, reprinted in the *Inquirer* (Philadelphia), September 10, 1864.
8. Diane Miller Sommerville, "A Burden Too Heavy to Bear," *New York Times*.
9. Rachel Maddow. *Drift: The Unmooring of American Military Power*, 43.
10. Oliver Wendell Holmes, Jr., "The Soldier's Faith."
11. Holmes, "The Soldier's Faith."
12. British Broadcasting Corporation, "Historic Figures: Siegfried Sassoon (1886–1967)," http://www.bbc.co.uk/history/historic_figures/sassoon_siegfried.shtml.
13. Siegfried Sassoon, "Statement against the Continuation of the War—1917," http://web.viu.ca/davies/h482.WWI/sassoon.statement. against.war.1817.htm.
14. Sassoon, "Statement."
15. Siegfried Sassoon, *The War Poems of Siegfried Sassoon*, 39.
16. Kenneth C. Davis, *Don't Know Much about History*, 245.
17. Davis, *Don't Know Much about History*.
18. Jo Knox and David H. Price, "Healing America's Warriors: Vet Centers and the Social Contract."
19. Butler's comments were made in a letter that was reprinted in the *VVA Veteran*, April 1995. The *VVA Veteran* is a publication of the Vietnam Veterans of America.
20. James Bradley with Ron Powers. *Flags of Our Fathers*, 292.
21. Bradley with Powers, *Flags of Our Fathers*, 10.

22. Bradley with Powers, *Flags of Our Fathers*, 307.

23. Bradley with Powers, *Flags of Our Fathers*, 324.

24. Bradley with Powers, *Flags of Our Fathers*, 332.

25. Bradley with Powers, *Flags of Our Fathers*, 344.

26. Bradley with Powers, *Flags of Our Fathers*, 345–46.

27. Bradley with Powers, *Flags of Our Fathers*, 346.

28. Richard Schickel, "Clint's Double Take," *Time*, October 23, 2006.

29. Bradley with Powers, *Flags of Our Fathers*, 343.

30. Bradley with Powers, *Flags of Our Fathers*, 334. John Bradley, the last survivor, died in 1994 at age seventy, also from a heart attack.

31. Reinhart Char, "Philip Sheridan 3rd Leaps to Death from Golden Gate Bridge."

32. Christian Goeschel, *Suicide in Nazi Germany*, 152.

33. Dave Grossman, *On Killing*, 214.

34. Goeschel, *Suicide in Nazi Germany*, 158.

35. Goeschel, *Suicide in Nazi Germany*, 64.

36. Goeschel, *Suicide in Nazi Germany*, 158.

37. Goeschel, *Suicide in Nazi Germany*, 160.

38. Goeschel, *Suicide in Nazi Germany*, 170.

39. James Brooke, "Okinawa Suicides and Japan's Army: Burying the Truth?"

40. Maddow, *Drift*, 211.

41. Rod Nordland, "Risks of Afghan War Shift from Soldiers to Contractors."

42. Laurie B. Slone and Matthew J. Friedman, *After the War Zone*, 220.

43. Nordland, "Risks of Afghan War Shift from Soldiers to Contractors."

44. Doug Robinson, "Hidden War Zone Scars Claim Another Soldier's Life."

45. Robinson, "Hidden War Zone Scars Claim Another Soldier's Life."

46. Letter from Barb Dill to American Contractors in Iraq and Afghanistan, 2007, www.americancontractorsiniraq.org.

47. Letter from Barb Dill to American Contractors in Iraq and Afghanistan.

48. Letter from Barb Dill to American Contractors in Iraq and Afghanistan.

49. Maddow, *Drift*, 250.

50. T. Christian Miller, "A Journey That Ended in Anguish."

51. Terry J. Allen, "America's Child Soldier Problem."
52. Allen, "America's Child Soldier Problem."
53. Lindsay Wise, "A Soldier's Tragic Tale."
54. Wise, "A Soldier's Tragic Tale."
55. Wise, "A Soldier's Tragic Tale."
56. Siegal, "After a Marine's Suicide, a Family Recalls Missed Red Flags."
57. Siegel, "After a Marine's Suicide."
58. Siegel, "After a Marine's Suicide."
59. Siegel, "After a Marine's Suicide."
60. Sherr, "Coming Home."
61. Meagher, *Moving a Nation to Care*, 24.
62. Meagher, *Moving a Nation to Care*, 24.
63. DeVrieze, "Questions Swirl around Life, Suicide of Quad-City Veteran Pat Gibbs Jr."
64. DeVrieze, "Questions Swirl around Life."
65. DeVrieze, "Questions Swirl around Life."
66. "The Life and Death of Clay Hunt."
67. Lindsay Wise, "A Poster Boy for Suicide Prevention, Houstonian Becomes Another Statistic."
68. Wise, "A Poster Boy for Suicide Prevention."
69. Wise, "A Poster Boy for Suicide Prevention."

Chapter 6

1. Mike Tucker, *Ronin: A Marine Scout/Sniper Platoon in Iraq*, 4.
2. William Finnegan, "The Last Tour: A Decorated Marine's War Within."
3. Twiggs, "PTSD: The War Within: A Marine Writes about His PTSD experience."
4. Twiggs, "PTSD: The War Within."
5. Twiggs, "PTSD: The War Within."
6. Twiggs, "PTSD: The War Within."
7. Finnegan, "The Last Tour."
8. Finnegan, "The Last Tour."
9. Finnegan, "The Last Tour."

10. Diane Miller Sommerville, "A Burden Too Heavy to Bear," *New York Times*.

11. William H. Younts memoirs, Indiana Historical Society, 98–100, http://www.indianahistory.org.

12. Younts memoirs, 143.

13. Penny Coleman, *Flashback*, 26.

14. Kevin Sites, *The Things They Cannot Say*, 156.

15. Musil, "The Truth about Deserters."

16. Spencer C. Tucker, ed., *Encyclopedia of the Vietnam War* (New York: Oxford University Press, 2001), 4.

17. James Maycock, "War within War," *Guardian Unlimited*, September 15, 2001.

18. Martin Luther King, Jr., "Declaration of Independence from the War in Vietnam," speech delivered at Riverside Church in New York City, April 4, 1967.

19. Kenneth C. Davis, *Don't Know Much about History*, 391.

20. Coleman, *Flashback*, 87.

21. Coleman, *Flashback*, 88.

22. Coleman, *Flashback*, 113.

23. Ben Shephard, *A War of Nerves*, 343.

24. Richard Kulka et al., *Trauma and the Vietnam War Generation: Report of the Findings from the National Vietnam Veterans Readjustment Study*, 13.

25. Kulka et al., *Trauma and the Vietnam War Generation*, 186–87.

26. Margaret E. Noonan and Christopher J. Mumola, "U.S. Department of Justice, Bureau of Justice Statistics Special Report: Veterans in State and Federal Prison, 2004, May 2007."

27. William E. Calvert and Roger L. Hutchinson, "Vietnam Veteran Levels of Combat: Related to Later Violence?" *Journal of Traumatic Stress* 103 (1990): 104.

28. Thomas L. Hafemeister and Nicole A. Stockey, "Last Stand? The Criminal Responsibility of War Veterans Returning from Iraq and Afghanistan with Post-Traumatic Stress Disorder."

29. Barry L. Levin, "Defense of the Vietnam Veteran with Post-Traumatic Stress Disorder," *American Jury Trials* 441 (1993).

30. American-Statesman Investigative Team, "After Returning Home, Many Veterans Get into Motor Vehicle Accidents."

31. Ilona Meagher, *Moving a Nation to Care*, 120.
32. David Finkel, *Thank You for Your Service*, excerpted in *The Week*, November 22, 2013.
33. Barry R. Schaller, *Veterans on Trial*, 11.
34. Tony Dokoupil, "Moral Injury."
35. Stan Goff, "KIA in Alabama."
36. Goff, "KIA in Alabama."
37. Goff, "KIA in Alabama."
38. Phil Trexler, "Mom Remembers Son Who Died at InfoCision Stadium."
39. Trexler, "Mom Remembers Son Who Died at InfoCision Stadium."
40. Trexler, "Mom Remembers Son Who Died at InfoCision Stadium."
41. Mary Esther, "Nearly a Year after Her Husband Committed Suicide, Air Force Widow Still Wonders Why."
42. Esther, "Nearly a Year after Her Husband Committed Suicide."
43. Anderson, "Home Front Casualties."
44. "Killer Sentenced," *The Week*, September 6, 2013.
45. Murphy, "A 'Base on the Brink,' as Is the Community."
46. James McKinley, "Despite Army Efforts, Soldier Suicides Continue."
47. Sig Christenson, "GI's War Followed Him Home."
48. McKinley, "Despite Army Efforts, Soldier Suicides Continue."
49. Gregg Zoroya, "Thousands Strain Fort Hood's Mental Health System."
50. Margaret C. Harrell and Nancy Berglass, "Losing the Battle: The Challenge of Military Suicide."
51. Sullivan Rutledge Kissell, "Did War Vet Kill Self to Make a Statement?"
52. Glantz, "VA Delay in Aiding Veterans Growing."
53. Meagher, *Moving a Nation to Care*, 125.
54. E-mail communication with Ndidi Mojay, March 13 and March 14, 2014.
55. Steve Vogel, "VA's Shinseki Has His Critics as He Tries to Remake Agency, Cut Disability Claims Backlog."
56. Vogel, "VA's Shinseki Has His Critics as He Tries to Remake Agency."
57. U.S. Department of Veterans Affairs, "Compensation and Pension Historical Data," February 21, 2014.

58. U.S. Department of Veterans Affairs, "Compensation and Pension Historical Data."

59. Steve Vogel, "VA Trims 34% from Its Disability Claims Backlog."

60. Jayne Keedle, "Justin Eldridge's Battle with PTSD Ended in Tragedy Last Night."

61. Leo Shane, "Living through Nine Suicides," *Stars and Stripes*, September 11, 2013.

62. D'Souza, "Aleida Bordas, 38, Lincoln HS Teacher, Served in Iraq and Afghanistan."

63. D'Souza, "Aleida Bordas."

64. Nicholas D. Kristof. "A Veteran's Death, the Nation's Shame."

Chapter 7

1. Eric T. Dean, Jr., *Shook Over Hell*, 151.

2. Affidavit of Sanford Fortner, August 31, 1888, cited by Dean in *Shook Over Hell*.

3. Kenneth C. Davis, *Don't Know Much about History*, 177.

4. Affidavit of Charles E. Triplett, April 18, 1889, cited by Dean, *Shook Over Hell*.

5. Dean, *Shook Over Hell*, 152.

6. Commitment note, Indiana State Hospital for the Insane, National Archives, November 28, 1874.

7. Letter of Dr. George L. Andrew to Dr. O. Overts, superintendent of the Indiana Hospital for the Insane, November 30, 1874, cited by Dean in *Shook Over Hell*.

8. Federal pension file of Newell Gleason, National Archives.

9. The National Defense Authorization Act for FY 2011, Public Law 111–383, section 1062, January 7, 2011.

10. Margaret C. Harrell and Nancy Berglass, "Losing the Battle: The Challenge of Military Suicide," Center for a New American Security, October 2011.

11. Kristina Wong, "New Report: Military Losing the Battle against Suicide."

12. Elisabeth Bumiller, "Active-Duty Soldiers Take Their Own Lives at Record Rate."

13. Wong, "New Report."

14. Fran Lowry, "Army Psychiatrist Battles the War on Military Suicide."

15. Lowry, "Army Psychiatrist Battles the War on Military Suicide."

16. Jennifer Senior, "The Prozac, Paxil, Zoloft, Wellbutrin, Celexa, Effexor, Valium, Klonopin, Ativan, Restoril, Xanax, Adderall, Rotalin, Haldol, Risperdal, Seroquel, Ambien, Lunesta, Elavil, Trazodone War."

17. "US Troops in Iraq: 72% Say End War in 2006," Truth Out, February 28, 2006 press release.

18. Nicole Bowmer, "The Face of Military Suicide."

19. Phuong Le, "Widow: Ranger Killed Self to Avoid Another Tour."

20. James Dao, "White House Changes Policy on Condolence Letters for Military Suicides."

21. Pauline Jelinek and Lolita C. Baldor, "U.S. Shifts War Suicide Policy."

22. "Deaths by Suicide while on Active Duty, Active and Reserve Components, U.S. Armed Forces, 1998–2011," Armed Forces Health Surveillance Center, June 2012, www.ncbi.nlm.gov/pubmed/22779434.

23. Bowmer, "The Face of Military Suicide."

24. Bowmer, "The Face of Military Suicide."

25. Shawne K. Wickham, "Friends, Family Coping with a Hero's Suicide."

26. Wickham, "Friends, Family Coping with a Hero's Suicide."

27. Remarks delivered at the annual departments of Defense and Veterans Affairs conference on suicide prevention, June 22, 2012, Washington, D.C., http://www.defense.gov/speeches/speech.aspx?speechid=1686.

28. Wong, "New Report."

29. Wong, "New Report."

30. Jim Rendon, "Post-Traumatic Stress's Surprisingly Positive Flip Side."

31. Rendon, "Post-Traumatic Stress's Surprisingly Positive Flip Side."

32. "S.S.S. Intrepid: The Story of the 'Fighting I,'" A&E Television Networks, 1995.

33. Dean, *Shook Over Hell*, 214.

34. Rhonda Cornum, as told to Peter Copeland, *She Went to War*, 14.

35. Cornum, *She Went to War*, 17–18.

36. Cornum, *She Went to War*, 108.

37. Cornum, *She Went to War*, 194.

38. Daryl S. Paulson and Stanley Krippner, *Haunted by Combat*, 156–57.

39. Rendon, "Post-Traumatic Stress's Surprisingly Positive Flip Side."

40. Information provided by Peter Gutierrez of the VA in a March 5, 2014, e-mail.

41. Pauline Jelinek, "Panetta: Defense, VA must 'kick ass' to help military, veterans."

42. Kevin Freking, "Panel Urges Annual PTSD Screenings for Returned Military."

43. Benedict Carey, "Sleep Therapy Seen as an Aid for Depression."

44. Kim Tingley, "The Suicide Detective."

45. Kim Murphy, "A 'Base on the Brink,' as Is the Community."

46. Penny Coleman, "Military Suicides: Those We Might Yet Save."

47. Corey Mead, *War Games: Video Games and the Future of Armed Conflict*, 115.

48. "Pursuing Perfect Depression Care."

49. C. Edward Coffey, "Pursuing Perfect Depression Care: A Model for Eliminating Suicide and Transforming Mental Healthcare."

50. Maria Seyrig, "Depression Care Program Eliminates Suicide."

51. Hampton, "Depression Care Effort Brings Dramatic Drop in Large HMO Population's Suicide Rate," 1903–5.

52. Charles W. Hoge, Carl A. Castro, et al, "Combat Duty in Iraq and Afghanistan, Mental Health Problems, and Barriers to Care."

53. Swank and Marchand, "Combat Neuroses: Development of Combat Exhaustion," 236–47.

54. David Philipps, *Lethal Warriors*, 94–95.

55. Harrell and Berglass, "Losing the Battle."

56. The National Defense Authorization Act for FY 2010, Public Law 111-84, section 708.

57. Erin Emory, "Major General Mark Graham: The Commander's Shared Scars."

58. Emory, "Major General Mark Graham."

59. Vickie Bane, " 'They Were Great Boys.' "

60. Yochi J. Dreazen, "A General's Personal Battle."

61. Philipps, *Lethal Warriors*, 232.

62. Dreazen, "A General's Personal Battle."

63. Harrell and Berglass, "Losing the Battle."
64. Timothy Williams, "Suicides Outpacing War Deaths for Troops."
65. Penny Coleman, *Flashback*, 19.
66. Jonathan Shay, *Odysseus in America: Combat Trauma and the Trials of the Homecoming*, 4.
67. Paulson and Krippner, *Haunted by Combat*, 22.
68. Dave Grossman, *On Killing*, 88–89.
69. Ben Shephard, *A War of Nerves*, 244.
70. Harrell and Berglass, "Losing the Battle."
71. Craig J. Bryan and Kelly C. Cukrowicz, "Associations between Types of Combat Violence and the Acquired Capability for Suicide."
72. Kang and Bullman, "Risk of Suicide among US Veterans after Returning from the Iraq or Afghanistan War Zones," 652–53.
73. Kang and Bullman, "Risk of Suicide among US Veterans."
74. Bryan et al., "A Preliminary Test of the Interpersonal-Psychological Theory of Suicidal Behavior in a Military Sample," 347–50.
75. Bryan and Cukrowicz, "Associations between Types of Combat Violence and the Acquired Capability for Suicide."
76. Dexter Filkins, "Atonement."
77. Dexter Filkins, "Atonement."
78. James Dao, "Veterans Wait for Benefits as Claims Pile Up."
79. Peterson and Emmons, "Vexing Problem: Bridging Scores of Military Veterans into Civilian Jobs."
80. Joe Klein, "Ten Years After: A National Disgrace."
81. James Dao, "Veterans Wait for Benefits as Claims Pile Up."
82. Ann Jones, *They Were Soldiers*, 114.
83. Senior, "The Prozac, Paxil…War."
84. Mark Benjamin and Michael De Yoanna, "Kill Yourself. Save Us the Paperwork."
85. Helen Benedict, "Why Soldiers Rape."
86. Jones, *They Were Soldiers*, 123.
87. Philipps, *Lethal Warriors*, 97.
88. Kyle Henley and Tom Roeder, "Carson Soldier Kills Wife, Himself."
89. Philipps, *Lethal Warriors*, 117.

90. Philipps, *Lethal Warriors*, 117.

91. Philipps, *Lethal Warriors*, 118.

92. Deborah Sontag and Lizette Alvarez, "Across America, Deadly Echoes of Foreign Battles."

93. Philipps, *Lethal Warriors*, 123.

94. Philipps, *Lethal Warriors*, 215.

95. Philipps, *Lethal Warriors*, 138.

96. Cindy Piester, *On the Dark Side in Al Doura—A Soldier in the Shadows*, Maverick Media, December 17, 2011, http://youtube/watch?v=9mEjOGjvsQ.

97. Philipps, *Lethal Warriors*, 223.

98. Michael De Yoanna, "When War Kills at Home," *Salon*, November 12, 2011, http://salon.com/2011/11/12/when_war_kills_at_home.

99. Hugo Gye, "Purple Heart War Hero Kills Himself and His Wife after Suffering from Posttraumatic Stress Disorder."

100. Philipps, *Lethal Warriors*, 9.

101. Barry R. Schaller. *Veterans on Trial: The Coming Court Battles over PTSD*, 158.

102. R. Blaine Everson, "Quality of Life among U.S. Army Spouses: Parenting and Family Stress during Operation Iraqi Freedom," 2005 dissertation at Florida State University, http://diginole.lib.fsu.edu/etd/433.

103. David Brown, "Motor Vehicle Crashes: A Little-Known Risk to Returning Veterans of Iraq and Afghanistan."

104. Rebecca Clay, "Preventing Suicide among Veterans."

Afterword

1. Rosen, "PTSD Root of Deadly Spree?"

2. Rosen, "PTSD Root of Deadly Spree?"

3. Weissert and Coto, "Argument May Have Set off Attack."

4. Sanchez and Brumfield, "Fort Hood Shooter Was Iraq Vet Being Treated for Mental Illness."

5. Sanchez and Brumfield, "Fort Hood Shooter War Iraq Vet."

6. Rosen, "PTSD Root of Deadly Spree?"

7. Sanchez and Brumfield, "Fort Hood Shooter Was Iraq Vet."
8. Weissert and Coto, "Argument May Have Set off Attack."
9. Sanchez and Brumfield, "Fort Hood Shooter Was Iraq Vet."
10. Sanchez and Brumfield, "Fort Hood Shooter Was Iraq Vet."
11. Sanchez and Brumfield, "Fort Hood Shooter Was Iraq Vet."
12. Rosen, "PTSD Root of Deadly Spree?"
13. Jonsson, "Spc. Ivan Lopez, before Fort Hood Attack: 'My Spiritual Peace Has GoneAway.' "
14. Jonsson, "Spc. Ivan Lopez."
15. Zarembo, "Ft. Hood Shooting Puts Army Resilience Training to the Test."
16. Sanchez and Brumfield, "Fort Hood Shooter Was Iraq Vet."
17. Sanchez and Brumfield, "Fort Hood Shooter Was Iraq Vet."
18. Sanchez and Brumfield, "Fort Hood Shooter War Iraq Vet."
19. Baldor, "Suicides Down for Troops on Active Duty."
20. Baldor, "Suicides Down for Troops on Active Duty."
21. Baldor, "Suicides Down for Troops on Active Duty."
22. Daly and Tang, "Additional Veteran Deaths Reported in Phoenix Area."
23. Daniel Somers, "I Am Sorry That It Has Come to This': A Soldier's Last Words," Gawker, June 22, 2013, http://gawker.com/i-am-sorry-that-it-has-come-to-this-a-soldiers-last-534538357.
24. Somers, "I Am Sorry That It Has Come to This."
25. Somers, "I Am Sorry That It Has Come to This."

Appendix A

1. Centers for Disease Control and Prevention, "Deaths and Mortality," www.cdc.gov/nchs/fastats/deaths.htm.
2. George Howe Colt, *November of the Soul*, 54.
3. Pamela S. Hyde, "Suicide: The Challenges and Opportunities behind the Public Health Problem."
4. Hyde, "Suicide: The Challengers and Opportunities behind the Public Health Problem."
5. Aaron Levin, "Clinic Visits Common before Service Members' Suicide."

6. Quin and Nordentoff, "Suicide Risk in Relation to Psychiatric Hospitalization."
7. American Foundation for Suicide Prevention, "Facts and Figures: Suicide Deaths," http://afsp.org/understanding-suicide/facts-and-figures (2014).

Bibliography

Books

Alvarerz, A. *A Savage God*. New York: W. W. Norton, 1971.

Barnham, Peter. *Forgotten Lunatics of the Great War*. New Haven, CT: Yale University Press, 2007.

Baskir, Lawrence M., and William A. Strauss. *Chance and Circumstance: The Draft, the War and the Vietnam Generation*. New York: Random House, 1978.

Bateson, John. *The Final Leap: Suicide on the Golden Gate Bridge*. Berkeley: University of California Press, 2012.

Bierce, Ambrose. *The Civil War Short Stories of Ambrose Bierce*. New York: Bison Books, 1988.

Bilmes, Linda J., and Joseph E. Stiglitz. *The Three Trillion Dollar War: The True Cost of the Iraq Conflict*. New York: W. W. Norton & Co., 2008.

Bradley, James, with Ron Powers. *Flags of Our Fathers*. New York: Bantam Books, 2006.

Brandt, Dennis W. *Pathway to Hell: A Tragedy of the American Civil War*. Lincoln: University of Nebraska Press, 2008.

Brocke, Rita N. *Soul Repair: Recovering from Moral Injury after War*. Boston: Beacon Press, 2012.

Chambers, John Whiteclay II. *The Oxford Companion to American Military History*. New York: Oxford University Press, 1999.

Coleman, Penny. *Flashback: Posttraumatic Stress Disorder, Suicide, and the Lessons of War*. Boston: Beacon Press, 2006.

Colt, George Howe. *November of the Soul: The Enigma of Suicide*. New York: Scribner, 2006.

Cornum, Rhonda, with Peter Copeland. *She Went to War*. Novato, CA: Presidio Press, 1993.

Cott, Nancy, ed. *No Small Courage: A History of Women in the United States*. New York: Oxford University Press, 2000.

Crane, Stephen. *The Red Badge of Courage*. New York: Harper and Row, 1968.

Cumming, Kate. *The Journal of Kate Cumming: A Confederate Nurse, 1862–1865*. Ed. Richard Harwell. Savannah, GA: Beehive Press, 1975.

Davis, Kenneth C. *Don't Know Much about History*. New York: Crown Publishers, 1990.

Dean, Chuck. *Nam Vet: Making Peace with Your Past*. Puyallup, WA: Green City Productions, 1987.

Dean, Jr., Eric T. *Shook Over Hell: Post-Traumatic Stress, Vietnam, and the Civil War*. Cambridge, MA: Harvard University Press, 1999.

Durkheim, Emile. *Suicide*. New York: Free Press, 1951.

Faust, Drew Gilpin. *This Republic of Suffering: Death and the American Civil War*. New York: Vintage Books, 2008.

Finkel, David. *Thank You for Your Service*. New York: Farrar, Straus and Giroux, 2013.

Gabriel, Richard A. *No More Heroes: Madness and Psychiatry at War*. New York: Hill and Wang, 1987.

Gabriel, Richard A. *The Painful Field: The Psychiatric Dimension of Modern War*. Westport, CT: Greenwood Press, 1998.

Gibbs, Nancy, and Michael Duffy. *The President's Club*. New York: Simon & Schuster, 2012.

Gibbs, Philip. *Now It Can Be Told*. New York: Garden City Publishing, 1920.

Glatthaar, Joseph T. *Forged in Battle: The Civil War Alliance of Black Soldiers and White Officers*. New York: Free Press, 1990.

Goeschel, Christian. *Suicide in Nazi Germany*. Oxford: Oxford University Press, 2009.

Greene, Bob. *Homecoming: When the Soldiers Returned from Vietnam*. New York: Putnam, 1989.

Grossman, Dave. *On Killing: The Psychological Cost of Learning to Kill in War and Society*. New York: Back Bay Books, 2009.

Guarnere, William "Wild Bill," and Edward "Babe" Heffron, with Robyn Post. *Brothers in Battle, Best of Friends*. New York: Berkeley, 2007.

Heckler, Richard A. *Waking Up, Alive*. New York: Ballantine Books, 1994.

Hedrick, David T., and Gordon Barry, Jr. *I'm Surrounded by Methodists: Diary of John H. W. Stuckenberg, Chaplain of the 145th Pennsylvania Volunteer Infantry*. Gettysburg, PA: Thomas Publications, 1995.

Isenberg, David. *Shadow Force: Private Security Contractors in Iraq*. Westport, CT: Prager Security International, 2009.

Jamison, Kay Redfield. *An Unquiet Mind*. New York: Knopf, 1995.

Jamison, Kay Redfield. *Night Falls Fast: Understanding Suicide*. New York: Alfred A. Knopf, 1999.

Jobes, David A., and Edwin S. Shneidman. *Managing Suicidal Risk: A Collaborative Approach*. New York: Guilford Press, 2006.

Joiner, Thomas. *Myths about Suicide*. Cambridge, MA: Harvard University Press, 2010.

Joiner, Thomas. *The Perversion of Virtue*. New York: Oxford University Press, 2014.

Joiner, Thomas. *Why People Die by Suicide*. Cambridge, MA: Harvard University Press, 2005.

Jones, Ann. *They Were Soldiers: How the Wounded Return from America's Wars—The Untold Story*. Chicago: Haymarket Books, 2013.

Junger, Sebastian. *War*. New York: Twelve, 2010.

Kulka, Richard A., et al. *Trauma and the Vietnam War Generation: Report of the Findings from the National Vietnam Generation*. Levittown, PA: Brunner/Mazel, 1990.

Kurian, George Thomas, ed. *A Historical Guide to the United States Government*. New York: Oxford University Press, 1998.

Kutchins, Herb, and Stuart A. Kirk. *Making Us Crazy: DSM: The Psychiatric Bible and the Creation of Mental Illness*. New York: Simon and Schuster, 1997.

Kyle, Chris, Scott McEwen, and Jim DeFelice. *American Sniper: The Autobiography of the Most Lethal Sniper in U.S. Military History*. New York: Harper Collins, 2013.

Lande, R. Gregory. *Madness, Malingering, and Malfeasance: The Transformation of Psychiatry and the Law in the Civil War Era*. Washington, DC: Potomac Books, 2003.

Ledbetter, James. *Unwarranted Influence: Dwight D. Eisenhower and the Military Industrial Complex*. New Haven, CT: Yale University Press, 2011.

Lembcke, Jerry. *The Spitting Image: Myth, Memory, and the Legacy of Vietnam*. New York: New York University Press, 2000.

Lessing, Doris. *A Small Personal Voice*. New York: Alfred A. Knopf, 1974.

Linderman, Gerald. *Embattled Courage: The Experience of Combat in the American Civil War*. New York: Free Press, 1989.

Lindy, Jacob. *Vietnam: A Casebook*. Levittown, PA: Brunner/Mazel, 1988.

Lord, Francis A. *Civil War Collector's Encyclopedia*. Mineola, NY: Dover, 2004.

Maddow, Rachel. *Drift: The Unmooring of American Military Power*. New York: Crown Publishers, 2012.

Marcus, Eric. *Why Suicide?* New York: HarperCollins, 2010.

Marlantes, Karl. *What It Is Like to Go to War*. New York: Atlantic Monthly Press, 2011.

Marshall, S. L. A. *Men against Fire: The Problem of Battle Command in Future War*. Gloucester, MA: Peter Smith Publications, 1975.

Mead, Corey. *War Play: Video Games and the Future of Armed Conflict*. Boston: Houghton Mifflin Harcourt, 2013.

Meagher, Ilona. *Moving a Nation to Care: Post-Traumatic Stress Disorder and America's Returning Troops*. Brooklyn: Ig Publishing, 2007.

Myers, Charles S. *Shell Shock in France: Based on a War Diary*. Cambridge: Cambridge University Press, 1940.

Paulson, Daryl S., and Stanley Krippner. *Haunted by Combat: Understanding PTSD in War Veterans*. Lanham, MD: Rowman & Littlefield, 2010.

Perry, John G. *Letters from a Surgeon of the Civil War*. Ed. Martha Derby Perry. Boston: Little Brown and Company, 1906.

Philipps, David. *Lethal Warriors: Uncovering the Tragic Reality of PTSD*. New York: Palgrave Macmillan, 2010.

Powers, Kevin. *The Yellow Birds*. New York: Little Brown, 2012.

Provine, Charles M. *The Unknown Patton*. New York: Random House, 2009.

Quintard, Charles T. *Doctor Quintard, Chaplain C.S.A. and the Second Bishop of Tennessee: Being His Story of the War*. Ed. A. H. Noll. Sewanee, TN: University Press of Sewanee, 1905.

Ramchand, Rajeev, Joie Acosta, et al. *The War Within: Preventing Suicide in the U.S. Military*. Santa Monica, CA: RAND Center for Military Health Research Policy, 2011.

Robertson, Robert S. *Diary of the War*. Ed. Charles N. Walker and Rosemary Walker. Scottsville, KY: Allen County Historical Society, 1965.

Ryan, Cornelius. *The Last Battle: The Classic History of the Battle for Berlin*. New York: Touchstone, 1995.

Schaller, Barry R. *Veterans on Trial: The Coming Court Battles over PTSD*. Washington, DC: Potomac Books, 2012.

Shay, Jonathan. *Achilles in Vietnam: Combat Trauma and the Undoing of Character*. New York: Scribner, 1994.

Shay, Jonathan. *Odysseus in America: Combat Trauma and the Trials of Homecoming*. New York: Scribner, 2002.

Shea, Shawn C. *The Practical Art of Suicide Assessment*. Hoboken, NJ: John Wiley and Sons, 2002.

Shephard, Ben. *A War of Nerves: Soldiers and Psychiatrists 1914–1994*. London: Pimlico, 2002.

Shields, David, and Shane Salerno. *Salinger*. New York: Simon and Schuster, 2013.

Shneidman, Edwin S. *The Suicidal Mind*. New York: Oxford University Press, 1996.

Silkenat, David. *Moments of Despair: Suicide, Divorce, and Debt in Civil War Era North Carolina*. Chapel Hill: University of North Carolina Press, 2011.

Singer, P. W. *Wired for War: The Robotics Revolution and Conflict in the 21st Century*. New York: Penguin, 2009.

Singer, P. W. *Corporate Warriors: The Rise of the Privatized Military Industry*. Ithaca, NY: Cornell University, 2003.

Sites, Kevin. *The Things They Cannot Say: Stories Soldiers Won't Tell You about What They've Seen, Done or Failed to Do in War.* New York: HarperCollins, 2013.

Slone, Laurie B., and Matthew J. Friedman. *After the War Zone: A Practical Guide for Returning Troops and Their Families.* Philadelphia, PA: Da Capo Press, 2008.

Stiglitz, Joseph E., and Linda J. Bilmes. *The Three Trillion Dollar War: The True Cost of the Iraq Conflict.* New York: W. W. Norton, 2008.

Tucker, Mike. *Ronin: A Marine Scout/Sniper Platoon in Iraq.* Mechanicsburg, PA: Stackpole Books, 2008.

Tucker, Spencer C., ed. *Encyclopedia of the Vietnam War.* New York: Oxford University Press, 2001.

Turse, Nick. *Kill Anything That Moves: The Real American War in Vietnam.* New York: Henry Holt, 2013.

Williams, Kayla. *Love My Rifle More Than You: Young and Female in the U.S. Army.* New York: W. W. Norton, 2005.

Winter, Denis. *Death's Men: Soldiers of the Great War.* London: Penguin, 1978.

Wyatt-Brown, Bertram. *Southern Honor: Ethics and Behavior in the Old South.* New York: Oxford University Press, 2007.

Youngson, Robert, and Ian Schott. *Medical Blunders: Amazing True Stories of Mad, Bad, and Dangerous Doctors.* New York: NYU Press, 1998.

Articles and Studies

Abbot, Sebastian, and Munir Ahmed. "Pakistan's Drone Toll Claim Met with Skepticism." Associated Press, October 31, 2013.

"After a Marine's Suicide, a Family Recalls Missed Red Flags." National Public Radio, June 19, 2013.

Agent Orange Review 2(2) (June 1993): 1.

Allen, Terry J. "America's Child Soldier Problem." *In These Times,* May 15, 2007.

Alvarez, Lizette. "Army and Agency Will Study Rising Suicide Rate among Soldiers." *New York Times,* October 29, 2008.

Amarante, Joe. "Pentagon: Active-Military Suicides Almost One a Day in U.S." *New Haven Register,* January 26, 2013.

American Legion. "Dying in Line: VA's Trial of Patients." www. legion.org, May 6, 2014.

American-Statesman Investigative Team. "After Returning Home, Many Veterans Get into Motor Vehicle Accidents." *Austin American-Statesman*, September 29, 2012.

Anderson, R. "Vietnam Legacy: Veteran's Suicide Toll May Top War Casualties." *Seattle Times*, March 18, 1981.

Anderson, Rick. "Home Front Casualties." *Seattle Weekly*, August 31, 2005.

"An Enslaved Man's Noble Suicide." *The Liberator*, October 20, 1843.

Appel, John W., and Gilbert W. Beebe. "Preventive Psychiatry: An Epidemiological Approach." *JAMA* 131 (1946).

Archibald, Herbert C., and Read D. Tuddenhan. "Persistent Stress Reaction after Combat: A 20-Year Follow-up." *Archives of General Psychiatry*, May 1965.

Armed Forces Health Surveillance Center. "Deaths by Suicide while on Active Duty, Active and Reserve Components, U.S. Armed Forces, 1998–2011." *Medical Surveillance Monthly Report*, June 2012.

"Army Says 22-Year-Old Fort Campbell Special Forces Soldier Has Died From Self-Inflicted Gunshot." Associated Press, April 17, 2012.

"Army STARRS Preliminary Data Reveal Some Potential Predictive Factors for Suicide." National Institute of Mental Health, March 22, 2011, http://www.nimh.nih.gov/science-news/2011/army-starrs-preliminary-data-reveal-some-potential-predictive-factors-for-suicide.shtml.

Ashlock, Alex. "A Marine's Suicide and a Family's Fight for Compensation." *Here & Now*, February 28, 2012.

Atkinson, Michael P. et al. "A Dynamic Model for Post-Traumatic Stress Disorder among U.S. Troops in Operation Iraqi Freedom. *Management Science* 55 (September 2009).

Australian Institute of Health and Welfare. *Morbidity of Vietnam Veterans: Suicide in Vietnam Veterans' Children (Supplementary Report 1)*, 2000.

Avalona-Butler, Amber. "Combating the Stigma of Suicide: An Army Story." *Paraglide*, September 16, 2010.

Baker, Mike. "Alleged Gunman Found Dead." Associated Press, January 3, 2012.

Baldor, Lolita C. "APNewsBreak: Military Suicides Drop; Unclear Why." Associated Press, November 11, 2013.

Baldor, Lolita C. "Military Faces Character Issues." Associated Press, February 16, 2014.

Baldor, Lolita C. "Suicides Down for Troops on Active Duty." Associated Press, April 26, 2014.

Baldor, Lolita C. "This Is What It's Like to Be an Army Woman in Combat." Associated Press, February 26, 2014.

Baldor, Lolita C., and Deb Riechmann. "Army Charges Bales in Afghan Killings, Plans Proceedings at Lewis-McChord." *Seattle Times*, March 23, 2012.

Bane, Vickie. " 'They Were Great Boys.' " *People Magazine*, August 17, 2009.

Barlow, Nikita. "Philip Henry Sheridan, III." Find a Grave, March 26, 2008, http://genforum.genealogy.com/sheridan/messages/2386.html.

Basu, Moni. "Why Suicide Rate among Veterans May Be More Than 22 a Day." CNN, November 14, 2013.

Baum, Dan. "The Price of Valor." *New Yorker*, October 13, 2004.

Benedict, Helen. "Why Soldiers Rape." *In These Times*, August 13, 2008.

Benjamin, Mark. "Is the U.S. Army Losing Its War on Suicide?" *Time*, April 13, 2010.

Benjamin, Mark. "Seventh Iraq War Veteran Kills Himself." United Press International, March 16, 2004.

Benjamin, Mark. "The V.A.'s Bad Review." Salon.com, October 26, 2005, http://salon.com/2005/10/26/suicide_22.

Benjamin, Mark, and Michael De Yoanna, Michael. "Coming Home: The Conclusion." Salon.com, February 14, 2009, http://salon.com/2009/02/14/coming_home_five.

Benjamin, Mark, and Michael De Yoanna. " 'The Death Dealers Took My Life' " Salon.com, February 9, 2009, http://salon.com/2009/02/09/coming_home_one.

Benjamin, Mark and Michael De Yoanna. " 'He Hears Sounds Which Seem to Be Voices.' " Salon.com, February 13, 2009, http://salon.com/2009/02/13/coming_home_four_marko.

Benjamin, Mark, and Michael De Yoanna. " 'Kill Yourself. Save Us the Paperwork.' " Salon.com, February 10, 2009, http://salon.com/2009/02/10/coming_home_two.

Benjamin, Mark, and Michael De Yoanna. "Mark Waltz, Kenneth Lehman, Chad Barrett." Salon.com, February 10, 2009, http://salon.com/2009/02/10/coming_home_two_sidebar.

Benjamin, Mark, and Michael De Yoanna. " 'That Young Man Never Should Have Come into the Army,' " Salon.com, February 13, 2009.

Benjamin, Mark, and Michael De Yoanna. " 'You're a Pussy and a Scared Little Kid.' " Salon.com, February 12, 2009.

Bergen, Peter. "Drone Wars." New America Foundation, April 24, 2013.

Bickley, Harriet, Isabelle M. Hunt, et al. "Suicide within Two Weeks of Discharge from Psychiatric Inpatient Care: A Case-Control Study." *Psychiatry Online*, July 1, 2013.

"Bid to Limit Marine Suicides," *Los Angeles Times*, February 27, 2009.

Birk, Chris. "Veterans Benefits Bill Brings Big Changes to VA Loan Program." *Zillow*, August 6, 2012.

Blow, Frederic C., Amy S. B. Bohnert, et al. "Suicide Mortality among Patients Treated by the Veterans Health Administration From 2000 to 2007." *American Journal of Public Health* 102 Suppl (March 2012): 1:S98–104.

Bonner, Raymond. "The Case against Sgt. Bales." *Newsweek*, November 5, 2012.

Bourne, Peter G. "From Boot Camp to My Lai." In *Crimes of War*. Ed. Richard A. Falk, Gabriel Kolko, and Robert Jay Lifton. New York: Random House, 1971.

Bowmer, Nicole. "The Face of Military Suicide." *Socialist Worker*, September 12, 2011, socialistworker.org.

Boyle, Coleen A., Pierre Decoufle, et al. "Post Service Mortality among Vietnam Veterans." U.S. Department of Health and Human Services, Public Health Service, Centers for Disease Control, Atlanta, February 1987, 257.

Brauser, Deborah. "Postdischarge Period Linked to Very High Suicide." *Medscape*, April 12, 2013.

Bravin, Jess. "Army Report Omitted Prison Details." *Wall Street Journal*, June 4, 2004.

Bremner, J. Douglas, Steven M. Southwick, et al. "Chronic PTSD in Vietnam Combat Veterans: Course of Illness and Substance Abuse." *American Journal of Psychiatry* 153(3) (March 1996): 369–75.

British Broadcasting Corporation. "Historic Figures: Siegfried Sassoon (1886–1967), http://www.bbc.co.uk/history/historic_fig ures/sassoon_siegfried.shtml

Brock, Rita N. "Moral Injury: The Crucial Missing Piece in Understanding Soldier Suicides." *Huffington Post*, July 23, 2012.

Brock, Rita N. "New Soul Repair Center at Brite Divinity School Aims to Help Veterans Recover from Moral Injuries from War." *Star-Telegram*, October 30, 2012.

Brogan, Beth. "BNAS Suicide Report Released." *Times Record*, May 6, 2008.

Bronstein, Scott, and Drew Griffin. "A Fatal Wait: Veterans Languish and Die on a VA Hospital's Secret List." CNN, April 23, 2014.

Brooke, James. "Okinawa Suicides and Japan's Army: Burying the Truth?" *New York Times*, June 20, 2005.

"Brother of Sgt. Kirkland: 'Army Mental Health Care Is a Joke.' " *March Forward*, July 1, 2011.

Brown, David. "Motor Vehicle Crashes: A Little-Known Risk to Returning Veterans of Iraq and Afghanistan." *Washington Post*, May 5, 2013.

Brunswick, Mark. "Battle on Home Front Is Guard's Most Perilous." *Star Tribune*, June 25, 2011.

Bryan, Craig J., and Kelly C. Cukrowicz. "Associations between Types of Combat Violence and the Acquired Capability for Suicide." *Suicide and Life-Threatening Behavior* 41(2) (April 2011).

Bryan, Craig J., et al. "A Preliminary Test of the Interpersonal-Psychological Theory of Suicidal Behavior in a Military Sample." *Personality and Individual Differences* 48 (2009).

Buchanan, Christopher. "A Reporter's Journey." *Frontline*, March 1, 2005.

Bumiller, Elisabeth. "Active-Duty Soldiers Take Their Own Lives at Record Rate." *New York Times*, January 19, 2012.

Bumiller, Elisabeth, and Thom Shanker. "Pentagon Is Set to Lift Combat Ban for Women." *New York Times*, January 23, 2013.

Burkett, Jon. "Gun Range Owner Haunted by Recent Suicide on Premises." *WTVR*, July 24, 2012.

Burns, Robert. "Army Active-Duty Suicides Double in July." Associated Press, August 17, 2012.

Burns, Robert. "General Foresees End to Grim Rise in Army Suicides." Associated Press, March 7, 2013.

Burns, Robert. "Number of Military Suicides Up." Associated Press, January 15, 2013.

Calvert, Scott. "A Soldier's Grim Homecoming." *Baltimore Sun*, February 18, 2004.

Calvert, William E., and Roger L. Hutchinson. "Vietnam Veteran Levels of Combat: Related to Later Violence?" *Journal of Traumatic Stress* 103 (1990).

Canham, Matt. "Researcher: Deployed Military Need Tailored Mental Health Care." *Salt Lake Tribune*, July 24, 2012.

Carey, Benedict. "Sleep Therapy Seen as an Aid for Depression." *New York Times*, November 18, 2013.

Carey, Benedict. "Suicidal Tendencies Are Evident before Deployment, Study Finds." *New York Times*, March 3, 2014.

Carter, Chelsea J. "Were Bonuses Tied to VA Wait Times? Here's What We Know." CNN, May 30, 2014.

Cave, Damien. "Tracking a Marine Lost at Home." *New York Times*, March 31, 2008.

"CBS Reports: The Wall Within." CBS News, June 2, 1988.

Char, Reinhart. "Philip Sheridan 3d Leaps to Death from Gate Bridge." *San Francisco Chronicle*, March 12, 1948.

"Charles E. Dane, 37." *Eagle Tribune*, July 3, 2009.

Chedekel, Lisa, and Matthew Kauffman. "Army's Suicide Struggles Continue: 2006 Rate of Self-Inflicted Deaths in Iraq Could Exceed Record Set in 2005." *Hartford Courant*, January 31, 2007.

Chedekel, Lisa, and Matthew Kauffman. "Did Military Withhold Correct Treatment for Mentally Ill? Troops Got Antidepressants but Not Needed Counseling." *Hartford Courant*, May 22, 2006.

Christenson, Sig. "GI's War Followed Him Home." *San Antonio Express-News*, February 18, 2011.

"Civilian Drone Deaths Rise, Government Says." Associated Press, October 31, 2013.

Clay, Rebecca A. "Preventing Suicide among Veterans." *SAMHSA News*, May/June 2006.

Cogan, Sandy D. "What Military Patients Want Civilian Providers to Know." *SAMHSA News*, Fall 2011.

Cohen, Tom, Drew Griffin, Scott Bronstein, and Nelli Black. "Shinseki Resigns, but Will That Improve Things at VA Hospitals?" CNN, May 31, 2014.

Coker, Eric. "Historian Focuses on Civil War Suicides." *Discover-e,* Binghamton University, http://discovere.binghamton.edu/faculty-spotlights/sommerville-3571.html, February 15, 2011.

Cole, David. "Obama and Terror: The Hovering Questions." *New York Review,* July 12, 2012.

Cole, Ronald H. *Operation Urgent Fury: The Planning and Execution of Joint Operations in Grenada, 12 October–2 November, 1983.* Joint History Office, Office of the Chairman of the Joint Chiefs of Staff, 1997.

Coleman, Penny. "120 War Vets Commit Suicide Each Week." *AlterNet,* November 26, 2007.

Coleman, Penny. "Military Suicides: Those We Might Yet Save." Justice Policy Institute, January 24, 2012.

Colliver, Victoria. "Researchers Use Brain Imaging to Study PTSD." *San Francisco Chronicle,* August 1, 2012.

Conger, Dave. "Shockwave." *Carolina Reporter,* September 12, 2001.

Contrada, Fred. "Army Report Released to Newspaper Says Smith College Graduate Shot Herself in Iraq." *Republican,* January 21, 2009.

"Cost of U.S. Wars Linger for Over 100 Years." Associated Press, March 19, 2013.

Crane, P. J., et al. "Mortality of Vietnam Veterans." *The Veteran Cohort Study: A Report of the 1996 Retrospective Cohort Study of Australian Vietnam Veterans,* 1997.

Czekalinski, Stephanie. "Black Women Key to Easing Military Suicides?" *National Journal,* June 12, 2012.

Daly, Matthew, and Terry Tang. "Additional Veteran Deaths Reported in Phoenix Area." Associated Press, June 6, 2014.

Dao, James. "As Suicides Rise in U.S., Veterans Are Less of a Total." *New York Times,* February 1, 2013.

Dao, James. "Taking Calls from Veterans on the Brink." *New York Times,* July 30, 2010.

Dao, James. "Veterans Wait for Benefits as Claims Pile Up." *New York Times,* September 27, 2012.

Dao, James. "White House Changes Policy on Condolence Letters for Military Suicides." *New York Times,* July 6, 2011.

Davidson, Michael P. "Post-Traumatic Stress Disorder: A Controversial Defense for Veterans of a Controversial War." *William and Mary Law Review* 29 (Winter 1988).

"Deaths by Suicide while on Active Duty, Active and Reserve Components, U.S. Armed Forces, 1998–2011." Armed Forces Health Surveillance Center, June 2012, www.ncbi.nlm.gov/pubmed/22779434.

Dempsey, James. "Man's Wife Sensed Crisis Was Brewing: 'He Wasn't a Happy Man.'" *Worchester Telegram & Gazette*, June 24, 1996.

Department of Defense Personnel and Military Casualty Statistics. "Casualty Summary by Reason, October 7, 2001 through August 18, 2007." Defense Manpower Data Center.

Department of Veterans Affairs, Office of Facilities Management. "70 Years of VA History." April 2001.

DeVrieze, Craig. "Questions Swirl around Life, Suicide of Quad-City Veteran Pat Gibbs Jr." *Quad-City Times*, May 30, 2010.

De Yoanna, Michael. "Despite PTSD, Soldier Was Determined to Return to Iraq." *Rocky Mountain News*, April 21, 2008.

De Yoanna, Michael. "Vet's War Continued at Home." *Colorado Springs Independent*, April 12, 2007.

De Yoanna, Michael. "When War Kills at Home." Salon.com, November 12, 2011, http://salon.com/2011/11/12/when_war_kills_at_home.

"A Disservice to Disabled Troops." *New York Times*, May 27, 2012.

"Documentary on Veterans to Open on Web." *Washington Post*, May 24, 2012.

Dokoupil, Tony. "Moral Injury." *Newsweek*, December 10, 2012.

Dreazen, Yochi J. "A General's Personal Battle." *Wall Street Journal*, March 28, 2009.

Drescher, Kent D., Craig S. Rosen, et al. "Causes of Death among Male Veterans Who Received Residential Treatment for PTSD." *Journal of Traumatic Stress* 16(6) (December 2003): 535–43.

D'Souza, Charles. "Aleida Bordas, 38, Lincoln HS Teacher, Served in Iraq and Afghanistan." *Yonkers Daily Voice*, April 25, 2013.

Duhigg, Charles. "'Enemy Contact. Kill'em, Kill'em.'" *Los Angeles Times*, July 18, 2004.

Dykes, Brett Micheak. "Report: Mental Health of U.S. Soldiers in a Freefall." *Los Angeles Times*, February 7, 2011.

Egelko, Bob. "Judge Told VA Stalls on Care while 18 Veterans a Day Commit Suicide." *San Francisco Chronicle*, April 22, 2008.

Egelko, Bob. "Military Veterans Backed on Claims for Mental Health Care." *San Francisco Chronicle*, May 11, 2011.

Egelko, Bob. "VA Faulted in Diagnosing Suicide Candidates." *San Francisco Chronicle*, April 23, 2008.

Egelko, Bob. "Women Return from Battle, Sue over Combat Ban." *San Francisco Chronicle*, November 28, 2012.

Eisenhower, Dwight D. Farewell Address to the Nation, July 17, 1961. http://mcadams.posc.mu.edu/ike.htm.

Eisenhower, Dwight D. "Public Papers of the Presidents." The American Presidency Project. http://www.presidency.ucsb.edu/us.

Elias, Paul. "Court Orders Mental Health Overhall." Associated Press, May 5, 2011.

Ellison, Jesse. "Nineteen Veterans, Service Members File New Lawsuit over Military Sexual Assault." *Daily Beast*, September 28, 2012.

Emmons, Mark. "Who Was Abel Gutierrez?" *San Jose Mercury News*, March 25, 2012.

Emory, Erin. "Major General Mark Graham: The Commander's Shared Scars." *Denver Post*, March 9, 2008.

Esther, Mary. "Nearly a Year after Her Husband Committed Suicide, Air Force Widow Still Wonders Why." *Northwest Florida Daily News*, September 17, 2011.

Evans, Martin C. "War Experience Changed Marine, Family Says." *Newsday*, March 31, 2012.

Evans, Nate. "Their Battle Within." *Los Angeles Times*, June 16, 2013.

Everitt, Lauren, Andrew Theen, et al. "Efforts Lag to Improve Care for National Guard Troops." *Washington Post*, February 14, 2012.

Everson, Ronald Blaine. "Quality of Life among U.S. Army Spouses: Parenting and Family Stress during Operation Iraqi Freedom." PhD diss., Florida State University, 2005. http://diginole.lib.fsu.edu/etd/433.

"Ex-Marine Kills 2 Co-Workers before Committing Suicide." Associated Press, September 1, 2012.

Fagan, Kevin. "President to Send Condolences for War-Zone Suicides." *San Francisco Chronicle*, July 7, 2011.

Fagan, Kevin. "Tragedy Shows Extreme Result of Postwar Stress." *San Francisco Chronicle*, March 17, 2012.

Fagan, Kevin. "Vet's Belated Victory." *San Francisco Chronicle*, January 25, 2014.

Fagan, Kevin, and Vivian Ho. "Iraq Vet Kills His Sister, 11, Then Self." *San Francisco Chronicle*, March 16, 2012.

Falk, Richard J. "U.S. Military Suicides and Palestinian Hunger Strikes." *Guernica*, June 14, 2012.

Fantz, Ashley. "At Last, Suicides among Military Family Members Could Be Tracked." CNN.com, February 6, 2014.

Farmer, Blake. "Record High Army Suicides Prompt Action." National Public Radio, May 6, 2009.

Farrell, Warren. "Behind the Rise in Male Suicide." *San Francisco Chronicle*, June 28, 1996.

"Father Says Military Support System Failed Suicidal Soldier." Associated Press, December 19, 2007.

Faust, Drew Gilpin. "'Numbers on Top of Numbers': Counting the Civil War Dead." *Journal of Military History* 70 (October 2006): 95–1009.

Feeney, Lauren. "The Military Suicide Epidemic," July 27, 2012. www.billmoyers.com.

Fernandez, Manny, and Michael Schwirtz. "Untouchable in Iraq, Ex-Sniper Dies in Shooting Back Home." *New York Times*, February 3, 2013.

Filkins, Dexter. "Atonement." *New Yorker*, October 29, 2012, and November 5, 2012.

Finkel, David. "The Return." *New Yorker*, September 9, 2013.

Finnegan, William. "The Last Tour: A Decorated Marine's War Within." *New Yorker*, September 29, 2008.

Fiore, Kristina. "Suicide, Mental Illness Climb in Military." *Medpage Today*, March 7, 2012.

Flip, Julia. "War Widow Blames VA Neglect for Her Husband's Suicide." Courthouse News Service, October 18, 2011.

Freedman, Dan. "Hunt for Motive Turns up a 'Pattern of Misbehavior.'" *San Francisco Chronicle*, September 18, 2013.

Freedman, Samuel G. "Faith Leaders Training to Help with Moral Injury among Veterans." *New York Times*, January 13, 2013.

Freedman, Samuel G. "Tending to Veterans' Afflictions of the Soul." *New York Times*, January 11, 2013.

Freking, Kevin. "Panel Urges Annual PTSD Screenings for Returned Military." Associated Press, July 13, 2012.

Freking, Kevin. "VA under Fire over Mental Health Laws." Associated Press, March 4, 2012.

Frosch, Dan. "Fighting the Terror of Battles That Rage in Soldiers' Heads." *New York Times*, May 13, 2007.

Frueh, B. Christopher, and Jeffrey A. Smith. "Suicide, Alcoholism, and Psychiatric Illness among Union Forces during the U.S. Civil War." *Journal of Anxiety Disorders* 26(7) (2012): 769–75.

"Full Military Honors Planned for Marine." *WMUR*, July 2, 2009.

Gafni, Matthias. "The 'Black Hole' for U.S. Veterans." *Contra Costa Times*, May 11, 2012.

Gamel, Kim. "U.N.: Drone Strikes in Afghanistan Climb." Associated Press, February 20, 2013.

Grer, Darrock. "County Civil War Casualties, Week-by-Week, for the Abraham Lincoln Presidential Library and Museum." BRC Imagination Arts, 2005.

Gibbs, Nancy A., and Mark Thompson. "The War on Suicide?" *Time*, July 23, 2012.

Glantz, Aaron. "After Service, Veteran Deaths Surge." *Bay Citizen*, October 18, 2010.

Glantz, Aaron. "Are Local Vets Getting the Help They Need?" *Bay Citizen*, March 24, 2012.

Glantz, Aaron. "Long Wait for Compensation Claims a Growing Problem in Urban Areas." *San Francisco Chronicle*, August 29, 2012.

Glantz, Aaron. "Suicide Rates Soar among WWII Vets, Records Show." *Bay Citizen*, November 11, 2010.

Glantz, Aaron. "Suicides Highlight Failures of Veterans' Support System." *New York Times*, March 24, 2012.

Glantz, Aaron. "VA Delay in Aiding Veterans Growing." *San Francisco Chronicle*, March 16, 2013.

Goff, Angie. "Soldier's Recent Suicide May Not Have Been Isolated Incident." *WISTV*, September 10, 2006.

Goff, Stan. "KIA in Alabama." *Huffington Post*, January 20, 2006.

Gold, Hadas. "CNN Anchor Breaks Down over Vet's Suicide." Politico, May 30, 2014, http://www.politico.com/blogs/media/2014/05/cnn-anchor-breaks-down-over-vets-suicide.

Goode, Erica. "After Combat, Victims of an Inner War." *New York Times*, August 2, 2009.

Goodman, Amy. "Soldier Killed Herself after Objecting to Interrogation Techniques Being Used on Iraqi Prisoners." *Democracy Now*, November 7, 2006.

Goodman, Amy. "The War and Peace Report." *Democracy Now,* May 28, 2012.

Goodwin, Jim. "The Etiology of Combat-Related Posttraumatic Stress Disorders," *Posttraumatic Stress Disorders of the Vietnam Veteran.* Ed. Tom Williams. 1987.

Great War Society. "Charles Whittlesey: Commander of the Lost Battalion." 2000. http://www.worldwar1.com/dbc/whitt.htm.

Greenbergon, Benjamin T. "Silent Witnesses." *Hungry Blues,* November 28, 2006.

Griffin, Drew, Nelli Balck, Scott Bronstein, and Greg Botelho. "Daughter: Vietnam Vet Waited and Waited, Only to Die before Getting VA Appointment." CNN, May 23, 2014.

Gross, Liza. "Rising Rates of Military Suicides Reveal Complex Effects of Service on Soldiers' Health." *KQED,* August 14, 2013.

Grossman, Lev. "Rise of the Drones." *Time,* February 11, 2013.

Gugliotta, Guy. "New Estimate Raises Civil War Death Toll." *New York Times,* April 2, 2012.

Gye, Hugo. "Purple Heart War Hero Kills Himself and His Wife after Suffering from Post-Traumatic Stress Disorder." *Daily Mail Reporter,* February 6, 2012.

Hafemeister, Thomas L., and Nicole A. Stockey. "Last Stand? The Criminal Responsibility of War Veterans Returning from Iraq and Afghanistan with Post-Traumatic Stress Disorder." *Indiana Law Journal* 85(1) (2010).

Hall, Kristin M. "APNewsBreak: Suit Claims VA Negligent In Suicide." Associated Press, October 12, 2011.

Hampton, Tracy. "Depression Care Effort Brings Dramatic Drop in Large HMO Population's Suicide Rate." *JAMA* 393(19) (2010).

Harrell, Margaret C., and Nancy Berglass. "Losing the Battle: The Challenge of Military Suicide." Center for a New American Security, October 2011.

Hawley, Chris. "Eight Charged in Death of Fellow Soldier." Associated Press, December 22, 2011.

Hayes, Christopher. "The Good War on Terror." *In These Times,* September 8, 2006.

Hayes, Jr., Major Timothy P. "Post-Traumatic Stress Disorder on Trial." *Military Law Review* 190/191 (2006/2007): 67–110.

Hearst, Norman, Thomas B. Newman, and Stephen P. Hulley. "Delayed Effects of the Military Draft on Mortality: A Randomized Natural Experiment." *New England Journal of Medicine 314* (1986).

Hearst, Norman, et al. "Correspondence." *New England Journal of Medicine* 317(8) (1987).

Hefling, Kimberly. "Iraq War Vets' Suicide Rates Analyzed." Associated Press, February 13, 2008.

Hefling, Kimberly. "VA Mental Health Chief Sorry about 'Shh' on Suicidal Vets." Associated Press, May 7, 2008.

Hendley, Matthew. "Phoenix VA Director, Two Others Placed on Leave." *Phoenix New Times*, May 2, 2014.

Hendricks, Larry. "Flag Soldier Died Deeply Conflicted." *Arizona Daily Sun*, March 10, 2007.

Henley, Kyle, and Tom Roeder. "Carson Soldier Kills Wife, Himself." *Colorado Springs Gazette*, August 5, 2005.

Herring, George C. " 'Cold Blood': LBJ's Conduct of Limited War in Vietnam." In *An American Dilemma: Vietnam 1964–1973*. Military History Symposium Series of the United States Air Force Academy, by Dennis E. Showalter and John G. Albert, 1993.

Hill, Christian, and Adam Ashton. "Is Lewis-McChord Really 'Most Troubled Base in the Military?' " *Miami Herald*, March 18, 2012.

"Hiroshima Bomb Pilot Dies Aged 92." BBC News, November 1, 2007.

Hoffman, Michael, "Guard, Reserve Suicide Rate Sees Big Spike." *Army Times*, January 19, 2011.

Hoge, Charles W., Carl A. Castro, et al. "Combat Duty in Iraq and Afghanistan, Mental Health Problems, and Barriers to Care." *New England Journal of Medicine* 351(1) (2004): 13–22.

Holmes, Oliver Wendell. Jr., "The Soldier's Faith." Address given at Harvard University, May 30, 1895.

Hurst, Lynda. "Troops in Iraq on Suicide Watch." *Toronto Star*, April 11, 2004.

Hyer, Lee, Patrick A. Boudewyns, et al. "Three Tier Evaluation of PTSD among Vietnam Combat Veterans." *Journal of Traumatic Stress* 4(2) (1991).

Hyer, Lee, Edward W. McCranie, et al. "Suicidal Behavior among Chronic Vietnam Theatre Veterans with PTSD." *Journal of Clinical Psychology* 46(6) (1990).

Jaffe, Greg. "Marine's Suicide Is Only Start of Family's Struggle." *Washington Post*, February 11, 2012.

Jaffe, Greg. "VA Study Finds More Veterans Committing Suicide." *Washington Post*, January 31, 2013.

Jaffe, Greg, and Ed O'Keefe. "VA Chief Takes Blame for Employees' Missteps." *Washington Post*, May 31, 2014.

Jelinek, Pauline. "Army's Efforts Fail to Quell Suicide Rate." Associated Press, February 1, 2008.

Jelinek, Pauline. "Glint of Hope on Suicide Rate." Associated Press, November 18, 2009.

Jelinek, Pauline. " 'I'm a Monster': Veterans 'Alone' in Their Guilt." Associated Press, February 22, 2013.

Jelinek, Pauline. "Panetta: Defense, VA Must 'Kick Ass' to Help Military, Veterans." Associated Press, July 25, 2012.

Jelinek, Pauline. "Report: Troop Morale Higher in Afghanistan." Associated Press, February 3, 2014.

Jelinek, Paulina. "Suicides May Top Combat Deaths, Army Says." Associated Press, February 6, 2009.

Jelinek, Pauline, and Lolita C. Baldor. "U.S. Shifts War Suicide Policy." Associated Press, July 7, 2011.

Jonsson, Patrik. "Spc. Ivan Lopez, before Fort Hood Attack: 'My Spiritual Peace Has Gone Away.' " *Christian Science Monitor*, April 5, 2014.

"Joshua Omvig Veterans Suicide Prevention Act of 2007." *Harvard Journal on Legislation*, June 11, 2008.

Judis, John. "An American Suicide: What War Did to Jeffrey Lucey." *New Republic*, August 6, 2007.

Kaiser, David. "War Crimes and American Strategy." *History Unfolding*, January 26, 2009.

Kang, Han K., and Tim A. Bullman. "Risk of Suicide among US Veterans after Returning from the Iraq or Afghanistan War Zones." *JAMA* 300(6) (2008).

Kaplan, Mark S., Nathalie Huguet, Bentson H. McFarland, and Jason T. Newsom."Suicide among Male Veterans: A Prospective Population-Based Study." *Journal of Epidemiology and Community Health* (July 2007).

Kay, Lindell, and Hope Hodge. "Mental Healthcare for Troops Draws Criticism." *Daily News*, May 14, 2010.

Keedle, Jayne. "Justin Eldridge's Battle with PTSD Ended in Tragedy Last Night." *Waterford Patch*, October 29, 2013.

Kelley, Michael. "Report Finds Despite VA's Record Funding, Enrolled Veterans Attempting Suicide at Rate of 48 per Day." *Military Suicide Report*, July 26, 2012.

Kelley, Michael. "The US Government Is Failing Miserably at Helping Veterans." *Business Insider*, July 26, 2012

Keteyian, Armen. "Suicide Epidemic among Veterans." CBS News, November 13, 2007.

Kilner, Peter. "Military Leaders' Obligation to Justify Killing in War." *Military Review*, March–April 2002.

King, Martin Luther, Jr. "Declaration of Independence from the War in Vietnam." Speech Delivered at Riverside Church in New York City, April 4, 1967.

Klein, Joe. "Ten Years After: A National Disgrace." *Time*, March 25, 2013.

Knox, Jo, and David H. Price. "Healing America's Warriors: Vet Centers and the Social Contract." Paper presented at After the Cold War: Reassessing Vietnam (conference), University of Texas at Arlington, April 18–20, 1996.

Kramer, Andrew E. "A New Hotel, Where the Stay Used to Be Mandatory." *New York Times*, December 3, 2011.

Kristof, Nicholas. "A Veteran's Death, the Nation's Shame." *New York Times*, April 14, 2012.

Kristof, Nicholas D. "Veterans and Brain Disease." *New York Times*, April 25, 2012.

Lande, R. Gregory. "Felo De Se: Soldier Suicides in America's Civil War." *Military Medicine* 176(5) (May 2011): 531–36.

Larraneta, Izaskun E. "Former Marine's Suicide in Waterford Standoff Shocks Friends." *The Day*, October 29, 2013.

Le, Phuong. "Widow: Ranger Killed Self to Avoid Another Tour." *Seattle Times*, August 24, 2011.

Lepore, Jill. "The Force." *New Yorker*, January 28, 2013.

Lester, David. "Suicide in Vietnam Veterans." *Archives of Suicide Research* 9(4) (2005).

Levin, Aaron. "Army Gets Closer to Pinpointing Soldiers at Risk for Suicide." *Psychiatry News*, May 6, 2011.

Levin, Aaron. "Clinic Visits Common before Service Members' Suicide." *Psychiatry Online*, April 6, 2012.

Levin, Barry L. "Defense of the Vietnam Veteran with Post-Traumatic Stress Disorder." *American Jury Trials* 441 (1993).

"The Life and Death of Clay Hunt." *60* Minutes. CBS News. Byron Pitts reporting, March 3, 2013.

Litz, Brett T., and William E. Schlenger. "PTSD in Service Members and New Veterans of the Iraq and Afghanistan Wars: A Bibliography and Critique." *PTSD Research Quarterly* 20(1) (Winter 2009).

Litz, Brett T., Nathan Stein, et al. "Moral Injury and Moral Repair in War Veterans: A Preliminary Model and Intervention Strategy." *Clinical Psychology Review* 29(8) (December 2009): 695–706.

Lowry, Fran. "Army Psychiatrist Battles the War on Military Suicide." *Medscape Medical News*, November 26, 2010.

Lubin, Gad, Nomi Werbeloff, et al. "Decrease in Suicide Rates after a Change of Policy Reducing Access to Firearms in Adolescents." *Suicide and Life-Threatening Behavior*, November 2010.

MacPherson, Myra. "McNamara's 'Moron Corps.'" Salon.com, May 30, 2002. www.salon.com/2002/05/30/mcnamara.

Maguen, Shira, and Brett Litz. "Moral Injury in Veterans of War." *PTSD Research Quarterly* 23(1) (2012): 1–3.

Maltais, Michelle. "Anti-Suicide Effort Joined by Facebook." *Los Angeles Times*, May 10, 2012.

Mann J. John, Alan Apter, Jose Bertolote, et al. "Suicide Prevention Strategies: A Systematic Review." *Journal of the American Medical Association* 294(16) (October 26, 2005).

Marshall, Konrad. "In Their Minds It's Never Gonna Go Away. The War Is Still There." *Indianapolis Star*, September 1, 2009.

Martin, David. "Army Suicide Widows: Too Little, Too Late." CBS News, August 16, 2012.

Martin, Gary, and Viveca Novak. "U.S. Fast-Tracks Widespread Use of Drones." *San Francisco Chronicle*, November 27, 2012.

Matson, John. "Legacy of Mental Health Problems from Iraq and Afghanistan Wars Will Be Long-Lived." *Scientific American*, June 27, 2011.

Maurer, Kevin, and Julie Watson. "Marines Tackle Mental Health." Associated Press, August 25, 2010.

Maycock, James. "War within War." *Guardian Unlimited*, September 15, 2001.

Mazzetti, Mark. "A Secret Deal on Drones, Sealed in Blood." *New York Times*, April 6, 2013.

McCumber, David. "Shooter's Plight Sparks Talk on Vets' Treatment." *San Francisco Chronicle*, February 14, 2013.

McFarland, Bentson H., Mark S. Kaplan, and Nathalie Huguet, "Datapoints: Self-Inflicted Deaths among Women with U.S. Military Service: A Hidden Epidemic?" *Psychiatry Online*, December 1, 2010.

McKinley, Jr., James C. "Despite Army Efforts, Soldier Suicides Continue." *New York Times*, October 10, 2010.

McManus, Reed. "A Missing Piece: Can Wilderness Adventure Repair the Ravages of War?" *Sierra*, July/August 2011.

McNally, Richard J. "Are We Winning the War against Posttraumatic Stress Disorder?" *Science*, May 18, 2012.

McNally, Richard J. "The Ontology of Posttraumatic Stress Disorder: Natural Kind, Social Construction, or Causal System?" *Clinical Psychology: Science and Practice* 19(3) (September 2012).

McNally, Richard J. "Psychiatric Disorder and Suicide in the Military, Then and Now: Commentary on Frueh and Smith." *Journal of Anxiety Disorders* 26 (October 2012).

Menefee, Samuel P. "The 'Vietnam Syndrome' Defense: A G.I. Bill of Criminal Rights?" *Army Law*, February 1985.

"Middletown Soldier Kills Wife, Self: Apparent Murder-Suicide on a Texas Army Post." *WPRI*, September 29, 2010.

Mikkelson, Barbara, and David Mikkelson. "M-16." Urban Legends Reference Pages, Snopes.com, July 7, 2002, snopes.com/military/m16.asp.

"The Military-Civilian Gap: Fewer Family Connections." Pew Research Center, November 23, 2011.

Miller, Matthew, Catherine Barber, et al. "Suicide among US Veterans: A Prospective Study of 500,000 Middle-aged and Elderly Men." *American Journal of Epidemiology* 170(4) (May 19, 2009): 494–500.

Miller, T. Christian. "Ex-Cop Who Killed N.C. Deputy Found Dead." *Charlotte Observer*, September 26, 2008.

Miller, T. Christian. "A Journey That Ended in Anguish." *Los Angeles Times*, November 27, 2005.

Miller, T. Christian. "The Other Victims of Battlefield Stress; Defense Contractors' Mental Health Neglected." *ProPublica*, February 26, 2010.

Mitchell, Greg. "General Petraeus's Link to a Troubling Suicide in Iraq: The Ted Westhusing Story." *The Nation*, June 27, 2011.

Mitchell, Greg. "Revealed: U.S. Soldier Killed Herself after Objecting to Interrogation Techniques." *Editor & Publisher*, November 1, 2006.

Mitchell, Greg. "She Survived Iraq—The Shot Herself at Home." *Editor & Publisher*, November 13, 2006.

Mitchell, Greg. "The Soldier Who Killed Herself after Refusing to Take Part in Torture." *Huffington Post*, September 14, 2011.

Mitchell, Greg. "A Suicide in Iraq—Part II." *Editor & Publisher*, November 7, 2006.

Mitchell, Greg. "U.S. Soldier Killed Herself—After Refusing to Take Part in Torture." *Huffington Post*, April 15, 2013.

Mitchell, Hannah. "Caldwell Killing Suspect Known as Peaceable." *Charlotte Observer*, September 23, 2008.

"Mother of Iraq Veteran Who Committed Suicide: 'Honor the Dead, Heal the Wounded, Stop the Wars.'" *Democracy Now*, May 28, 2012.

"Mother of Sgt. Kirkland Speaks Out: 'The Army Killed My Son.'" *March Forward*, April 19, 2011.

Moulton, Kristen. "Experiencing Assault a Possible Risk Factor for Military Suicide." *Salt Lake Tribune*, January 24, 2013.

Moulton, Kristen. "Study: Seeing Heavy Combat Carries High Risk of Suicide, PTSD." *Salt Lake Tribune*, July 24, 2012.

Moulton, Kristen. "U. Study: Combat Puts Soldiers at High Suicide, PTSD Risk." *Salt Lake Tribune*, July 23, 2012.

Moulton, Kristen, and Gary Peterson. "Nineteen Veterans, Service Members Sue over Military Sexual Assault." *Salt Lake Tribune*, September 28, 2012.

Mudd, Roger, "Supreme Court Upholds Law Restricting Legal Fees in Veterans Benefit Claims Cases." *NBC Nightly News*, June 28, 1985.

Mueller, Mark, and Tomas Dinges. "Military Suicides: Army Sgt. Coleman Bean's Downward Spiral Ends with Gunfire." *New Jersey Star-Ledger*, November 22, 2009.

Mulrine, Anna. "Sgt. Robert Bales and Multiple Tours of Duty: How Many Is Too Many?" *Christian Science Monitor*, March 23, 2012.

Murphy, Kim. "A 'Base on the Brink,' as Is the Community." *Los Angeles Times*, December 26, 2011.

Musil, Robert K. "The Truth about Deserters." *The Nation*, April 16, 1973.

Nalpathanchil, Lucy. "Marine's Family Decides to Talk Openly about His Suicide." National Public Radio, November 7, 2013.

Natelson, Rachel, and Sandra S. Park. "Exposing the Ugly Details of the Military Violence Epidemic." *Huffington Post*, March 1, 2012.

National Humanities Center. "Suicide among Slaves: A 'Very Last Resort.'" *The Making of African-American Identity*, volume 1, 1500–1865 (2007), 1, http://nationalhumanitiescenter.org/pds/maai/emancipation/text2/suicide.pdf.

Nauert, Rick. "Veterans Risk for Depression and Suicide." *Psych Central*, November 1, 2007.

"New National Strategy Paves Way for Reducing Suicide Deaths." *SAMHSA News*, September 10, 2012.

News21 Staff. "Back Home: Nearly 1 in Every 5 Suicides Is a Veteran." *Denver Post*, August 28, 2013.

News21 Staff. "Back Home: VA System Ill-Prepared for Residual Effects of War." *Denver Post*, August 25, 2013.

News21 Staff. "Back Home: Women Warriors Face Daunting Challenges in Civilian Life." *Denver Post*, August 29, 2013.

Noonan, Margaret E., and Christopher J. Mumola. "U.S. Department of Justice, Bureau of Justice Statistics Special Report: Veterans in State and Federal Prison, 2004," May 2007.

Nordland, Rod. "Risks of Afghan War Shift from Soldiers to Contractors." *New York Times*, February 11, 2012.

"Operation Iraqi Freedom Mental Health Advisory Team. *Annex D: Review of Soldier Suicides*. Falls Church, VA, U.S. Army Surgeon General, 2003.

"Parents Mourn Son's Suicide after Returning from Iraq Duty: 'He's a Casualty of War but He'll Never Be Known as That.'" *Democracy Now*, August 11, 2004.

Parrish, Kevin. "Decorated Soldier, Suicide Victim, Is Remembered at Calif. Service." *Stockton Record*, August 17, 2012.

Parrish, Melvin M. "Florence Native Commanded Famed Lost Battalion." *Florence Mining News*, August 26, 1980.

"Partial Transcript of President Obama's Roundtable with Military Reporters." *Stars and Stripes*, August 4, 2009.

Payton, Brenda. "Readjusting from War Can Be Hell, Too." *San Francisco Chronicle*, April 14, 2013.

Pelkey, Stefanie. "In His Boots." American Widow Project, January 8, 2010, http://americanwidowproject.org/stories/in-his-boots.

Pelkey, Stefanie. "Statement of Stefanie E. Pelkey before the Committee on Veterans Affairs, House of Representatives," July 25, 2005, http://veterans.house.gov/hearings/schedule109/jul05/7-27-05f/spelkey.html.

Perrin, Megan A., et al. "Differences in PTSD Prevalence and Associated Risk Factors among World Trade Center Disaster and Recovery Workers." *American Journal of Psychiatry* 164(9) (September 2007).

Peterson, Gary. "Disabled Veterans Wait for Action on Oakland VA Backlog." *Contra Costa Times*, July 30, 2012.

Peterson, Gary. " 'Fix-It' Event Fixes Little." *Contra Costa Times*, July 29, 2012.

Peterson, Gary. "Vets Scoff at VA Promise." *Contra Costa Times*, April 20, 2013.

Peterson, Gary, and Mark Emmons. "Death, Fears Trailed Veteran." *Contra Costa Times*, March 17, 2012.

Peterson, Gary, and Mark Emmons. "Vexing Problem: Bridging Scores of Military Veterans into Civilian Jobs." *San Jose Mercury News*, October 18, 2013.

Peterson, Gary, and Mark Emmons. "The War of Waiting." *Contra Costa Times*, April 17, 2013.

Peterson, Gary, and Mark Emmons. "Where Warriors Heal." *Contra Costa Times*, June 22, 2012.

Pickler, Nedra, and Donna Cassata. "Obama to Military: Stop Sex Assaults." Associated Press, December 21, 2013.

Pizzaro, Judith, Roxane Cohen Silver, and JoAnn Prouse. "Physical and Mental Costs of Traumatic War Experience among Civil War Veterans." *Archives of General Psychiatry* 63 (2006).

Pols, Hans. "Waking Up to Shell Shock: Psychiatry in the U.S. Military during World War II." *Endeavor* 30 (December 2006).

Prah, Pamela M. "Backlogs for Veterans Could Spike under Shutdown." *USA Today*, October 4, 2013.

"PTSD Doesn't Prevent Combat Duty." Associated Press, March 24, 2012.

"PTSD Marine Kills Brother, Self." Associated Press, February 11, 2009.

"Pursuing Perfect Depression Care." *Psychiatry Online* 57(10) (October 2006).

Qin, Ping, and Merete Nordentoft. "Suicide Risk in Relation to Psychiatric Hospitalization." *JAMA Psychiatry* 62(4) (April 2005).

Reinberg, Steven. "U.S. Army Suicides Rising Sharply, Study Finds." *Health Day News*, March 8, 2012.

Remnick, David. "Going the Distance: On and Off the Road with Barack Obama." *New Yorker*, January 27, 2014.

Renderman, Vanessa. "Victims of War: Hammond Man among Growing Number of Military Suicides." *Military Suicide Report*, July 21, 2012.

Rendon, Jim. "Post-Traumatic Stress's Surprisingly Positive Flip Side." *New York Times*, March 22, 2012.

Reno, Jamie. "Nearly 30% of Vets Treated by V.A. Have PTSD." *Daily Beast*, October 21, 2012.

Repard, Pauline, and Susan Shroder. "Murder-Suicide at Serra Mesa Military Housing." *San Diego Union-Tribune*, December 21, 2011.

"Report: Texas Vets Dying Young at Alarming Rate." Associated Press, September 29, 2012.

Riker-Coleman, Erik Blaine. "Reflection and Reform: Professionalism and Ethics in the U.S. Army Officer Corps, 1968–1975." PhD diss., University of North Carolina, 1997, www.unc.edu/ffichaos1/reform.pdf.

Roberts, John. "Marine Corps Steps up Suicide Prevention Efforts to Halt Deadly Trend." Fox News, March 30, 2011.

Roberts, Kate. "Reservist Commits Suicide over City Job." Associated Press, March 19, 2004.

Roberts, Kristin. "U.S. Army Suicides Hit Highest Rate since Gulf War." Reuters, August 16, 2007.

Robinson, Doug. "Hidden War Zone Scars Claim Another Soldier's Life." *Deseret News*, June 5, 2012.

Robinson, Stephen L. "Hidden Toll of the War in Iraq." Center for American Progress, September 2004.

Rock, Nicholas L., James W. Stokes, et al. "U.S. Army Combat Psychiatry." In *War Psychiatry: Textbook of Military Medicine*, chapter 7.

Rosen, James. "PTSD Root of Deadly Spree?" McClatchey Newspapers, April 4, 2014.

Rosenberg, Mike. "Three Marines Charged in Death." *San Jose Mercury News*, October 27, 2011.

Rotstein, Arthur. "'That Was Not My Husband.'" Associated Press, May 17, 2008.

Ruiz, Rebecca. "Memorial Day 2012: Honoring Service Members Who Died by Suicide." *Urban Christian News*, May 26, 2012.

Ruzek, Josef. "The Struggle Within." *San Francisco Chronicle*, April 8, 2012.

Sadler, Anne G., et al. "Factors Associated with Women's Risk of Rape in the Military Environment." *American Journal of Industrial Medicine* 43 (2003): 262–273.

Sanborn, Kathy. "The Suicide Rush." *Counter Punch*, February 13–15, 2009.

Sanchez, Ray, and Ben Brumfield. "Fort Hood Shooter Was Iraq Vet Being Treated for Mental Illness." CNN, April 4, 2014.

"San Diego, CA: Navy Couple Found Shot Dead in Murder-Suicide after Three-Hour Stand-Off with Swat Officers." *Daily Mail Reporter*, December 22, 2011.

Sassoon, Siegfried. "Statement against the Continuation of the War—1917." http://web/viu.ca/davies/h482.WWI/sassoon.state ment.against.war.1917.htm.

Sassoon, Siegfried. *The War Poems of Siegfried Sassoon*. Create Space, http://www.createspace.com.

Satcher, David. "The Surgeon General's Call to Action to Prevent Suicide." U.S. Public Health Services, 1999, http://profiles.nlm. nih.gov/ps/access/NNBBBH.pdf.

Satel, Sally. "Stressed Out Vets: Believing the Worst about Post-Traumatic Stress Disorder." *Weekly Standard*, August 21, 2006.

Savacool, Julia. "Rising Suicide Rates among Female Veterans Show How Deep the Emotional Wounds Can Be." *Women's Health*, May 25, 2012.

Savage, Charlie. "As Acts of War or Despair, Suicides Rattle a Prison." *New York Times*, April 24, 2011.

Schickel, Richard. "Clint's Double Take." *Time*, October 23, 2006.

Schmidle, Nicholas D. "In the Crosshairs." *New Yorker*, June 3, 2013.

Schwartz, Jeremy. "Deadly Appointments: Vets Increasingly Arriving at VA Hospitals...to Kill Themselves." *Austin American-Statesman*, September 9, 2013.

Scott, Larry. " 'They're Sending Me Back to Hell Again.' " *OpEd News*, October 23, 2005.

"Senator Questions Post-Traumatic Stress Denials." McClatchy Newspapers, March 29, 2012.

Senior, Jennifer. "The Prozac, Paxil, Zoloft, Wellbutrin, Celexa, Effexor, Valium, Klonopin, Ativan, Restoril, Xanax, Adderall, Ritalin, Haldol, Risperdal, Seroquel, Ambien, Lunesta, Elavil, Trazodone War." *New York Magazine*, February 6, 2011.

"Sexual Assault Now an Epidemic, Pentagon Reports." Associated Press, May 8, 2012.

Seyrig, Maria. "Depression Care Program Eliminates Suicide." Henry Ford Health Services press release, http://www.henryford.com/body.cfm?id=46335&action=detail&ref=1104, downloaded April 16, 2013.

Shane, Leo. "Living through Nine Suicides." *Stars and Stripes*, September 11, 2013.

Shane, Scott. "Obama Working on Drone Rules." *New York Times*, November 25, 2012.

Shapiro, Nina. "Derrick Kirkland, Iraq War Veteran, Hung Himself after Being Mocked by Superiors, Say Lewis-McChord Soldiers." *Seattle Weekly*, November 8, 2010.

Shapiro, Nina. "Derrick Kirkland, Soldier Who Hung Himself, Was Deemed a 'Low-Moderate Risk' after Attempting Suicide Three Times Before. *Seattle Weekly*, January 5, 2011.

Shapiro, Nina. "Jared Hagemann's Hell." *Seattle Weekly*, November 9, 2011.

Sherr, Lynn. "Coming Home." *Parade*, October 21, 2012.

Siegel, Robert. "After a Marine's Suicide, a Family Recalls Missing Red Flags." National Public Radio, June 19, 2013.

Siegel, Robert. "At a Texas Base, Battling Army's Top Threat: Suicide." National Public Radio, June 20, 2013.

Siegel, Robert. "Seeking Mental Health Help Can Be Hard in Military Culture." National Public Radio, June 21, 2013.

Slater, Dashka. "Standing Up for Vets." *California Lawyer*, April 2013.

"Soldier's Widow Sues U.S. over Suicide." CBS News, October 8, 2008.

"Soldiers with Mental Illness More Often Get PTSD." Reuters, May 2, 2011.

Somers, Daniel. "'I Am Sorry That It Has Come to This': A Soldier's Last Words." Gawker, June 22, 2013, http://gawker.com/i-am-sorry-that-it-has-come-to-this-a-soldiers-last-534538357.

Sommerville, Diane Miller. "A Burden Too Heavy to Bear." *New York Times*, April 2, 2012.

Sommerville, Diane Miller. "A Burden Too Heavy to Bear: War Trauma, Suicide and Confederate Soldiers." *Civil War History*, December 2013.

Sontag, Deborah, and Lizette Alvarez. "When Strains on Military Families Turn Deadly." *New York Times*, February 15, 2008.

Sowers, Tommy. "Misinformation about VA Ill Serves Deserving Veterans." *Contra Costa Times*, March 2, 2014.

Speier, Jackie. "PTSD: Roadblocks to Recovery." *San Francisco Chronicle*, April 8, 2012.

Spiegel, Alix. "Study: Female Vets Especially Vulnerable to Suicide." NPR, December 4, 2010.

Spiller, Roger J. "Shellshock." *American Heritage Magazine* 41 (May/June 1990).

"S.S.S. Intrepid: The Story of the 'Fighting I,'" A&E Television Networks, 1995.

Standifer, Cid. "PTSD Diagnosis Rates Rise among Female Troops." *Navy Times*, May 12, 2012.

Stanton, Sam. "Website Helps Veterans Reconnect, Tell Stories." *Sacramento Bee*, May 30, 2011.

Starr, Barbara. "Behind the Scenes: Triumph and Tragedy for Two Wounded Soldiers." CNN.com, July 27, 2009.

Stauffer, Cindy. "The War Within: Some Iraq Vets Coming Home with Emotional Scars That Are Difficult to Heal." *Lancaster News*, February 19, 2007.

Steinhauer, Jennifer. "Military Sexual Assaults Increase." *New York Times*, May 8, 2013.

Sternhagen, Beth. "Florence Native Commanded Famed Lost Battalion in World War I." *Florence Mining News*, August 26, 1980.

Stetka, Bret, Richard H. Weisler, et al. "At War with Mental Illness: Caring for Troops and Veterans." *Medscape*, February 2, 2011.

Stevens, John. "Army Ranger Took His Life after Eight Deployments to Iraq and Afghanistan Because He Thought 'There Was No Way That Any God Would Forgive Him.'" *Daily Mail Reporter*, August 15, 2011.

Stopczynski, Kelli. "South Bend Native Dies at Fort Campbell in Apparent Domestic Violence Incident." *WSBT*, April 18, 2012.

Suczek, Noreen. "VA: Making System Easier to Navigate." *San Francisco Chronicle*, April 8, 2012.

"Suicide Brings a Decade of War Home." *NineMSN*, August 23, 2011.

"Suicide in the Armed Forces." *Washington Post*, July 23, 2009.

"Suicide Rate for Veterans Twice that of Other Americans." CBS News, November 13, 2007.

Sulek, Julia Prodis, Lisa Fernandez, et al. "Iraq Vet Snaps, Kills Girl, 11." *Contra Costa Times*, March 16, 2012.

Sullivan, Lucas, and Margo Rutledge Kissell. "Did War Vet Kill Self to Make a Statement?" *Dayton Daily News*, April 16, 2010.

Susman, Tina. "8 Charged in Soldier's Afghanistan 'Suicide.'" *Los Angeles Times*, December 22, 2011.

"Suspect's History Sparks Debate about Multiple Tours." *New York Times*, March 18, 2012.

Swank, Roy L., and Walter E. Marchand. "Combat Neuroses: Development of Combat Exhaustion." *Archives of Neurology and Psychology* 55 (1946).

Swofford, Anthony. "'We Pretend the Vets Don't Even Exist.'" *Newsweek*, May 28, 2012.

Tanielian, Terri, Lisa Jaycox, et al. "Invisible Wounds: Mental Health and Cognitive Care Needs of America's Returning Veterans." RAND Corporation, April 17, 2008.

Tarrant, David. "Couple Shares Their Story to Raise Awareness about Suicide, Depression." *Dallas Morning News*, October 3, 2010.

Tavernise, Sabrina. "Suicides Account for Most U.S. Gun Deaths." *New York Times*, February 14, 2013.

Thompson, Mark. "Is the U.S. Army Losing Its War on Suicide? *Time*, April 13, 2010.

Thompson, Mark. "A Troubled Marine's Final Fight." *Time*, February 10, 2014.

Tingley, Kim. "The Suicide Detective." *New York Times*, June 26, 2013.

Toohey, Marty. "Did Army Do Enough to Prevent Soldier's Death?" *American Statesman*, February 6, 2007.

"Tragic Iraq Veteran, 25, Shoots Himself Dead in Front of Father in Family's Back Yard after Battle with PTSD." *Daily Mail Reporter*, July 26, 2012.

Trexler, Phil. "Mom Remembers Son Who Died at InfoCision Stadium." *Akron Beacon Journal*, November 5, 2011.

"Troops Need Yearly Screening for PTSD, Medical Panel Says." Associated Press, July 14, 2012.

"The Trouble with Drones." *New York Times*, April 7, 2013.

Turan, Kenneth. "John Huston's 'Let There Be Light' Online." *Los Angeles Times*, May 24, 2012.

Twiggs, Travis N. "PTSD: The War Within: A Marine Writes about His PTSD Experience." *Marine Corps Gazette*, January 2008.

"The Unfinished War: A Decade since Desert Storm," CNN.com, Gulf War Facts, 2001.

Unger, Laura. "Suicide Takes Growing Toll among Military, Veterans." *Courier-Journal*, September 13, 2009.

"US Troops in Iraq: 72% Say End War in 2006." *Truth Out*, February 28, 2006.

"US Veterans 'High Suicide Risk.'" BBC News, June 11, 2007.

"Vietnam 101." *60 Minutes*, CBS, October 4, 1987.

Vogel, Steve, "VA's Shinseki Has His Critics as He Tries to Remake Agency, Cut Disability Claims Backlog." *Washington Post*, November 10, 2013.

Vogel, Steve. "VA Trims 34% from Its Disability Claims Backlog." *Washington Post*, November 8, 2013.

"The War That Has No Ending." *Discover* 6 (June 1985): 44–47.

Watson, Julie. "Navy Pilot John Robert Reeves Killed Self in San Diego Murder-Suicide." *Huffington Post*, January 4, 2012.

Weissert, Will, and Danica Coto. "Argument May Have Set off Attack." Associated Press, April 5, 2014.

"What Has the North to Do with Slavery?" *Southern Gazette*, September 23, 1837.

Wickham, Shawne K. "Friends, Family Coping with a Hero's Suicide." *New Hampshire Sunday News*, August 14, 2011.

Wiegand, David. "How the Bloodiest of Wars Changes the Way We Look at Death and Dying." *San Francisco Chronicle*, September 17, 2012.

Williams, Timothy P. "Suicides Outpacing War Deaths for Troops." *New York Times*, June 8, 2012.

Wilson, Scott. "Obama: Korean War Is 'Forgotten Victory.'" *Washington Post*, July 28, 2013.

Wiltrout, Kate. "Walk Brings Light to Dark Subject of Suicide in the Military." *Virginian-Pilot*, September 11, 2009.

"Wings of Valor: The Lost Battalion in the Argonne Forest," http://www.homeofheroes.com/wings/part1/3_lostbattalion.html.

Wise, Lindsay. "A Poster Boy for Suicide Prevention, Houstonian Becomes Another Statistic." *Houston Chronicle*, April 9, 2011.

Wise, Lindsay. "A Soldier's Tragic Tale." *Houston Chronicle*, May 18, 2008.

Wong, Kristina. "New Report: Military Losing the Battle against Suicide." ABC News, November 2, 2011.

Wood, David. "Obama Drone War 'Kill Chain' Imposes Heavy Burden at Home." *Huffington Post*, May 5, 2013.

Yeoman, Barry. "Women Vets: A Battle All Their Own." *Parade*, November 13, 2013.

Youker, Darrin. "Did Lingering Pain Cause Suicide of Civil War Vet?" *Reading Eagle*, May 22, 2011.

Younts, William H. Memoirs, Indiana Historical Society, 98–100, http://www.indianahistory.org.

Youssef, Nancy A. "Army Braces for Rise in Soldiers' Suicides." McClatchy Newspapers, November 18, 2009.

Youssef, Nancy A. "Suicides Soared in 2010 for Army Reserve, National Guard." McClatchy Newspapers, January 16, 2011.

Zarembo, Alan. "Ft. Hood Shooting Puts Army Resilience Training to the Test." *Los Angeles Times*, April 5, 2014.

Zoroya, Gregg. "Army Suicides Rise as Time Spent in Combat Increases." *USA Today*, January 12, 2009.

Zoroya, Gregg. "Female Soldiers' Suicide Rate Triples When at War." *USA Today*, March 18, 2011.

Zoroya, Gregg. "Repeated Deployments Weigh Heavily on U.S. Troops." *USA Today*, January 13, 2010

Zoroya, Gregg. "Thousands Strain Hood Mental Health System." *USA Today*, August 23, 2010.

Presentations

Aaen, Tanya R. B., and Pamela Planthara. "Targeted Applications of Prolonged Exposure and Cognitive Processing Therapy with Combat-Related PTSD." Veteran Affairs Northern California, March 30, 2012.

Baker, Michael. "Care of Returning Casualties from the Mideast Wars: The Good, the Bad, and the Ugly." Walnut Creek, CA, June 12, 2012.

Coffey, C. Edward. "Pursuing Perfect Depression Care: A Model for Eliminating Suicide and Transforming Mental Healthcare." Henry Ford Health Services, http://www.rcpsych.ac.uk/pdf/Pursuing%20Perfect%20Depression%20Care-1-2.pdf, downloaded April 16, 2013.

Hyde, Pamela S. "Suicide: The Challenges and Opportunities behind the Public Health Problem." SAMHSA presentation, Tucson, AZ, August 2, 2011.

Joseph, David M. "Vicarious Traumatization: Understanding and Managing Compassion Fatigue in Working with Veterans." Front Line to Home Front Conference, Pleasant Hill, CA, March 30, 2012.

Kemp, Janet E. "Suicide Rates in VHA Patients through 2011 with Comparisons with Other Americans and Other Veterans through 2010." Veterans Health Administration, January 2014.

Manley, Stephen V. "Veterans Treatment Courts: Improving Outcomes for Our Military Service Personnel." Front Line to Home Front Conference, Pleasant Hill, CA, March 30, 2012.

Panetta, Leon E. Speech delivered at the Department of Defense/Veterans Affairs Conference on Suicide Prevention, U.S. Department of Defense, Washington, DC, June 22, 2012.

Thompson, Caitlin. "Suicide Prevention and Crisis Intervention with Veterans." Veterans Crisis Line and Chat Service, Baltimore, July 26, 2011.

Movies

Hearts and Minds. Produced and directed by Peter Davis, 1974.

Let There Be Light. Produced by the U.S. Army, directed by John Huston, part of the FedFlix Collection, 1946.

On the Dark Side in Al Doura—A Soldier in the Shadows. Produced and directed by Cindy Piester, Maverick Media, December 17, 2011, http://youtube/watch?v=9mEjOGj5vsQ.

Wartorn: 1861–2010. Produced by HBO Documentary Films, 2011.

Index

Note: "n." indicates material in notes.